# A Basic Bible Dictionary

**Other titles in the Basic Dictionary series, available from the Canterbury Press:**

*A Basic Catholic Dictionary* Alan Griffiths

*A Basic Church Dictionary* Tony Meakin

*\* Now in its fifth edition\**

*A Basic Dictionary of Bible People* Julien Chilcott-Monk

*A Basic Dictionary of Saints* Kathleen Jones

**Other books by Michael Counsell**

*Prayers for Sundays* (HarperCollins*Religious*)

*More Prayers for Sundays* (HarperCollins*Religious*)

*Kieu by Nguyen Du, bilingual edition* (Thé Gio'i Press, Hanoi)

*Every Pilgrim's Guide to Oberammergau and its Passion Play* (Canterbury Press)

*Two Thousand Years of Prayer* (Canterbury Press and Morehouse Publishing) (an edited version of this in Swedish is published by Libris as *Stora Bönboken*)

*All Through the Night* (Canterbury Press and Westminster John Knox Press)

*Every Pilgrim's Guide to the Journeys of the Apostles* (Canterbury Press and Morehouse Publishing)

*The Little Book of Heavenly Humour* by Syd Little with Chris Gidney and Michael Counsell (Canterbury Press)

*Every Pilgrim's Guide to England's Holy Places* (Canterbury Press)

Michael Counsell also headed the translators of The Four Gospels into Seychelles Creole

# A Basic Bible Dictionary

*Compiled by*
Michael Counsell

CANTERBURY
PRESS
Norwich

British Library Cataloguing in Publication Data

A catalogue record for this book is available from
the British Library

ISBN 1-85311-475-8

Typeset by Regent Typesetting, London
and printed by
Bookmarque, Croydon

# Contents

# Contents

# Preface

The Bible is the most exciting and stimulating book in the world, and, properly understood, can guide us to 'life in all its fulness' (John 10.10). Philip the Evangelist found the Ethiopian official reading the Scriptures, and asked him 'Do you understand what you are reading?' (Acts 8.30). It is easy to misunderstand the Bible or impose our own views upon it, if we do not understand the background situation in which it was written: a text without a context is a pretext. It is in the hope of filling in some of this background, unravelling difficulties, helping readers to find what they are looking for and explore areas they were unaware of, that this book has been compiled, in the same series as Tony Meakin's *A Basic Church Dictionary*, also published by Canterbury Press. I have also tried to help readers to interpret the meaning of the Bible for today. Different parts of the Bible may be 'true' in different ways; in the first section of this book I list people and events as the Bible describes them; in the second part I give some suggestions as to which parts of the Bible should be regarded as historical, and how accurate it is. There are many opinions about the Bible held with equal sincerity among believers and unbelievers; many of them can neither be proved nor disproved, and I leave users of this book to make up their own minds, while resisting the suggestion that only one interpretation is valid.

The first part of this book is arranged alphabetically; the second section has longer notes on individual books of the Bible and Apocrypha and other aspects of the background. I have used standard abbreviations for the books of the Bible which can be looked up in the alphabetical section. I have also given a rough indication of the pronunciation of the names of the various books and their full titles for those who have to read them aloud, but with most Hebrew and Greek words there is no agreed English pronunciation, and so long as readers put the stress on

# Preface

the penultimate (last but one) or ante-penultimate (last but two) syllable and pronounce 'ch' as 'k', it would be wrong to criticize their pronunciation. If puzzled about the meaning of a word which is not listed here, Bible readers should look it up in another translation or an English dictionary; to find a full list of the occurrence of different words in the Bible, a cross-referenced Bible, a Concordance, or a searchable computer text is necessary. I use the words Canaan or Israel to describe the geographical area which used to be called Palestine and is now called by some the Holy Land, by others the State of Israel, and by others Israel and the Occupied Territories, without intending any judgement on the politics involved. Place names are sometimes given in the Hebrew form, sometimes the Arabic name is used.

Michael Counsell, Athens 2003

# A Time Line of the Bible

c. means *circa*, about; all dates are approximate, though where biblical events can be linked to those in other civilizations they are accurate to within a year or two. The abbreviations BCE, meaning Before the Common Era, and CE, for Common Era, are often used instead of the traditional BC (Before Christ) and AD (*Anno Domini*, year of our Lord)

**BC (or BCE)**

| | |
|---|---|
| c. 5000 | Stone and copper age, first Mesopotamian civilization |
| c. 2400 | Akkadian civilization in Mesopotamia, see Mesopotamia and Persia, p. **165** |
| c. 1900 | Abraham migrates to Canaan |
| c. 1700–c.1250 | Israelites enslaved in Egypt |
| c.1250 | Israelite Exodus from Egypt, led by Moses |
| c.1210–c.1030 | Period of Joshua and the Judges |
| c.1030–c.1010 | Reign of Saul |
| c.1010–c.970 | Reign of David, conquest of Jerusalem |
| c. 970–931 | Reign of Solomon. On his death the nation splits into two kingdoms, the Northern Kingdom known as Israel and the Southern Kingdom known as Judah |

Kings of Israel: Jeroboam I 931–910; Nadab 910–909; Baasha 909–886; Elah 886–885; Zimri 7 days in 885; Omri 885–874; Ahab 874–853; Ahaziah 853–852; Joram 852–841; Jehu 841–814; Jehoahaz 814–798; Jehoash 798–783; Jeroboam II 783–743; Zechariah 6 months in 743; Shallum 1 month in 743; Menahem 743–738; Pekahiah 738–737; Pekah 737–732; Hoshea 732–723; Fall of Samaria to the Assyrians in 722

Ministry of Prophets in Israel: Elijah 875–840; Elisha 850–790; Amos 790–750; Hosea 760–740

Kings of Judah: Rehoboam 931–913; Abijah 913–911; Asa 911–870; Jehoshaphat 870–848; Jehoram 848–841; Ahaziah 841; Athaliah 841–835; Joash 835–796; Amaziah 796–781; Azariah or Uzziah 781–740; Jotham 740–736; Ahaz 736–716; Hezekiah 716–687; Manasseh 687–642; Amon 642–640; Josiah 640–609; Jehoahaz 3 months in 609; Jehoiakim 609–598; Jehoiachin 3 months in 598; Zedekiah 598–587; Fall of Jerusalem to the Babylonians around 587 – the Jews taken to Babylonia, see 'Exile'

Ministry of Prophets in Judah: Isaiah 740–700; Micah 730–720; Jeremiah 630–586; Zephaniah 630; Nahum 610; Habakkuk 600; Ezekiel 587–575

# A Time Line of the Bible

| | |
|---|---|
| 550 | Cyrus unites Medes and Persians |
| 538 | Cyrus allows Israel to return from Exile in Babylon |
| 537–516 | New Temple built in Jerusalem |
| 445–433 | Nehemiah Governor of Jerusalem, restoration of the walls |

Ministry of Prophets after the return from Exile: Haggai and Zechariah 525; Obadiah 500; Malachi 500; Joel 410

| | |
|---|---|
| 334–323 | Alexander the Great conquers, and spreads Greek culture in, Asia Minor (Turkey), Persia, Syria, Egypt and parts of India |
| 323 | On Alexander's death his empire divided between Ptolemies in Egypt, Seleucids in Antioch-on-the-Orontes, and Antigonids in Greece and Asia Minor who are soon defeated by the Seleucids, see 'Seleucid kings' |
| 279 | Celts set up Galatia |
| 198–166 | Seleucids conquer Syria from the Ptolemies |
| 166–163 | Jewish revolt against Seleucid Greeks led by Judas Maccabeus, see 'Hasmoneans' |
| 129 | Romans establish Province of Asia with capital at Ephesus |
| 63 | Pompey captures Jerusalem for the Romans |
| 42 | Antony and Octavius defeat Cassius and Brutus at Philippi |
| 37–4 | King Herod the Great, an Idumean, see 'Herod Family', 'Judea' |
| 27 | Octavius renamed Augustus and declared to be a god. |
| 6–4 BC | Birth of Jesus (see p. **168**) |

**AD (or CE)**

| | |
|---|---|
| 14–37 | Tiberius is Roman Emperor |
| c. 27 | Ministry of John the Baptist and beginning of the public ministry of Jesus |
| c. 28 | Saul is student of Gamaliel at Jerusalem |
| 30 or 33 | Crucifixion and Resurrection of Jesus |
| 33–41 | Ministry of Peter and Philip |
| c. 33 | Martyrdom of Stephen (Acts 7–8); Conversion of Saint Paul (Acts 9.4–19) |
| 35–37 | Paul visits Jerusalem (Gal. 1.18; Acts 9.26) and returns to Tarsus in Cilicia (Acts 9.30) and Syria (Gal. 1.21; 2 Cor. 11.33; Acts 19.21) |
| 37–41 | Caligula is Roman Emperor |
| 39 | Herod Antipas exiled by Caligula |
| 41–54 | Emperor Claudius |
| 41 or 49 | Expulsion of Jews from Rome by Claudius (Acts 17.2) |
| 44 | Martyrdom of James, son of Zebedee; Peter freed from prison, goes to Caesarea (Acts 12); Death of Herod Agrippa I (Acts 12.23) |
| 45–46 | Paul called by Barnabas to teach in Antioch-on-the-Orontes (Acts 11.26) |
| 46 | First Missionary Journey: Paul, Barnabas and John Mark sent from Antioch to Cyprus and Galatia: Perga (John Mark leaves them), Antioch-of-Pisidia, Iconium, Lystra and Derbe, and back through Attalia to Antioch-on-the-Orontes (Acts 13–14) |

| | |
|---|---|
| 48 | The Council in Jerusalem agrees that Gentile (non-Jewish) Christians need not be circumcised (Acts 15.1–35, not mentioned in Galatians) |
| 49–50 | Second Missionary Journey: Paul and Silas to Syria and Cilicia, Derbe and Lystra (Timothy joins them), Phrygia and Galatia, Troas (Luke joins them), Neapolis, Philippi, Thessalonica, Berea, and Athens (Acts 15.36–16.40) |
| 50–51 | In Corinth (Acts 17.1) Paul writes two Letters to the Thessalonians |
| 51–52 | Hearing before Gallio in Corinth (this is a fixed date because an inscription discovered in Delphi shows that this was the year when Gallio was proconsul) Acts 17.12. Return via Ephesus (where Paul leaves Priscilla and Aquila) to Jerusalem (Acts 17.22; Gal. 2) |
| 52–60 | Felix procurator of Judea |
| 52 | Third Missionary Journey: Paul from Antioch-on-the-Orontes to Galatia and Phrygia (Acts 17.23) |
| 52–54 | Paul in Ephesus, (Acts 19.1–20.1). Around this time he writes his Letter to the Galatians, a lost 'previous letter' to the Corinthians, then the First Letter to the Corinthians, then the 'sorrowful letter'. Possibly he makes a visit to Corinth (2 Cor. 12.14; 13.1–2; not mentioned in Acts) |
| 54–68 | Emperor Nero |
| 54 | Riot in Ephesus (Acts 19.21–41) |
| 54–55 | Paul, with his companions, to Macedonia (Acts 20.1–4) (where he wrote his Second Letter to the Corinthians 1–9 and later 10–13), and maybe Troas (2 Cor. 2.12–13) and Illyricum (Romans 15.19) |
| 55–57 | Paul in Corinth (where he wrote his Letter to the Romans) (Acts 20.2), back to Philippi, Troas, Assos, Miletus, Patara, Tyre, Ptolemais, Caesarea-on-Sea, Jerusalem (Acts 20; 21.1–26) |
| 57–61 | Paul's arrest in Jerusalem, imprisonment in Caesarea (Acts 21.27–23.35). Trial before Felix (Acts 24) |
| 59–60 | Festus succeeds Felix as procurator of Judea. Trial before Festus, appeal to Caesar (Acts 25). Appearance before Agrippa II (Acts 26) |
| 61–62 | Departure for Rome, shipwreck, winter on Malta (Acts 27; 28.1–15) |
| 62–64 | Arrival and house-arrest in Rome (Acts 28.16–31). Paul writes the 'Captivity Epistles' (Ephesians, Philippians, Colossians and Philemon); possibly Luke writes The Gospel according to Luke and The Acts of the Apostles |
| 64 | Paul released (some say executed), travels to Spain and / or revisits Asia Minor |
| 64 | The Fire of Rome and persecution under Nero. |
| 66 | Paul arrested (2 Tim. 1.12; 4.13) |
| 67 | Peter and Paul martyred in Rome |
| 68 or 95 | The Revelation to John written in Patmos |
| 69–79 | Emperor Vespasian |

# A Time Line of the Bible

4

# A Dictionary of the Bible from A to Z

Probable translations of names are given in brackets, preceded by the following abbreviations: *Ak* = Akkadian (the language of Assyria and Babylon), *Ar* = Aramaic, *Eg* = Egyptian, *H* = Hebrew, *G* = Greek, *L* = Latin

**Aaron** (*H* = enlightened) the brother of Moses, was appointed the first High Priest, Ex. 4; before Pharaoh, Ex. 5; his rod became a snake, and caused the plagues, Ex. 7–9; held up Moses' hands, Ex. 17.12; made the golden calf, Ex. 32; priestly duties, Ex. 28–30; Lev. 8–10; Num. 16–17; sedition, Num. 12; death, Num. 20; descendants inherit the priesthood, Lev.10.1; Num. 3.4; 1 Chron. 6.49–52; compared to Christ, Heb. 5.7

**Abaddon and Apollyon** ('Destruction' is *Abaddon* in Hebrew, *Apoleia* in Greek, so this may be a slur on the god Apollo) Abaddon is synonymous with death in the Hebrew Scriptures, Job 26.6; 28.22; 31.12; Ps. 88.11; Prov. 15.11; 27.20; the angel of the bottomless pit in the New Testament, Rev. 9.11; see 'Hell 1.'

**Abana and Pharpar** rivers of Damascus; Naaman wished to wash his leprosy in them, 2 Kings 5.12; probably now called Barada and Nehr el-Awaj

**Abarim, Mount** (*H* = regions beyond) range north-east of the Dead Sea, on the edge of the Moabite Plateau, including Nebo, Pisgah and Hor, now in the Hashemite Kingdom of Jordan west of Amman, Num. 27.12; 33.47–48; Deut. 32.49

*Abba* the name by which children first call their fathers, used by Jesus in speaking to God, Mark 14.36; quoted in Rom. 8.15, Gal. 4.6

**Abednego** (*H* from *Ak Arad-nabu* = servant of Nebo) name given to Azariah, one of three Israelites thrown into the fiery furnace in Babylon; Mishael was called Meshach, Hananiah was called Shadrach, Dan. 1.7; 2.49; 3.12–30; 1 Macc. 2.59, and see Prayer of Azariah and Song of the Three Jews, p. **147**

**Abel** (*H* = breath) second son of Adam; offered the firstborn animals, which pleased God; murdered by his brother Cain, Gen. 4; Wisd. 10.3; 1 John 3.12; Jude 11; his death compared to the sacrifice of Christ, Matt. 23.35; Heb. 11.4; 12.24

**Abel-Beth-Maacah** (*H* = meadow of the house of Maacah) city where the rebel Sheba was beheaded, 2 Sam. 20.14–22; captured by Damascus in around 829 BC, 1 Kings 15.20; and by Tiglath-Pileser III in 733, 2 Kings 15.29. Identified with Tell Abil al-Qamh, on Israel's northern border near Metulla

**Abel-Meholah** (*H* = meadow of the dance) birthplace of Elisha, 1 Kings 4.12; 19.16

**Abiathar** (*H* = my father is excellent) priest; escaped from Saul, 1 Sam. 23.9; 22.20; faithful to David, 1 Sam. 23.6; 30.7; 2 Sam. 15.24; deposed by Solomon, 1 Kings 1.7; 2.26

**Abigail** (*H* = my father rejoices) turned away David's anger at her husband Nabal's churlishness, and became David's wife after Nabal died, 1 Sam. 25

**Abihu** (*H* = my father is he) son of Aaron; with his brother Nadab he offered unholy fire before the LORD and was consumed by fire, Lev. 10.1–3; no satisfactory explanation of this passage has been found

**Abijah** or **Abijam** (*H* = my father is Jah) nine different people with this name are mentioned: Abijah son of Rehoboam was king of Judah 913–911 BC, 1 Kings 15.1; 2 Chron. 12–13

**Abimelech** (*H* = my father is king) **1.** King of Gerar, tricked into thinking Abraham's wife was his sister, Gen. 20. **2.** King of Gerar, tricked into thinking Isaac's wife was his sister, Gen. 26. **3.** Son of Gideon, killed his brothers to become king, Judg. 8–9. **4.** Priest to David, 1 Chron. 18.16

**Abiram** (*H* = my father is high) and his brother Dathan joined Korah's revolt against Moses, Num. 16

**Abishag** (*H* = my father a wanderer) young woman from Shunem, cared for David in his old age, 1 Kings 1.1–4; 2.17–25

**Abishai** (*H* = father exists) one of David's warriors, 1 Sam. 26; 2 Sam. 2–3; 10.9–14; 16.5–14; 18–21; 23.18–19

**Abner** (*H* = father of light) cousin of Saul, member of his army, 1 Sam. 14.50; taunted by David, 1 Sam. 26; made Ish-bosheth king, then went over to David and was killed by Joab, 2 Sam. 2–3; David's lament, 2 Sam. 3.31–39

**Abomination of Desolation** (*H* = blasphemous thing which defiles the Temple), Dan. 9.27; 11.31; 12.11: the erection in the Temple of an altar to Zeus and burning of pig-meat on it by Antiochus Epiphanes in 168 BC, 1 Macc. 1.54. Jesus predicted that this would precede the destruction of Jerusalem, Matt. 24.15; Mark 13.14; he may have predicted the raising of Roman standards in the Temple in AD 70, or more generally the foreseeable wrath of the Romans

**Abraham** (*H* = father of many), originally called Abram (*H* = high father), called by God to Canaan, then to Egypt, Gen. 11–12; separated from Lot, Gen. 13; received a promise from God, Gen. 13.15; 15.5; blessed by Melchizedek, Gen. 14.19; Heb. 7.1; his faith counted as righteousness, Gen. 15.6; Rom. 4.3–16; Gal. 3.6–29; Heb. 11.8–12; James 2.21–23; God's covenant with Abraham and his descendants, Gen. 15.18; 17.1–27; Ps. 105.9; Luke 1.55; welcomed angels, Gen. 18; offered his son Isaac for sacrifice, Gen. 22; made arrangements for his death, Gen. 23–25

**Absalom** (*H* = father of peace) son of David, 2 Sam. 3.3; conspired against his father, 2 Sam. 15; caught by the hair in an oak and killed by Joab, 2 Sam. 18; David's moving lament over Absalom, 2 Sam. 18–19; Absalom's pillar, 2 Sam. 18.18. (The monument called Absalom's pillar in Jerusalem today is a first-century BC tomb, one of the few buildings remaining from the time of Jesus)

**Acacia** spiny species of trees adapted for desert climates, producing a wood used to make the Ark of the Covenant and other furnishings for the Tabernacle, Ex. 25–38; Deut. 10.3. God promises that acacia trees will grow in the wilderness when he makes it fertile, Isa. 41.19; see 'Shittim'

**Achaia** Roman Province in Greece, with Corinth as its capital, Acts 18.12; Rom. 15.26; 1 Cor. 16.15; 2 Cor. 9.2

**Achan** (*H* = troubler) executed for keeping booty devoted to God, Jos. 7

**Acre 1.** See 'Akko'. **2.** See 'Measures of length'

**The Acts of the Apostles** (usual abbreviation Acts), see p. **151**

**Adam** (*H* = humankind; resembles *H adamah* = dust, earth) **1.** The first man, created by God, Gen. 1; placed in the garden of Eden, Gen. 2; disobeyed God and was punished, Gen. 3; Jesus described as the Second Adam who makes a fresh start for humanity, 1 Cor. 15, see 'Obedience'. **2.** City on the delta of the River Jabbok where it joins the Jordan, at Tell ed-Damiyeh, Josh. 3.9–17

**Additions to Esther** (Add. Esth.), see p. **146**

**Additions to the Book of Daniel** see p. **147**

**Admah** see 'Plain'

**Adonijah** (*H* = my Lord is Jah) David's fourth son; rebelled against him; pardoned by Solomon, 1 Kings 1; asked to marry his father's wife and was killed, 1 Kings 2

**Adoption** rich men who were childless often adopted sons to inherit their wealth; the Bible says that God has adopted us and loves us as his children, John 1.12; 2 Cor. 6.18; Gal. 4; Eph. 1.5; 1 John 3

**Adramyttium** home-port of the ship on which Paul sailed, Acts 27.2; the site was near the modern town of Edremit, in Turkey

**Adria** the 'Gulf of Adria' was the Adriatic Sea between Greece and Italy; the 'Sea of Adria', where Paul endured a storm, included the Mediterranean as far as Crete and the north coast of Africa, Acts 27.27

**Adullam** (*H* = a refuge) cave in the hills north of Hebron where David hid from Saul, 1 Sam. 22.1; 1 Chron. 11.15

**Adultery** having sexual relations with someone one is not married to, forbidden; punishable by stoning to death. Jesus used the tradition that only an innocent person could accuse another to save the woman caught in adultery, Ex. 20.14; Lev. 20.10; Deut. 22.23–29; John 8.3–11. A metaphor for being unfaithful to God, Hos. 1–2 etc. See also 'Divorce','Fornication', 'Levirate Marriage', 'Marriage'

**Advocate** see 'Paraclete'

**Agabus** (*H* = locust) prophet from Jerusalem; foretold a famine, Acts 11.28; predicted that Paul would suffer in Jerusalem, Acts 21.10

**Agag** (*H* = violent) king of the Amalekites, spared by Saul but killed by Samuel, 1 Sam. 15

**Agrippa I** in AD 53 made Tetrarch of Abilene, Galilee, Iturea and Trachonitis; listened to Paul's defence, Acts 25–26. See 'Herod Family'

**Ahab** (*H* = father's brother) king of Israel 874–853 BC; married Jezebel; worshipped idols; had Naboth killed so that he could seize his vineyard; rebuked by Elijah; killed at Ramoth-Gilead; buried in Samaria, 1 Kings 16.29–33; 20.1–22.40

**Ahasuerus 1.** Father of Darius the Mede, Dan. 9.1. **2.** King of Persia, supposed to be Xerxes I (485–465 BC), Ezra 4.6; see Esther, p. **139**

**Ahaz** (*H* = grasped) king of Judah 736–716 BC; worshipped idols; sacrificed his son; stole gold from the Temple; rearranged the worship there. Isaiah brought him a message of encouragement but Ahaz refused to ask for a sign, so Isaiah gave him the sign of Immanuel, 2 Kings 16; Isa. 7

**Ahaziah** (*H* = Jah preserves) **1.** Son of Ahab, king of Israel 853–852 BC, condemned by Elijah, 1 Kings 22.40, 49–53; 2 Kings 1.1–17. **2.** Son of Jehoram and Athaliah, king of Judah 841, killed by Jehu, 2 Kings 8.25; 9.27–28

**Ahijah** (*H* = Jah is my brother) prophet who denounced Solomon and Rehoboam, 1 Kings 11.31; 14.7

**Ahimelech** (*H* = my brother is king) priest killed by Saul for helping David, 1 Sam. 21–22

**Ahithophel** (*H* = brother of foolishness) gave bad advice to Absalom and hanged himself, 2 Sam. 15.31–17.23

**Aholah and Aholibah** see 'Oholah, Oholibah'

**Ai** (*H* = heap of stones, pronounced AY-eye) Canaanite city near Bethel, whose

7

inhabitants defeated the Israelites, and were destroyed by Joshua; possible locations either et-Tell or Beitin have been suggested, Josh. 7–8

**Aijalon** (*H* = place of stags) valley where Joshua made the sun and moon stand still, now at Yalo near 'Imwas, 13 miles WNW of Jerusalem, Josh. 10.12

**Ain Karem** village 5 miles west of Jerusalem, where traditionally Mary went to visit her cousin Elizabeth; birthplace of John the Baptist, Luke 1.39–56

**Akeldama** or **Hakeldama** (*H* = field of blood) the potters' field in the Valley of Hinnom, where Judas Iscariot died, Matt. 27.8; Acts 1.19

**Akkad** or **Accad** capital city of the Akkadian civilization; its site is not identified, Gen. 10.10; Akkadian was a Semitic language spoken in Assyria and Babylonia, see Mesopotamia, p. **165**

**Akko** port on the north-east coast of Israel, Judg. 1.31; called Ptolemais in Greek times, 2 Macc. 13.24–26; Paul visited it on his way from Tyre to Caesarea, Acts 21.7; called Saint-Jean-d'Acre by the Crusaders, whose fortress, now underground, may be visited

**Alabaster** white stone used for making perfume bottles etc. The Greek word *alabastron* was used for a type of perfume bottle, whatever it was made from, and when the woman was said to 'break' it, this meant simply breaking the wax seal to pour the ointment over Jesus's feet, Matt. 26.7; Mark 14.3; Luke 7.37

**Alexander** (*G* = defender of men) **1.** Alexander the Great, Macedonian conqueror of Asia; reigned 336–323 BC; defeated Persia at Issus 333; then conquered Palestine and made it part of the Province of Coele-Syria; Dan. 11.3–4; 1 Macc. 1.1–8; 6.2. **2.** Son of Simon of Cyrene, Mark 15.21. **3.** Member of the Sanhedrin, Acts 4.6. **4.** Jew in Ephesus, Acts 19.33. **5.** Coppersmith who did Paul great harm, 1 Tim. 1.20; 2 Tim. 4.14

**Alexandria** port on the Nile delta and for long capital of Egypt, with the world's greatest library, where the Hebrew Scriptures were translated into Greek (see Septuagint, p. **178**) and many Jews including Philo, born 25 BC, expressed Judaism in Greek terms. Apollos the apostle came from Alexandria, Acts 18.24. Grain ships from Alexandria supplied food to Rome, Acts 27.6; 28.11

**Aliens** or foreigners, to be accepted as having rights in the community, Ex. 23.9–12; Num. 15.15–16; Deut. 1.16; 27.19. 'You are no longer strangers and aliens', Eph. 2.19

**All** in all, 1 Cor. 15.28; all things to all men, 1 Cor. 9.9; all things work together for good, Rom. 8.28

**Alleluia** see 'Hallelujah'

**Almighty** in Gen. 17.1, and elsewhere in the Hebrew Scriptures, 'God Almighty' translates the Hebrew *El-Shaddai*, the meaning of which is uncertain. This name is translated in the Septuagint as *pantokrator* (*G* = ruler over all); in the New Testament this word is found in 2 Cor. 6.18 and the Book of Revelation. Later it corresponded to the Latin *omnipotens* (= source of all power)

**Almond** type of peach tree valued for its nuts. In Jer. 1.11–12 there is a pun on the Hebrew name *shaqed*, which sounds like the word *shoqed* meaning 'watching'. In Eccles. 12.5 the white almond blossom may be compared to the white hairs of old age.

**Almsgiving** giving money to the poor, from the Greek *eleemosune* (= compassion). Commended in the books of Tobit and Ecclesiasticus, and by Jesus in Matt. 6.2; Luke 11.41; 12.33

**Almug** or **algum wood** probably red sandalwood, from Ophir, supplied by the king of Tyre for building the Jerusalem Temple and making musical instruments, 1 Kings 10.11; 2 Chron. 2.8; 9.10

**Aloes** see 'Spices'

**Alpha** first letter of the Greek alphabet, written α and A, used as a title of Jesus 'the first and the last' in Rev. 1.8, 11; 21.6; 22.13; see also 'Omega'

**Alphaeus** (*Ar* = leader of 1,000) father of James and Levi-Matthew, two of the Twelve Disciples, Matt. 10.3; Mark 2.14; this could be another form of the name Cleopas, the disciple who walked with the risen Christ to Emmaus, and Clopas, the husband of one of the Marys at the foot of the cross, Luke 24.18; John 19.25; the theory that these were all the same person is possible but unprovable

**Altar** place for meeting with God, usually by sacrificing an animal on it. Sometimes it is a platform or sanctuary, or it can be a mound of earth or a table made of uncarved stone, wood or bronze; some altars have projections at the corners called 'horns'. The first reference is to the altar made by Noah, Gen. 8.20; rules for making and using altars are in Ex. 20; 27; 30

**Amalek, Amalekites** (*H* = warlike) Canaanite tribe inhabiting the wilderness region around Kadesh, Gen. 14.7; at war with Israel up until the time of David, 1 Sam. 30. An Amalekite resident in Israel killed the wounded King Saul, and was executed for doing so, 2 Sam. 1

**Amarna** between Memphis and Thebes on the east bank of the Nile, capital of Egypt for only one generation in the fourteenth century BC. A large number of cuneiform tablets found at Tell el-Amarna are examples of the business and political correspondence of the times, giving considerable detail of the social life, tribal makeup and language of Canaan before the Exodus

**Amasa** (*H* = burden-carrier) David's nephew; supported Absalom; reconciled with David; killed by Joab, 2 Sam. 17.25; 19–20

**Amaziah** (*H* = Jah is strong) son of Joash, king of Judah 796–781 BC, killed at Lachish, 2 Kings 14.1–20

**Ambassadors** those sent as representatives from one nation to another, Josh. 9.4; 2 Chron. 32.31; Isa. 39. Apostles are called ambassadors for Christ, 2 Cor. 5.20; Eph. 6.20

**Amen** (*H* = true) word said at the end of a prayer signifying 'may it be so', 'yes, I agree', Num. 5.22; 1 Cor. 14.16 etc. Jesus began solemn statements with 'Amen, amen, I tell you', John 1.51 etc. Christ is called the Amen, who confirms the truth of God's promises, Rev. 3.14

**Ammonites** tribe living in Gilead, east of the River Jordan, around the city of Rabbath-Ammon, now called Amman, Deut. 2.19. They quarrelled with the Israelites, Judg. 11; 1 Sam. 11; 2 Sam. 10; 12.26. Prophecies concerning them are in Jer. 49.1–6; Ezek. 21.28–32; 25.1–7; Amos 1.13–15; Zeph. 2.8–11

**Amnon** (*H* = faithful) son of David; raped his half-sister Tamar; killed by her brother Absalom, 2 Sam. 13

**Amon** (*H* = trustworthy) son of Manasseh, king of Judah 642–640 BC, 2 Kings 21.19–26

**Amorites** group of tribes with their own Semitic language. By the eighteenth century BC, Amorite dynasties ruled many cities in Mesopotamia and Syria. Sihon the Amorite King, reigning east of the Jordan by the river Arnon, was defeated by the Israelites, Num. 13.29; 21.21–31, see Mesopotamia, p. **165**

**Amos** (*H* = burden-carrier) (Am.) The Book of the Prophet Amos (AY-moss), see p. **143**

**Amphipolis** gold-mining town on the Egnatian Way between Philippi and Thessalonica, capital of the first district of Macedonia, which Paul visited on his second missionary journey, Acts 17.1. A huge marble lion found there has been re-erected beside the River Strymon

**Anakim** (*H* = long-necked) tribe of giants in Canaan who frightened the Israelites and were destroyed by Joshua, Num. 13.33; Deut. 1.28; 9.2; Josh. 11.21

**Ananias** (*H* = Jah protects) **1.** Husband of Sapphira; held back money from the apostles; fell down dead, Acts 5. **2.** Disciple in Damascus; healed Paul's blindness, Acts 9; 22.12–16. **3.** High Priest AD 47–59, led the case against Paul, Acts 23.2; 24.1

**Anathema** (*G* = accursed, translates *H cherem* = 'put under a ban'), Rom. 9.3; 1 Cor. 16.22; Gal. 1.8–9; Rev. 22.3; see 'Ban'

**Anathoth** (*H* = answers) village 2.5 miles north-east of Jerusalem; birthplace of Jeremiah; its inhabitants are condemned for threatening him, Jer. 1.1; 11.21

**Ancient of Days** translates Aramaic phrase for the vision of God as an extremely old person, Dan. 7.9–22

**Andrew** (*G* = manly) Galilean fisherman, one of The Twelve, who brought his brother Simon Peter to Christ, Matt. 4.18–20; John 1.40–42; 6.8–9; 12.22

**Angel** (*G* = messenger) **1.** 'The Angel of the LORD' often signifies God himself, Ex. 3.2–15; Num. 22.23–35; Judg. 2; Matt. 28.2–7; Acts 10.3–4. **2.** Race of beings of a spiritual nature much lower than God but a little higher than human beings, Ps. 91.11–12; 103.20; Dan. 6.22; Matt. 24.31; Luke 2.13; Heb. 1.6–14 etc. **3.** Guardian angels: every church has its heavenly representative, and Jesus said that each of 'his little ones' has an angel, speaking on our behalf to God, Let. Jer. 6.7; Matt. 18.10; Rev. 2.1. **4.** Named angels: Michael, Dan. 10.13; 12.1; Jude 9; Rev. 12.7; Gabriel, Dan. 8.16; 9.21; Luke 1.19; 1.26; Raphael in Tobit; Uriel, 2 Esd. 4.1. **5.** Ranks of heavenly beings: Seraphim, Isa. 6.2–7; Rev. 4.8; Cherubim, Gen. 3.24; Ex. 25.18; Ezek. 1.5–12; Heb. 9.5; Thrones or Wheels, Ezek. 1.15; Col. 1.16; Rev. 20.4; Dominions or Dominations and Rulers or Virtues, Col.1.16; Titus 3.1; Principalities and Powers, Rom. 8.38; Col. 1.16; 2.10; Archangels, 1 Thess. 4.16; Jude 9; Watchers and Holy Ones, Dan. 4.13; Angels' Choirs, Job 38.7; Luke 2.13. **6.** The Devil is described as a fallen angel and has his own angels, Matt. 25.41; Luke 10.18; 2 Cor. 11.14; 2 Peter 2.4; Jude 6; Rev. 12.7–9. See also 'Hosts', Revelation, p. **159**

**Anna** (*G* form of *H Hannah* = grace), aged prophetess who waited for Christ, Luke 2.36

**Annas** (*G* form of *H Hanan* = grace; Josephus calls him Ananas) High Priest AD 6–15; still powerful when five of his sons and his son-in-law Caiaphas succeeded him; present when Jesus, Peter and John were tried, Luke 3.2; John 18.13–24; Acts 4.6

**Annunciation** when the archangel Gabriel announced to the Virgin Mary that she would have a son, to be named Jesus, Luke 1.26–38

**Anointing 1.** Oil poured on the head as a sign of appointing someone a king or priest, 1 Sam. 15.1; Lev. 6.20. **2.** Perfumed oil used to prepare a body for burial, Mark 14.8. **3.** Oil used to welcome a guest, Luke 7.46. **4.** Oil used in healing, James 5.14. **5.** Symbolic of the coming of the Holy Spirit, 2 Cor. 1.21; 1 John 2.20. See also 'Messiah'

**Ant** insect symbolizing busy foresight, Prov. 6.6; 30.25

**Antichrist** opponent of Christ, 1 John 2.18, 22; 4.3; 2 John 7. Possibly the same as the lawless one in 2 Thess. 2.9

**Anti-Semitism** see 'Jews'

**Antioch** (*G* = opposer) sixteen cities were named by Seleucus Nicator in honour of his father Antiochus, see 'Seleucid kings'. **1.** Antioch-on-the-Orontes was known as Syrian Antioch, though it is now in south-eastern Turkey and called Antakya. It was the centre of the Seleucid Empire and the capital of the Roman Province of Syria. Nicholas of Antioch was a Greek converted to Judaism and then to Christianity, Acts 6.5; in Antioch the followers of Jesus were first called 'Christians', Acts 11.26; Barnabas brought Saul (Paul) to help with the work there, Acts 11.26; the church there sent Paul out on his missionary journeys, Acts 13.1; 18.22. **2.** Pisidian-Antioch was a colony in the Roman Province of Galatia, on the borders of the regions of Pisidia, Phrygia and Lycaonia, intended to pacify the tribes and bring Roman civilization; the extensive ruins of the city, near Yalvaç on the high Anatolian plain of Central Turkey, contain what may be the foundations of the synagogue where Paul preached. Here Paul first 'turned to the Gentiles', Acts 13.14–49

**Antipas** (short for *G Antipatros* or *Antipater* = against father) **1.** Herod Antipas, see 'Herod Family', 'Judea'. **2.** Christian martyr in Pergamon, Rev. 2.13

**Antipatris** town rebuilt by Herod the Great and named after his father Antipater, on the site of Aphek 1.; where Paul stopped on his way under detention to Caesarea, Acts 23.31

**Antonia Fortress** rebuilt in 35–37 BC by Herod the Great on the north side of the Temple courtyard, and named after Mark Antony; traces of the rock foundations can be seen in the Haram es-Sharif; this was the 'Barracks', where Paul was taken after he was arrested, Acts 21.34–37; 22.24; 23.10, 16, 32

**Aphek 1.** Site now called Rosh Ha'ayin, in the Plain of Sharon, north of Lod airport, 1 Sam. 4; 29.1; see 'Ebenezer', 'Antipatris'. **2.** Town east of Lake Galilee associated with Ben-hadad and Elisha, 1 Kings 20.26–30; 2 Kings 13.17

**Apocalypse** (uh-POCK-uh-lips) (*G* = no longer hidden) or **The Revelation** (Rev.), see p. **159**

**Apocalyptic** see p. **175**

**Apocrypha** (uh-POCK-riff-uh) (*G* = hidden), see p. **145**

**Apollonia** town on the Egnatian Way which Paul and Silas passed though on their way to Thessalonica; today signs in the village point to large rock called Apostle Paul's Pulpit, Acts 17.1

**Apollos** (*G* = belonging to Apollo) Jew from Alexandria, converted to Christianity, who was an eloquent preacher but incompletely instructed. Paul welcomed him as a fellow apostle, and refused to regard him as leader of a rival faction, Acts 18.24–28; 19.1; 1 Cor. 1.12; 3.4

**Apollyon** (*H* = destroyer) see 'Abaddon'

**Apostle** (*G* = sent out) **1.** Jesus is an apostle, sent by God, Heb. 3.2. **2.** General word for all Christian missionaries (missionary is from the *L* word for someone sent out). Saint Paul is the greatest apostle, sent out by the church in Antioch, and by Christ, to convert the Gentiles, Rom. 1.1 etc. Others who are called apostles include James the brother of the Lord, Gal. 1.19; Barnabas, Acts 14.14; Andronicus and Junia (a woman), Rom. 16.7; Titus, 2 Cor. 8.23; and Peter, Gal. 2.8; 1 Peter 1.1; 2 Peter 1.1. **3.** All followers of Jesus are called 'disciples', but among them were chosen 'The Twelve' to 'judge the twelve tribes of Israel'; i.e. to rule the Jewish Christian Church, Matt. 19.28. To maintain the symbolism of the twelve sons of Jacob they had to be male. After the persecution in Jerusalem they began to do missionary or apostolic work. They are usually called The Twelve, but Mark 3.14 says they were 'also called apostles', and the word is used for The Twelve also in Matt. 10.2; Mark

6.30; Rev. 21.14; and in the writings of Paul, and Luke his companion. Possibly Paul was the first to apply the term 'apostles' to The Twelve, to show that they were all equal in missionary service

**Appii Forum** (*L* = market place of the Appius family) place on the Appian Way where believers from Rome came out to meet Paul as he travelled under arrest towards the city. It is identified as Borgo Faiti on the SS7 about 43 miles from Rome, Acts 28.15

**Apple** translates the Hebrew *tappuach*, which is probably the apricot, S. of Sol. 2.3; 7.8; Prov. 25.11; Joel 1.12

**Apple of the eye** pupil; as one would protect one's eyes from being touched or harmed, so God protects those who are dear to him, Deut. 32.10; Ps. 17.8; Zech. 2.8; Ecclus. (Ben Sira) 17.22

**Aquila** (*G* = eagle) husband of Priscilla, Jewish tent-makers expelled from Rome under Emperor Claudius, with whom Paul stayed in Corinth. They travelled with Paul to Ephesus, where they instructed Apollos, and hosted a church in their house; when Paul writes to Rome, however, they have moved back there, Acts 18.2; 18.26; Rom. 16.3; 1 Cor. 16.19. They may have returned to Ephesus later, 2 Tim. 4.19

**Arabah** (*H* = the plain) the Great Rift Valley, especially from the Dead Sea to Eilat, Deut. 2.8; 3.17; 1 Sam. 23.24

**Arabah Wadi** see 'Zered'

**Arabia** refers both to the whole area east of the River Jordan, and the Arabian Peninsula between the Red Sea and the Persian Gulf, 1 Kings 10.15; 2 Chron. 9.14; Acts 2.11; Gal. 1.17. Arabs were present at Pentecost, Acts 2.11

**Aram, Aramean, Aramaic** Arameans were a west-Semitic semi-nomadic people who settled in Syria, named *Aram*, and Mesopotamia, called *Aram-naharaim*. Aramaic is a language closely related to Hebrew, in which much of the Book of Daniel is written, and was spoken by Jesus, Gen. 25.20; Num. 23.7; Deut.26.5; 2 Kings 18.26; Isa. 7.8; Dan. 2.4

**Aram-naharaim** (*H* = High Place of Two Rivers) Hebrew name for Mesopotamia, Gen. 24.10; Deut. 23.4; Judg. 3.8; 1 Chron. 19.6; see 'Paddan-aram'

**Ararat** mountainous region, now in eastern Turkey, where Noah's ark is described as coming to rest after the flood, Gen. 8.4; 2 Kings 19.37; Jer. 51.27

**Araunah** (*H* = Jah is firm, called Ornan in 1 Chron.) Jebusite who owned a threshing floor on the windy ridge above Jerusalem, where the plague was stopped, and where David planned to build the Temple. The rock surface under the Dome of the Rock may be the threshing floor, 2 Sam. 24.16; 1 Chron. 21.15–22.1

**Archangel** see 'Angel'

**Archelaus** (*H* = commanding the people) king of Judea, feared by Joseph, Matt. 2.22; see 'Herod Family', 'Judea'

**Archippus** (*G* = ruler of horses) Christian minister, Col. 4.17; see Philemon, p. **157**

**Areopagus** (*G* = hill of Ares, translated Mars Hill in some versions) slope on the north-west of the Acropolis in Athens, where the god Ares (Mars) was supposed to have been tried for murder. It became the site of the court which dealt with murder trials and religious disputes, and Paul was questioned there; Dionysius the Areopagite, a member of the court, was converted, Acts 17.19–33

**Aretas IV** (*G* = goodness) king of Arabia 9 BC to AD 40, whose governor tried to seize Paul, 2 Cor. 11.32

**Ariel** (*H* = hearth of God) poetic name for Jerusalem, Isa. 29.1–7

**Arimathea** home of Joseph of Arimathea who buried Jesus in his own tomb;

identified as either Ramathain or Rentis, which are 15 and 20 miles east of Tel-Aviv respectively, Matt. 27.57–60; Mark 15.43; Luke 23.51; John 19.38

**Aristarchus** (*G* = noble ruler) a Christian from Thessalonica, travelling companion and fellow-prisoner with Paul, Acts 19.29; 20.4; 27.2; Col. 4.10; Philemon 24

**Ark 1.** Boat in which Noah and the animals survived the flood, Gen. 6.14. **2.** Basket of bulrushes in which baby Moses was found by Pharaoh's daughter, Ex. 2.3. **3.** Box containing the stone tablets with the Ten Commandments, with carrying poles, a cover, and figures of two cherubim, called the Ark of the Covenant. It was captured by the Philistines, retrieved, carried to Jerusalem and placed in the Temple there, Ex. 25.10–22; Josh. 6.11; 1 Sam. 4–6; 2 Sam. 6; 1 Kings 8.3; Heb. 9.4–5. It is claimed that Jeremiah hid it, 2 Macc. 2.4–8; a pattern of the ark is in heaven, Rev. 11.19

**Armageddon** (*H* = the hill of Megiddo) the Valley of Jezreel or Plain of Esdraelon, near Megiddo, is where many major battles were decided, and is described as the site of the final battle on the Day of God, Rev.16.16

**Armour** Isa. 59.17 describes the armour which God wears. Paul, who may have been chained to a Roman soldier wearing full armour, writes that we also must wear God's armour, and describes it piece by piece, Eph. 6.11; Rom. 13.12; 2 Cor. 6.7

**Arnon** (*H* = rushing) river, in Arabic Wadi al-Mujib, which flows through a half-mile-deep canyon south of Madaba in Jordan, entering the Dead Sea from the east; in early times the border between Moab and Ammon, Num. 21.13; Deut. 3.12; 4.48; Josh. 13.16

**Artaxerxes** kings of Persia; the names and chronology in the Bible are confused, see 'Exile', Mesopotamia, p. **165**

**Artemis** fertility goddess worshipped at Ephesus; the success of Paul's preaching reduced the sales of silver models of her temple, and led to a riot, Acts 19.23–41. Although given the Latin name Diana, she was very different from the 'chaste huntress'; only one pillar of her enormous temple remains.

**Artists** see 'Craftsmen'

**Asa** (*H* = healer) king of Judah, 911–870 BC, praised for reforming worship, 1 Kings 15.8–24; 2 Chron. 14–16

**Asaph** (*H* = collector) Temple musician, 1 Chron. 6.39; 15.17–16.37; Ps. 50; 73–83

**Ascension of Christ** an account, story, or vision to indicate the end of the time when Jesus was visible on earth, and his exaltation to a position of authority in the spiritual realm, Luke 24.51; John 20.17; Acts 1.9

**Ascents** psalms probably sung while processing up the road to Jerusalem, Ps. 120–134

**Ashdod** (*H* = stronghold) one of the five towns of the Philistines, where the Ark of the Covenant was taken after it was captured; later called Azotus; now an important port, between Gaza and Tel-Aviv, 1 Sam. 5; 2 Chron. 26.6; 1 Macc. 4.15; Acts 8.40

**Asher** (*H* = happy) one of the twelve sons of Jacob, ancestor of a tribe which occupied the northern Mediterranean coast, south of Tyre, Gen. 30.13; Deut. 33.24–25; Josh. 19.24; Judg. 5.17

**Asherah** mother goddess, partner to El and mother of Baal, probably represented by a wooden post, and connected with Ashtoreth-Astarte, the Phoenician moon goddess, Judg. 3.7; 6.25; 1 Sam. 12.10; 2 Kings 23.14

**Ashkelon, Askalon** or **Ascalon** one of the five towns of the Philistines, between Ashdod and Gaza, by the sea but without a harbour; birthplace of Herod the Great, who beautified it, Judg. 1.18; 14.19; 1 Sam. 6.17; 2 Sam. 1.20

**Ashkenaz** (*H* = spreading fire) see 'Scythians'

**Asia 1.** Continent stretching from the Aegean Sea to the Indian Ocean. **2.** Roman Province in what is now western Turkey, with its capital at Ephesus, ruled by Asiarchs, Acts 19.31. People from Asia were present at Pentecost, Acts 2.9. The Seven Churches addressed in Rev. 2–3 were all in the Province of Asia, Acts 19.10; 19.22; 27.2; 1 Cor. 16.19

**Asia Minor** not a Province, but the whole Anatolian Peninsula between the Mediterranean and the Black Sea

**Asp** (*H pethen*) poisonous snake, probably the cobra, Deut. 32.33; Job 20.14; Isa. 11.8; Rom. 3.13 quoting Ps. 140.3; see also 'Vipers'

**Ass** see 'Donkey'. Wild asses were the ancestors of the domestic donkey, Job 24.5; Ps. 104.11; Dan. 5.21

**Assassins** Jewish revolutionary group named *sicarii*, Latin for short daggers. Paul was mistaken for one of their leaders, Acts 21.38

**Assos** important city south of Troy, where the philosopher Aristotle taught, and Cleanthes the Stoic was born. The site, with impressive ruins, is beside Behramkale village on the Turkish coast, south of the Hellespont. Paul walked there on his third missionary journey, Acts 20.13

**Ashur** or **Assur** capital city of Assyria, near modern Qal'at Sherqat on the west bank of the Tigris in northern Iraq. The name is also used for the deity and the nation of Assyria, Ezek. 27.23; Num. 24.22–24; see Mesopotamia, p. **165**

**Assyria** see Mesopotamia, p. **165**

**Astrologers** people who attempted to predict the future from the stars; Isa. 47.13–15 mocks the powerlessness of the Chaldean astrologers, but the Magi were also astrologers, Matt. 2.1–12

**Athaliah** (*H* = Jah is strong) Queen Regent of Judah 841–835 BC; massacred almost all the royal family; had herself proclaimed sovereign; was executed when Joash was proclaimed king, 2 Kings 8.26; 9.11; 11.1, 13–16

**Athens** capital city of Greece, founded before 1000 BC when Theseus brought together a federation of states with Athens as head. From 700 it became the home of Greek philosophy and democracy, and from 500 to 400 was a time of great building, under Pericles, and some of the greatest philosophers. When Paul visited Athens it was ruled by the Romans but was known as a university city, where he was willing to take their existing beliefs as a starting-point for commending Christianity to them, Acts 17.15–34; 1 Thess. 3.1

**Atonement** translates the Hebrew word *kippur* (as in 'Yom Kippur') meaning covering, covering over sins so that they will be seen no more. The Bible translator William Tyndale invented the word atonement, at-one-ment, meaning reconciling humans to become 'at one' with God, Ex. 29.33; Rom. 3.25; Heb. 2.17 etc. The ritual for the Day of Atonement, Lev. 16, see 'Calendar'

**Attalia** now Antalya, port on the southern coast of Turkey, founded in the second century BC by Attalus II, king of Pergamon. In 25 BC it was made the capital of the Roman Province of Pamphylia. Paul left from Attalia at the end of his first missionary journey, Acts 14.25–26

**Augustan Cohort** either a unit of auxiliary soldiers stationed in the Province of Syria, or a unit of *frumentarii*, special messengers who among other duties escorted prisoners, to which Julius, the centurion who escorted Paul to Rome, belonged, Acts 27.1

**Augustus Caesar** born 63 BC, first Roman Emperor. Octavius was one of those who plotted against his uncle Julius Caesar; he was named Augustus in 27 BC by the Roman Senate and declared to be a god. He reigned until his death in AD 14, Luke 2.1

**Author** (*G archegon*) pioneer, or initiator, and perfecter of our life and faith, Jesus begins and completes the process of bringing us to God, Acts 3.15; Heb. 12.2

**Azariah** (*H* = Jah helps) **1.** Also called Uzziah, king of Judah 781–740 BC, he was called a good king; in the year Uzziah died, Isaiah was in the Temple praying about the future. Azariah was stricken with 'leprosy', seen as a punishment for attempting to make sacrifices which only priests were allowed to offer. His tomb has been discovered on the Mount of Olives, 2 Kings 15.1–7; 2 Chron. 26; Isa. 6.1. **2.** One of the three Jews thrown into the fiery furnace in Babylon, see 'Abednego'. **3.** Name adopted by the angel Raphael in Tobit

*Azazel* (*H* = God is strong) see 'Scapegoat'

**Azotus** see 'Ashdod'

**Baal** (*H* = husband, owner, lord) plural Baalim or Baals, the local male fertility and storm gods; eventually they were combined into one as Baal the sun-god. As with all fertility gods, the worship of Baal involved sexual excesses, and was opposed by the prophets who called Israel to be loyal to Jah, their true husband, Num. 25; 1 Kings 18.17–40; Isa. 54.5

**Baal-berith** (*H* = lord of the covenant), god worshipped at Shechem, which became the centre for the annual renewal of the covenant of Israel with YHWH, Judg. 8.33; Josh. 8.30–35; 24; 1 Kings 12.25–33

**Baal-hazor, Mount** summit now called Jebel Ashur, about 6 miles north-east of Bethel, 3,300 feet above sea level; here Absalom had sheep-shearers, and murdered his brother Amnon, 2 Sam. 13.23

**Baal-Zephon** (*H* = lord of the north) Israelite camp 'in front of Pi-hahiroth, between Migdol and the sea'; possibly = Tahpanhes, Ex. 14

**Baasha** (*H* = Baal hears) king of Israel 909–886 BC, 1 Kings 15.16–33; 16.1–13; 2 Chron. 16.1–6

**Babbler** translates Greek *spermologos*, meaning 'seed-logic', an insult to Paul from the Athenian philosophers, who saw him as gathering unrelated ideas like a sparrow pecking in the gutter, Acts 17.18

**Babel** (*H* = gate of God) where a tower was built with its top in the heavens, which God destroyed. The name sounds like *balal* (*H* = confuse). The story is told to rebuke human arrogance, and to explain why different areas speak different languages; it may refer to the tall *ziggurat* buildings of Babylon, Gen. 11.1–9

**Babylon 1.** Capital city of the Babylonian Empire; the site is beside the River Euphrates, 56 miles south of Baghdad in present-day Iraq, see Mesopotamia, p. **165**. **2.** Code name for Rome, 1 Peter 5.13; symbol of all that is evil, Rev. 14.8; 16.19; 17–18

**Badger** see 'Coney'

**Balaam** (*H* = conqueror of the people) prophet from the Euphrates region; summoned by Balak, king of Moab to curse the Israelites; when his donkey spoke to him, he blessed them instead, Num. 22–24; Deut. 23.4–5; Judg. 11.25; Micah 6.5. In a separate tradition he is said to have tempted the Israelites to sin – by eating meat offered to idols – at Peor, Num. 31.16; 2 Peter 2.15; Jude 11; Rev. 2.14

**Balm in Gilead** resin from the styrax tree, Jer. 8.22

**Ban** command from God that booty captured in battle is to be destroyed; the consequences of disobedience are serious, Deut. 7.2–6; Lev. 27.28; Josh. 6.17–19; 7; 8.2

**Baptism** (*G* = washing) ritual arising from the regular purification required of pious Jews (Mark 7.1–5; John 2.6), especially of non-Jewish converts before they joined the covenant community of Israel. John the Baptist said that even Jews needed to be baptized, relying not on their parentage but on 'a baptism of repentance for the remission of sins', Mark 1.4–11. Jesus was baptized by John to show his membership of the community, and those who wished to become his disciples did so by baptism, Acts 2.38; 8.36–39; Rom. 6.3–4. Possible references to infant baptism, Acts 16.15; 16.33; 18.8. Jesus said that he is the living water, and Christian baptism was distinguished from John's, because it is baptism in the Spirit, Mark 16.16; John 3.5–8; 4.10–15; 1 Peter 3.21; see 'Water'. Baptism is a metaphor for being plunged into suffering, Mark 10.39

**bar-** Aramaic for 'son of', e.g. the prophet bar-Jesus (= son of Joshua), Acts 13.6; Simon Peter bar-Jonah (= son of Jonah), Matt.16.17

**Barabbas** (*Ar* = son of the father), Jesus Barabbas was a rebel, bandit and murderer, who was chosen by the crowd to be released rather than Jesus Christ, Matt. 27.20–26; Mark 15.7–15; Luke 23.18–25; John 18.40

**Barbarian** term of contempt for one who cannot speak proper Greek, but only make 'bar-bar' noises; Paul says we must despise nobody because Christ is in everybody, Col. 3.11

**Barley** cereal crop harvested in April–May, before the wheat-harvest, Ruth 1–3; 2 Kings 7; Judith 8.2; made into barley-bread, Judg. 17.13; 2 Kings 4.42; John 6.9–13

**Barnabas** Levite from Cyprus, first name Joseph; sold his possessions when he became a Christian; preacher at Antioch; invited Paul to help and went with him on his first missionary journey; went his own way after a disagreement over Barnabas's nephew John Mark. Acts says his name means 'son of encouragement' but probably it is 'son of prophecy', Acts 4.36–37; 11.22–26; 13–15; Gal. 2.13

**Barracks** see 'Antonia Fortress'

**Bartholomew** (*Ar* = son of Tolmai) one of The Twelve; as he is not mentioned in John, and Nathanael is mentioned in John but not in the other Gospels, it is suggested that Bartholomew may have been the family name of Nathanael, Acts 1.13

**Bartimaeus** (*Ar* = son of Timai) blind beggar in Jericho, healed by Jesus, Mark 10.46–52

**Baruch** (*H* = blessed) scribe whom Jeremiah entrusted with the deeds of his property, and to whom he dictated his prophecies. The seal with which Baruch sealed documents, bearing his name, has been found. He was taken to Egypt, and given a special message of encouragement, Jer. 32.12–16; 36; 43.3–6; 45

**Baruch** (Bar.) The Book of Baruch (BA-rook), see p. 146

**Barzillai** (*H* = son of iron) old man who helped David but refused any reward, 2 Sam. 17.27; 19.31–39

**Bashan** (*H* = fruitful) large area east of Jordan, corresponding today to the Golan Heights and the area of Syria to the east; famous for fertility, trees and cattle; King Og was defeated by the Israelites, Deut. 3.1–13; Ps. 22.12; Isa. 2.13; Amos 4.1

**Bathsheba** (*H* = daughter of the oath) wife of Uriah the Hittite, to gain whom David had Uriah killed. She was the mother of Solomon, 2 Sam. 11–12; 1 Kings 1.15–31; 2.13–21

**Beam** or Log, large piece of wood, e.g. to support a roof; it is absurd to imagine someone not noticing that one was stuck in their eye, Matt. 7.3; see also 'Mote'

**Beating** see 'Scourging'

**Beatitudes** (from *L beati* = blessed) eight descriptions of a truly happy person which begin Jesus's Sermon on the Mount, Matt. 5.3–12

**Bed** the old translation for the Greek word meaning sleeping-mat, which could be rolled up and carried on one shoulder, Mark 2.4–12; John 5.8–11

**Beelzebub** or **Beelzebul** Ahaziah, who was injured, was rebuked by Elijah for sending a messenger to ask the god of Ekron whether he would recover, 2 Kings 1.2–6. The god's name was probably *baal zebul* (*H* = god, the exalted one) but the Hebrew writers use the insulting name *baal-zebub* (*H* = Lord of the flies). In the New Testament the Prince of Demons, in most Greek manuscripts, is called Beelzebul, but Jerome adopted Beelzebub for the Vulgate Latin translation. In Matt. 10.25 Jesus says, 'If they have called the master of the house Beelzebul, . . .' which may be a play on words, for 'master of the house' is another possible translation. Matt. 9.34; 12.24; Mark 3.22; Luke 11.15

**Beer-lahai-roi** (*H* = well of the Living One who sees me) well in the wilderness, northern Sinai Peninsula, where Hagar saw the LORD, Gen. 16.14

**Beer-sheba** (*H* = well of the oath) city with a well on the edge of the wilderness in the extreme south of Canaan, so that the full extent of the land was described as 'from Dan to Beersheba'. The site is at Tell es-Seba east of the modern city. Abraham, Hagar, Jacob and Elijah all spent some time there, Gen. 21.14; 21.31–33; 46.1–5; Judg. 20.1; 1 Kings 19.3

**Behemoth** (*H* = beasts) usually regarded as the hippopotamus, but it has taken on a mythical character in Job 40.15–24; 2 Esd. 6.49–52

**Bel** (*Ak* form of *H Baal* = Lord) Father of the Assyrian-Babylonian gods, identified with Marduk, the god of Babylon, Isa. 46.1; Jer. 50.2; 51.44

**Bel and the Dragon** (usual abbreviation Bel.) The Story of Bel and the Dragon, see p. **147**

**Belial** or **Beliar** (*H* = hell, wickedness) in the Hebrew Scriptures used in the combination 'children of Belial' or 'sons of Belial', meaning 'hellions', Deut. 13.13; Judg. 19.22; 1 Sam. 10.27. Another name for Satan in the New Testament and the Dead Sea Scrolls, 2 Cor. 6.15

**Believe** means to accept as true; **Believe in** means to trust, John 11.25–26, see 'Faith'

**Beloved** the name of King David is from a Hebrew root meaning 'beloved'. The firstborn is often called the 'beloved son'; God says of Jesus at his baptism and transfiguration 'This is my son, my beloved', Ex. 4.22; 2 Sam.13.21; Matt. 3.17; 17.5; Eph. 1.6

**Beloved Disciple** unnamed disciple who reclined next to Jesus at the Last Supper; commanded to care for Jesus's mother at the crucifixion; the first to enter the empty tomb, John 13.23–25; 19.26–27; 20.2–10; 21.20–23. John 21.24 states that the fourth Gospel is based on his account; he is usually identified as John, son of Zebedee; Lazarus has also been suggested

**Belshazzar** (*Ak Bel-shar-utsur* = Bel protect the king) portrayed in a story designed to teach God's judgement on the arrogant, as the king who held a great feast and saw the writing on the wall; an inscription in the British Museum shows that he was actually the son of King Nabonidus who held authority during his father's absence, and second in the kingdom, which is why Daniel was made third, Dan. 5; 8.1; see Mesopotamia, p. **165**

**Belteshazzar** (probably *Ak Balatsu-uzur* = preserve his life) name given to Daniel in Babylon, Dan. 1.7

**Ben-hadad** (*H* = son of Hadad) **1.** Syrian god, 1 Kings 15.18. **2.** Kings of Syria, probably three successors: the first signed a treaty with Asa, 1 Kings 15.16–22; the second fought with Ahab, was baffled by Elisha, besieged Samaria, and was killed by Hazael, 1 Kings 20; 2 Kings 6.8–24; 7.1–7; 8.7; and the third was the son of Hazael, who fought with Israel, 2 Kings 13.3; 13.25; Jer. 49.27; Amos 1.4

**Benjamin** (*H* = son of the right hand, or son of the south) youngest son of Jacob, and the tribe descended from him which settled in the south of Canaan around Jerusalem; King Saul was from the tribe of Benjamin, and so was Saul of Tarsus or Paul, Gen. 35.18; 44; 49.27; Deut. 33.12; 1 Sam. 9.16; Phil. 3.5

**Bernice** (*G* = bringer of victory) daughter of Herod Agrippa, who heard Paul's defence, Acts 25.13–26.32, see 'Herod Family'

**Beroea or Berea** town in Macedonia, now called Verea in Greece, where Paul preached, and converted Sopater, Acts 17.10–15; 20.4

**Bethany** (*H* = house of dates, or house of the afflicted) **1.** Village 2 miles from Jerusalem on the Mount of Olives, home of Lazarus (it is now called el-Azariyeh) and his sisters Martha and Mary, near to which Jesus ascended into heaven, Matt. 26.6; Luke 19.29; 24.50–51; John 11.18–44; 12.1–8. **2.** Ford on the River Jordan where John baptized, rediscovered on the Jordanian side in 1996, John 1.28; because the site was unknown the text was changed to Bethabara (*H* = house of the ford)

**Beth-aven** (*H* = house of wickedness) either another (insulting) name for Bethel; or the town near the sanctuary, Josh. 7.2; Hos. 4.15; 10.5

**Bethel** (*H* = house of God) place, formerly called Luz, 12 miles north of Jerusalem, now Beit El in the Palestinian Territories, where Jacob had a vision of a ladder; an important sanctuary of the Northern Kingdom, Gen. 28.19; 1 Kings 12.25–13.10; 2 Kings 23.15; Amos 4.4; 5.5; 7.10

**Bethesda** (*H* = house of mercy or house of the stream) or **Beth-zatha** (*H* = house of olives) in some manuscripts, pool in Jerusalem, with five 'porches', where Jesus healed a paralysed man. A short distance inside the Lion Gate, where the sheep market was held until recent times, is the entrance to the Greek–Catholic Seminary, occupied by the French White Fathers, and inside is St Anne's Church and the site of the pool, though today there is only a little water under a vault. Excavations show that as well as the colonnade along each of the four sides there was a fifth colonnade on a causeway across the centre, as described in John 5.1–13

**Bethlehem** (*H* = house of bread) **1.** Bethlehem in Zebulun, now called Beit Lahm, 7 miles north-west of Nazareth; Josh. 19.15; Judg. 12.8–10. **2.** Bethlehem in Judah, village 5 miles south of Jerusalem, where Rachel was buried; birthplace of King David and of Jesus Christ; where the children were slaughtered on the orders of King Herod. It is on a hillside so that a stable might well have been under the house. A cave, identified in the early second century, can now be reached below the sixth-century (with fourth-century foundations) Church of the Nativity, Gen. 35.19; Ruth 1–4; 1 Sam. 16.1–13; Micah 5.2; Matt. 2.1–12; Luke 2.1–20

**Bethphage** (*H* = house of figs) village near Bethany, where Jesus was when he sent the disciples to find a donkey for him to ride, Matt. 21.1; Mark 11.1; Luke 19.29

**Bethsaida** (*H* = house of fishing) city on the north shore of Lake Galilee, where the River Jordan enters, where Jesus healed a blind man and fed five thousand people; native town of Philip, Peter and Andrew. The walls have been excavated a short distance inland at et-Tell, Mark 8.22; Luke 9.10–17; John 1.44; 12.21

**Beth Shan** or **Bet-shean** (*H* = house of rest) city west of the River Jordan just south of Lake Galilee, where Saul's body was fastened to the wall after he was killed; extensive remains have been found of the city which the Romans called Scythopolis, including a theatre, 1 Sam. 31.10–12

**Beth-Shemesh** (*H* = house of the sun) see 'Sorek'

**Bethulia** town in the hill country of Samaria, which is the setting for the book of Judith, but it may be more symbolic than historical, Judith 4.6; 6.11–12; 7.12–13; 11.19

**Betrothal** commitment to marry which was considered binding; adultery while betrothed was punishable by stoning; in Galilee, unlike Judea, betrothed couples did not have intercourse until married, Deut. 20.7; 22.23–27; Matt. 1.18; Luke 2.5

**Beulah** (*H* = married) prophetic name for Israel in its future happiness, Isa. 62.4

**Bier** stretcher for carrying a dead body, 2 Sam. 3.31; Luke 7.14

**Bildad the Shuhite** (*H* = Bel has loved) one of Job's 'friends', from the tribe of Shuah, Job 2.11; 8.1 etc.

**Binding** and **loosing** forbidding or permitting an action, or condemning or forgiving it, Matt. 16.19; 18.18; John 20.23

**Birth pangs** pain of a woman in childbirth, used as a metaphor for the suffering which we must endure now before God brings his work to a joyful culmination, Micah 4.10; Mark 13.8; John 16.20–22; Rev. 12.1–6

**Birthright** right of the firstborn son to inherit a double share, twice as much as the other sons, of their father's property; despised by Esau, Gen. 25.31–34; Deut. 21.15–17

**Bishop** (*G episkopos* = overseer) leader in the Church; the term is first used in Phil. 1.1, where the terms 'bishops and deacons' may reflect the 'overseers and servants' in Lydia's household; the qualifications are outlined in 1 Tim. 3.1–7; Tit. 1.7–9; the same word is used of the Ephesian elders, Acts 20.28; and of Jesus 'the bishop of your souls', 1 Peter 2.25

**Bithynia** and **Pontus** Roman Province along the southern coast of the Black Sea. Paul was prevented by the Spirit of Jesus from preaching there, Acts 16.7; but 1 Peter 1.1 is addressed to Christians there; Pliny in his letter to Trajan in about AD 110 asks advice what to do about them.

**Bitter herbs** eaten at Passover to remember the bitterness of slavery, Ex. 12.8

**bitter waters** of Marah made sweet, Ex. 15.23–25

**Bitumen** pitch, tar-like substance obtained from the Dead Sea region, used in building, Gen. 11.3; Ex. 2.3; Isa. 34.9

**Blasphemy 1.** Cursing God, pronouncing the sacred name of God, or claiming equality with God; punishable by death; this was the crime for which the priests condemned Jesus and sent him to Pilate, Lev. 24.15–16; 1 Kings 21.10; Matt. 9.3; 26.65; Acts 6.11. **2.** Jesus said that all sins can be forgiven except blasphemy against the Holy Spirit, by which he probably meant rejecting good deeds done in the power of God as being works of the Devil, thereby declaring oneself unwilling to receive God's all-forgiving love; it has been said that if you are worried about having committed the unforgivable sin, then you certainly haven't, because those who have wouldn't worry, Mark 3.28–30. **3.** See 'Swearing'

**Blemish 1.** Defect or injury, which makes an animal undesirable for human consumption; worshippers are forbidden to sacrifice second-rate animals to God, Ex. 12.5. **2.** Priests must not be deformed, Lev. 21.16. **3.** Christ is described as an unblemished sacrifice, and the Church must be pure and holy also, Eph. 5.27; 1 Pet. 1.19

**Bless 1.** To thank God, Ps. 103.1. **2.** See 'Beatitudes'. **3.** When God gives his blessing we receive material and spiritual benefits, Num. 6.22–27

**Blind** people healed by Jesus: Matt. 9.27–30; 12.22; 20.29–34; Mark 8.22–25; 10.46–52; Luke 7.21; 18.35–43; John 9; a fulfilment of the prophecy in Isa. 35.5. Metaphor for inability to see God's truth, Isa. 56.10; Matt. 15.14; John 9.39–41

**Blood** in Hebrew thought represented the life of the body; the law forbad them to shed the blood of another human being in murder, Deut. 21.1–9; or to eat meat with blood in it, Lev. 17.11–14; Deut. 12.23. When the blood of an animal was offered in sacrifice, it represented also the life of the worshipper offered to God, Ex. 23.18, Heb. 9.12–14; and a covenant was sealed by sprinkling blood on the worshippers and on the altar, as though it was signed in blood by both God and the people, Ex. 24.6–8. Jesus at the Last Supper said of the wine, 'This is my blood of the covenant', Mark 14.24 etc.

**Boanerges** (*H bene regez* = sons of thunder) the nickname that Jesus gave to the brothers James and John, because of their fiery temper, Mark 3.17; 9.38; 10.35–41; Luke 9.54

**Boat** a fishing boat from around the time of Jesus has been discovered and preserved near the shore of Lake Galilee, Matt. 8.23–27; 13.2; 14.22–33; John 6.17–24

**Boaz** (*H* = cheerfulness) **1.** Landowner of Bethlehem; married Ruth; ancestor of Jesus, Ruth 2–4. **2.** A pillar in the Temple, 2 Chron. 3.17

**Body 1.** The instrument through which the human personality is recognized, communicates and works; Paul wrote that the Christian's body is the temple of the Holy Spirit, 1 Cor. 3.16; 6.19; 2 Cor. 6.16. **2.** Jesus came to give God a body to work through, Col. 1.15. **3.** At the Last Supper he said of the bread, 'This is my body', Matt. 26.26. **4.** Paul said the Church is 'the body of Christ', which must be united if he is to work through it, Rom. 12.4–5; 1 Cor. 12.12–27; Eph. 3.6; 4.12; Col. 3.15. **5.** In the resurrection we shall have a 'spiritual body', Rom. 12.34; 1 Cor. 15.35–49; Eph. 5.30. **6.** In 1 Cor.15.50 Paul distinguishes the 'body' from the 'flesh'. See 'Members', 'Unity of the Church'

**Bones** the vision of the Valley of Dry Bones teaches that, though the Jewish leaders and people seem to be spiritually dead and hopeless, the Spirit of God (Spirit and Wind are the same word in Hebrew) can breathe new life into them; this led to the hope of individual resurrection, Ezek. 37

**Book** originally a scroll, then a codex of folded pages. The book of life is a list of those who will inherit eternal life, Phil. 4.3; Rev. 3.5; 13.8; 20.12–15

**Booths** (*H succoth*) small shelters built out of branches, called in older translations tabernacles, for those gathering the harvest to overnight in the fields. During the autumn festival, they commemorated the shelters of the Israelites in the wilderness after the Exodus, Ex. 23.16; 34.22; Lev. 23.33–44. At this festival, the High Priest poured water over the bronze altar, so it was at Tabernacles that Jesus referred to rivers of Living Water, John 7.2, 37–38; see also 'Calendar'

**Born again** better translated 'born from above', in the discussion with Nicodemus, means making a fresh start in life, depending no longer on our own achievements but on the love of God; 'born of the Spirit' means that our salvation is the work of God within us; Christians differ about whether this requires a particular type of conversion experience, John 3.3–8; 1 Peter 1.23

**Bosom** see 'Reclining'

**Bottles 1.** Liquids were transported by ship in pottery amphoras, and an earthenware jug was broken by Jeremiah as a sign of God's judgement; older translations call it a bottle, Jer. 19.1. **2.** Glass and other precious materials were used for perfume bottles, see 'Alabaster'. **3.** Wine bottles for home use were usually made of leather; the skin of a dead goat was peeled off without splitting it, and tanned with bark; such a bottle would expand when it was new to hold the fermenting new wine, but once it had been emptied it dried out and became brittle, so Jesus said that the ferment of his new teaching could only be contained in new social structures: 'new bottles for new wine', Matt. 9.17 etc.

**Boundary-marker** see 'Landmark'

**Bow** flexible piece of wood with a leather thong, used to fire arrows. When God promised Noah there would be no more floods, he said he had hung up his battle-bow in the clouds; we call it a rainbow, Gen. 9.12–17

**Bowels** seat of pity or kindness in Hebrew thought, Gen. 43.20; 1 Kings 3.26; S. of Sol. 5.4; Phil. 1.8; 2.1; Col. 3.12; 1 John 3.17

**Bozrah** (*H* = fortified place) the principal city in Edom, south of the Dead Sea, modern Buseirah in Jordan, whence one who has fought with God's enemies returns covered in blood, Isa. 63.1; Christians use this paradoxically to describe Christ on the cross

**Branch** the striking image of a tree which has been cut down to a stump, from which a new shoot appears with promise of new life, in Isa. 11.1 expresses hope for a new ruler coming from the royal family of David, son of Jesse. Possibly the 'righteous branch' of Jer. 23.5; Zech. 3.8; 6.12, is also a promise of a Messiah; Jesus said, 'I am the vine, you are the branches', John 15.5

**Brand** burning piece of wood; it is snatched from the fire just in time to prevent it being consumed, Amos 4.11; Zech. 3.2; Jude 23

**Brass** alloy of copper and zinc; **Bronze** is of copper and tin; bronze was discovered about 2600 BC, brass not until much later. The same word *H nechosheth* or *G chalkos* is used for both, as in the 'brazen serpent', Num. 21.9, Goliath's 'helmet of brass', 1 Sam. 17.5, and the 'sounding brass' gong, 1 Cor. 13.1, which were all probably made of bronze

**Bread** the staple diet, could be made of wheat or barley, see 'Lord's Prayer', 'Manna', 'Unleavened bread'. Jesus used unleavened bread at the Last Supper, and described himself as the Bread of Life, John 6.35; 1 Cor. 11.23; see also 'Body', 'Loaves and fishes'

**Bread of the Presence** or Showbread, placed daily in the Temple as food for the deity, but eaten by the priests, Ex. 25.30; Lev. 24.5–9; in an emergency given to David, 1 Sam. 21.1–6; Matt. 12.4

**Bricks made without straw** were more likely to crumble as the clay baked in the sun, than if straw was mixed in to bind it together, Ex. 5.7

**Bride of Christ** description of the Church, 2 Cor. 11.12; Rev. 19.7; 21.2; see 'Marriage'

**Bridegroom** title of Christ, Matt. 9.15; 25.1–12; Mark 2.19–20; John 3.29

**Brimstone** (*H gophrith, G theion*) used in old translations for sulphur, found on the brim of a volcano's crater, Gen. 19.24; Deut. 29.23; Isa. 30.33; Rev. 9.17

**Bronze** see 'Brass'

**Brook** see 'Wadi'

**Brothers of Jesus** James, Joseph, Simon and Judas are described as brothers of Jesus, together with some sisters, and before his crucifixion tried to persuade him to withdraw from his ministry, Matt. 12.46–49; 13.55; Mark 3.20–21, 31–34; 6.3; Luke

8.19–21; John 2.12; 7.3–10; but they are with The Twelve in Acts 1.14; 1 Cor. 9.5; see also 'James'. Those who believe in the perpetual virginity of Mary argue that these were half-brothers or cousins. Jesus calls all believers his brothers and sisters, Mark 3.35; John 20.17

**Buckler** small shield held in the hand or strapped to the arm to ward off a sword-stroke, Ps. 35.2; 91.4

**Bulrushes** The 'ark' in which baby Moses was placed, and the reeds where it was found, were both *papyrus antiquorum*, the plant from which paper was made, Ex. 2.3

**Burden** see 'Oracle'

**Burning bush** God appeared to Moses in a bush which burned but was not burnt up, Ex. 3.2; Mark 12.26; Luke 20.37; Acts 7.35

**Burnt offerings** (*L holocaustum* comes from *G holokatauma* = whole burnt). Animals which were sacrificed were usually roasted, then the meat was eaten by the priests and the worshippers; but in a burnt offering it was totally destroyed, Ex. 29.38–42; Lev.1.1–17; Mark 12.33; Heb. 10.5–10

**Bushel** basket or pot containing a measure of grain; it would be absurd to put an oil-lamp under an upturned measure where it would shed no light and might go out, Matt. 5.15; Mark 4.21, see 'Measures in other systems'

**Butler** Pharaoh's 'butler' in old translations, is called 'cup-bearer' in newer versions, Gen. 40

**'Butter** in a lordly dish', better translated curds, made from coagulated milk, Judg. 5.25

**Caesar** (SEE-suh) family name of Gaius Julius Caesar; Augustus Caesar made it a title for Roman Emperors, Luke 2.1; Tiberius, Luke 3.1; Claudius, Acts 11.28; Nero, Acts 25.11; see also 'Money'

**Caesarea** (SEE-suh-REE-uh) **1.** Caesarea-Maritima, port and administrative capital on the coast of the Roman Province of Judea. Remains visible today, 25 miles north of Tel-Aviv, include a large Roman theatre; a stone with Pontius Pilate's name on it; the foundations of Herod's Palace; the Roman aqueduct and underwater harbour foundations. There Peter met the Roman centurion Cornelius, Acts 10; Paul stayed, Acts 21.8–15; Paul was tried by Felix and imprisoned, Acts 23.23–26.32. **2.** Caesarea-Philippi, a town named Paneas after the god Pan, one of the sources of the River Jordan, later refounded by Tetrarch Philip and named after Augustus, today called Banyas, with recently excavated Roman remains. Here Peter recognized that Jesus was the Messiah, Matt. 16.13–20; Mark 8.27–33

**Caiaphas** (K-EYE-uh-fass, probably from *Ar kepha*, a rock) High Priest from about AD 18 to 36, who condemned Jesus, Matt. 26.3; 26.57–68; John 11.49–52. In 1990 his tomb was found in Jerusalem

**Cain** (KAYN, *H* = get) see 'Abel'

**Calah** or **Kalakh** ancient capital of Assyria, now called Nimrud near the Tigris and Zab rivers in Iraq, Gen. 10.11–12; see Mesopotamia, p. **165**

**Caleb** (*H* = dog) and Joshua were the only two of the spies sent by Moses to survey Canaan to bring back a favourable report, and the only people in the Exodus group to enter the promised land, Num. 13.1–14.10; Deut. 1.36; Josh. 14.6–14

**Calendar** Different calendars have been used at different periods. The Israelites at first adopted the agricultural calendar of its Canaanite neighbours, based on a 7-day week and 7 × 50 day periods in the year. Each community held a 7-day Feast of Unleavened Bread before the first sheaf of the spring harvest was cut, which was declared the local New Year. In Jerusalem King David processed to a sanctuary on the Mount of Olives at the beginning of the Feast of Unleavened Bread, and back to his throne at New Year as the ram's horn was blown, 2 Sam. 15.32. The ram's horn was also blown when the new moon was first sighted. This calendar continued in agricultural communities for many centuries.

King Solomon adopted the calendar of Tyre, based on the sun. New Year was at the autumn equinox, when the rising sun shone through the East Gate of the Temple onto the Sanctuary. This was preceded by the 7-day Feast of Booths. At the New Year the King, representing YHWH, was enthroned in the Temple, with lighting of the new fire and blowing of the ram's horn. It was followed by 12 months of 30 days each.

In the seventh century, an Assyrian calendar was adopted with months numbered from the spring equinox; New Year became the tenth day of the seventh month.

During the Exile a mixed sun / moon calendar emerged, with New Year on the first day of the first month (the spring equinox) and 12 months of 30 days, with extra days inserted every 3 months. This continued among sectarian groups including Qumran.

Ezra and Nehemiah reverted to the Assyrian calendar, with New Year on the first day of the seventh month, and the High Priest replacing the King as YHWH's representative. There are 12 months of 29 and 30 days alternately, plus a thirteenth month called Ve-Adar whenever the priests (later the rabbis) decided it was necessary. The months were at first called by number, later by their Babylonian names. This is the Jewish year until now.

*Nisan* (or Tyrian name *Abib*), in approximately March–April, 14th day is Passover (with which are combined the agricultural festivals of Firstfruits (Wave-offering) and Unleavened Bread). Latter or spring rains, barley harvest begins

*Iyyar* (or *Ziv*), April–May, barley harvest continues

*Sivan*, May–June, 6–7th day is Pentecost (Feast of Weeks or Harvest Festival). Wheat harvest

*Tammuz*, June–July

*Ab*, July–August

*Elul*, August–September. Grape harvest

*Tishri* (or *Ethanim*), September–October, 1st day is New Year, or *rosh ha-shanah*, 10th is Day of Atonement, 15th–22nd Feast of Tabernacles or Booths. Grape and olive harvest, former or early rains, ploughing begins

*Marchesvan* (or *Bul*), October–November, wheat and barley sown

*Chislev*, November–December, 25th day is *Hanukkah*, Feast of Lights, Dedication of the Temple

*Tebet*, December–January

*Shebat*, January–February

*Adar*, February–March, 14th–15th day is Feast of *Purim*. Almond tree blossoms

The Talmud introduced the system of numbering the years from the date of creation. The Jewish day runs from sunset to sunset, Lev. 23.32

**Calf** Golden, image of a bull, made by Aaron for the people to worship while Moses was on Sinai, Ex. 32; worshipped in Bethel and Dan by King Jeroboam, 1 Kings 12.28. **2.** Fatted, specially fed ready to be eaten on a special occasion, killed by the father of the Prodigal Son for a feast to welcome him home, Luke 15.23

**Call** of Noah, Gen. 6.13; Abraham, Gen. 12; Jacob, Gen. 28.12; Moses, Ex. 3; Gideon, Judg. 6.11; Samuel, 1 Sam. 3; Elijah, 1 Kings 17; Elisha, 1 Kings 19; Isaiah, Isa. 6; Jeremiah, Jer. 1; Ezekiel, Ezek. 1; Hosea, Hos. 1; Amos, Amos 1; 7.14–15; Jonah, Jonah 1; Peter and others, Matt. 4.18; Mark 1.16; Luke 5; John 1.39; Paul, Acts 9; Rom. 1.1; Gal. 1.15

**Calvary** (*L calvaria*, *G kranion*; *G from Ar Golgotha* = a skull) place in Jerusalem where Jesus was crucified. Excavations at the Church of the Holy Sepulchre show that there was a quarry, outside the city walls, with cave tombs cut into the walls, and a skull-shaped piece of rock left unused because of a crack in it. It is unlikely that Jews would allow skulls from previous executions to remain, but there is a legend that the skull of Adam was buried there, and the blood of Christ trickling through the crack raised Adam to life. Emperor Trajan built a shrine to Jupiter and Venus over the site, unintentionally identifying it, enabling Constantine to build a church for pilgrims. Gordon's Calvary, however, is a good place for meditation, Matt. 27.33; Mark 15.22; Luke 23.33; John 19.17

**Camel** when domesticated in about the eleventh century BC, became a principal means of transport and sign of wealth among nomads, Judg. 7.12; 1 Chron. 5.21; Job 1.3; Matt. 3.4. Jesus said it is easier for a camel to pass through the eye of a needle than for a rich man to enter the kingdom of heaven. Alternative explanations have been proposed, but most likely this is an example of humorous but challenging exaggeration, Matt. 19.24; Mark 10.25. Gnat and camel are a play on words in Aramaic, Matt. 23.24. See also 'Sackcloth'

**Cana of Galilee** (KAY-nuh, *H* = reed) traditionally identified with Kafr Kanna, north-east of Nazareth on the road to Tiberias, though more likely is Khirbat Qana, 9 miles north-west of Nazareth; town where at a wedding feast Jesus turned water into wine; where a royal official came to Christ to ask healing for his son; hometown of Nathanael, John 2; 4.47; 21.2

**Canaan** (KAY-nun, *H* = low land) area between the Mediterranean coastal plain and the River Jordan; occupied by many tribes called in general Canaanites, and promised to Abraham, Gen. 12.6–7 etc. The discovery of writing on clay tablets at Tell el-Amarna in Egypt and Ras Shamra in Syria has given an insight into Canaanite society and religion before the settlement of the Israelite tribes. See also 'Syro-Phoenician'

**Cananaean** (KAY-nuh-NEE-un) alternative name of Simon, one of The Twelve Disciples, possibly the Aramaic equivalent of the Greek 'Zealot', Matt. 10.4; Mark 3.18

**Candace** (CAN-duh-see) Queen of Ethiopia, whose servant Philip baptized, Acts 8.27

**Candle** misleading term in the old translations for an oil lamp; for 'candlestick' read 'lamp-stand', see 'Lamp'

**Canon of Scripture** see p. 133

**Canticles** see Song of Songs, p. 140

**Capernaum** or **Capharnaum** (kuh-PURR-nee-um or ka-fur-NAY-um, *H Kfar Nahum* = Nahum's village) small village on the north shore of Lake Galilee, where Jesus stayed at Peter's house, taught and healed, but which he also rebuked.

Foundations of houses from Jesus's time can be seen, including one identified by early graffiti as Peter's house. An inscription in Aramaic includes the personal names Alphaeus, Zebedee and John. Under the fourth-century synagogue can be seen traces of the synagogue where Jesus preached, Matt. 4.13; 8.5; 11.23; 17.24; Mark 1.21; 2.1; 9.33; Luke 4.23; 4.31; 7.1; John 2.12; 4.46; 6.17; 6.24; 6.59

**Caphtor** Crete and the Aegean region, Gen. 10.14; Deut. 2.23; Jer. 47.4; Amos 9.7

**Cappadocia** (kapp-uh-DOH-see-uh) Province of the Roman Empire in what is now central Turkey; people from there were present on the Day of Pentecost, Acts 2.9; they are among those to whom Peter wrote, 1 Peter 1.1–2

**Captivity** see 'Exile', Captivity Epistles, p. **154**

**Carchemish** (KAR-kuh-mish, *H* = fortress of Chemosh) battle in 605 BC where Neco II, Pharaoh of Egypt, fighting alongside the Assyrians, was defeated by Nebuchadnezzar, thus ending the Assyrian Empire and Egyptian hopes of dominance; the site is on the Euphrates on the Turkey–Syria border and is occupied by a Turkish military base, called Karkamiş, 2 Kings 23.28–30; 2 Chron. 35.20–24; Jer. 46.2–12; see Mesopotamia, p. **165**

**Carmel** (KAR-mul, *H* = garden land) **1.** Mountain near the sea in northern Israel, where Elijah held a contest with the prophets of Baal, 1 Kings 18; and where the Shunammite woman asked Elisha to heal her son, 2 Kings 2.25; 4.25–30. **2.** Village 7 miles SSE of Hebron, where Nabal rejected David, 1 Sam. 15.12; 25; 2 Sam. 2.2; 3.3

**Carpenters** built temples, 2 Sam. 5.11; Jesus and Joseph probably made anything from yokes, Matt. 11.30, to houses, Matt.7.24; 13.55

**Cassia** see 'Spices'

**Castor and Pollux** (*G dioscouroi*) twin gods of Greek and Roman mythology, after whom the ship was named in which Paul sailed from Malta, Acts 28.11

**Caterpillars** one of the plagues of Egypt in Ps. 78.46, not mentioned in Exodus; probably a type of locust or stage in their development, see also 1 Kings 8.37; Isa. 33.4

**Cauda** (KOW-duh) island 23 miles south of Loutro in Crete, now called Gavdos; provided temporary shelter from the storm for Paul's ship, Acts 27.16

**Cenchreae** (KEN-cree-ay) port 7 miles east of Corinth, from which Paul sailed for Syria, after having his hair cut at the conclusion of a Nazirite vow, Acts 18.18; Num. 6.2–21. The church there was served by a deaconess named Phoebe, Rom. 16.1–2. Today called Kechries, 2.5 miles south of Isthmia, there are remains of quayside buildings and underwater structures.

**Censer** small dish of bronze or gold filled with burning charcoal from the altar; over which aromatic spices and gums were heated, Lev. 10.1; 16.12; 1 Kings 7.50; Rev. 8.3

**Census** counting the adult males capable of joining the army; commanded in Ex. 30.11–16, including the payment of a half-shekel tax so that a plague should not break out. The plague after David's census was probably because this was not done, 2 Sam. 24. Emperor Augustus ordered frequent censuses on which the income expected from taxation was calculated. Mary and Joseph had to go to Bethlehem because of a census, though there is no other evidence of this particular census, Luke 2.1. There was one in Egypt in 4 BC, and in AD 104 people had to go to their home-town for a census, see also 'Quirinius'

**Centurion** (*L* = commander of 100 soldiers), highest rank of non-commissioned officer, in fact in charge of 80 men. **1.** A centurion asked Jesus to heal his servant, Matt. 8.5–13; Luke 7.1–10; see also 'Nobleman 2.'. **2.** A centurion in charge of the crucifixion spoke favourably of Jesus, Matt. 27.54; Mark 15.39; Luke 23.47. **3.** Cornelius, a centurion, received the Holy Spirit, convincing Peter that even non-Jews can be baptized as Christians, Acts 10. **4.** Centurions escorted Paul to Caesarea and then to Rome to be tried, Acts 23.23; 27.43

**Cephas** (SEE-fass, *Ar kefa* = a rock) nickname which Jesus gave to Simon, translated into Greek as Peter, John 1.42; 1 Cor. 1.12; 9.5; Gal. 2.9

**Chaldea** (kawl-DEE-uh) province in the south of Babylonia, near 'Ur of the Chaldees', from which came Nabopolassar who replaced the Assyrians as rulers of Babylon. Thereafter 'Chaldeans' means Babylonians, though it is especially applied to their wise men, Gen. 11.28–31; Jer. 37–39; Dan. 2.2–10; 5.7–11; see Mesopotamia, p. **165**

**Chamberlain** in older translations, a court official, called in modern translations a eunuch, 2 Kings 23.11; Esth. 1.10; 6.2

**Charger** large dish on which the head of John the Baptist was placed; in modern translations a platter or dish, Matt. 14.8

**Chariot** small fast horse-drawn cart, introduced by the Egyptians, which changed the character of warfare, Ex. 14.6–7; 1 Sam 13.5; 2 Sam.10.18; Ps. 20.7; Elijah was taken up to heaven in a chariot of fire, and chariots of fire were sent to defend Elisha, 2 Kings 2.11–12; 6.17; Ps. 68.17

**Charity** old translation of the Greek word *a-ga-pe*, 1 Cor. 13, see 'Love'

**Chebar** (KEE-bar) navigable canal forming part of the Euphrates irrigation system; it ran for 186 miles from Sippar through Nippur to Uruk, and the Jewish exiles may have been used to dig it; some identify it with the Shatt en-Nil. Beside the 'River Chebar' Ezekiel saw his visions, Ezek. 1.1

**Chedorlaomer** (tched-or-lay-OH-mur) one of four kings who took Lot and the other inhabitants of the Cities of the Plain captive; were defeated by Abraham and driven out of the area which had been promised to him. No such names are known from other sources; they are probably symbolic of Israel's later enemies: Elam in the east, Babylonia south, Assyria north and Hittites west, Gen. 14

**Cheek** to strike someone on the cheek is a common insult, 1 Kings 22.24; Job 16.10; Ps. 3.7; Micah 5.1. It is good to give one's cheek to the smiter and bear insults, Lam. 3.30. The Suffering Servant of God gave his cheeks to those who pulled out the beard, Isa. 50.6. Although someone insulted would usually retaliate, Jesus tells us to turn the other cheek, Matt. 5.39

**Cherethites** and **Pelethites** (TCHE-ru-thigh-ts) David's bodyguard; the name Keret was found on a tablet at Ras Shamra, suggesting they may have been Phoenician tribes, possibly Cretans, who were in Canaan before the arrival of the Philistines or the Israelites, 1 Sam. 4.1; 30.14; 2 Sam. 8.18; 15.18

**Cherith** (TCHE-rith) where Elijah was fed by ravens during a drought, is traditionally the Wadi Kelt near Jericho, though 1 Kings 17.3 says it is east of the Jordan, so more likely is the Wadi el-Yabis, entering the Jordan south of Lake Galilee

**Cherubim** (TCHE-roo-bim) plural of Cherub, and see 'Seraphim'. **1.** Mythical guardians of the Garden of Eden preventing humans from returning to paradise; God flies on the cherubim, Gen.3.24; Ps. 18.10. **2.** Two images of winged cherubim were placed on top of the Ark of the Covenant, Ex. 25.18; 37.7–9. **3.** Ezekiel had a vision of cherubim, winged beings with two or four faces, Ezek. 1; 10; 28.14; 41.18–19; Rev. 4.7; they may have been related to the sphinx of Egypt and the winged creatures shown in front of Assyrian Temples. The vision of the wheels showed that God is not found only in one place, but can meet us where we are

**Children 1.** A gift from God, Ps. 127; 128. **2.** The boy Samuel in the Temple, 1 Sam. 3. **3.** The streets of Jerusalem shall be full of children playing, Zech. 8.5. **4.** Welcomed by Jesus, Matt. 19.13–15. **5.** Relationship with parents to be one of mutual self-sacrifice, Eph. 6.1–4; Col. 3.20–21

**Chios** (KEE-oss) Greek island in the Aegean close to the Turkish coast; Paul arrived 'opposite Chios', most likely at Erythrae (Ildır in Turkey, which has a theatre and a Temple to Athena) on his way to Samos, Acts 20.15

**Chloe** (KLOH-ee, *G* = tender shoot) leading Christian in Corinth; she was probably manager of a business which had travelling representatives, who reported the situation to Paul, 1 Cor. 1.11

**Chorazin** (KORR-uh-zinn) town rebuked by Jesus for unresponsiveness, Matt. 11.21; the site is at Khirbat Karazeh, 2 miles north-west of Capernaum

**Christ** see 'Messiah'

**Christian** term first applied in Antioch-on-the-Orontes to followers of Christ, Acts 11.26; 26.28; 1 Pet. 4.16

**1 & 2 Chronicles** (1 Chr. & 2 Chron.) The First Book of Chronicles & The Second Book of Chronicles, known as 1 & 2 Paralipomenon in Greek, see pp. **138–9**

**Church** In Athens the *ekklesia demos* was the democratic assembly of citizens; *ekklesia* was the word used in the Greek translation of the Hebrew Scriptures for the 'congregation' of Israel. Paul wrote to the church in a town, or the church which meets in someone's house, Rom. 16.1, 5; but also refers to the worldwide Church, which must be built up, and must not be divided, 1 Cor. 14.4; Eph. 5.27. Jesus speaks of building his Church on the rock; some say that is the person of Peter, others that it means his faith, Matt. 16.18. See 'Unity of the Church'

**Cilicia** (sigh-LISS-ee-uh) Roman Province at the north-eastern corner of the Mediterranean, on the southern coast of what is now Turkey. The 'Cilician Gates', a narrow pass through the Taurus mountains, were of strategic importance on the road to the east. Paul was born at Tarsus in Cilicia, and he passed though on his second and probably third missionary journeys, Acts 15.41; 18.23; 21.39; Gal. 1.21

**Cinnamon** see 'Spices'

**Circumcision, Circumcise** (sur-kum-SIZH-un, SUR-kum-size) small surgical operation to remove the foreskin from the penis. Originally a hygienic precaution in sandy conditions, it came to be a sign to the Israelites of their membership of the covenant community. Performed when baby boys were eight days old, it was also imposed on adult converts and vanquished enemies, Gen. 17.10–27; 21.4; 34.15–24; Ex. 12.48; 1 Macc. 2.46; Luke 2.21. The Council of Jerusalem decided it was not necessary for Gentiles to be circumcised when they became Christians, Acts 15.1–29; Paul argued for the implementation of this decision, so that there could be unity between Jewish and Gentile Christians, Gal. 2.3; 5.6; 6.15. A disobedient attitude is called an uncircumcised heart, Lev. 26.41; Deut. 10.16; Jer. 4.4; Rom. 2.28–29

**Citizenship** of the Roman Empire gave protection against unjust punishment and the right to appeal to Caesar; it had probably been granted to Paul's parents by the authorities in Tarsus, whereas the tribune at Paul's arrest had to pay for his; Paul told the Christians in the Roman colony of Philippi that we are 'citizens of heaven', Acts 21.39; 22.25–29; 23.27; Phil. 3.20

**Claudius** (CLOR-dee-us) **1.** Roman Emperor AD 41–54, expelled Jews from Rome in 41 or 49, according to the Roman historian Suetonius because of riots about someone called 'Chrestus'; Suetonius also mentions the famine during Claudius's reign, Acts 11.28; 18.2. **2.** Claudius Lysias, tribune in Jerusalem who sent Paul, for his own safety, to Governor Felix in Caesarea, Acts 23.26

**Clean** and **Unclean** unconnected with modern ideas of sanitary and insanitary, are descriptions of what may be used in worship and what disqualifies a person from worship, see 'Food laws', 'Leprosy', 'Menstruation', 'Purification'

**Cleansing the Temple** see 'Money-changers'

**Clement** (*L* = merciful) co-worker with Paul, Phil. 4.3. Possibly the Clement who was a leading presbyter in the church at Rome at the end of the first century. There are remains of first-century houses under the Church of San Clemente in Rome, one of which might have been his; the First Letter of Clement might be by him, see p. **163**

**Cleopas** (KLEE-oh-pass, probably short for *G Cleopatros* = famous father) one of two disciples who met the risen Christ on the road to Emmaus, Luke 24.13–32; probably = Clopas, John 19.25, see 'Alphaeus'

**Cnidus** port on the coast of what is now Turkey, 21 miles from Datça on a peninsula near Marmaris. There is an island connected to the mainland by a causeway which provides two harbours. It was famous for the statue of Aphrodite by Praxitiles, and the Lion of Cnidus now in the British Museum. Paul was forced to change direction off Cnidus, Acts 27.7

**Coal** meaning burning charcoal, symbolizes the cauterizing of Isaiah's sinful words, Isa. 6.6; and the painful guilt produced in your enemy when you treat them kindly, Prov. 25.21–22; Rom. 12.20

**Coastlands** see 'Isles'

**Cockcrow** third watch, from roughly midnight to 3 a.m., Mark 13.35; Peter, after he denied Jesus, heard the crowing and was remorseful, Matt. 26.34

**Cohort** Roman army unit, 600 men, one tenth of a legion. The cohort in Jerusalem at the time of the crucifixion had barracks in the Antonia Fortress north of the Temple, Matt. 27.27; Acts 21.31; see also 'Augustan Cohort', 'Italian Cohort'

**Colossae** once a great city in the Lycus Valley in Asia Minor, it declined with the growth of nearby Laodicea, and is now an unexcavated mound near Honaz in Turkey, Col. 1.2

**Colossians** (Col.) The Letter of Paul to the Colossians (kuh-LOSS-yuns), see p. **155**

**Comfort 1.** Comfort from God, Isa. 66.13; 2 Cor. 1.3–4. **2.** We are to comfort or console others, 2 Cor. 1.4–7. **3.** Comforter, in older translations, means fortifier, strengthener, see 'Paraclete'

**Commandment** something which God orders us to do, see 'Ten Commandments'. Ps. 119 alternates the other names for the law, 'ordinances', 'decrees', 'precepts', 'statutes', 'word'. There are hundreds of commandments in the Hebrew Scriptures; Jesus reduced them to two: love God and love your neighbour, Mark 12.30; John 13.34

**Communion** see 'Last Supper'

**Concubine** woman permanently belonging to her husband, but with a status lower than a wife, 1 Kings 11.3

**Coney** (KOH-nee) the rock badger, *Hyrax syriacus*, a small mammal, the size of a large rabbit but with short ears, which can still be seen on the rocky cliffs of mountains and valleys, Lev.11.5; Ps. 104.18; Prov. 30.26

**Confess, confession 1.** Accept one's responsibility for wrongdoing, Lev. 16.21; Ps. 32.5; James 5.16; 1 John 1.9. **2.** Agree with the truth of a statement, John 1.20; Heb. 11.13. **3.** Declare one's belief, 1 Kings 8.33; John 9.22; Rom. 10.9; 1 John 4.3

**Coniah** see 'Jehoiachin'

**Corban** (*H* = offering) tradition whereby a man who quarrelled with his parents could dedicate all he had to God, thus avoiding his duty under the Ten Commandments to care for them; Jesus puts the word of God above tradition, Lev. 1–7; Mark 7.11

**Corinth** (KO-rinth) city near the narrow isthmus which joins the large peninsula of the Peloponnese to the mainland of Greece. To avoid several days' sailing around the peninsula, many ships approached Corinth up the Saronic Gulf and either their contents or the whole ship were transported over the isthmus to the Gulf of Corinth, or vice versa, requiring thousands of slaves. There were extremes of wealth and poverty, many prostitutes, and the Isthmian Games were held nearby. The Temple of Apollo, the Bema where Paul was tried, the Lecheon Road, an odeon and a theatre can be seen in the ancient city, together with Acro-Corinth towering above it, and parts of the *diolkos* along which the ships were wheeled. Paul made several visits and formed a congregation of Christians there, Acts 18.1–18; 18.24–19.1; 20.2–3

**1 Corinthians** (1 Cor.), Paul's First Letter to the Corinthians (kuh-RINN-thyuns), see p. **153**

**2 Corinthians** (2 Cor.), Paul's Second Letter to the Corinthians, see p. **154**

**Corn** in older translations means wheat; maize had not yet been brought from America

**Cornelius** see 'Centurion'

**Cornerstone** either a large boulder in the foundations of a building to make a firm corner, or the keystone of an arch, Ps. 118.22; Isa. 28.16; Matt. 21.42; Eph. 2.20; 1 Peter 2.6

**Cos** Greek island in the Aegean, birthplace of Hippocrates who originated the physicians' oath; Paul stayed there one night after leaving Miletus, 1 Macc. 15.23; Acts 21.1

**Council** see 'Sanhedrin'

**Council of Jerusalem** meeting of church leaders who produced a letter stating that the whole Law of Moses was not binding on Gentile Christians, only four essentials: to 'abstain from what has been sacrificed to idols, from blood, from what is strangled, and from fornication', Acts 15; 21.25; and probably Gal. 2.1–10; based on God's covenant with Noah, Gen. 9.4–7

**Covenant** (KUH-vuh-nunt) contract, treaty or agreement between a great monarch and subordinate kings; Testament means the same, though, as with a Last Will and Testament, it is one in which the giver decides the terms. Covenants began by naming the persons involved, a promise to protect, and a list of conditions which must be kept, including that of not making a similar contract with any other monarch. This is the form of the Covenant between God and the Israelites at Mount Sinai, Ex. 20–24; God promised to protect them; the Ten Commandments were the conditions; and instead of signing it, the Israelites sacrificed an animal and sprinkled the Blood of the Covenant, half on the altar representing God, and half on the people. Other covenants are compared to this: with Noah, Gen. 9.1–17; Abraham, Gen. 15.18; 17.2–14; Joshua and the twelve tribes, Josh. 24.14–27; David, 2 Sam. 23.5; Ps. 89.3–4. Because nobody has ever fully kept the commandments, prophets dreamt of a new covenant, written not on tablets of stone but on our hearts, Jer. 31.31–34; Heb. 7–13; 2 Cor. 3.3–6. Jesus said at the Last Supper that his blood shed on the cross, and the wine passed around, resemble the Blood sprinkled on the signatories of a Covenant, of which the only conditions were faith and love; so the book about

Jesus is called the New Testament, 1 Cor. 11.25; Matt. 26.28; Mark 14.24; Luke 22.20

**Cover** old translation for atone, 1 Peter 4.8; see 'Atonement', 'Mercy-seat'

**Covet** (KUH-vitt) wanting something which belongs to another, Ex.20.17; Eph. 5.5

**Craftsmen** inspired by the Holy Spirit and essential to civilization, Ex. 31.1–11; Ecclus. (Ben Sira) 38.24–34

**Creation** the making of the universe; 'Creationists' believe that Gen. 1–2 is a literal description of what happened in seven days, see Fundamentalism, p. **177**; though Job 38.14–41; Ps. 19.4–6; 104.2–9; Isa. 11.12 etc. are accepted as metaphorical. 'Liberals' hold that there are two accounts in Gen. 1–2, 'P' and 'J', see p. **134**; and that the Israelites took stories of *how* the world began from surrounding cultures, retelling them to emphasize *why* the world was created, and the character of the Creator

**Crete** southernmost and largest Greek island; Cretans were present at Pentecost, Acts 2.11; Paul visited Crete on his way to Rome, Acts 27.7–16; Titus, the first bishop, is buried there, Titus 1.5, see 'Caphtor'

**Crippled woman** healed by Jesus, Luke 13.10–17

**Crown 1.** Gold circlet worn on the head by royalty, e.g. Saul, 2 Sam. 1.10; Jesus, Rev. 19.12. **2.** Laurel wreath placed on the head of the winner of a race, thus symbolically promised to Christians who perform their tasks diligently, James 1.12; 1 Peter 5.4; Rev. 2.10. **3.** Crown of thorns placed in mockery on Jesus's head before his crucifixion, Matt. 27.29; Mark 15.17; John 19.2

**Crucifixion** the most painful method of execution ever invented, was introduced by the Romans for slaves and rebels. The skeleton of a crucified man was found in Jerusalem, with a nail sideways through the ankles; nails will also have been driven through the wrists as the palms would tear, and death will have been from suffocation because every breath would require pulling oneself up on the nails, though the legs might be broken as a *coup de grâce*. The crucifixion of Jesus is described in Matt. 27.32–56; Mark 15.21–41; Luke 23.26–49; John 19.17–37; and the cross, meaning Christ's voluntary self-sacrifice, is the centre of Paul's theology, 1 Cor. 1.23 etc. John says Jesus died on a Friday, the day before Passover; the other Gospels suggest the Friday was the day when Passover began at sunset. There may be confusion over the Feast of Unleavened Bread, or the writers may have changed the story to teach its significance; the only suitable years when Passover fell on a Saturday were AD 30 and 33

**Cruse** called a jug in modern translations; the widow's cruse, where she kept her oil, never became empty, 1 Kings 17.12

**Crystal** either quartz or glass, Job 28.18; Ezek. 1.22; Rev. 4.6; 22.1

**Cubit** distance from a man's elbow to his finger-tips, from the Latin for 'elbow', or perhaps the time it would take to walk this distance, Matt. 6.27; Luke 12.25, see 'Measures of Length'

**Cucumber** watery fruit eaten as a vegetable, remembered nostalgically in the wilderness, Num. 11.5; grown in a field where the watchman made a small shed to protect himself from the sun, Isa. 1.8

**Cummin** the small aromatic fruit of *Cuminum sp.*, used as a spice, Isa. 28.25–27; Jesus rebukes those who pay tithes of this tiny crop and ignore more important matters, Matt. 23.23

**Cuneiform writing** (*L* = wedge-shaped) impressing marks in tablets of soft clay and baking them

**Curse 1.** Curse by God, Gen. 8.21; Deut. 11.20. **2.** Curse by Israel's enemies, Gen.12.3; Num. 22.6. **3.** We are not to curse others, Ex. 22.28; Lev. 26.9; Luke 6.28; Rom. 12.14. **4.** We are not to curse God, Job 1.11. **5.** The disobedient are accursed, Matt. 25.41; 1 Cor. 16.22, see 'Anathema', 'Ban'. **6.** Peter said something like, 'May God's curse be on me if I am telling a lie', Matt. 26.74

**Cush** the Upper Nile region of Nubia, including modern Ethiopia, Eritrea and Sudan, Num. 12.1; 2 Sam. 18.21–32; 2 Chron. 14.9–15; Esth. 1.1; Isa. 18; Jer. 13.23; 38.7–16; Acts 8.28–40

**Custom** toll; Matthew was sitting at the receipt of custom, Matt. 9.9, collecting taxes from everyone who carried goods from Galilee, ruled by Herod Antipas, to the Decapolis, ruled by Herod Philip II, and vice versa, see 'Tax-collectors'

**Cyaxares** (sigh-uh-KSAH-rees) (624–585 BC) king of Media, who freed the Medes from Scythian rule. Together with Nabopolassar of Babylon, he captured and destroyed Nineveh in 606, Isa. 13.17–22; Tob. 14.15; see Mesopotamia, p. **165**

**Cyprus** large island in the Mediterranean, source of copper (*G cypros*). **1.** Called Chittim or Kittim in the Hebrew Scriptures, from the city of Kition, some remains of which can be seen in Larnaca, Num. 24.24; Isa. 23.1, 12; Jer. 2.10; Ezek. 27.6. **2.** Home of Barnabas, Mnason and other Christians, Acts 4.36–37; 11.19–20; 21.16. **3.** Starting-point for Paul's first missionary journey, Acts 13.4. **4.** Paul, Barnabas and John Mark preached in the synagogue in Salamis; extensive remains of Salamis can be seen near Famagusta, in north Cyprus, Acts 13.5. **5.** Paphos, in the south-west of the island, is where Paul and Barnabas met Elymas the magician and the Governor Sergius Paulus, Acts 13.6–12

**Cyrene** (sigh-REE-nee) city (the dramatic remains can be viewed near modern Shahat in Libya) and Roman Province on the north African coast, 2 Macc. 2.23. Simon of Cyrene carried the cross for Jesus, Mark 15.21; people from Cyrene were present at Pentecost, Acts 2.10; disciples from Cyrene and Cyprus were the first to evangelize Greeks, Acts 11.20; 13.1

**Cyrus II** (SIGH-russ) king of Babylonia. A Persian, in 550 BC he defeated the Median king; formed a combined empire of the Medes and Persians, Esth. 10.2; Isa. 13.17–22; Dan. 6.8–15. In 538 he invaded Babylonia, defeating Nabonidus and entering Babylon in 539, Jer. 50.2–3; 51.11, 28; where he ruled until 530. He is praised in the Bible because he allowed the first group of Jewish exiles to return home, 2 Chron. 36.22–23; Ezra 1; Isa. 44.28–45.13; Jer. 16.14–15; see 'Exile', Mesopotamia, p. **165**

**D** the 'Deuteronomist', believed by some to have edited the books from Deuteronomy to Kings, see p. **135**

**Dagon** national god of the Philistines, Judg. 16.23; 1 Sam. 5.2–5; 1 Chron. 10.10; 1 Macc. 10.83–84

**Dalmanutha** name given in Mark 8.10 to the place called Magdala in Matt. 15.39

**Dalmatia** (dal-MAY-shuh) Roman Province to the north-east of the Adriatic, 2 Tim. 4.10, see 'Illyricum'

**Damascus** capital city of Syria, 2 Sam. 8.5; David subdued it, 2 Sam. 8.6; Rezin occupied it, 1 Kings 11.24; Naaman the leper worshipped there in the House of Rimmon, 2 Kings 5.1–14; Elisha prophesied there, 2 Kings 8.7; Jeroboam captured it, 2 Kings 14.28; Tiglath-Pilezer conquered it, 2 Kings 16.9; Paul was converted on his way there, then healed in the Street called Straight, Acts 9.1–21; 22.6; and lowered from the walls in a basket, 2 Cor. 11.33. Today the walls of the old town follow the lines of the Roman walls, and two streets, joined by a Roman arch, correspond to Straight Street; the beautiful Ummayad mosque is on the site of a Roman Temple, and probably also of the House of Rimmon

**Dan** 1. Son of Jacob, Gen. 30.6; ancestor of one of the twelve tribes of Israel, Gen. 49; Deut. 33. 2. Capital town of the tribe of Dan and one of the sanctuaries of the Northern Kingdom, originally called Laish. It is one of the sources of the River Jordan, and walls, a sacred way and the base of a throne from the time of King Ahab can be seen, Gen. 30.6; 49.16–17; Deut. 33.22; Judg. 18; 1 Kings 12.29–30. One theory suggests that the Psalms of Korah, Ps. 42–49; 84–88, with many references to water, were used at an autumn festival at Dan, then adapted for Jerusalem

**Dancing** to celebrate a victory, Ex. 15.20–21; at pagan worship, Ex. 32.19; 1 Kings 18.26; David dances before the Ark, 2 Sam. 6; dancing to praise God, Ps. 87.7; 150.4; at harvest-time, Jer. 31.12–13; at weddings, Matt. 11.17; at birthdays, Matt. 14.6; at the return of the prodigal, Luke 15.25

**Daniel** (*H* = God is my judge) (Dan.) The Book of Daniel (DAN-yul), see p. **142**

**Darius** Kings of Babylon, 1. Darius 'the Mede', Dan. 5.31; 9.1; 11.1, probably = Cyrus II. 2. Darius I (522–486 BC), during whose reign the Jerusalem Temple was rebuilt and dedicated; he overcame the Greeks at Thermopylae but was defeated at Marathon; Ezra 4.24–6.15; Dan. 11.2; Hag. 1.1–2.19; Zec. 1.1, 7; 7.1; 1 Esd. 3–4. 3. Darius II called Nothus (424–404); condemned Daniel to the lion's den, then wrote a decree in favour of Daniel's God, Neh. 12.22; Dan. 6. 4. Darius III called Codomanus, was defeated by Alexander the Great in 335, 1 Macc. 1.1. See Mesopotamia, p. **165**

**Darnel** see 'Tares'

**Dathan** (*H* = strong) see 'Abiram'

**Daughters and Fathers** Ecclus. (Ben Sira) 42.9–14

**David** (*H* = beloved) King of the united kingdom of Israel and Judah c.1010–c.970 BC. Son of Jesse, Ruth 4.22; anointed by Samuel, 1 Sam. 16.1–13; played the harp for Saul, 16.14–23; killed Goliath, 17; Saul's jealousy, 18–20; friendship with Jonathan, 18.1–23.16; loved by Michal, 18.20–19.17; ate the temple bread, 1 Sam. 21; Matt. 12.3–4. At Adullam, 1 Sam. 22. Lament over Saul and Jonathan, 2 Sam. 1; king of Judah, 2; David and Abner, 3; and Ishbaal, 4; king of all Israel, 5; brought the Ark, and danced, 6; not allowed to build a temple, 7; David and Mephi-bosheth, 9; had Uriah killed to marry Bath-Sheba, 11; rebuked by Nathan, 12; quarrelled with Absalom, 13.23–18.32; lament for Absalom, 18.33–19.8; appointed Solomon his successor, 1 Kings 1–2; ancestor of Jesus, Matt. 1.1

**Day of the LORD** 1. Day of battle when the LORD's armies score a notable victory, Ezek. 13.5; 30.3; Zep. 1.14–16. 2. Day when God judges the wicked among his people, Joel 2.31; 3.14; Amos 5.18–20; Mal. 4; 1 Cor. 1.8; 5.5; 2 Peter 3.10

**Dayspring** the dawn, Luke 1.78

**Deacon** (*G diakonos* = servant) position in the Church; term first used in Phil. 1.1, where the terms 'bishops and deacons' may reflect the 'overseers and servants' in Lydia's household; the qualifications are outlined in 1 Tim. 3.8–13; verse 11 could refer to wives of deacons, but more likely means women deacons, treated as equals: Phoebe was a deacon of the church at Cenchreae, Rom. 16.1. 'The Seven' in Acts 6.1–6 are often described as the first deacons, though that word is not used of them in the Bible

**Dead Sea** 400 metres (1,300 feet) below Mediterranean sea level, lowest point on the earth's surface, in the rift valley; the River Jordan runs into it from the north and then evaporates, so it is saturated with salts and has no outlet and no fish, Gen. 14.3; Num. 32.3; 34.12 etc. See also 'Siddim'

**Dead Sea Scrolls** see p. 162

**Deaf** healed, Isa. 29.18; 35.5; Matt. 11.5; Mark 7.32; 9.25

**Death** see 'Crucifixion', 'Mourning', 'Resurrection'

**Debir 1.** town between Hebron and Beer-Sheba, conquered by Joshua and again by Othniel, Josh. 10–11; Judg. 1.11 **2.** Town near Gilgal, Josh 15.7. **3.** See 'Lo-Debar'

**Deborah** (*H* = bee) prophetess and leader of Israel, whose song following the defeat of Jabin, written c.1125 BC, is one of the oldest poems in the Hebrew language, Judg. 4–5

**Debt 1.** Charging interest on loans is forbidden, Lev. 25.36–37; Deut. 23.19; Ps. 15.15; Ezek. 18.8–17; forbidden when lending to the poor, Ex. 22.25; Neh. 5; forbidden when exorbitant, Prov. 28.8; permitted when lending to foreigners, Deut. 23.20; expected, Matt. 25.27. **2.** Debtors could lose their pledge, Neh. 5.3–5; be sold as slaves, 2 Kings 4.1; or put in prison, Matt. 18.30. **3.** See 'Jubilee'. **4.** Debt is used as a metaphor for sin in parables and the Lord's Prayer to teach divine and human forgiveness, Matt. 6.12–15; 18.23–35; Luke 7.41–50

**Decalogue** see 'Ten Commandments'

**Decapolis** (*G* = ten towns) region east of the Jordan where non-Jews outnumbered Jews, consisting of Canatha; Damascus; Dion or Dium; Gadara; Gerasa; Hippos; Pella; Philadelphia (the site of Amman); Raphana; and Scythopolis (Bethshan west of the Jordan), Matt. 4.25; Mark 5.20; 7.31

**Deceiver** 2 John 1.7, see 'Devil 3.'

**Decision** or Verdict, Valley of, where the LORD judges the nations, Joel 3.14, see 'Jehoshaphat'

**Dedication 1.** Of the Temple by Solomon, 1 Kings 8. **2.** Rededication of the Temple by Judas Maccabeus in 164 BC, origin of the Feast of the Dedication in November–December, 1 Macc. 4.36–59; John 10.22; see 'Calendar'

**Deer** red, fallow and roe deer were known in Bible times; hart and hind mean the male and female (stag and doe) red deer, but Hebrew terminology is inexact, Deut. 14.5; Ps. 18.33; 42.1; S. of Sol. 8.14; Isa. 35.6

**Delilah** (*H* = dainty) Philistine wife of Samson; betrayed him by having his head shaved, Judg. 16

**Demas** (*G* = popular) Paul's fellow-worker, Col. 4.14; Philemon 24; who deserted him, 2 Tim. 4.10

**Demetrius 1.** Silversmith who led riot in Ephesus, Acts 19.24–38. **2.** A good Christian, 3 John 12

**Demons** Tobit; Matt. 9.33; 11.18; 15.22; 17.18; Luke 4.33–35; 8.29; John 10.20–23; see 'Devil 1.'

**Denarius** see 'Money'

**Denial** when Peter swore he did not know Jesus, Matt. 26.69–75

**Derbe** small town in Lycaonia to which Paul fled from Lystra on his first missionary journey, Acts 14.20–21; probably among the Galatian towns he revisited on his second and third journeys; hometown of Gaius, one of Paul's companions, Acts 20.4. Its site is an unmarked mound about 2 miles north of the village of Ekinözü, north-east of Karaman in Turkey

**Descent into hell** belief stated in the Apostles' Creed that Jesus 'descended into hell' (meaning the world of the dead, not a place of suffering) to bring those who died before his time back to life, based on 1 Peter 3.19, 'Christ visited the spirits in prison', and Eph. 4.9, Christ 'also descended into the lowest parts of the earth'. See also Ps. 139.8; Matt. 27.52; John 5.25–29; 8.56. It brings comfort to Christians worried about the fate of those who had no chance to hear the gospel attractively presented before they died, see 'Hell'

**Desert 1.** (pronounced DEZZ-urt) land deserted, with no human inhabitants; see 'Wilderness'. **2.** For 'the desert road' see 'Gaza'. **3.** (pronounced dizz-URT) to go away and leave someone, Matt. 26.33

**Deuteronomy** (G = second law) (Deut.) The Book of Deuteronomy (pronounced dew-ter-O-no-me or DEW-ter-o-NO-me, with short 'o's), see p. **136**

**Devil 1.** One of a multitude of evil spirits; some cases then called demon-possession might today be called madness, see 'Spirit 1'. **2.** Power opposed to God, also called Satan, who brought death into the world, Wisd. 2.24; Heb. 2.14; tempts Jesus in the wilderness, Matt. 4.1–11; Mark 1.13; Luke 4.1–13; tries to entrap Judas, Peter and others, Luke 22.3, 31; John 6.70; 13.2; Acts 5.3; 1 Cor. 7.5; 2 Cor. 2.11; 12.7; Eph. 4.27; 1 Tim. 3.6–7; 2 Tim 2.26; James 4.7; 1 Peter 5.8; 1 John 3.8–10; Rev. 2.10; sowed weeds in God's field, Matt. 13.39; Luke 8.12; is the father of lies but can disguise himself as an angel of light, John 8.44; 2 Cor. 11.14; and is defeated when Jesus heals the sick, Luke 10.18; 11.18; 13.16. Those who are excommunicated are handed over to Satan, 1 Cor. 5.5; 1 Tim. 1.20; Jews who persecute Christians are a synagogue of Satan, Acts 13.10; Rev. 2.9; 3.9. Satan is the supreme enemy of God, Acts 26.18; 1 Thess. 2.18; 2 Thess. 2.9; Jude 9. In the end the Devil will be defeated, Matt. 25.41; 1 John 3.8; Rev. 12.9, 12; 20.2–10. See also 'Satan'. **3.** Also called Abaddon and Apollyon, Rev. 9.11; a fallen angel, 2 Cor. 11.14; 2 Peter 2.4; Jude 6; Rev. 9.11; 12.7–9; Antichrist, 1 John 2.18, 22; 4.3; 2 John 1.7; Beelzebub, or Beelzebul, Prince of demons, Matt. 9.34; 10.25; 12.24, 27; Mark 3.22; Luke 11.15–19; Belial, or Beliar, 2 Cor. 6.15; the Deceiver, 2 John 1.7; Rev. 12.9; the dragon, Rev. 12; 13; 16.13; 20.2; the enemy, Matt. 13.25–39; Luke 10.19; the evil one Matt. 5.37; 6.13; 13.19; John 17.15; Eph. 6.16; Lucifer, Isa. 14.12; Luke 10.18; Rev. 9.1–11; Prince of this world, John 12.31; 14.30; 16.11; Prince of the Power of the air, Eph. 2.2; the Old Serpent, Gen. 3; Isa. 27.1; Rev. 12.9; 20.2; the tempter, Matt. 4.3; 1 Thess. 3.5; Wormwood, Rev. 8.11

**Diana** Latin name of the Greek goddess Artemis of Ephesus, Acts 19

**Dibon** capital city of Moab, present Dhiban, 40 miles south of Amman in Jordan, where the 'Moabite Stone' was found, Num. 21.26; 32.34; Isa. 15.2

**Didymus** (G = twin), another name for Thomas (H = twin), one of The Twelve disciples, John 11.16

**Dill 1.** Black cummin, *Nigella sativa*, Isa. 28.25–27. **2.** Parsley-like herb, *Anethum graveolens*; its seeds are used in cooking; Jesus rebuked the Pharisees for troubling to tithe this crop while neglecting love, Matt. 23.23

**Dinah** (H = justice) daughter of Jacob, raped by Shechem, avenged by her brothers Simeon and Levi, Gen. 34

**Dionysius** member of the Court of Areopagus in Athens, named after Dionysos the god of wine, vegetation and drama, he was converted to Christianity by Paul's preaching, Acts 17.34

**Disciple** (L, translates G *mathetes* = one who is taught) **1.** All the followers of Jesus, before the name Christians was applied to them, John 6.60–66; Acts 6.1. **2.** The disciples of John the Baptist, John 1.35. **3.** Disciples of the Pharisees, Matt. 22.16. **4.** The Twelve, Matt. 10.1.

**Disobedience** of Adam and Eve, its effects overcome by the obedience of Christ, Gen. 3; Rom. 5.19

**Dispersion** Jews living outside Judea, John 7.35; James 1.1; 1 Peter 1.1

**Divers** old spelling of diverse, meaning many types of, Matt. 4.24 etc.

**Divination** predicting the future by contacting the dead, forbidden Deut. 18.14–15; 1 Sam. 28.7; Isa. 44.25. The slave-girl in Philippi had 'a spirit of the Python', the dragon which inspired the priestess at Delphi, Acts 16.16

**Divorce 1.** Permitted in the Hebrew Scriptures when a wife displeased her husband; he had only to give her a certificate and send her away. The rabbis said that it must be done in the presence of two witnesses, and some said that burning the food was a sufficient reason. The wife was allowed to remarry, but not to remarry her first husband, Deut. 24.1–4. **2.** Because easy divorce left many women with no choice but prostitution, Jesus opposed it to protect women, and described a man who divorced his wife in this way and married another as an adulterer, Mark 10.2–11, although in Matt. 5.31–32; 19.9 (unless this clause was added later) he allows divorce in cases of 'unchastity'; which could be adultery, or if the wife was not a virgin when they married. **3.** Mark 10.12 about a wife divorcing her husband would have been impossible under Jewish law, and appears to have also been added later. **4.** The principle that marriage is intended to be for life is certain; but one should be cautious about applying teaching intended for one society to a different situation, see also 'Adultery', 'Fornication', 'Levirate Marriage', 'Marriage'

**Doctors** old translation of teachers or teachers of the law, Luke 2.46; 5.17; see 'Scribes'

**Donkey** more often used as a beast of burden and for riding than horses or camels; so valuable that its firstborn offspring was the only animal apart from humans which could be bought back instead of being sacrificed; Jesus rode a donkey rather than a war-horse into Jerusalem at the triumphal entry to show he was Prince of Peace, Ex. 14.13; Matt. 21 etc.

**Door 1.** Door of the sheepfold, see 'Gate 5.'. **2.** Doors of the Temple, which may have had an upper section which could be raised to allow the Ark of the Covenant to be carried in in procession, Ps. 24.7–9; 100.4. **3.** Doorposts, Ex. 12.7; Isa. 6.4. **4.** Doorkeeper, Ps. 84.10

**Dorcas** Greek for Tabitha (*Ar* = gazelle), woman devoted to acts of charity and sewing, raised from the dead in Joppa by Peter, Acts 9.36–42

**Dothan** where Joseph was thrown into a well, and Elisha was besieged, Gen. 37.17; 2 Kings 6.13. Tell Dotha has been excavated 10 miles north of Samaria

**Dove 1.** Doves or pigeons (*H yonah*) and turtledoves (*H tor*) were domesticated; even the poorest could keep a dovecote and offer them as sacrifices, Lev. 12.6–8; Luke 2.22–24. **2.** A dove was sent out from Noah's ark and returned with an olive branch; they became symbols of peace, Gen. 8.8. **3.** The Holy Spirit descended on Jesus in the form of a dove, Matt. 3.16 etc. **4.** 'Oh, for the wings of a dove', Ps. 55.6. **5.** 'The voice of the turtledove is heard in our land', S. of Sol. 2.12

**Dragon 1.** Mythical sea-monster, connected with Leviathan, Rahab of Egypt, and Canaanite and Babylonian myths of creation by slaying a monster, Job 7.12; Isa. 27.1; 51.9; Ezek. 29.3; 32.2; Bel. **2.** The Dragon's Spring, near the Dung Gate in Jerusalem, Neh. 2.13. **3.** A name for the Devil or Satan, Rev. 12; 13; 16.13; 20.2

**Draught** old word for dragged or drawn. **1.** Miraculous draught or catch of fish, Luke 5.4–6; John 21.6–11. **2.** Drain or latrine, Matt. 15.17; Mark 7.19

**Dreams** used by God to reveal truth to Jacob, Gen. 10.12–17; Joseph, Gen. 37.5;

Pharaoh, Gen. 41; Solomon, 1 Kings 3.5; Nebuchadnezzar, Dan. 2.4; Joseph, Matt. 1.20; 2.13; Magi, Matt. 2.12; Pilate's wife, Matt. 27.19

**Dropsy** swelling because of an excess of watery fluid retained in the cavities or tissues of the body; on the sabbath day, Jesus healed a man suffering from dropsy, Luke 14.1–6

**Drunkenness** condemned, Isa. 5.11; Joel 1.5; Luke 21.34; Rom. 13.13; Gal. 5.21

**Drusilla** see 'Herod Family'

**Dumb 1.** Zechariah made dumb, Luke 1.22. **2.** Dumb man healed by Jesus, Matt. 9.32–34; 12.22; fulfilling Isa. 35.6

**Dura** where Nebuchadnezzar erected an image, Dan. 3.1; location unknown; it is a common place-name, and is unlikely to be identified with Dura-Europos

**Duty** our whole duty is to reverence God and keep his commandments, Eccles. 12.13

**E** one of the sources believed by some to lie behind the books from Genesis to Numbers; originating in Ephraim; using Elohim as the name of God, see p. **135**

**Eagle** (*H nesher*) can mean either an eagle or a vulture, Ex. 19.4; Ps. 103.5; Isa. 40.31; Matt. 24.28

**Earnest** (*G arrabon*) small amount paid as a first instalment, to pledge or guarantee that full payment will follow: the gift of the Holy Spirit is the guarantee that God will dwell in us fully, 2 Cor. 1.22; Eph. 1.14

**Ebal** (*H* = stony) see 'Gerizim'

**Ebed-nego** (*H* = servant of Nebo) see 'Abednego'

**Ebenezer** (*H* = stone of help) stone commemorating the scene of battles between Philistines and Israel, 1 Sam. 4.1–11; 7.12, either near Aphek 1. or Mizpah

**Ebony** dark, hard heartwood of an Indian tree, Ezek. 27.15

**Ecbatana** capital city of Media, today called Hamadan in Iran; Ezra 6.2; Tob. frequently; Judith 1.1–14; see Mesopotamia, p. **165**

**Ecclesiastes** (Eccl.) The Book called Ecclesiastes (eck-lees-ee-ASS-tees), see p. **140**

**Ecclesiasticus** or The Wisdom of Jesus Son of Sirach (Ecclus. or Ben Sira or Sirach) The Book called Ecclesiasticus (eck-lees-ee-ASS-tick-us), see p. **146**

**Eden** (*H* = delight) paradise garden where the first man and woman were placed after their creation; the rivers are Pishon, which if Havilah (in Arabia) includes India, could be the Ganges; Gihon, if Cush is Ethiopia, could be the Nile; Hiddekel is the Tigris; and the fourth is Euphrates, Gen. 2.8–3.24; Isa. 51.3; Ezek. 28.13; 36.35; Joel 2.3.

**Edom** (*H* = red) region south-east of the Dead Sea; its inhabitants were regarded as descendants of Esau, Gen. 25.30; Num. 20.14–21; 1 Kings 11.14–16; 2 Kings 3; 8.20–22; Ps. 60.8 = 108.9 (see 'sandals'); Isa. 63.1; Jer. 49.7–22; Obadiah. Later called Nabatea, 1 Macc. 5.25, 9.35, see 'Idumea'

**Egypt** great power in the ancient world, dependent on the Nile; the chronology of the Pharaohs is still debated so we cannot be certain who was the ruler in the time of Abraham, Gen. 10.6; Joseph, Gen. 37–46; and Moses, Ex. 1–14. Egyptian civilization influenced the court of Solomon and the Wisdom literature. The infant Jesus went to Egypt, Matt. 2.13. People from Egypt were present at Pentecost, Acts 2.10

**Egypt, Brook of** Wadi Al-Arish which flows north across the Sinai Peninsula and enters the Mediterranean at the Egyptian town of Al-Arish, south-west of Gaza, 1 Kings 8.65; 2 Kings 24.7; Isa. 27.12; Ezek. 47.19

**Ehud** (*H* = united) left-handed man who by trickery stabbed the grossly fat King Ekron of Moab, Judg. 3.12–30

**Ekron** northernmost of the five towns of the Philistines; frequently changed hands between them and the Israelites, Judg. 1.18; 1 Sam. 5.10; 7.14; 17.52. It was destroyed by Nebuchadnezzar; the ruins are at Tel Miqne, near Khirbat el-Muqanna', 35 miles south-west of Jerusalem

*El, Elohim* Hebrew words for God. El was the name of a Canaanite god, and occurs in Ps. 18.31; Isa. 9.6; also in personal names such as 'Israel'; it is the root of the Arabic Allah. *Elohim* is plural in form; it can refer to a number of gods, Ex. 12.12; more often it means the one true God. The plural, like the royal 'we', indicates importance; it takes a singular verb, and became the normal word for God in the Northern Kingdom of Israel and in the 'E' source. *Elohim* is also used for the spirits of the dead, 1 Sam. 28.13

**Elah** (*H* = oak) **1.** Valley where David fought Goliath, now Wadi es-Sant, 9 miles WSW of Bethlehem, 1 Sam. 17. **2.** King of Israel 886–885 BC, assassinated by Zimri, 1 Kings 16.6–14

**Elam** (*H* = highland) **1.** Son of Shem, Gen. 10.22; see 'Chedorlaomer'. **2.** Region now in the highlands of Iran around the city of Shiraz; its capital in ancient times was Anshan, now Tal-i-Malyan, east of the Persian Gulf. It was a powerful threat to the Mesopotamian empires from the earliest times, and was at its greatest between 1400 and 1100 BC; it was defeated by Nebuchadnezzar I of Babylon (1119–1098), and again in 640 by Assurbanipal of Assyria. Elamite archers fought for the Babylonians, Isa. 22.6. **3.** From time to time, Elam annexed Susiana with its capital at Susa, so Susa is wrongly described as being in Elam, Dan. 8.2. **4.** Elamites were present at Pentecost, Acts 2.9; see Mesopotamia, p. **165**

**Elath** (*H* = grove of tall trees) now the seaside resort of Eilat at the head of the Gulf of Aqabah, Deut. 2.8; 2 Kings 14.22; 16.6; it is described as next to Ezion-Geber but in fact was the later name for the same city, Num. 33.35–36; 1 Kings 9.26; 22.48

**Eldad** (*H* = God loves) prophesied with Medad, Num. 11.26–30

**Elders** (*G presbyteroi*) **1.** Leaders of Israel, Ex. 3.16; 24.1, 9; Num. 11.16–25; Matt.21.23. **2.** Leaders of the Church, Acts 11.30; 14.23; 15.2–6, 22–23; 16.4; 21.18; 1 Tim. 4.14; 5.17–22; James 5.14. In some places the term was interchangeable with 'bishops', Acts 20.17, 28; Titus 1.5, 7. **3.** Twenty-four elders surround the throne of God in heaven, probably representing the twelve tribes of Israel and the Church, the new Israel, Rev. 4.4, 9–11; 5.6–14

**Elect** chosen by God, Rom. 8.33; 2 John 1; see 'Predestination'

**Elemental spirits of the universe** see 'Spirits 2.'

**Elephant** only in the Apocrypha, where a Jewish suicide attacker stabs one from below, which collapses on top of him, 1 Macc. 6.35, 46; 2 Macc. 13.15; 3 Macc. 5.45

**Eli** (EE-lie, *H* = uplifted) priest at Shiloh who trained the boy Samuel but could not control his own sons, 1 Sam. 1–4

**Eliakim** (uh-LIE-uh-kim, *H* = God raises) see 'Jehoiakim', 2 Kings 23.34

**Elihu** (*H* = my God is he) one of Job's 'friends', Job 32–37

**Elijah** (*H* = Jah is my God; *G Elias*) from an unknown town called Tishbe, prophet in the Northern Kingdom of Israel; predicted a drought, in punishment for Ahab's sins; survived it with help from the widow's cruse of oil which never ran out; healed her son, 1 Kings 17. Helped by Obadiah, challenged Ahab; challenged the prophets of Baal to a rain-making competition; ran from Carmel to Jezreel, 10 miles by the sheer drop, 18. Fled from Jezebel, met God at Mount Horeb, 19. Jezebel arranged with forged letters for Naboth to be killed so Ahab her husband could have his vineyard; Elijah pronounced sentence: they would both die horribly, 21. Predicted the death of Ahaziah, 2 Kings 1. Ascended into heaven in a chariot of fire, 2 Kings 2. Representative of the prophets at the Transfiguration, Matt. 17.3; Mark 9.4; Luke 90.30; compared to John the Baptist, Matt. 11.14; 16.14; Luke 1.17; 9.8; 9.19; John 1.21; see 'Prophets'

**Eliphaz** (*H* = my God is strength) one of Job's 'friends', Job 4; 5; 15; 22

**Elisha** (*H* = my God saves) prophet in Israel; when Elijah ascended into heaven in a chariot of fire, his mantel fell upon Elisha, 2 Kings 2. Elisha performed miracles, predicted the defeat of Moab, 3. The widow's oil and the widow's son at Shunem; feeding a crowd of 100, 4. Healed Naaman the leper, 5. more miracles; warned the king which way the enemy were approaching, 6. Claimed justice for the Shunammite, anointed Jehu, 9

**Elizabeth** (*H* = I swear by my God) elderly mother of John the Baptist; cousin of the Virgin Mary, Luke 1.5; 1.42

***Eloi, Eloi, lema sabachthani?*** (traditional pronunciation ee-LOH-eye, ee-LOH-eye, LAH-muh sa-back-THAR-nee, but more accurate would be ell-OH-ee, ell-OH-ee, luh-MAH suh-back-tha-NEE; *Ar* translation of *H* = My God, my God, why have you abandoned me?) words of Jesus on the cross, Mark 15.34 quoting Ps. 22.1; Matt. 27.46 reverts to the Hebrew word *Eli* (EEL-eye, better el-LEE); a cry of desolation from one who had relinquished his sense of oneness with his Father; yet the Psalm quoted ends triumphantly

**Elymas** Jewish false prophet in Paphos, the meaning and origin of his name is lost; it is not a translation of Bar-Jesus, Acts 13.8

**Emerods** old word for haemorrhoids, see 'Tumours'

**Emmanuel, Immanuel** (*H* = God is with us) see 'Virgin'

**Emmaus** (*H* = hot springs) village near Jerusalem, where Jesus was seen by two disciples after his Resurrection; its identification is uncertain, Amwas or Latrun (19 miles west of Jerusalem), Abu Gosh (7 miles, see 'Kiriath-Jearim'), El Qubeibah (7 miles), and the village of Qalunieh (4 miles, destroyed in 1948) have been suggested, Luke 24.15

**Emperor worship** by burning a pinch of incense before a bust of the Roman Emperor, who was declared to be a god; refusing it led to suspicion of disloyalty. Jews were a 'legal religion'; anyone who could prove they were of the Jewish race could be excused from sacrificing to the Emperor. Christianity was not, and its members were of many different races. Their refusal to join in emperor worship led to martyrdoms at the end of the first century, Rev. 2.13

**En-dor** (*H* = spring of Dor) town near Mount Tabor, where Barak destroyed the army of Sisera, Ps. 83.10; and Saul consulted a witch or medium, 1 Sam. 28.7, see 'Divination'

**Endurance** see 'Patience'

**Enemy 1.** Christians are command to love our enemies, Matt. 5.43; Rom. 12.14–21. **2.** Satan described as The Enemy, Matt. 13.25–39; Luke 10.19; see 'Devil 3.'

**En-Gedi** (*H* = spring of the kid) oasis west of the Dead Sea where David stayed while fleeing from Saul, 1 Sam. 23.29; 24.1; S. of Sol. 1.14; Ezek. 47.10

**English translations of the Bible** see p. 179

**Enoch** (EE-nock, *H* = dedicated) **1.** Son of Cain, Gen. 4.17–18. **2.** Son of Jared, who walked with God, lived to the age of 365, then God took him, Gen. 5.18–24; Heb. 11.5; Jude 14

**Enoch, books of** see p. 161

**En-Rogel** (*H* = fullers' spring) spring near Jerusalem, where Jonathan gathered information, and Adonijah held a sacrificial feast; usually identified as Bir Ayyub, south of where Hinnom Valley enters the Kidron Valley, Josh. 15.7; 18.16; 2 Sam. 17.17; 1 Kings 1.9

**Enuma Elish** Mesopotamian legend describing the creation of the world by the god Marduk, who destroyed chaos

**Epaphras, Epaphroditus** (*G* = belonging to the goddess Aphrodite) **1.** Epaphras, a native of Colossae who founded the church there, Col. 1.7; 4.12; Philemon 23. The name is short for **2.** Epaphroditus, Paul's fellow-worker who was a leader at Philippi and carried messages and gifts, Phil. 2.25–30; 4.18. It is possible but unlikely that they were the same person

**Ephah** (*H* = dark) **1.** Son of Midian, Gen. 25.4. **2.** Place in or near Midian, Isa. 60.6. **3.** Measure, see 'Measures of Capacity'

**Ephesus** capital city of the Province of Asia, visited by Paul, whence he wrote to the Corinthians, and where a riot broke out over his teaching, Acts 18.19–21; 19.1–41; 20.17–38; 1 Cor. 16.8; 2 Tim. 4.12. Timothy ministered in Ephesus, 1 Tim. 1.3; it was one of the seven churches addressed in Rev. 2–3. There are extensive remains, including the theatre where the riot ended, near Selçuk on the Aegean coast of Turkey, but all that is left of the Temple to Artemis is one pillar in a swamp.

**Ephesians** (Eph.) The Letter of Paul to the Ephesians (if-FEES-ee-uns), see p. **155**
**Ephod 1.** Elaborate garment worn by the High Priest, Ex. 28.6–14; 39.2–7. **2.** Linen garment worn by priests and kings, 1 Sam. 2.18; 22.18; 2 Sam. 6.14. **3.** An idol? Judg. 8.27; 17.5; 1 Sam. 21.9. **4.** Something for foretelling the future, possibly carried in the pocket of an ephod, 1 Sam. 23.9–12; 30.7–8

**Ephphatha** (= be opened) Aramaic word spoken by Jesus when he healed a deaf man, Mark 7.34

**Ephraim** (*H* = two fruits) **1.** One of the sons of Joseph, Gen. 41.50–52; 48.8–22; the tribes of Ephraim and Manasseh together counted as the Joseph tribe, Gen. 49.22–26; Deut. 33.13–17. **2.** The hill-country of Ephraim, Josh. 17.15. **3.** Northern of the two kingdoms after the split, 1 Kings 12.25. **4.** Town where Jesus retreated after raising Lazarus, John 11.54; 2 Sam. 13.23; probably the same as Ophrah, Josh. 18.23; 1 Sam. 23.6; Ephron, 2 Chron. 13.19; Aphairema, 1 Macc. 11.34; identified as Et-Taiyibeh, 14 miles north of Jerusalem

**Ephrath** Rachel died and was buried beside the road to Ephrath, and some distance from there, Gen. 35.16–20. The note in Gen. 35.19 and 48.7 led to the building of Rachel's Tomb near Bethlehem by the Crusaders on a site dating from the fourth century AD. But Jer. 31.15 locates Rachel's tomb at Ramah, 5 miles north of Jerusalem, and 1 Samuel 10.2 puts it at an unknown place called Zelzah

**Ephrathah** (EFF-ra-tha, *H* = fruitful) region around Bethlehem in Judah, 5 miles south of Jerusalem; word used to distinguish the hometown of the royal family of David from Bethlehem in Zebulun, Ruth 4.11; Micah 5.2. Ps. 132.6 links Ephrathah with Jaar (Kiriath Jearim) 9 miles west of Jerusalem, and may be another form of Ephraim

**Epicureans** followers of the philosopher Epicurus (341–270 BC), who taught that everything happens by chance, the gods are too remote to be interested in us, and death is the end of everything, so we should devote ourselves to seeking happiness – though this was to be an intellectual rather than a sensual happiness, Acts 17.18

**Epilepsy** disorder of the nervous system, sometimes leading to fits. Jesus healed epileptics, Matt. 4.24; 17.14–18; Mark 9.14–27; Luke 9.37–42

**Epistles**  see Letters in the New Testament, p. **152**

**Erastus**  (*G* = beloved) town clerk of Corinth where there is an inscription with his name, Acts 19.22; Rom. 16.23; also, if they are the same person, Acts 19.22; 2 Tim. 4.20

**Esar-haddon**  (*Ak Asur-ahha-iddina* = Ashur has given a brother) king of Assyria 681–669 BC, 2 Kings 19.37; Ezra 4.2; see Mesopotamia, p. **165**

**Esau**  (*H* = hairy) elder son of Isaac; sold his birthright to his twin brother Jacob; ancestor of the Edomites, Gen. 25–36

**Esdraelon**  central plain between northern and southern Israel, also called the Valley of Jezreel, Judith 1.8

**1 Esdras**  (1 Esd.) The First Book of Esdras, see p. **148**

**2 Esdras**  (2 Esd.) The Second Book of Esdras, see p. **148**

**Eshcol**  (*H* = cluster) valley near Hebron, possibly below Burj Haskeh; whence the spies brought a huge cluster of grapes, Num. 13.23–24

**Essenes**  sect in Judaism, who may have written some of the Dead Sea Scrolls, see p. **162**

**Esther**  (*Persian* = star, or perhaps from the goddess Ishtar) (Esth.) The Book of Esther (ESS-tur), see p. **139**

**Eternity**  when God created the universe, time, like space, was 'without form'; then God divided it into measurable periods. To each empire and kingdom he gave its proper period (*H* = *'olam*, *G* = *aeon*); then would come the Day of the LORD which would begin the age to come, the kingdom of God. Those who survived or were resurrected into the next age would receive 'the life of the age'. But with the Resurrection of Jesus the new age had already begun, and the life of the age was available to believers here and now, John 3.36; 17.3; 1 John 5.13; to continue after death when we share it with God, Mark 10.30. Life with God the creator of time is not divided into moments or days, so we call it eternity, Isa. 57.15. 'Eternal life' is an approximate translation for the 'life of the age'; 'everlasting' should be understood to mean that it has no end, not that it goes on for a long time, see 'Life'

**Ethbaal**  (*H* = Baal is with him, also called *Ittobaal*) priest-king of Tyre and Sidon 889–856 BC, father of Jezebel, and grandfather of Dido who founded Carthage; there was a drought throughout the region during Ittobaal's reign, as predicted by Elijah, 1 Kings 16.31; 17.1

**Ethiopia**  see 'Cush'

**Eunice**  (YOU-niss, *G* = good victory) Jewish woman, mother of Timothy, Acts 16.1; 2 Tim. 1.5

**Eunuch**  (YOU-nuck) man who is deliberately or accidentally castrated; they were in charge of the harem in oriental courts, Esth. 2.3. They were not admitted to Jewish worship, Deut. 23.1; though Isa. 56.3 is prepared to relax this; so the baptism of the Ethiopian eunuch in Acts 8.27–39 is a sign that the Church accepts the unacceptable. In Matt. 19.12, Jesus refers rather to celibacy

**Euodia**  (*G* = good journey) and **Syntyche**  (*G* = fortunate) (you-OH-dee-a and SIN-tick-ee) two women in the church at Philippi, fellow-workers with Paul, whose continued disagreement was hindering the spread of the gospel, Phil. 4.2–3

**Euphrates**  river flowing from Lake Van in Turkey through Iraq to The Gulf, see Mesopotamia, p. **165**

**Euroclydon**  (KJV) (*G Eurakylon* from Greek–Latin hybrid *Euraquilo* = north-east wind), winter tempest sweeping down from the south coast of Crete, Acts 27.14

**Eutychus**  (*G* = fortunate) (YOU-tick-us) young man at Troas; falling asleep during

Paul's sermon, he fell two storeys from a window; Paul restored him to life, Acts 20.7–12

**Evangelism** the task of spreading the good news to those who have not heard it, commanded in the Great Commission, Matt. 28.18–20

**Evangelist** (*G* = bringer of good news) preacher of the gospel, Acts 21.8; Eph. 4.11; 2 Tim. 4.5. The same word is used for those who wrote the four Gospels

**Eve** (*H* = life-giver) the first woman, Gen. 1–3

**Evil** harming others; arises when humans, given the power of choice, selfishly choose to disobey God, symbolized in the Eden story, Gen. 2; John 3.19. Jesus, the self-sacrificing Saviour, bring's God's love and forgiveness, shames us into loving others, and gives his Spirit, enabling us to love, Matt. 6.13; Rom. 5.20; Gal. 1.4; 3 John 11. God cannot destroy evil without destroying good as well, Gen. 5–8; Matt. 13.25–36. The evil of physical suffering is often due to human sin and could sometimes be avoided; it can always be used to build character, Job; Rom. 5.3–4

**Evil-Merodach** (*Ak Awil-Marduk*) king of Babylon 562–560 BC, 2 Kings 25.27; Jer. 52.31, see Mesopotamia, p. **165**

**Evil spirits, the Evil One** see 'Devil'

---

**Exile** or captivity of the Jews in Babylon about 586–538 BC, see Mesopotamia, p. **165**. It took place in several stages.

**605 BC** or thereabouts it was predicted by Jeremiah, Jer. 25.1–14

**599** Nebuchadnezzar deported 3,023 Jews to Babylon, Jer. 52.28

**598** King Jehoiachin, who had reigned 3 months in Jerusalem, was taken as a captive to Babylon, 2 Kings 24.12–16; 2 Chron. 36.10; Zedekiah was enthroned in his place, 2 Kings 24.17–19

**588** Zedekiah rebelled, Nebuchadnezzar besieged Jerusalem, Jer. 21.1–10; 32.1–2; Zedekiah was blinded, he and 832 people were deported, Jer. 39; 52.29; 2 Kings 25; 2 Chron. 36.10–20

**587** Jerusalem was destroyed, 2 Kings 25.8–21; Jer. 52.12–13

**583** 745 Jews deported, Jer. 52.30

**562** Jehoiachin received by Evil-Merodach, the new king of Babylon, Jer. 52.31–34

**538** Cyrus II signed an edict for the return of the Jews, 2 Chron. 36.22–23; Ezra 1; Isa. 44.28–45.13; Jer. 16.14–15

**537** Zerubbabel started to restore the Temple, Ezra 3.8–12; but the work was interrupted, Ezra 4.1–5, 24

**520** work resumed on the Temple, with permission from Darius, Ezra 5.13–6.12; Hag. 1.1–2.19

**516** restoration of the Temple completed, Ezra 6.15–22

**486–458** opposition to the Jews continued under Xerxes I and Artaxerxes I, Ezra 4.6–23

**445** Nehemiah became governor of Judah, rebuilt the walls of Jerusalem, Neh. 1–7; 12–13

**433** Nehemiah paid a visit to Persia, Neh. 13.6

**397** under Artaxerxes II, Ezra returned to Jerusalem, to reform the Jewish nation and its worship, Ezra 8.31–10.5; Neh. 8

The Exile was predicted as a national disaster, but from this experience the Jews learnt that God works through the suffering of his servants, and that his activity is not limited to one land only, see also Ps. 137; Isa. 40; 43; Ezek. 10; 12; 43; Dan. 1–6

# Exodus

**Exodus** (*G* = way out) the salvation of the Jewish slaves when they escaped from Egypt under Moses, Ex. 14. The date is uncertain; 1250 and 1450 BC are suggested, or even 1645 when the natural phenomena could have been caused by the volcanic explosion of Santorini. The route, described in Num. 33, is hard to establish, see 'Red Sea', 'Sinai', and Sources, p. **134**. The Greek word *exodos* is also used for the salvation that Jesus will accomplish by his death, Luke 9.31

**Exodus** (Ex.) The Book of the Exodus, see p. **136**

**Eye for an eye** law designed to prevent excessive revenge, by limiting the punishment to one proportionate to the crime; but Jesus ruled out all revenge, Ex. 21.24; Lev. 24.20; Deut. 19.21; Matt. 5.38

**Ezekiel** (*H* = God strengthens) (Ezek.) The Book of the Prophet Ezekiel (e-ZEEK-yul), see p. **142**

**Ezion-Geber** see 'Elath'

**Ezra** (*H* = help) (Ezra) The Book of Ezra, see p. **139** (see also 1 & 2 Esdras, p. **148**)

**Face** see 'Presence of God'

**Fair Havens** harbour on the south coast of Crete, today called by the same name, in Greek *Kaloi Limenes*. The ship carrying Paul as a prisoner to Rome stopped here just before the winter gales began. They set off from there hoping to reach Phoenix, but were blown offshore by the gales, Acts 27.6

**Faith 1.** A trusting relationship with God, the key to salvation history in Heb. 11; and the means of justification in Rom. 3.28 etc. **2.** Assent to a set of doctrines, 1 Tim. 5.8; Jude 3. **3.** Faithfulness in humans and in God is enduring trustworthiness, Gal. 5.22; 1 Thess. 5.24

**Family** can be a good environment for learning self-sacrificing love, but can also restrict the freedom of the members to follow God's call, Ex. 20.12; Luke 14.26; Eph. 6.1–4

**Fasting** abstaining from food, Matt. 6.16; 9.14; 17.21; 1 Cor. 7.5

**Father 1.** To be honoured, see 'Parents'. **2.** God the father of Israel, Isa. 63.16; 64.8; Jer. 31.9; Hos. 11.3–4. **3.** God who cares for each individual like a father caring for his children, Matt. 5.16; Mark 14.36; Luke 11.2; 15.11–32. **4.** The Creator's relationship with Jesus like that of Father and Son, Mark 13.32; Luke 10.22; John 1.14; 3.35; 6.46, see '*Abba*'

**Fear** of God; from the early human experience of awe towards the unknown, fear progresses to a relationship of respect, which is unconnected with fright, to a powerful but loving father, Ps. 2.11; Prov. 9.10; Luke 1.50; 1 Peter 2.17; 1 John 4.18

**Feast 1.** Jews were commanded to observe three annual festivals: Passover (Unleavened Bread), Weeks (Harvest, concluding with Pentecost) and Tabernacles (Succoth, Booths or Ingathering), Ex. 23.14–17, see 'Calendar'. **2.** The kingdom of Heaven compared to a great feast, Matt. 8.11; 22.2–10; 23.6; 25.10

**Feet 1.** 'How beautiful upon the mountains are the feet of him that brings good news', Isa. 5.27. **2.** 'Feet of clay', Dan. 2.33–34. **3.** Euphemism for the genitals, Ex. 4.25; Deut. 11.10; Judg. 3.24; Isa. 6.2; 11.20

**Felix** (*L* = happy) Procurator of Judea AD 52–59; heard Paul's defence but did not release him, Acts 23.23–24.27

**Fertility religions** claimed to ensure the essential fertility of crops, herds and family; often they aimed to do so by sympathetic magic, providing temple prostitutes and orgies. Baal and Asherah were fertility gods. This was abhorrent to Judaism and Christianity, Judg. 2.13; Hos. 2.16; 1 Cor. 6.15–20; Acts 19.21–41

**Festus** (*L* = joyful) Procurator of Judea 59–62; heard Paul's defence; allowed him to appeal to Caesar, Acts 24.27–26.32

**Fetters** chains to bind the feet, 2 Kings 25.7; Ps. 149.8

**Fever** healed by Jesus, Matt. 8.14; John 4.46–53

**Fig tree 1.** Jeremiah's vision of good and bad figs teaches God's opinion of the exiles and those who remained, Jer. 24. **2.** Jesus curses a fig tree, Matt. 21.18–22; Mark 11.12–14. **3.** Parable of the Barren Fig Tree; this and the cursing incident teach that God's patience with his people is running out, Luke 13.6–9. **4.** Lesson of the fig tree, to know that the Kingdom is near, Matt. 24.32–33; Luke 21.29. **5.** Jesus sees Nathanael under a fig tree; this was recommended by the rabbis as a place to meditate on the law, John 1.48

**Firmament** the sky conceived of as a solid dome; this universal belief of pre-scientific people should not distract from the message of Genesis, that all that is, however we describe it, is made by God, Gen. 1.6–8

**Firstborn 1.** The first male offspring of humans and animals were killed by the final plague in Egypt, so among the Israelites they were sacrificed to the LORD, though firstborn donkeys and humans could be bought back ('redeemed') when another sacrifice was killed in their place, Ex. 11.5; 13.2–16; 34.19–20; Luke 2.22–24. **2.** The firstborn son inherited his father's position and twice as much of his father's property as the other sons, see 'Birthright', Deut. 21.15–17; 2 Chron. 21.3; Col. 1.15; Heb. 12.23

**Firstfruits** the first sheaves of any crop grown in the field, the first fruit from any tree, the first wine and the first oil in each season were given to the priests, Lev. 23.9–14; Num. 18.13; 28.26–31; Deut. 18.4; 26.1–11; see 'Calendar'

**Fish 1.** Jonah was swallowed by a fish; see p. **144**. **2.** Fishing in Lake Galilee was by a circular throwing net; a seine-net dragged along the bottom; a long gill-net or trammel-net pulled out in a circle or semicircle and drawn together; or by hook and line, Matt. 4.18–22; 13.47–48; 17.27; Luke 5.1–11; John 21.1–14. **3.** Jesus called fishermen to be his disciples and told them they would now draw in people, Matt. 4.19. **4.** See 'Loaves and fishes'

**Flesh 1.** Living people are defined as flesh and blood, implying mortality, Ps. 65.2; Isa. 40.6; Matt. 16.17; Luke 24.39; John 1.14; Heb. 2.14. **2.** Flesh is contrasted with body: flesh is our animal-like bone and muscle, body is a God-given means of expressing our personality, 1 Cor. 15.50. **3.** Flesh is contrasted with spirit: flesh is human nature, weak and potentially sinful, spirit is human nature filled with the power of God, Matt. 26.41; John 6.63; Rom. 8.9; Gal. 5.17. **4.** Different categories or species of created things are described as different flesh, 1 Cor. 15.19. **5.** In marriage and sexual intercourse a man and woman are described as becoming a single person, 'one flesh', Gen. 2.24; Mark 10.8; 1 Cor. 6.16

**Flogging** see 'Scourging'

**Flood** see 'Noah'

**Food laws** became one of the distinguishing marks of Israel, together with circumcision and the sabbath. Since 'the blood is the life' Jews are not allowed to eat meat until the blood has drained out of it, Lev. 17.10–14; only quadrupeds who chew the cud and have a divided hoof are allowed, 11.3–7; only fish with both fins and scales, 11.9–12; and pig-meat is definitely disallowed, 11.7. The genitals must be removed, Gen. 32.32. To guard against accidentally breaking the rule against 'seething a kid in its mother's milk', in a kosher kitchen the areas and utensils used for meat and dairy products are rigidly separated, Ex. 23.19. Jesus questioned the basis of the food laws,

Mark 7.14–23. Strict observance of these laws meant that Jewish Christians could never share a meal with Gentile Christians, even the Holy Communion, so Paul challenged his fellow-Jews to admit that they are not all-important, Gal. 2.11–14. See also 'Meat offered to idols'

**Fool** see 'Wisdom'. 'The fool says there is no God', Ps. 14.1; 53.1. The Rich Fool, Luke 12.20

**Foreigners** see 'Aliens'

**Forgiveness 1.** Forgiveness by God was sought through sacrifice, but could also be begged through prayer, Lev. 4; 5; 1 Kings 8.30; Ps. 79.9. **2.** Jesus taught the outcast and sick that their guilty feelings are unnecessary, as God has already forgiven them, Luke 7.48. **3.** Paul says the sacrifice of Jesus on the cross is all that is necessary, Eph. 1.7. **4.** Because God has forgiven us, we must forgive each other; sin matters, but reconciliation matters more, Matt. 6.12–15; 18.21–35; Luke 6.37; 17.3–4, see also 'Binding'

**Fornication 1.** If a man seduces a virgin he is to marry her, Ex. 22.16. **2.** Promiscuous sex is denounced when it is associated with the worship of fertility gods, Num. 25. **3.** Seducers, rapists, and women who are not virgins when they are married, are to be stoned to death, according to Deut. 22; but Jesus showed in John 8.3–11 that enforcement of this is incompatible with belief in a compassionate, all-forgiving God. **4.** No girl from a respectable family was allowed out her father's sight: the usual meaning of fornication (*G porneia*) is paying for sex with a prostitute (*G porne*), Mark 7.21; Acts 15.29; 1 Cor. 6.13–18; Gal. 5.19; Eph. 5.3; Col. 3.5; 1 Thess. 4.3. **5.** 'Fornication' is also used metaphorically for idolatry, being unfaithful to God, especially in fertility cults, Ezek. 16.29; Hos. 1–3; Rev. 2.14 etc., see also 'Adultery', 'Divorce', 'Levirate Marriage', 'Marriage', 'Prostitutes'

**Forty** used as a round number, for the flood, Gen. 7.17; Moses on Mount Sinai, Ex. 24.18; the Israelites' wanderings, 16.35; spying the land of Canaan, Num. 13.25; Goliath's challenge, 1 Sam. 17.16; Elijah's journey, 1 Kings 19.8; Jonah's preaching, Jonah 3.4; the temptation of Jesus, Matt. 4.2 etc.; his appearances after the Resurrection, Acts 1.3. Forty lashes less one, see 'Scourging'

**Four living creatures** seen by Ezekiel, Ezek. 1.5–14; 10.10–14; Rev. 4.6–8; 5.14; 6.1–7; they had the faces of a lion, an ox, an eagle and a man, and probably represent all that live on land or in the air: wild animals, domesticated animals, birds and humans. Christians have used them as symbols of the four Gospels: Mark's forcefulness; Luke's gentleness; John's vision and Matthew's humanity

**Foxes** the 400 animals caught by Samson were probably jackals which hunt in packs, Judg. 15.4; whereas foxes have solitary holes, Matt. 8.20

**Frankincense** see 'Spices'

**Freedmen, Synagogue of the** Jews who had been deported and made slaves, then given their freedom, but spoke Greek rather than Hebrew, Acts 6.9; synagogue inscriptions in Greek have been found in Jerusalem

**Friend** Abraham, James 2.23; Moses, Ex. 33.11; Jonathan and David, 1 Sam. 18.1–23.16; a friend who sticks closer than a brother, Prov. 18.24; Jesus, John 15.15

**Fringe** the knotted tassels on the outer garment, required by Num. 15.38–39; Matt. 9.20; 14.36; 23.5

**Fruit** produce of grain, animals, plants and trees, see 'Harvest'. The fruit of the body are children, Ps. 132.11; the fruit of the lips are words, Heb. 13.15; the fruit of faith is good deeds, proving that we have repented, Matt. 3.8; 7.16; the 'fruit of the

Spirit' is the crop of virtues which grow gradually in those within whom the Holy Spirit flows like the sap of a tree, Gal. 5.22

**Fuller** craftsman who cleans, shrinks, thickens and bleaches cloth by washing, treading, alkalis and sunlight, 2 Kings 18.17; Mal. 3.2; Mark 9.3

**Fullness** or completeness, the whole of God dwells in Christ and his Church, needing nothing more to bring it to completion, Eph. 1.23; 3.19; 4.13; Col. 1.19; 2.9

**Gabbatha** (*H* = high ground) the platform (*G lithostroton* = paved with stones) where Pilate sat in judgement on Jesus; probably in front of Herod's palace, west of the Temple, which Pilate used when in Jerusalem (the impressive pavement in the Convent of Our Lady of Zion is from a later date), John 19.13, see 'Praetorium 1.'

**Gabriel** (*H* = God is my hero) archangel who brought messages to Daniel, Zacharias and Mary, Dan. 8.16; 9.21; Luke 1.19; 1.26

**Gad** (*H* = good fortune) son of Jacob and Zilpah, Gen. 30.9–11; ancestor of one of the twelve tribes of Israel, Gen. 49; Deut. 33

**Gadarene swine** herd of pigs (unclean to Jews) which ran into Lake Galilee when Jesus cast out demons from a madman; Gadara (Umm Qeis) was one of the Decapolis towns but 6 miles from the lake; some manuscripts read Gerasene, some Gergesene: Gerasa or Jerash was even further; Gergesa (Kersa or Gerge) was nearer but not so well known, but any of them could have owned land on the lakeshore, Matt. 8.28–34; Mark 5.1–20; Luke 8.26–39

**Gaius** (*G* form of *L Caius* = commended) **1.** Paul's companion from Macedonia, Acts 19.29. **2.** Paul's companion from Derbe, Acts 20.4. **3.** Baptized by Paul in Corinth, and his host there, Rom. 16.23; 1 Cor. 1.14. **4.** Recipient of a letter from John, 3 John 1

**Galatia** Roman Province in Asia Minor, at one time settled by people from Gaul, which stretched from Pisidian Antioch (Yalvaç in Turkey) to Gordion, west of modern Ankara; Paul visited the southern towns of Antioch, Iconium, Lystra and Derbe on his first missionary journey, and most people think it is to them that he wrote his letter, Acts 13.14–14.23

**Galatians** (Gal.) The Letter of Paul to the Galatians (guh-LAY-shuns), see p. **154**

**Galilee** (*H* = circle) **1.** Lake in the north of Israel, with the River Jordan flowing in at the north and out at the south, also called Lake Tiberias, Chinnereth (*H* = harp) and Genessaret. **2.** Territory west of the lake, despised by Judeans as 'Galilee of the Gentiles' because, situated on a trade route, it attracted non-Jewish settlers and mixed marriages; here Jesus spent most of his life, Isa. 9.1; Matt. 2.22; 4.12–16; John 7.52; 21

**Gall** bile excreted by the gall bladder; also a poisonous herb, probably hemlock; metaphor for bitterness, Job 16.13; Lam. 3.19; Tob. 11.8; Acts 8.23. At Golgotha, according to Matt. 27.34, Jesus was offered wine mixed with gall, which may be a confusion between the bitter bread of Ps. 69.21; the myrrh of Mark 15.23; and the acidic wine of Mark 15.36

**Gallio** (*G* = milk-drinker) refused to try Paul in Corinth, Acts 18.12–17; praised by his brother the orator Seneca; an inscription found at Delphi shows that he served as Roman proconsul in charge of Achaia in AD 51–52

**Gamaliel** (*H* = God is my reward) Pharisee and teacher; grandson of the liberal rabbi Hillel; advised the Sanhedrin not to oppose Christianity; taught Paul, Acts 5.34; 22.3; his tomb is at Beth Shearim

**Games** athletics, wrestling and races were important in Greek and Roman life; an example of the determination needed to succeed as a Christian; every city had its stadium, and the Isthmian Games were held near Corinth, 1 Cor. 9.24–27; Phil. 3.12–14; 2 Tim. 2.5; 4.7–8; Heb. 12.1–2

**Garden 1.** Places for growing edible crops, trees for shade, olives and flowers, 1 Kings 21.2; Isa. 1.8; 61.11; Jer. 52.7; Sus. 1.5–27. **1.** See 'Eden'. **2.** See 'Gethsemane'. **3.** The garden of the Resurrection, John 19.41–42; 20.1–17

**Garlands** wreaths of flowers wound into the horns of sacrificial bulls at Lystra, seen in many local carvings, Acts 14.13

**Gate 1.** Gates of the city, where legal and commercial business was done, Gen. 34.20–24; Deut. 21.19; Ruth 4.1–11. **2.** Gates of the Temple, see 'Door 2.' **3.** The Beautiful Gate of the Temple, where Peter healed a lame man, probably the Nicanor Gate into the Court of Israel, made of Corinthian bronze, Acts 3.2–10. **4.** Wide and narrow gates, Matt. 7.13–14. **5.** Gate of the sheepfold; sometimes a shepherd would himself lie down across the entrance to the place where the sheep were penned to protect them; a robber would have to climb over the wall or fence, John 10.7–10. **6.** Jesus suffered outside the gate, Lev. 16.27; Heb. 13.11–12. **7.** Gates of death, Ps. 107.18; Isa. 38.10; Wisd. 16.3; Matt. 16.18. **8.** Gates of heaven, Gen. 28.17; Rev. 21.12–25

**Gath** (*H* = winepress) one of the five Philistine cities, home of Goliath, Josh. 11.2; 1 Sam. 17.4; 2 Sam. 1.20. There were four or five other towns called Gath

**Gaza** (*H* = strong) one of the five Philistine cities, where Samson carried away the gates, and, blinded, pulled down the temple on himself; 'the desert road', where Philip met the Ethiopian, means the road to Deserted Gaza, the ruins of the old city destroyed in 93 BC, Judg. 16.1–3; 16.21–30; Acts 8.26

**Geba** (*H* = hill) **1.** Modern Jeba, 6 miles NNE of Jerusalem, was in Benjamin's tribal area and allocated to the Levites, Josh. 18.24; 21.17; it was rebuilt by Asa, 1 Kings 15.22; and formed the north boundary of Judah, 2 Kings 23.8; it was resettled after the Exile, Neh. 7.30; 12.29; Isa. 10.29. **2.** Geba in the Plain of Esdraelon, Judith 3.10. **3.** Possibly an error for Gibeah, Judg. 20.33; 1 Sam. 13–14; 2 Sam. 5.25

**Gedaliah** governor of Jerusalem under Nebuchadnezzar, Jer. 40.6–41.3. His seal was discovered at Lachish

**Gehazi** (*H* = valley of vision) servant of Elisha, punished for his greed, 2 Kings 4.12–15; 5.20–27

**Gehenna** (*G* from *H* = Valley of Hinnom) see 'Hell 2.'

**Genealogies** lists of ancestors and descendants, show movements of tribes and relationships in society. The genealogy of Jesus shows that he was the descendant of David, of Abraham, and of Adam, Gen. 5; 10; 25; 1 Chron. 1–9; Matt. 1; Luke 3.23–38. Misuse of genealogies under rabbinic or gnostic influence, is condemned, 1 Tim. 1.4; Titus 3.9

**Genesis** (Gen.) The Book of Genesis (JEN-nee-sis), see p. **136**

**Gennesaret** (H = garden of the prince) see 'Galilee 1.'

**Gentiles** (*L* = nations; *H goi-im*, *G ethne*) all non-Jews. Between Jew and Gentile there was mutual loathing, but some prophets looked forward to their conversion; Paul's vocation was to preach the gospel to the Gentiles, making Jew and Gentile one, Isa. 42.8; 49.6; Acts 18.6; Gal. 3.28; Eph. 3.8

**Gentle gentleness** see 'Meek'

**Gerasene Gergesene** from Gerasa or Gergesa, see 'Gadarene swine'

**Gerizim** and **Ebal** two peaks above Shechem, modern Nablus, symbolizing the choice between following YHWH or disobeying him, Deut. 11.26–30; Josh. 8.33; Gerizim is the sacred mountain of the Samaritans, John 4.20

**Gethsemane** (*H* = oil-press) olive orchard in the Kidron Valley west of Jerusalem, where Jesus prayed that he would not have to die, and was arrested; the Rock of the Agony is inside the Church of All Nations, John 18.1–26 etc.

**Gezer** (*H* = precipice) Tel Gezer, 10 miles south of Lod, site of city which was held by Egypt, then given to Solomon as dowry when he wed Pharaoh Shishak's daughter, 1 Kings 9.15–17. Known later as Gazara, it was captured by Simon during the Maccabean wars, 1 Macc. 13.43. A tenth-century BC tablet found here gives an agricultural calendar in an early form of Hebrew

**Ghost** old English word for 'Spirit', see 'Holy Spirit', 'Spirits' and The Holy Spirit, p. **174**

**Giants** Gen. 6.4; Num. 13.33; Deut. 2.10; 3.11–13; 9.2–20; 2 Sam. 21.16–22; 1 Chron. 20.6; Wisd. 14.6; Ecclus. (Ben Sira) 16.7

**Gibbethon** (*H* = high place) Philistine town where Baasha assassinated Nadab, 1 Kings 15.27; 16.15–17

**Gibeah** (*H* = hill), **1.** Where Saul was born, either 3 miles north of Jerusalem at Tell el-Ful, or 6 miles north-east of Jerusalem at Jaba'; destroyed in Israel's battles against Benjamin, Judg. 19.12–16; 20.4–43; Saul's capital 1 Sam. 10–26; held up as a bad example, Hos. 5.8; 10.9. **2.** Gibeah of God, probably the same as 1., 1 Sam. 10.5. **3.** In the hill-country of Judah, possibly el-Jeba' 7 miles south-west of Bethlehem, Josh. 15.57. **4.** Unknown site in Ephraim, Josh. 24.33. **5.** Hill at Kiriath-Jearim, 1 Sam. 7.1–2; 2 Sam. 6.3–4

**Gibeon** (*H* = hill) el-Jib 5 miles NNW of Jerusalem, with a pool; where the sun stood still, Josh. 9–10; David struggled with Saul, 2 Sam. 2.2–17; Solomon had a dream, 1 Kings 3; and the Ark of the Covenant was kept until the Jerusalem Temple was built, 1 Chron. 16.39–42

**Gideon** (*H* = tree feller) leader who saw an angel; was given the signs of the fire and the fleece; reduced the size of his army; defeated the Midianites, Judg. 6–8

**Gihon** (*H* = gushing) **1.** The Virgin's Spring, which gushes irregularly, in a cave east of the City of David in Jerusalem; today it is called 'En Sitti Maryam or 'Ain Umm ed-Darag. The 'water shaft' for drawing water from the spring, through which David attacked the Jebusites, is today called Warren's Shaft, leading to Hezekiah's Tunnel, 2 Sam. 5.8; 1 Kings 1.38–45; 2 Chron. 32.30; 33.14. **2.** See 'Eden'

**Gilboa, Mount** barren group of hills between the Valley of Jezreel and the River Jordan, where Saul and Jonathan were killed, 1 Sam. 31; 2 Sam. 1.21

**Gilead** (*H* = rocky) land east of the River Jordan between Lake Galilee and the Dead Sea, once occupied by the Reubenites; birthplace of Jair, Jephthah, Jehu and Elijah; now in Jordan, where Mount Gilead is known as Jebel Jilad and Jebel Osha, Num. 32; Judg. 10.3; 11.1–29; 1 Kings 17.1; see also 'Balm in Gilead', 'Ramoth-Gilead'

**Gilgal** (*H* = stone circle) site near Jericho where Joshua crossed the River Jordan, Josh. 4.19; 9.6. Like the other places called Gilgal in the Bible its site is impossible to identify

**Gilgamesh Epic** story written in the Akkadian language, about a king of Uruk who survived a great flood

**Gleaning** gathering ears of grain left behind by the reapers, a privilege for the poor, aliens and widows, Deut. 24.19–22; Ruth 2.2

**Glory** what we praise about someone: their power, reputation, wealth or wisdom; the glory or splendour of God is often represented by a bright light, see '*Shekinah*', Ex. 24.16–17; Ps. 19.1; John 1.14

**Glutton and a drunkard**, accusation of eating and drinking excessively made against Jesus, because he enjoyed parties with the outcasts, Matt. 11.19; Luke 7.34

**Gnats** plague in Egypt, also translated as lice, mosquitoes or fleas; probably the sand-fly which carries dengue fever, Ex. 8.16–18; Ps. 105.31; Matt. 23.24

**Goad** the Risen Christ told Paul at his conversion that it was painful for Paul to kick against the goad, like an animal kicking the pointed stick which is used to guide it, Acts 26.14

**Goat** *Capra hircus*, kept in the same flock with the sheep and separated at shearing time; the wild goat was a long horned ibex, *Capra beden*, which lived in the mountains, Ps. 104.18; Matt. 25.32–33; see also 'Scapegoat'

**God** see p. **174**, see also 'Presence of God'

**God-fearers** non-Jews who were sympathetic to Judaism but unwilling to become converts; they were called 'proselytes of the porch', and were among the first converts to Christianity; in the theatre at Miletus one bench is inscribed 'For the Jews and God-fearers', Acts 10.2, 22; 13.16; 16.14; 17.4, 12; 18.7

**Gog** (*H* = mountain) and **Magog** Ezekiel prophesies about God calling Gog, chief prince of Meshech and Tubal, from the unidentified land of Magog in the north, against Israel; then God destroys Gog's forces with natural disasters; the vision is obscure, but suggests that the nations who had exiled the Jews would not last for ever, Ezek. 38–39; in Rev. 20.8 Gog and Magog are both mythical nations

**Golden Rule** 'do to others what you would have them do to you', Matt. 7.12; Luke 6.31

**Golgotha** (*G* from *Ar gulgalta* = place of a skull) where Jesus was crucified, see 'Calvary'

**Goliath** (*H* = soothsayer) Philistine giant killed by David, though another version gives Elhanan as the name of his killer, 1 Sam. 17.4–51; 21.9; 22.10; 2 Sam. 21.19

**Gomorrah** see 'Sodom'

**Good Samaritan** The Parable of the Good Samaritan who rescued a traveller on the road to Jericho, teaches that Christian neighbourliness knows no boundaries of race or religion, Luke 10.25–37

**Gopher Wood** from which Noah's Ark was made, possibly cypress or cedar, Gen. 6.14

**Goshen** part of Egypt where the Hebrew slaves lived; one suggestion is Wadi Tumilat which leads from the delta to the Bitter Lakes, Gen. 45.10; 46.28; 47.4; Ex. 8.22

**Gospel** (old English god-spell, *G euangelion* = good news) the message of God's universal all-forgiving love, brought us by the sacrifice of Jesus for each of us on the cross, Mark 1.1, 15; 13.10; Rom. 1.16; Eph. 6.15. The Gospels according to Matthew, Mark, Luke and John are the four canonical books which contain this good news, see pp. **149–50**

**Gospel of the Hebrews** see p. **163**

**Gospel of Thomas** see p. **162**

**Gourd** probably *Cucurbita pepo*, which grows quickly, is used to cover arbours for shade, and a worm in the root would cause it rapidly to wither, Jonah 4.6–10; the wild gourd may be *Citrullus colocynthis*, which has a bitter taste, 2 Kings 4.38–40

**Governor** someone who rules over a territory under a king: Joseph, Gen. 42.6;

Gedaliah, 2 Kings 25.22; Tattenai, Ezra 5.3; Nehemiah, Neh. 5.14; Zerubbabel, Hag. 1.1. There were legates, directly under the Emperor, such as Quirinius, Luke 2.2; proconsuls, under the senate, Sergius Paulus, Acts 13.7; Gallio 18.12; the prefect, Pontius Pilate, Matt. 27.2; and two procurators of Judea, Felix, Acts 23.24; Festus, 24.27, see 'Judea'

**Grace** (from *L gratia* = favour) **1.** Like 'mercy' and 'loving-kindness', translates Hebrew *hesed*, God's love for us, Ps. 45.2; 84.11; Prov. 3.34; Jer. 31.2; Zech. 4.7. **2.** Greek *charis*, the free gift of God's forgiveness which we can never earn ('free, gratis and for nothing'), and the power to show love to others which this brings, John 1.17; Acts 4.33; Rom. 3.24; 6.14; Eph. 2.5–8

**Grafting** Paul describes the non-Jews as like a shoot from a wild olive, grafted onto the root of the tree of Israel; horticulturally improbable, the metaphor is another illustration of grace, Rom. 11.17–24

**Grapes 1.** 'The fathers have eaten sour grapes, and the children's teeth are set on edge', proverb for the effects of sin on later generations, contradicted in Jer. 31.29; Ezek. 18.2. **2.** Grapes cannot be gathered from thorn bushes, so good deeds can only come from a good heart, Matt. 7.16; see 'Vine'

**Grass** 'all flesh is grass', we cannot be saved by mortal humans, only by the word of the LORD, Isa. 40.6

**Graven image** carved representation worshipped as an idol, Ex. 20.4; Lev.26.1; Isa. 42.17; 44.15

**Greeks** 'Hellenes' were from Greece, but since Greek language and culture were used all over the Roman Empire, anyone who spoke Greek or followed a Hellenistic life-style was called a Greek or 'Hellenist', Acts 6.1. Greeks came to see Jesus, John 12.20; Greek-speaking Jewish Christians grumbled about unfair charitable distribution; in Antioch the gospel was first preached to Greeks, Acts 11.20; in Christ there is neither Jew nor Greek, Gal. 3.28

**Grove** old translation for the goddess 'Asherah', which see

**Guest-room** many houses would have one, if only a raised area at one end of the single room; some would rent them out. Jesus sent disciples to find a guest-room where he could eat the Passover, Mark 14.14; and he said that in his Father's house are many guest-rooms (with room for everyone), John 14.2; the same word is translated 'inn' in the story of his birth, Luke 2.7

**Habakkuk** (*H* = wrestler) (Hab.) The Book of the Prophet Habakkuk (HAB-uh-cuk), see p. **144**

**Hades** (*G* = the unseen) (HAY-deez) see 'Hell 1.'

**Hagar** (*H* = fugitive) slave-girl from Egypt, given to Abraham by his wife Sarah; mother of Ishmael; fled to the wilderness where an angel promised her many descendants; sent away again when Isaac was born; see 'Ishmael' Gen. 16; 21.8–21. She is an allegory for slavery to the Law in Gal. 4.21–31

**Hagarenes** or **Hagrites** enemies of Israel living east of Gilead during Saul's reign, 1 Chron. 5.10–20; Ps. 83.6

**Haggai** (*H* = festive) (Hag.) The Book of the Prophet Haggai (HAG-a-eye), see p. **145**

**Hakeldama** see 'Akeldama'

**Hallelujah** (*H* = praise Jah) Hebrew call (in the plural) for all people to praise the LORD, used in Jewish and Christian worship, Ps. 104–106; 111–113; 115–117; 135; 146–150; Rev. 19.1–6

**Hallow** to make something holy, by keeping the sabbath separate for God, and by praising his name, Ex. 20.11; Matt. 6.9

**Ham** (*H* = black) son of Noah, ancestor of the Canaanites, Assyrians, Egyptians and Ethiopians, Gen. 7.13; 9.18–27; 10.6; Ps. 105.23

**Haman** chief servant of the Persian king, see Esther, p. **139**

**Hamath** (*H* = fortress) today called Hamah in Syria; town and kingdom on the River Orontes north of Riblah; Lebo-Hamath or The Entrance of Hamath was the northern boundary of Israel during Solomon's reign, Num. 13.21; 2 Sam. 8.9; Isa. 10.9; Jer. 39.5

**Hamstring** making a horse lame by cutting the tendon of its leg, Gen. 49.6; Josh. 11.6; 2 Sam. 8.4

**Hananiah** (*H* = Jah is gracious) **1.** False prophet, Jer. 28. **2.** Also called Shadrach, one of three Israelites thrown into the fiery furnace, see 'Abednego'

**Hands** laying on of hands was a symbol of identifying oneself with one's representative, in sacrifice, ordination, initiation or healing, Lev. 1.4; Num. 8.10–12; 27.18; Matt. 9.18; Mark 7.32; Acts 6.6; 8.17; 13.3; 1 Tim. 4.14; 2 Tim. 1.6

**Hannah** (*H* = grace) childless woman who prayed for a son and became the mother of Samuel, 1 Sam. 1.1–2.21

**Haran** (*H* = way) northern Mesopotamian town; here Abram settled before setting off for the promised land; Jacob married Rachel and Leah; now called Altınbaşak, 24 miles south-east of Şanlıurfa (Edessa) in Turkey, Gen. 11.31–12.4; 27.43–31.21, see also 'Paddan-aram', Mesopotamia, p. **165**

**Harlots** see 'Prostitutes'

**Harod, the Spring of** (*H* = fear) small lake, now called Ein Jalud, in the Valley of Jezreel, at the foot of Mount Gilboa, where Gideon reduced the size of his army by testing how they drank the water, Judg. 7

**Harp** or lyre or lute, played by descendants of Jubal, Gen. 4.21; played by David, 1 Sam. 16.16–23; 2 Sam. 6.5; used in the Temple, Ps. 33.2; 81.2; 150.3; to be played distinctly, 1 Cor. 14.7; heard in heaven, Rev. 5.8; 14.2; 15.2, see also 'Musical instruments'

**Harvest** promise to Noah, Gen. 8.22; harvest festival, Ex. 23.16; 34.21–22, see 'Calendar'; harvest of souls into heaven, Matt. 9.37–38; 13.30; Mark 4.29; John 4.35–38

---

**Hasmoneans** descendants of Mattathias
**167–160** BC Judas Maccabeus, son of Mattathias
**160–142** Jonathan Apphus, son of Mattathias, 1 Macc. 9.23–12.48
**142–134** Simon Thassi, son of Mattathias, 1 Macc. 13–16
**134–104** John Hyrcanus I, son of Simon, 1 Macc. 16.18–24
**104–103** Judas Aristobulus I, son of John, the first to be called King
**103–76** Alexander Jannaeus, son of John
**76–66** Queen Alexandra, widow of Judas, then of Alexander
**66–63** Aristobulus II, son of Alexandra
After Pompey captured Jerusalem for the Romans in 63, it was ruled by puppet ethnarchs:
**63–40** Hyrcanus II, son of Alexandra, appointed by the Romans
**40–37** Antigonus Mattathias, son of Aristobulus II, appointed by the Parthians
**40–37** Herod the Great, from a non-Jewish Idumean family but related by marriage to the Hasmoneans; appointed king of Judea by the Romans; eventually supplanted Mattathias, see 'Herod Family'

**Hatred** as bad as murder, Matt. 5.21

**Hazael** (*H* = God sees) ninth century BC king of Syria, 1 Kings 19.15; 2 Kings 8.8–15; 9.14; attacked Israel, 10.32; received tribute from Judah, 12.17; death, 13.22–25

**Hazazon-Tamar** see 'Tamar 5.'

**Hazor** (*H* = castle) important Canaanite city; impressive remains can be seen north of Lake Galilee beside the road to Kiryat Shemona, Josh. 11.10; 15.25; 19.36; 1 Sam. 12.9

**Head 1.** 'burning coals on his head', metaphor for your enemy's shame when you are kind, Rom. 12.20, quoting Prov. 25.22. **2.** Christ the head of the Church, Col. 1.15–20. **3.** 'The husband is head of the wife', Eph. 5.23, see 'Women'

**Healing** the work of God, Ps. 103.3; Matt. 4.23; 10.8; 1 Cor. 12.9; James 5.13–16

**Heart** seat of reason and will, not of emotion, Judg. 5.16; 1 Kings 3.9; Job. 38.36; Ps. 51.10; Matt. 5.8; 15.19

**Heaven** originally the sky seen as a solid dome, Gen. 1.1, 8; then seven regions with different types of being, and God in the top one, 1 Kings 8.30; Matt. 6.9; 2 Cor. 12.2; place where the visionary can see truth revealed, John 1.51; Heb. 9.23; Rev. 4.1; synonym for God to avoid pronouncing the divine name, Matt. 13.24; eternal dwelling of those who have died, 2 Cor. 5.1; Rev. 19.1

**Hebrew** probably from *Habiru*, who in Mesopotamian, Canaanite and Egyptian inscriptions were stateless bandits. The Jewish race, nation and language, Ex. 3.18; 1 Sam. 4.6; Phil. 3.5

**Hebrews** (Heb.) The Letter to the Hebrews, see p. **157**

**Hebron** (*H* = association) ancient city 19 miles south of Jerusalem, alternative names Mamre and Kiriath-arba, where the Cave of Machpelah, containing the tombs of Abraham, Sarah and other patriarchs, is venerated by Jews and Muslims; it was King David's capital before he captured Jerusalem, Gen. 13.18; 23.2; Num. 13.22; Josh. 14.13–15; 2 Sam. 2.1–4; 5.1–5

**Heifer** young cow; sacrificing a red heifer was a ceremony of purification after a death, Num. 19.1–10; Deut. 21.1–9; Heb. 9.13

**Heir** one who inherits property following a death; we are heirs of God and inherit his promised kingdom following the death of Jesus, Rom. 8.17; Gal. 4.7; Eph. 3.6; James 2.5

**Heliopolis** see 'On'

**Hell 1.** (*H Sheol, G Hades*) where all people go after death; a shadowy place, with no joy or hope, Job 3.13–19. Greeks thought of the soul escaping the body and crossing the River Styx in Charon's ferry-boat, but Jews refused to separate the soul and body, Ps. 16.10; 88.3–12; Ezek. 32.17–32; Matt. 16.18; Rev. 20.13–14, see 'Descent into hell'. Unfortunately the same English word translates this and **2.** (*H Hinnom, G Ge-henna*) the municipal rubbish dump, beyond the Dung Gate, in a valley downhill and downwind from Jerusalem, now called Wadi Jehennam or Wadi er Rubeb. Prophets compared this place, 'where the fire never goes out and the worms never die', to God's destruction of the worthless among his people, Isa. 66.24; Ecclus. (Ben Sira) 7.17; Matt. 5.22; 10.28; 13.42; 18.8–9; Mark 9.48. **3.** Opinions vary as to whether this is a literal description of endless punishment in the next life, or implies immediate total destruction, Matt. 25.41, 46; Luke 16.23–31; Rev. 14.10–11

**Hellenes, Hellenists** see 'Greeks'

**Hem of a garment** see 'Fringe'

Hephzi-bah

**Hephzi-bah** (*H* = my delight is in her) **1.** King Hezekiah's queen, 2 Kings 21.1. **2.** Symbolic name for the restored Jerusalem, Isa. 62.4

**Hermes** Greek god, spokesman for the gods of Olympus. Paul, the preacher, was mistaken for Hermes at Lystra, Acts 14.12

**Hermon** or **Sirion**, high mountain (Jebel ash-Sheikh, 9,229 feet, 2,814 m.) now in Lebanon to the north of Israel, often visible from afar with snow on the summit, Deut. 3.9; Ps. 29.6; 89.12; 133.3

## The Herod Family Tree

An outline family tree of all the Herods mentioned in the New Testament, see 'Judea'
*(There were many more wives and offspring than there is space for here)*

Herod the Great (Matt. 2.1; Luke 1.5; Acts 23.35) an Idumean
Herod was made King of Judea in 40 BC; married ten times; died 4 BC

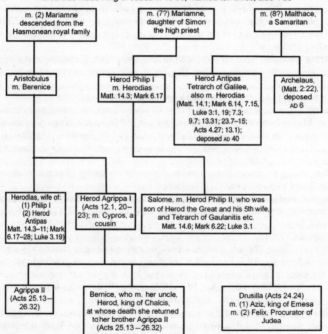

**Heshbon** capital city of the Amorites, now Tell Hesban, about 6 miles north of Madaba in Jordan, see 'Sihon'

**Hezekiah** (*H* = my strength is Jah) king of Judah 716–687 BC; abolished idolatry, reformed worship, was besieged by Sennacherib of Assyria, consulted Isaiah, was given the sign of the sundial, and was rebuked for showing his treasures to Babylonian envoys, 2 Kings 16–20; 2 Chron. 29–30; Isa. 38–39

**Hezekiah's Tunnel** built to bring water from the Gihon spring to within the city during a siege; it has been rediscovered, and the tablet describing how the teams of tunnellers met is now in a museum in Istanbul; provided the water is low, it is possible to walk through the tunnel from Gihon to the Pool of Siloam, 2 Kings 20.20; 2 Chron. 32.30

**Hidden Treasure** parable of Jesus teaching the priority of searching for the Kingdom, Matt. 13.44

**Hierapolis** (G = priests' city) town above Laodicea, now called Pamukkale, Turkey, Col. 4.12–13

**High Places** local sanctuaries, later destroyed in Hezekiah's and Josiah's reforms, Deut. 12.2; 1 Kings 3.2–4; 2 Kings 18.4; 23.5

**High Priest** the senior temple official, consecrated by anointing with oil, who wore a seamless robe, an 'ephod' and a jewelled breastplate; he alone entered the Holy of Holies on the Day of Atonement; the appointment was for life but the Romans replaced them every few years, Ex. 28–29; Lev. 4–9; 16; 21–22; Matt. 26.57–67

**Hinnom, Valley of** see 'Hell 2.'

**Hiram** (H = my brother is high) **1.** King of Tyre; sent building materials and crafts-men to David, 2 Sam. 5.11; 1 Chron. 14.1; and Solomon, 1 Kings 5; 9.11–14, 27; 10.11, 22. **2.** Brass-worker from Tyre who worked for Solomon, 1 Kings 7.13–45; 2 Chron. 2.13–14

**Hittites 1.** Settlers in Anatolia, see Mesopotamia, p. **165**. **2.** Canaanite tribe, whose territory included Hebron, Luz and Kadesh, Gen. 23; Josh. 1.4; 3.10; Judg. 1.26

**Hivites 1.** Canaanite tribe from Lebanon who settled in Gibeon and Shechem, Gen. 34.2; Ex. 3.17; Josh. 9.7; 11.3–19; 2 Sam. 24.7. **2.** See 'Horites 2.'

**Holy** idea supposed to have developed from awe before natural wonders and atmos-pheric places, 'the mystery which frightens and fascinates'; to the priests, places, days, utensils and vestments used in worship, to be kept apart from profane use; then to the moral purity required of those who approach God, 'you shall be holy because I am holy', Ex. 3.5; 20.8; Lev. 11.44–45; Isa. 6.3; 1 Cor. 3.17. The holiness code is a name for Lev. 17–26

**Holy Spirit** or **Holy Ghost** God inspiring and working through people, **1.** In the Hebrew Scriptures, Gen. 1.2; 6.3; 41.38; Ex. 31.3; Num. 11.25–29; 1 Sam. 10.6,10; 16.13; 2 Sam. 23.2; Isa. 61.1; Ezek. 11.19; 37; Joel 2.28–29; Zech. 4.6. **2.** In the life of Jesus, at his conception, Matt. 1.18–20; Luke 1.35; baptism, Matt. 3.11, 16; Mark 1.8, 10; Luke 3.16, 22; John 1.32, 3.5; temptation; Matt. 4.1; Mark 1.12; in his teaching, Matt. 10.20; 12.18; 22.43; 28.19; Mark 13.11; Luke 10.21; 12.12; John 7.39; 14.17; 15.26; 16.13; 20.22. **3.** At Pentecost, Acts 2; in Acts 4.31; 8.15–19; 9.17; 10.44–47; in the teaching of Paul, Rom. 5.5; 7.6; 8; 1 Cor. 3.16; 12.3–13; 2 Cor. 13.13; Gal. 5.22; Eph. 4.4; 6.17; in the rest of the New Testament, Heb. 2.4; 3.7; 2 Peter 1.21; Rev. 22.17, see also The Holy Spirit, p. **174**

**Homosexual acts** forbidden to Jews, a capital offence on a level with adultery, cursing parents, incest, eating non-kosher food and spiritualism, Lev. 20.13. Anthropologists disagree whether this prejudice was because they fail to ensure the survival of the tribe, or because they were distinctive of other religions. There is no evidence these laws were ever put into effect, and the Church declared that they do not apply to non-Jewish Christians, Acts 15.28. Homosexual prostitution in the temples of the fertility religions was abhorrent, Deut. 23.17; 1 Kings 14.24; 15.12; 22.46; 2 Kings 23.7; and the condemnation in 1 Cor. 6.9; 1 Tim. 1.10, probably refers to homosexual prostitution and rape. Faithful same-sex relationships like David's with Jonathan are praised, 1 Sam. 18.1. In Rom. 1.27 Paul quotes the Jewish belief that homosexuality is distinctive of Gentiles and is 'unnatural', but argues from this in Rom. 2.1 that the most unnatural vice of all is prejudice against those who are different

**Hope** a positive attitude to the future. **1.** See 'Covenant', 'Remnant', 'Resurrection'. **2.** Hope of eternal life, 1 Peter 1.3; 1 Cor. 13.13; 1 Thess. 5.8; Rom. 8.24–39; 15.3; Col. 1; 1 Peter 3.15

**Hophni** (*H* = boxer) and **Phinehas** dishonest priests, sons of Eli at Shiloh, 1 Sam. 1.3; 2.12–36; 4.1–11

**Hophra** (*Eg Haaibrah Wahibra*) Pharaoh (589–570 BC), Jer. 37.5; 44.30

**Hor, Mount** where Aaron died, Num. 20.22–29; usually identified as Jebel Haroun, near Petra in Jordan, though Jebel Madurah near Kadesh-Barnea is also suggested

**Horeb** name used in E and D sources, when J and P use Mount Sinai. Here God gave the Ten Commandments, 1 Kings 8.9; Moses brought water from the rock, Ex. 17.6; Elijah spent forty days, 1 Kings 19.8. Traditionally associated with one of the peaks of Jebel Musa, in the Sinai peninsula. However Ex. 3.1 places it near Midian; Deut. 33.2 associates Sinai with Seir; so some identify Horeb with Mount Hor. Interpreters differ over whether Horeb and Sinai were two mountains in different places, or only one mountain and one of the sources has changed its location. See Ex. 33.6; Deut. 1.2, 6; 4.10; 5.2; 9.8; 18.16; Mal. 4.4. See also 'Rephidim', 'Sinai'

**Horites** or **Horim 1.** Tribe living near Seir, Gen. 14.6; 36.20; Deut. 2.12, 20. **2.** The Hivites in Gen. 34.2; Josh. 9.7 are called in Greek Horites, and may be Hurrians, who took Mesopotamian civilization to Asia Minor

**Horns 1.** Of an animal, used as a container for oil, 1 Sam. 16.1; 1 Kings 1.39; as a trumpet, Josh. 6.4. **2.** Horn-shaped projections on the altar, to which those who sought sanctuary could cling, Ex. 27.2, 30.10; 1 Kings 1.50; 2.28. **3.** Poetic symbol for strength, Ps. 75.4–5; Jer. 48.25; Ezek. 29.21. **4.** Prophetic symbol for kings, Dan. 7.7–8; 8.21; Rev. 12.3; 13.1

**Horse** introduced by the Egyptians for chariots and cavalry; the war-horse was used in Israel from the time of David and Solomon. The Four Horsemen of the Apocalypse are a symbol of war, and the famine, epidemics and death which war brings, Ex. 15.21; 1 Kings 4.26; 2 Chron. 1.14–17; Job 39.19–25; Zech. 1.8–10; Rev. 6.2–8

**Hosanna** (*H* = save us, we pray) shouted by the crowds while Jesus rode into Jerusalem, Matt. 21.9–15; Mark 11.9–10; John 12.13; quoting Ps. 118.25

**Hosea** (*H* = Jah saves) (Hos.) The Book of Hosea (hoe-ZEE-uh), see p. **143**

**Hoshea** (*H* = may Jah save) son of Elah, killed Pekah to become last king of Israel 732–723 BC; imprisoned by Assyrians for seeking an alliance with Egypt (confirmed in cuneiform tablets of Tiglath-Pileser III), 2 Kings 15.30; 17.1–4

**Hosts** (*H sabaoth*) the armies of the LORD, the God of Hosts; originally Israelite soldiers; later thought of as invisible armies of angels, and the multitude of stars, Deut. 4.19; 1 Sam. 17.45; 1 Kings 22.19; Luke 2.13

**Hours of the day** divided the time from sunrise to sunset into twelve, so the third hour was approximately 9 a.m., Matt. 20.3; 27.45; Acts 3.1

**Housetops** most houses were single-storey with stairs leading to the flat roof made of mud and branches (easy to dig through) where people relaxed to gossip in the evening, Ps.129.6; Matt. 10.27; Luke 5.19; Acts 10.9

**Huldah** (*H* = weasel) prophetess at the time when Josiah discovered the law-book, 2 Kings 22.14–20

**Humility, humble** see 'Meek'

**Humour** in the Bible is mostly mocking satire, e.g. 1 Kings 18.27; there is also hyperbole or humorous exaggeration, e.g. Matt. 23.24; and many of the parables of Jesus must have struck the first hearers as extremely funny, e.g. Matt. 7.3–5; see also 'Laughter'

**Husbands** see 'Marriage'

**Husbandman** old word for a farmer, Matt. 21.33; John 15.1

**Hushai** (*H* = my brother's gift) David's friend, deceived Absalom with bad advice, 2 Sam. 15–17

**Husks** foot-long seed vessel of the carob-tree, Luke 15.16

**Hymenaeus** Paul's opponent at Ephesus, preached that the resurrection had already happened, 1 Tim. 1.19–20; 2 Tim. 2.14–19

**Hymn** Jesus and the disciples sang a 'hymn' after the Last Supper, probably the 'Hallel' Psalms 115–118 which conclude the Passover ceremony, Matt. 26.30; Mark 14.26. Paul and Silas sang hymns in prison, Acts 16.25; Paul recommends hymn-singing, Eph. 5.19; Col. 3.16. Examples of hymns are probably Phil. 2.6–11; 1 Tim. 2.5; 3.16; 2 Tim. 2.11–13; and frequently in Revelation

**Hypocrite** (*G* = under criticism) normal Greek word for an actor. Jesus accused some Pharisees of acting as though they were righteous but without sincerity, Matt. 6.2, 5, 16; 7.5; 15.7; 22.18; 23.13

**Hyssop** probably marjoram or the caper-plant, used for sprinkling blood for purifying rituals, Ex. 12.22; Lev. 14.4; Ps. 51.7; Heb. 9.19. As it could hardly support a wet sponge, what may have been used at the crucifixion was a javelin called in Greek *hyssos*, John 19.29

**I AM** the name of God: written in Hebrew it resembles YHWH, Ex. 3.14. Repeated use of 'I am' by Jesus may imply a claim to be God, Mark 14.62; John 6.35; 8.12, 58; 9.5; 10.7, 11; 11.25; 14.6; 15.1; Rev. 1.17; 22.13.

**Ichabod** (*H* = where is the glory?) child named because of the capture of the Ark of the Covenant, 1 Sam. 4.21

**Iconium** town, now Konya in Turkey, formerly in Lycaonia, in the Roman Province of Galatia, visited by Paul on his first, second and probably third missionary journeys, Acts 14.1–6, 21; 16.1–2; 18.23; 2 Tim. 3.11

**Idolatry** the worship of 'graven images' (carved statues) or 'molten images' (cast metal statues), forbidden by the First Commandment because it drew worshippers to gods with only local power, away from the one universal God, and was usually associated with immoral fertility practices; and by the Second Commandment because it lowered the invisible God to the level of his visible creation, Ex. 20.3–5; Isa. 40.18–20, see 'Meat offered to idols'

**Idumea** area west of the Dead Sea, to which many Edomites had been driven by invading Arabic Nabateans, 1 Macc. 4–6; 5.25; 9.35; 2 Macc.10.14; Mark 3.8

**Illyricum** Roman Province on the east coast of the Adriatic, Rom. 15.19

**Image of God** men and women created in, not visually but in having the power to choose and to love, Gen. 1.26–27; Rom. 8.29; 1 Cor.15.49; 2 Cor. 3.18; Col. 3.10. Jesus pointed out the image of the head and the name of the Emperor on a coin to show that it already belongs to him, just as human beings in the image of God belong totally to God, Matt. 22.15–22

**Immanuel** (*H* = God is with us) see 'Virgin'

**Immortality** not innate as Greeks believed, but the gift of God, Rom. 2.7; 1 Cor. 15.54

**Impossible** nothing is impossible with God, Matt. 17.20; Luke 1.37; 18.27

**Incense** mixture of resins which, when placed on burning sacrifices or charcoal, produces a fragrant smoke, Ex. 30.7–9; 30.34–38; Lev. 16.12–13; Mal. 1.11; Luke 1.9–11; see 'Spices'. Smoke ascending to heaven, a metaphor for prayer, Ps. 141.2; Rev. 5.8; 8.3

**Incest** sexual relations with a close relative, forbidden, Lev. 18; Mark 6.17–18; 1 Cor. 5.1

**Infants** or **Innocents** massacre of the children of Bethlehem by Herod's soldiers, Matt. 2.16–18

**Ingathering, Feast of** see 'Booths', 'Calendar'

**Inheritance** see 'Birthright', 'Earnest', and Num. 27.6–11. Inheritance of eternal life guaranteed to all believers, Acts 20.32; Col. 1.12; 3.24; Heb. 9.15; 1 Peter 1.4

**Inn** see 'Guest-room'. In the Parable of the Good Samaritan, the 'inn' is a different word meaning a place where all are received, Luke 10.34

**Inspiration of the Bible** see p. **176**

**Intercession** praying for other people, **1.** Intercession by Jesus, Luke 23.34; John 17; Rom. 8.34; 1 John 2.1. **2.** By the Holy Spirit, Rom. 8.26. **3.** We must pray for others, Eph. 6.18; 1 Tim. 2.1–2. **4.** Paul asks his friends to pray for him, Rom. 15.30; 2 Cor. 1.11; Col. 4.3; 1 Thess. 5.25; 2 Thess. 3.1. **5.** Effective prayer for the sick, James 5.14–16

**Invisible** Jesus makes the invisible God visible, Rom. 1.20; Col. 1.15; 1 Tim. 1.17; Heb. 11.27

**Isaac** (*H yitzhak* = laughter) so named because Sarah laughed at the idea that she would have a child, Gen. 18.12. He was offered in sacrifice by Abraham his father, Gen. 22. He married Rebekah, Gen. 24; his children were Esau and Jacob, Gen. 27. He died at Hebron, Gen. 35.27–29

**Isaiah** (*H* = Jah is salvation) (Isa.) The Book of the Prophet Isaiah (British pronunciation eyes-EYE-uh, American eye-ZAY-uh), see p. **141**

**Iscariot** Judas Iscariot was one of The Twelve; he betrayed Jesus to the priests when he told them they could find Jesus in Gethsemane. In remorse he hanged himself, according to Matt. 27.3–10, or fell headlong according to Acts 1.18. His name may be from Ish-Kerioth, man of Kerioth (possibly Khirbat el-Qaryatein in Judea); or from the Greek *sicarios*, the dagger used by the assassins, because he was trying to provoke a revolution, Matt. 10.4; 26.14–16, 47–49; Luke 22.3–6, 47–48; John 6.70–71; 12.4–6; 13.21–30; 18.2–5

**Ish-bosheth** Saul's son, whose name has probably been changed from Ish-Baal, Man of Baal, to Man of Shame. He led a rebellion against David, and was assassinated, 2 Sam. 2.8–10; 3.7–11; 4; 1 Chron. 8.33; 9.39

**Ishmael** (*H* = God hears) elder son of Abraham, but was banished to Arabia and became the ancestor of the Ishmaelites (Arabs), see 'Hagar', Gen. 16; 17.20–27; 21.8–21; 25.12–18; Gal. 4.21–31. Muslims believe he was more important than Isaac

**Isles** or coastlands, the distant areas where the Gentiles lived, probably meaning the whole Mediterranean and Red Sea coast, which will eventually be converted, Ps. 97.1; Isa. 24.15; 41.1–5; 66.19; Jer. 31.10

**Israel** (*H* = fighter with God) **1.** Name given to Jacob after he wrestled with God at Jabbok, Gen. 32.28; 35.10. **2.** General term for the whole Jewish people, slaves in Egypt, Ex. 1–13; saved through the Red Sea, Ex. 14; fed in the wilderness, Ex. 15–17; made a covenant with God, Ex. 19–20; entered Canaan, Josh. 1–19; ruled by

'Judges', Judg. 2–21; by David and Solomon, 1 and 2 Sam., 1 Kings 1–11. **3.** The Northern Kingdom of ten tribes after the division from Judah, 1 Kings 11.38; 12–22; 2 Kings 1–15; taken captive to Assyria, 2 Kings 17

**Issachar** (*H* = he brings reward) one of the twelve sons of Jacob, ancestor of a tribe occupying the Valley of Jezreel, Gen. 30.18; 49.14–15; Deut. 33.18–19; Josh. 19.17–23

**Italian Cohort** regiment in which Cornelius was a centurion, *Cohors II Italica Civium Romanorum*, mostly freedmen from Italy, in Caesarea AD 41–44, Acts 10.1

**Ivory** elephants' tusks, imported from Africa or India, used for decorating beds, palaces and thrones; 500 pieces were found at the 'ivory palace' of Ahab, excavated at Samaria, 1 Kings 10.18–22; 22.39; Ps. 45.8; Amos 3.15; 6.4


**J** one of the sources believed by some to lie behind the books from Genesis to Numbers, originating from the Southern Kingdom of Judah in Jerusalem and using the name Jah or YHWH for the LORD, see p. **134**

**Jaar** (*H* = woodland) Ps. 132.6, see 'Kiriath-Jearim'

**Jabbok** (*H* = pouring out) a wadi or river, tributary of the Jordan, entering on the east between Lake Galilee and the Dead Sea, now called the Zarqa River in Jordan, where Jacob wrestled with God, Gen. 32.22; Deut. 2.37; Judg. 11.13–22

**Jabesh-Gilead** (*H* = dry place in Gilead) town identified with ruins of ed-Deir, near the present-day Wadi Yabis, which enters the Jordan from the east, south of Lake Galilee; Judg. 20–21; 1 Sam. 11.1–11; 31.11

**Jacob** (*H* = takes by the heel, or supplanter) son of Isaac; cheated his brother Esau; dreamt of 'Jacob's ladder' at Bethel; married Leah and Rachel; made a covenant with Laban; was father of twelve sons, who were ancestors of the twelve tribes of Israel; wrestled with God; died in Egypt, Gen. 25–35; Hos. 12.2–4

**Jacob's well** where Jesus met a Samaritan woman, and spoke about living water; now within a church on the south of Nablus, Gen. 33.18–19; Josh. 24.32; John 4.4–30; see 'Shechem'

**Jael** (*H* = mountain goat) wife of Heber the Kenite; killed Sisera with a tent-peg, Judg. 4.17–22; 5.24–27

**Jah** the name of God, shortened from YHWH, Ps. 68.4, see 'LORD'

**Jailer** converted in Philippi, Acts 16.23

**Jair** (djah-eer, *H* = enlightens) Gileadite who ruled Israel, Judg. 10.3

**Jairus** (dj-EYE-russ) 'ruler of the synagogue' whose daughter was raised to life by Jesus, Matt. 9.18–26; Mark 5.22–43; Luke 8.41–56

**James** English form of Jacob, **1.** One of The Twelve, a Galilean fisherman, brother of John, son of Zebedee, present at the Transfiguration and in Gethsemane, Matt. 4.21–22; 10.2; 17.1–13; 20.20–24; 26.36–46; killed by Herod, Acts 12.2. **2.** Known as James the Less or 'Little James', also one of The Twelve, brother of Matthew, son of Alphaeus and Mary, Matt. 10.3; Mark 16.1; Acts 1.13. **3.** See 'Judas 4'. **4.** One of the brothers of Jesus who tried to dissuade him, see 'Brothers of Jesus'. **5.** James the brother of the Lord, leader of the church in Jerusalem, Acts 12.17; 15.13–29, 21.18; 1 Cor. 15.7; Gal. 1.19; 2.9–12. According to Josephus he was called James the Just and was martyred on the orders of High Priest Annas II around AD 60–62; the church historian Eusebius says he was martyred under Vespasian in 67; a first-century ossuary (limestone box for bones) has been found with the Aramaic words 'Of James son of Joseph and brother of Jesus'. **6.** The author of The Letter of James. These occurrences probably refer to six, but possibly as few as two, individuals.

**James** (James) The Letter of James, see p. **158**

**Jannes** and **Jambres** names given in 2 Tim. 3.8 for the unnamed Egyptian magicians who in Ex. 3.8 opposed Moses; the names are familiar in Jewish tradition

**Japheth** (*H* = beauty) son of Noah, ancestor of the Gentiles, Gen. 7.13; 9.18–27; 10.2–5

**Japho** (*H* = beauty) port on the Mediterranean coast, later called Joppa and Jaffa, now part of Tel Aviv-Yaffo; from which Jonah set sail; where Peter healed Dorcas, and stayed with Simon the Tanner, Jonah 1.3; Acts 9.36; 10.5; 11.5

**Jarmuth** kingdom of Canaan beside the River Yarmuk, which flows from the east into the Jordan south of Lake Galilee, Josh. 10.5; 21.29

**Jashar** (*H* = upright) book of national songs which has not survived, Josh. 10.13; 2 Sam. 1.18

**Jason** (*G*, after the leader of the Argonauts) Christian in Thessalonica who had to pay bail because he had given Paul hospitality, Acts 17.5–9; Rom. 16.21

**Jawbone of a donkey** Samson's weapon, Judg. 15.15–17

**Jealous God** graphic way of saying that God demands total allegiance; not implying petty emotions, Ex. 20.5; 34.14

**Jebusites** original inhabitants of Jerusalem; defeated when David climbed the water-shaft, Josh. 15.63; Judg. 19.11; 2 Sam. 5.6–8; 24.16–24

**Jeconiah** (*H* = Jah establishes) see 'Jehoiachin'

**Jehoahaz** (*H* = YHWH holds) **1.** Son of Jehoram and Athaliah, king of Judah 841 BC, also called Ahaziah, killed by Jehu at Megiddo, 2 Kings 8.25–29; 9.27–29; 2 Chron. 21.17; 22.1. **2.** Son of Jehu, king of Israel 814–798, also called Joahaz, 814–798, 2 Kings 10.35; 13.1–9; 14.1. **3.** Son of Josiah, king of Judah for 3 months in 609, 2 Kings 23.31–33; 2 Chron. 36.1, also called Shallum, Jer. 22.11–18

**Jehoash** (*H* = YHWH bestows) **1.** Son of Ahaziah, also called Joash, king of Judah 835–796 BC, 2 Kings 11.2, 21; 12.1–21. **2.** Son of Jehoahaz, also called Joash, king of Israel 798–783, 2 Kings 13.10–25; 14.8–17

**Jehoiachin** (*H* = YHWH strengthens) son of Jehoiakim, king of Israel for 3 months in 598 BC, then taken into exile in Babylon, 2 Kings 23.36–24.6; 25.27–30; 2 Chron. 36.8–9; Jer. 52.31–34; Ezek. 1.2. Also called Jeconiah, 1 Chron. 3.16–17; Esth. 2.6; Jer. 24.1; 27.20; 28.4; 29.2; Baruch 1.3–9; shortened to Coniah, Jer. 22.24–30; 37.1, see also 'Exile'

**Jehoiada** (*H* = YHWH knows) high priest in Israel; in about 835 BC killed Athaliah, restored Jehoash 2 or Joash 2, and repaired the Temple, 2 Kings 11.4–12.9; 2 Chron. 23–24

**Jehoiakim** (*H* = YHWH raises) son of Josiah, king of Israel 609–598 BC; revolted against Nebuchadnezzar, 2 Kings 23–24; 1 Chron. 3.15–16; 2 Chron. 36.4–8; Jer. 22.18–19; 26.21–23; 36; Dan. 1.1–2. Also called Eliakim, 2 Kings 23.34

**Jehoram** (*H* = YHWH is high) **1.** Son of Ahab, king of Israel 852–841 BC, also called Joram, killed by Jehu, 2 Kings 1.17; 3.1–5; 8.28–29; 9.14–26. **2.** Son of Jehoshapat, husband of Athaliah, king of Judah 848–841, also called Joram, 1 Kings 22.50; 2 Kings 8.16–26; 2 Chron. 21

**Jehoshaphat** (*H* = YHWH judges) **1.** Son of Asa, king of Judah 870–848 BC, 1 Kings 15.24; 22; 2 Kings 3; 2 Chron. 17–22. **2.** Son of Nimshi and father of Jehu, 2 Kings 9.2, 14

**Jehoshaphat, Valley of** where the LORD judges the nations; traditionally identified as the Kidron valley in Jerusalem, Joel 3.2, 12

**Jehovah** see 'LORD'

**Jehovah-jireh** (*H* = the LORD provides) the place where God provided a ram to sacrifice in place of Abraham's son, Gen. 22.14, see 'Moriah'

**Jehu** (*H* = Jah is he) son of 'Jehoshaphat 2.' above (sometimes 'son of Nimshi'), king of Israel 841–814 BC; anointed, 2 Kings 9.4–6; killed Joram of Israel, Ahaziah of Judah, and Jezebel, 2 Kings 9.14–31; killed the royal families of Israel and Judah and the worshippers of Baal, 2 Kings 10; Hos. 1.4–5; 'drove furiously', 2 Kings 9.20. He is portrayed on the Black Obelisk of Shalmaneser III

**Jemima** (*H* = dove) beautiful daughter, Job 42.14

**Jephtha** (*H* = Jah opens) leader of the Israelites in the district of Gilead; defeated the Ammonites; sacrificed his own daughter to fulfil a rash vow, Judg. 11, see 'Tammuz'

**Jeremiah** (*H* = Jah establishes) (Jer.) The Book of the Prophet Jeremiah (Jerry-MY-uh), see p. **141**

**Jericho** (*H* = city of palms) earliest known still-inhabited town in the world, and the lowest, 1,300 feet below sea-level, in the Jordan Valley about 10 miles from the north end of the Dead Sea; archaeological excavations reveal many layers of habitation. Here Rahab welcomed the spies, Josh. 2; the wall collapsed when Joshua's troops walked round blowing trumpets, Josh. 6; Elisha purified the water in the spring, 2 Kings 2.19–22; Jesus healed the blind, Matt. 20.29–34; Mark 10.46–52; Luke 18.35–43; dined with the tax-collector Zacchaeus, Luke 19.1–10; located the Parable of the Good Samaritan, Luke 10.30–37

**Jeroboam I** (*H* = struggler for the people) or Joboam, son of Nebat, servant of Solomon, rebelled against Rehoboam; became the first king of the Northern Kingdom of Israel 931–910 BC, 1 Kings 11.28–29; 12.20–28; 13.4; 14.7, 20

**Jeroboam II** son of 'Jehoash 2.', see above; king of Israel 783–743 BC, 2 Kings 13.13; 14.16, 23–29; condemned, Amos 7.11

**Jerub-baal** (*H* = fights with Baal) name given to Gideon when he destroyed the altar of Baal, Judg. 6.28–15

**Jerusalem** (*H* = foundation of peace?) city of the Jebusites; on the ridge in the centre of Canaan; city of Melchizedek; captured by David when he climbed the water shaft, 2 Sam. 5; capital city of the united kingdom; then of the Southern Kingdom of Judah; site of palaces, temples and mosques; fought over; scene of the ministry of prophets and the crucifixion of Jesus; metaphor for heaven, Isa. 65.18–25; Gal. 4.26; Rev. 21.2; see also 'Zion'

**Jeshua** Aramaic form of Joshua, translated into Greek as Jesus, 2 Chron. 31.15; Neh. 3.19; 10.9 etc.

**Jeshurun** (*H* = upright) poetic name for Israel, Deut. 32.15; 33.5, 26; Isa. 44.2

**Jesse** (*H* = Jah is) David's father, Ruth 4.22; 1 Sam. 16; dead-seeming tree-stump from which a new shoot appears, Isa. 11.1; ancestor of Jesus, Matt. 1.6

**Jesus** (*G* version of *Ar Jeshua* = Jah saves) **1.** Jesus son of Sirach, see Ecclesiasticus, p. **146**. **2.** Jesus Christ, named by the angel, Matt. 1.21; Luke 1.31; see The Life of Jesus, p. **168**; The Teaching of Jesus, p. **170**. **3.** Jesus Justus, a Jewish Christian, Col. 4.11

**Jethro** (called Reuel in Ex. 2.15–22, Hobab in Judg. 4.11) priest in Midian, one of whose seven daughters, Zipporah, married Moses, Ex. 3.1; Jethro advised Moses to delegate the task of deciding legal cases, Ex. 18

**Jewels** listed in Rev. 21.10–20 as the foundations of the New Jerusalem, representing the apostles, are modelled on the jewels in the breastplate of the high priest in Ex. 28.17–20 representing the twelve tribes; there is another list of jewels in Ezek. 28.13. Following is a list of the jewels in various translations; the Hebrew and Greek words, and possible modern equivalents.

Amethyst *'ahlamah, amethostos,* amethyst

Beryl *tarshish, berullos,* beryl

Carbuncle, emerald *bareketh, nophek, smaragdo,* deep red garnet

Chalcedony, agate *shebo, chalkedon,* chalcedony, a quartz of various colours

Chrysolite *pitdah, topazion, chrisolithos,* topaz, peridot

Chrysoprasus *chrusoprasos,* chrysoprase, apple-green chalcedony

Diamond *yahalom,* corundum, sapphire, ruby

Jacinth, ligure *leshem, huakinthos,* hyacinth, zircon, sapphire

Jasper *yashepeh, iaspis,* jade

Onyx, sardonyx *shoham, sardonux,* onyx

Sapphire *sappir, sapfiro,* lapis-lazuli

Sardius *'odem, sardios,* sard, carnelian

**Jews 1.** From the tribe of Judah; eventually used of all Israelites, Ezra 4.12; Esth. 2.5; Dan. 3.8; Zec. 8.23. **2.** Jesus, himself a Jew, said 'Salvation is from the Jews', John 4.22. **3.** Jews as distinguished from Gentiles, Mark 7.3; Judeans as distinguished from Galileans, John 7.1; Jewish-Christians as distinguished from Gentile-Christians, Rom. 10.12. **4.** The New Testament was mostly written by Jewish-Christians for readers many of whom were Jewish, so although they were being persecuted by non-Christian Jews (Matt. 10.17) it is unlikely to be deliberately anti-Semitic, whatever later generations have read into it

**Jezebel** (*H* = where is the Prince?) Sidonian wife of King Ahab of Israel, she encouraged worship of idols, caused the death of Naboth and many prophets of YHWH, met a violent end, and became a symbol of evil, 1 Kings 16.31; 18.4; 19.2; 21; 2 Kings 9.30–37; Rev. 2.20

**Jezreel** (*H* = God sows) **1.** Village (now Zer'in / Tel Yisre'el) on a spur of Mount Gilboa, where Naboth's vineyard was, 1 Kings 21.1; 2 Kings 9.30–37; Hos. 1.4. **2.** Large valley where Megiddo stands, Josh. 17.16; Judg. 6.33; see 'Esdraelon'

**Joab** (*H* = Jah is father) commander of David's army; killed Abner; pleaded for Absalom; killed him in an oak-tree; killed Amasa; supported Adonijah; was killed on Solomon's orders, 2 Sam. 8.16; 14; 18.10–16; 19.5–7; 20.7–23; 24.2–9; 1 Kings 2.28–34

**Joahaz** (*H* = Jah has grasped) king of Israel 814–798 BC, 2 Kings 14.1, see 'Jehoahaz 1.'

**Joanna** (*H* = Jah graciously gives) wife of Herod's steward Chuza; became a disciple; witness to the empty tomb, Luke 8.3; 24.10

**Joash** (*H* = Jah has given) **1.** Son of Ahaziah, king of Judah 835–796 BC, see 'Jehoash 1.' **2.** Son of Jehoahaz, king of Israel 798–783, see 'Jehoash 2.'

**Job** (Job) The Book of Job (pronounced with a long O), see p. **140**

**Joel** (*H* = Jah is good) (Joel) The Book of the Prophet Joel (JOE-ell), see p. **143**

**John** (*H yohanan* = Jah is gracious) **1.** John the Baptist, born a relative of Jesus, Luke 1. Preached a Baptism of Repentance in the wilderness, preparing the way for Jesus whom he baptized. Was arrested and beheaded by Herod, Matt. 3.1–4.12;

11.2–18; 14.2–12; 21.25–32; Luke 3.7–20; John 1.6–35; 3.23–27; Acts 19.3–4. **2.** John son of Zebedee, brother of James, one of The Twelve, Matt. 4.21; 17.1–13; Mark 9.38; 10.35–41; 14.33; Acts 3.1; 8.17–25; Gal. 2.9. **3.** Author of the Gospel according to John, John 21.24. **4.** Author of the Letters of John, 2 John 1; 3 John 1. **5.** Author of the Revelation, Rev. 1.1–9; 22.8. **6.** John Mark, see 'Mark'. **7.** Member of the high priest's family, Acts 4.6. **8.** Father of Simon Peter, John 1.42; 21.12–17, called Jonah in Matt. 16.17. **9.** Grandfather, brother and nephew of Judas Maccabeus, 1 Mac. 2.1; 8.17; 9.36; 16. Ancient tradition identifies 2, 3, 4, 5, and the 'Beloved Disciple' as one person, though it is unlikely that one man could have written in such different styles

**John**  (John) The Gospel according to John, see p. **150**

**1 John**  (1 John) The First Letter of John, see p. **158**

**2 John**  (2 John) The Second Letter of John, see p. **159**

**3 John**  (3 John) The Third Letter of John, see p. **159**

**Jonah**  (*H* = dove) (Jonah) The Book of Jonah (JOE-nuh), see p. **144**

**Jonathan**  (*H* = Jah gave) son of Saul; loved David; fought and killed by the Philistines; lamented by David, 1 Sam. 13–14; 18–23; 31.2; 2 Sam. 1.17–27

**Joppa**  see 'Japho'

**Joram**  (*H* = Jah is high) **1.** Son of Ahab, king of Israel 852–841 BC, see 'Jehoram 1.'. **2.** Son of Jehoshaphat, king of Judah 848–841, see 'Jehoram 2.'

**Jordan**  (*H* = descends) river descending the rift valley called the Arabah (formed by land sinking between two geological faults) between the Judean hills and the Arabian Desert, from its sources near Dan and Caesarea Philippi, through Lake Huleh (now reclaimed) and Lake Galilee to the Dead Sea (below sea-level) where it evaporates. Joshua divided the waters for the Israelites to enter the promised land, Josh. 3; Ps. 114.3–5; Elijah and Elisha crossed over, 2 Kings 2; John baptized there, Matt. 3

**Joseph**  (*H* = may Jah add) **1.** Son of Jacob, Gen. 30.22–24; dreamer; sold by his jealous brothers; became servant to Potiphar in Egypt; interpreted Pharaoh's dreams; made governor; prepared for the famine; welcomed his brothers and father to stay in Egypt, Gen. 37–50. His sons were Ephraim and Manasseh; their descendants formed the Joseph tribe among the twelve tribes of Israel, Deut. 33.13–17. **2.** Descendant of David, husband of the Virgin Mary, who was told in a dream to name her child Jesus, and took them to safety in Egypt, Matt. 1; 2.13–23; Luke 1.27; 2.4–51. **3.** See 'Brothers of Jesus'. **4.** See 'Arimathea'. **5.** Joseph Justus or Barsabas, who was considered but not selected to replace Judas, Acts 1.23. **6.** See 'Barnabas'

**Josephus**  see p. **163**

**Joshua**  (*H* = Jah saves) son of Nun, one of the spies who investigated Canaan, was appointed Moses' successor, led the Israelites across Jordan and in capturing Canaan, prayed for the sun to stand still at Aijalon, and divided the land between the tribes, Ex. 17.9–14; 24.13; 32.17; 33.11; Num. 13.16; 27.18–23; 34.17; Josh. 1–24

**Joshua**  (Josh.) The Book of Joshua, see p. **137**

**Josiah**  (*H* = Jah supports or Jah's fire) son of Amon, king of Judah 640–609 BC, instituted a reform based on a book of the law found in the Temple, destroying Bethel, eliminating fertility cults, and promoting the worship of YHWH in Jerusalem only, 1 Kings 13.2; 2 Kings 22–23; 2 Chron. 34; 35; 1 Esd. 1.25. See Deuteronomy, p. **136**

**Jot and tittle**  *yodh* (ʼ) the smallest letter of the Hebrew alphabet, and the *keraia*, a small mark like a serif which distinguishes the square corner in ד from the rounded corner in ר; Jesus said even such small details were not to be ignored in seeking God's will, Matt. 5.18; Luke 16.17

**Jotham** (*H* = Jah is perfect) **1.** Son of Gideon; in the parable of the trees he predicted the death of the mass-fratricide Abimelech, Judg. 9. **2.** Son of Uzziah, king of Judah 740–736 BC, 2 Kings 15.32–38

**Jubal** (*H* = sound) inventor of music, Gen. 4.21

**Jubilee** (*H yovel* = ram's horn) in the Year of Jubilee every fifty years, all the land was to lie fallow and be returned to its original owners, and all 'debt-slaves' were to be set free, Lev. 25.9–55; 27.17–24

**Judah** (*H Yehudah* = praise Jah) fourth son of Jacob, ancestor of the tribe of Judah, which gave his name to the Southern Kingdom, Roman Judea, and the race of the Jews, Gen. 29.35; 38; 49.8–12; Deut. 33.7; 1 Kings 12, see 'Jews 1.', 'Lion'

**Judas, Jude 1.** See 'Maccabeus'. **2.** See 'Brothers of Jesus'. **3.** See 'Iscariot'. **4.** Son or brother of James, one of The Twelve, probably the same as Thaddaeus, Matt. 10.3; Mark 3.18; Luke 6.16; John 14.22; Acts 1.13. **5.** Paul's host in Damascus, Acts 9.11. **6.** Judas Barsabbas, accompanied Paul and Barnabas to Antioch, Acts 15.22. **7.** The author of the Letter of Jude, who claims to be identical to 2 or 4 above, Jude 1. **8.** Judas the Galilean, who led a revolt at the time of the census of Quirinius, AD 6–7; the roads of Galilee were lined with the crosses on which the Romans executed his followers during the childhood of Jesus, Acts 5.37

**Jude** (Jude) The Letter of Jude, see p. **159**

---

**Judea** Greek name for the area of Judah, though under Herod the Great it was much larger. The rulers were:

**37–4 BC** Herod the Great, king of Judea (including Galilee, Samaria, Perea, Idumea and the Mediterranean coast)

**4 BC – AD 6** Archelaus, Ethnarch of Judea, Idumea and Samaria

**4 BC – AD 38** Herod Antipas, Tetrarch of Galilee and Perea

**AD 6–21** Quirinius, legate and consul of Syria

**6–40** Prefects as Governors of Judea (Pontius Pilate 26–36)

Tetrarchs of Gaulanitis and other regions east of the Jordan: Herod Philip II (4 BC– AD 34); Herod Agrippa I (AD 37–44); Herod Agrippa II (50–93)

**41–44** King Herod Agrippa I ruled the whole country

**44–66** Procurators of Judea and Galilee (Felix 52–59; Festus 59–62)

---

**Judge** settlement of disputes was the task of the leader of a tribe or nation, Ex. 18.13; early tribal leaders in Israel were called Judges, Judg. 2.16; Solomon prayed for wisdom in judgement, 1 Kings 3. The judgement of God means justice, which was longed for by the victims of injustice, Ps. 96.13. Christians are warned they should be able to settle disputes among themselves without going to law, 1 Cor. 6. For the Day of Judgement see Apocalyptic, p. **175**

**Judges** (Judg.) The Book of the Judges, see p. **137**

**Judging** criticizing others and counting yourself superior, a much worse sin than the behaviour being condemned, Matt. 7.1; Luke 6.37; Rom. 2.1–3; James 4.12; see also 'Revilers'

**Judith** (*H* = Jewess) (Judith) The Book of Judith, see p. **146**

**Julia** Christian woman in Rome to whom Paul sends greetings, Rom. 16.15

**Julius** centurion who escorted Paul to Rome, Acts 27

**Junia** Christian woman in Rome to whom Paul sends greetings, Rom. 16.7, probably the wife of Andronicus; she is described as 'prominent among the apostles'. It is extremely unlikely that this is an otherwise unknown masculine name

**Justify** to make someone righteous or to regard them as righteous, as when they win in a lawcourt. It is the verb from the noun righteous; there is no simple equivalent in English. Paul says God declares us 'not guilty', even though we are guilty, out of his generous love or grace – the sacrifice of Jesus has done all that is necessary; all we have to do is trust God: we are 'justified by grace through faith, not by works of the law', Rom. 3.24–28; Gal. 2.16; compare the penitent tax-collector in Luke 18.14; see also 'Righteousness'

**Kadesh-Barnea** (*H* = holy place of the desert) town in the Wilderness of Zin, where the Israelites sent out spies, and where Miriam was buried, probably Ain el-Qudeirat south-east of Beer-Sheba, Num. 13.26; 20.1; Deut. 32.51; Ps. 29.8

**Kebar** see 'Chebar'

**Kedar** (*H* = black) Ishmaelite tribe, wealthy Bedouin who lived in black tents, Ps.120.5; S. of Sol. 1.5; Isa. 60.7; Ezek. 27.21

**Kedesh** (*H* = holy place) **1.** City 6 miles north-west of Hazor in Upper Galilee, Josh. 20.7; 21.32; 2 Kings 15.29. **2.** Town in southern Galilee where Barak lived, probably Horvat Qedesh south-west of Lake Galilee, Judg. 4.6; 1 Macc. 11.63

**Kenites** tribe considered descendants of Cain, living south of Hebron, Judg. 4.11; 1 Sam. 15.6

**Key** could be large enough to carry on the shoulder; the bearer of the keys to the treasure-house was an important court official, Judg. 3.25, Isa. 22.22; Matt. 16.19; Luke 11.52, Rev. 1.18; 3.7; 9.1; 20.1

**Kidneys** seat of knowledge in Hebrew thought, Ps. 7.9; Jer.17.10; 20.12; Rev. 2.23

**Kidron Valley** (*H* = dark, torrent or cedars) eastern boundary of the old city of Jerusalem; crossed by David as he fled; by Jesus on his way to Gethsemane, 2 Sam. 15.23; John 18.1, see 'Jehoshaphat'

**King** some parts of the Bible praise the king, 1 Sam. 10; others say that kingship was granted reluctantly by God, 1 Sam. 8; God is our king, Ps. 74.12. 'Christ' or 'Messiah' mean anointed king, Luke 23.2; Jesus is called 'King of the Jews' Matt. 27.29; John 18.33–39; 18.3–21; and 'King of kings', Rev. 19.16. Parables include the king and his servants, the king and his guest, and the king going to war, Matt. 18.23–35; 22.2–14; Luke 14.31; see 'Messiah'

**Kingdom of God** (also called kingdom of Heaven, to avoid taking God's name in vain, Matt. 13.24–47), the rule or kingship of God in this world, a present reality among us; and the community of those who obey God, Luke 17.21; for its completion we pray, Matt. 6.10. Many parables show what the world would be like if we obeyed God as our king, e.g. Luke 13

**1–4 Books of Kingdoms** see '1 & 2 Samuel' and '1 & 2 Kings'

**1 Kings** (1 Kings) (3 Kingdoms in Greek) The First Book of Kings, see p. **138**

**2 Kings** (2 Kings) (4 Kingdoms in Greek) The Second Book of Kings, see p. **138**

**Kir-Hareseth** (*H* = city of potsherds) Moabite city, named Kerak by the Crusaders, 2 Kings 3.25; Isa. 15.1; 16.7; Jer. 48.31

**Kiriath-arba** (*H* = city of four) see 'Hebron', Gen. 23.2

**Kiriath-Jearim** (*H* = city of the woods) town where the Ark of the Covenant was left, after its recovery from the Philistines, until it could be brought to Jerusalem, 1 Sam. 6.21–7.2; 1 Chron. 13.6; 2 Chron. 1.4; also called 'the fields of Jaar', Ps.132.6;

the site is near Abu Ghosh, about 9 miles west of Jerusalem, where a large statue of the Virgin Mary indicates that, like the Ark, she 'contained God'

**Kishon** (*H* = winding) river traversing the Valley of Jezreel from Mount Tabor past Megiddo to the Mediterranean, Judg. 4.7; 5.21; 1 Kings 18.40; Ps. 83.9

**Kiss** common greeting, not erotic, Gen. 27.26; 29.11; Luke 15.20; 22.47–48 (Judas, echoes 2 Sam. 20.9); Rom. 16.16

**Kittim** see 'Cyprus 1.'

**Know 1.** To have sexual intercourse with, Gen. 4.1, etc. **2.** God knows all about us, yet knows us with affection, 2 Sam. 7.20; Matt. 6.8; Rom. 8.27; Gal. 4.9; 2 Tim. 2.19. **3.** We are called to know God, to recognize and love him, but on earth our knowledge is partial, 1 Chron. 28.9; John 17.3; 1 Cor. 13.12; 1 John 4.7

**Korah** (*H* = bald) **1.** Plotted with Dathan against Moses, Num. 16; 26.9–11; Jude 11. **2.** Singers in the Temple, 1 Chron. 9.19; Ps. 42–49; 84–88, see 'Dan 2.'

**Laban** (*H* = white) Aramean relation of Abraham; brother of Rebekah; father of Rachel and Leah, Gen. 24; 29–31

**Lachish** (*Ak* = impregnable) city which changed hands between Assyria and Judah, excavated at Tell ed-Duweir, 30 miles south-west of Jerusalem, Josh. 10; 2 Kings 14.19; 18.14–17; Micah 1.13. Excavations unearthed private letters written shortly before the Exile

**Lamb** sacrificed at Passover, the Day of Atonement etc.; hence Jesus is the Lamb of God who liberates from sin and death, Ex. 12.3; Num. 29.7–8; Isa. 53.7; John 1.29, 36; Rev. 5–6

**Lame 1.** Disqualified as priests, Lev. 21.18. **2.** Shall leap for joy, Isa. 35.6. **3.** Healed by Jesus and Peter, Matt. 11.5; 15.30–31; 21.14; Acts 3.2

**Lamentations** (Lam.) The Book of Lamentations, see p. **142**

**Lamp** container, usually of clay, for olive oil with a wick of flax (Isa. 42.3), placed in a niche in the wall called the lamp-stand, though richer houses and temples had ornate pedestals, Ps. 119.105; Matt. 5.15; 25.1–13; Rev. 1.12–13. The seven-branched candlestick in the Temple is known as the Menorah, Ex. 25.31–40; 37.17–24; Zech. 4.2; Heb. 9.2

**Land** nomadic Hebrews clung to God's promise that they should own land, Gen. 12.1; Deut. 32.49; Jer. 22.29; Ezek. 34.13; Mat. 5.5 (quoting Ps. 37.11); Heb. 11.9

**Landmark** stone or pile of stones marking a boundary, essential in settling inheritance disputes, never to be moved, Deut. 19.14; 27.17; Job. 24.2; Prov. 22.28; 23.10

**Languages 1.** Earth's inhabitants given many languages at the Tower of Babel, Gen. 11. **2.** This was reversed at Pentecost, when the Holy Spirit enabled believers to understand each other across language barriers, Acts 2. **3.** The Bible was originally written partly in Hebrew, one of the Semitic group of languages; partly in Aramaic, a later dialect of Hebrew; and the New Testament entirely in *koine* Greek, the rough dialect of the marketplace throughout the Roman Empire. **4.** See 'Tongues'

**Lantern** commonly made of oiled canvas stretched over a wooden frame with a lamp inside, John 18.3

**Laodicea** (named after the wife of Antiochus II, Laodike, *G* = justice of the people) city in the Lycus Valley, near Pamukkale in present-day Turkey. The letter from the Risen Christ in Rev. 3.14–22 punctures their pride in their wealth, black clothing, eye-salve, five gates and tepid baths; see also Philemon, p. **157**

**Lasea** city in Crete for which Fair Havens was the harbour; unexcavated remains have been surveyed east of Kaloi Limenes, Acts 27.8

**Last Days** The prophets looked forward to the Day of the LORD when God would punish, then reward Israel, and judge their enemies, Isa. 2.1–4; the New Testament refers to the final phase of God's plan for history, 2 Tim. 3.1; 2 Pet. 3.3; the last days have already begun, with the Resurrection of Jesus and the coming of the Holy Spirit, John 11.24–25; Acts 2.17; Heb. 1.2; the completion lies in the future, John 6.40; see Eschatology, p. **175**

**Last Supper** the Passover meal which Jesus ate with his disciples the night before he was crucified. The earliest account is 1 Cor. 10.16; 11.23–25; fuller accounts are Matt. 26.20–35; Mark 14.17–31; Luke 22.14–38. John 13–17 recounts the foot-washing, teaching on the true vine, and the High-Priestly Prayer; the bread of life is expounded in John 6. See also 'Blood','Body', 'Self-examination'

**Latin** official and legal language of the Roman Empire, used with Greek and Aramaic ('Hebrew') in the charge painted on a wooden tablet nailed to the cross; the initial letters of the Latin words for 'Jesus of Nazareth, King of the Jews' were I.N.R.I., John 19.20

**Lattice** when there was no glass in a window-frame, it was protected by diagonal strips of wood in a diamond pattern, Judg. 5.28; 2 Kings 1.2; Prov. 7.6; S. of Sol. 2.9; Ecclus. (Ben Sira) 42.11

**Laughter** at the promise of the birth of Isaac, Gen. 18.12–13; at calamity, Job 5.22; Prov. 1.26; at prosperity, Ps. 126.2; God laughs at the wicked, Ps. 2.4; laughter and tears, Prov. 14.13; Eccles. 2.2; 3.4; 7.3; Luke 6.25; see also 'Humour'

**Law** (*H torah*) **1.** Where rewards and punishments were at the whim of a ruler, a code of law was a blessing, Judg. 21.25. **2.** The Israelites rejoiced that their Scriptures were a collection of God's laws, though some doubt whether many of them were observed before the Exile, Ps. 119. **3.** Jesus said he had come to fulfil and supersede the law, Matt. 5.17–18; Luke 16.16; the law of love sums up and overrides all others, Matt. 22.40, 23.23–24; Mark 2.13–3.6; 7.1–23; 12.28–33; Luke 6.1–5; 13.10–17; see also 'Clean', 'Divorce', 'Sabbath'. **4.** Paul kept the Jewish law when he was among Jews, 1 Cor. 9.20; but argued that to impose it on Gentiles hindered their coming to God by grace through faith, Rom. 2–4; 6.14; 7.7–25; he persuaded the Council of Jerusalem to state that only four laws were binding on non-Jews, Acts 15; freedom is not an excuse for unloving, lawless behaviour, 1 Cor. 10.23; 1 Peter 2.16

**Lawsuits** by Christians in civil courts condemned, 1 Cor. 6

**Laying on of hands** see 'Hands'

**Lazarus** (short for Eleazar, *H* = God helps) **1.** Beggar in the parable of the rich man, Luke 16.19–31, see 'Reclining'. The unnamed rich man is known as Dives (*L* = wealth). **2.** The brother of Mary and Martha at Bethany, whom Jesus raised from the dead, John 11.1–12.10. There is a tradition that he later preached and was buried at Larnaca, Cyprus

**Leah** (*H* = gazelle?) Laban's daughter, married Jacob before Rachel, mother of six of his sons, Gen. 29–33; 49.31

**Leaven** portion of dough with live yeast still in it, used to start the next batch fermenting and rising. Image of the rapid spread of good or evil ideas, Matt. 13.33; 16.6; 1 Cor. 5.6–8, see 'Unleavened bread'

**Lebanon** (*H* = white) nation north of Israel, famous for cedar trees; the Mount Lebanon Range of mountains is in the north, and Mount Hermon in the south, 2 Kings 14.9; 2 Chron. 2.8; Ps. 92.12; S. of Sol. 3.9; Isa. 40.16; Hos. 14.5–6

**Legion** Roman army unit of 6,000 men; huge army of angels, Matt. 26.53; madman who felt he was possessed by an army of demons, Mark 5.9, Luke 8.30

**Lending** commended, Ex. 22.25–27; Ps. 37.26; 112.5; Prov. 19.17; Luke 6.34

**Leprosy** without medical knowledge, was the term for all skin diseases, which were considered 'unclean' and contagious. Lepers were excluded from the towns; only after proving to a priest that they had been healed could they be readmitted, Lev. 13–14. It was confused with blotches on clothes and walls, Lev. 13.47; 14.33. Elijah healed Naaman the leper, 2 Kings 5; Jesus was not afraid to approach and heal them, Matt. 8.3; Mark 1.41; Luke 5.12; 17.12. Today the term is applied only to 'Hansen's Disease'; the bacillus attacks nerves under the skin, leading to loss of feeling, paralysis and unfelt injury. To help modern sufferers seek early treatment and reintegrate into society, the Leprosy Mission teaches that with modern medicines and simple hygiene, Hansen's disease is curable and can be made non-contagious

**Letter and Spirit** Jesus went to the heart of God's will with his commandment to love, and gave us the Spirit to make love possible. Paul says concentration on the minutiae of a written code hinders the work of God's Spirit, Rom. 2.27; 7.6; 2 Cor. 3.6

**Letter of Jeremiah** (Let. Jer.), see p. 146

**Letters in the New Testament** see p. 152

**Levi** (*H* = clinging) **1.** Son of Jacob, ancestor of the Levites, who formed a second rank of priests below the descendants of Aaron, Gen. 29.34; 34.25–31; Ex. 32.26; Num. 3–4; 8; 18; 35; Deut. 12.19; 18; Josh. 21; Mal. 1–2. **2.** Son of Alphaeus; tax-collector; one of The Twelve; probably another name for Matthew, Mark 2.14; Luke 5.27–32

**Leviathan** (*H* = twisting) sea monster, perhaps derived from the Canaanite legend of the creator killing a monster and forming the creation from its corpse; later associated with the whale and the crocodile, Job 3.8; 41; Ps. 74.14; 104.26; Isa. 27.1; 2 Esd. 6.49–52

**Levirate marriage** The brother of a man who died was required to marry the widow, even if he already had a wife, to keep her from starvation and to continue the brother's family, Gen. 38.8; Deut. 25.5–10; Ruth 3.9–4.12; in these circumstances, polygamy was still required in the time of Jesus, who said that after the resurrection such considerations do not apply, Matt. 22.23–33, see also 'Marriage'

**Leviticus** (Lev.) The Book of Leviticus (le-VITT-ee-cuss), see p. 136

**Liars** telling lies is forbidden, Ex. 20.16; Eph. 4.25; Col. 3.9; the Devil is the father of lies, John 8.44; punishment of those who tell lies, Prov. 19.9; Rev. 21.8, 27; 22.15

**Liberal interpretation of Scripture** see p. 177

**Libnah** (*H* = white) town on the border of Judah and Philistia, probably the site of the Crusader fortress of Blanche-Garde, 2 Kings 8.22; 19.8

**Libya** people from this part of the north African coast were present at Pentecost, Acts 2.10

**Lice** plural of louse, see 'Gnats'

**Life** given when God breathed into the humans, Gen. 2.7; flowing water was called 'living water' because it gave life to the land around, S. of Sol. 4.15; Jer. 2.13; 17.13; John 4.10–11; 7.38; God is called the 'living God' in contrast to dead idols, Ps. 42.2; Matt. 16.16; 2 Cor. 3.3; 6.16; Heb. 10.31; Jesus promised 'life in all its fulness' now and in the age to come, John 10.10; the 'life of the age' is translated as 'eternal life', see 'Eternity'

**Light** created by God, Gen. 1.3; shows up the truth, Ps. 36.9; shows up evil deeds, John 3.19–21; Rom. 13.12; shows us the way to go, Ps. 119.105; John 11.10; replaces fear with hope, Luke 1.79; God is light, Isa. 60.1, Hab. 3.4; 1 John 1.5; Jesus the light of the world, John 1.4; 8.12; Rev. 21.23; his teaching sheds light, Luke 8.16; 11.33; 2 Cor. 4.4; calls us to shed light, Matt. 5.14–16; Rom. 2.19

**Lights, Feast of** see 'Calendar'

**Lilies of the Field** general term for wild flowers, whose beauty is given by God, showing how stupid it is to worry, Matt. 6.28; Luke 12.27; the anemone is abundant around Galilee

**Lineage** (LINN-ee-idj) old word for the ancestral line or family tree of descent, Luke 2.4

**Lion** extinct in Palestine since the Crusades, they were a terror to humans and animals, Judg. 14.5–6; 1 Sam. 17.34–35; Dan. 6.16–23; Judah is compared to a lion, Gen. 49.9; Jesus, from the tribe of Judah, is the Lion of Judah, Rev. 5.5

**Loaves and fishes** Jesus fed 5,000 people with 5 loaves and 2 fish, Matt. 14.13–21; Mark 6.30–44; Luke 9.10–17; John 6.1–13; and 4,000 with 7 loaves and a few fish, Matt. 15.32–38; boys are bread-sellers in the East, so the lad was sacrificing his stock-in-trade; the story looks back to God feeding his creation with the flesh of Leviathan, Ps. 74.17; 2 Esd. 6.52; and feeding the Israelites with manna in the wilderness, Ex. 16; and forward to the Last Supper, 1 Cor. 11.23–26, see also 'Bread'

**Locust** tropical grasshopper which migrates in huge swarms, casting a dark shadow and stripping plants completely of their leaves, Ex. 10.4–20; Joel 1.4; 2.25; Nahum 3.16–17; Rev. 9.3–10; eaten for food (interpretation of this word as carob-beans is unlikely), Lev. 11.22; Matt. 3.4

**Lo-Debar** town south of the River Yarmuk, where Mephibosheth stayed, 2 Sam. 9.4–5; 17.27; Amos 6.13; also called Lidebir or Debir, Josh 13.26

**Log** see 'Beam'

**Loins** literally the back between the hips and the ribs. **1.** Trembling of the loins is an image of fear, Ps. 38.7; 69.23; Isa. 15.4; 21.3. **2.** Putting sackcloth next to the flesh is 'binding it on your loins', Gen. 37.34. **3.** Putting on the minimum clothing to leave the house and start work is to 'gird up your loins', 1 Kings 18.46; Job 38.3; Jer. 1.17. **4.** The Passover meal to be eaten with loins girded, to show that they were ready to travel, Ex. 12.11. **5.** Euphemistically, the sexual organs, so that one's offspring are the 'fruit of the loins', Isa. 48.1; Heb. 7.10

**Lois** grandmother of Timothy, 2 Tim. 1.5

**Longsuffering** in older translations, see 'Patience'

**The LORD** (*H adonai* = my lord or ruler) The name of God used in documents from source J (see p. **135**) in the southern kingdom of Judah was written with the consonants YHWH, Gen. 2.4 etc. (shortened to Jah, Ps. 68.4, and in proper names). To avoid 'taking God's name in vain', this word was never pronounced; instead readers would say *Adonai*. To remind them to do so, the vowels of Adonai were written beneath the consonants of YHWH. These were never pronounced together; if they had been it would have produced the word 'Jehovah', which is unknown in Hebrew. In English translations it is usually printed as LORD in small capitals. In Greek, *kyrios* means mister or sir, Matt. 21.30, but it was used in the Greek translation of the Hebrew Scriptures to represent YHWH. When Jesus is addressed as sir or Lord, it means he is our ruler, and one with God, Matt. 7.21; 8.2; John 4.11; Rom. 10.9

**LORD of Hosts** see 'Hosts'

**Lord's day** Gentile Christians met not on the Jewish sabbath, the seventh day, but on the first day of the week, Sunday, to commemorate the Resurrection, John 20.1, 19; Acts 20.7; 1 Cor. 16.2; Rev. 1.10. Seventh Day Adventists may disagree

**Lord's Prayer** model prayer to our Father God which Jesus taught; intended as a set of headings to be expanded differently each time it is used in intimate personal prayer, it was soon used as a corporate recitation. The two versions may be intended for Greek or Aramaic-speaking audiences, or Jesus and his disciples may have revised it for other reasons, but the meaning is unchanged, Matt. 6.5–15; Luke 11.1–4

**Lost** Coin, Luke 15.8–10; Lost Sheep, Luke 15.1–7; Ps. 119.176; Lost (Prodigal) Son, Luke 15.11–32; God wants individuals, nations and races who are excluded from society brought back into fellowship with him

**Lot 1.** (*H* = concealed) Abraham's nephew; chose the Jordan Valley rather than the highlands, Gen. 13.8–13; was saved when Sodom was destroyed, Gen. 19.1–25; 2 Peter 2.6–8; whose wife was turned into a pillar of salt, Gen. 19.26; Luke 17.28–32. **2.** Lottery, when a choice was made by throwing onto the ground ('cast lots') or picking out of a bag ('drew lots') a marked piece of wood: tribal areas, Num. 26.55; Josh. 15; Saul, 1 Sam. 10.17; Christ's clothing, Matt. 27.35; Ps. 22.18; Matthias, Acts 1.26

**Love** God is love, 1 John 4.7–9; Eph. 3.14–19. God loves us, though we do not deserve it; we are given the power to love God in return, and our neighbours for his sake, 1 John 4.10–19; Matt. 22.34–40; even to love our enemies, Matt. 5.44. Love for God leads to forgiveness, and vice versa, Luke 7.47; 1 Peter 4.8. Christian love is distinguished by the self-sacrificing character of Jesus, who told us to love one another as he has loved us, John 13.34; and by the description of *a-ga-pe* given in 1 Cor. 13; Jesus uses the word translated *agapao* in Greek whereas Peter uses *philo* (be friends) in John 21.15–17

**Lovingkindness** see 'Steadfast love'

**Lucifer** (*L* = light-bringer) see 'Morning Star 3.'

**Lucius** (*L* = light) **1.** Lucius of Cyrene, member of the church in Antioch, Acts 13.11. **2.** Relative or compatriot of Paul who sends greetings to Rome, Rom. 16.21

**Luke** (*G Lukas*, probably from *L Lucius* or *Lucanus*) beloved physician; Gentile; fellow-worker with Paul in spreading the faith; and his attendant while Paul was a captive in Rome, Col. 4.14; 2 Tim. 4.11; Philemon 24. Early tradition holds that he wrote the Gospel according to Luke and the Acts of the Apostles

**Luke** (Luke) The Gospel according to Luke, see p. **150**

**Lukewarm** Christians at Laodicea, like their water brought in a long aqueduct, were neither cold nor hot, Rev. 3.16

**Lust** Jesus says unspoken sexual desire is as serious a sin as adultery, Matt. 5.28. Some interpreters say this only applies if there is deliberate calculation on how to accomplish the seduction; others say it was a warning that nobody is without sin

**Luz** (*H* = almond-tree) former name of the city near the sanctuary of Bethel, Gen. 28.19; 35.6; 48.3; Judg. 1.23–26

**LXX** abbreviation for the Greek translation of the Hebrew Scriptures, see Septuagint, p. **178**

**Lycaonia** region in the Roman Province of Galatia, still speaking a distinct language, containing Lystra and Derbe, Acts 14.6, 11

**Lycia** (*G* = wolf) district on the southern coast of Asia Minor, formerly an independent Lycian Federation, then a Roman Province, both having their capital at Patara, and a port at Myra, but later amalgamated with Pamphylia, Acts 21.1; 27.5

**Lydda** town near the Mediterranean coast of Israel, now reverting to the name of Lod and giving its name to Lod airport; here Peter found a Christian congregation and healed a paralysed man with the Greek name of Aeneas ($G$ = praise), Ezra 2.33; Acts 9.32–35

**Lydia 1.** Kingdom in Asia Minor (modern Turkey), where Croesus reigned 560–546 BC; subjugated by Cyrus the Persian and later conquered by the Romans, 1 Macc. 8.8; its capital was Sardis. **2.** Woman owning a business dealing in purple-dyed cloth; originally from Thyatira; settled in Philippi; became Paul's first convert there. She was the head of a household, where Paul stayed, and possibly the head of the church in Philippi, Acts 16.14–40

**Lying** see 'Liars'

**Lysanias** Tetrarch of Abilene, a small territory north-west of Damascus, Luke 3.1–2. Two tetrarchs called Lysanias are known, but neither reigned at the date of Jesus's birth

**Lysias** see 'Claudius 2.'

**Lystra** Roman colony, built to keep order in the district of Lycaonia, whither Paul and Barnabas fled when they were driven from Iconium on Paul's first missionary journey; the inhabitants mistook them for gods. Paul probably revisited it on all three journeys. The site is a mound about a mile north-west of the Turkish village of Hatunsarai, south of Konya. Here Paul recruited Timothy to join his missionary team, Acts 14.6–21

**Maccabeus** (mack-uh-BEE-us, $L$ from $H$ *maqebet* = hammer) nickname of Judas, leader of the revolt of the Jews against the Greek Seleucid kings in 167–161 BC, described in the Books of Maccabees, see 'Hasmoneans'

**1 Maccabees** (1 Macc.) The First Book of Maccabees, (MACK-uh-bees), see p. **147**

**2 Maccabees** (2 Macc.) The Second Book of Maccabees, see p. **148**

**3 Maccabees** (3 Macc.) The Third Book of Maccabees, see p. **148**

**4 Maccabees** (4 Macc.) The Fourth Book of Maccabees, see p. **149**

**Macedonia** large province in northern Greece, home of Alexander the Great. Paul visited Neapolis, Philippi, Amphipolis, Apollonia, Thessalonica and Berea, all in Macedonia, Acts 16.9–17.14; 20.1–3; Rom. 15.26; 2 Cor. 1.16; 8.1–5; Phil. 4.15; 1 Thess. 1.7–8; 4.10

**Machaerus** (muh-KEER-us, $G$ = knife) fortress 28 miles south-west of Madaba in Jordan, built by Herod the Great, where Herod Antipas had John the Baptist beheaded, Matt. 14.1–12

**Machpelah** (mack-PEE-luh, $H$ = doubling) cave in Hebron where Abraham, Sarah, Isaac, Rebekah and Jacob were buried, Gen. 23; 25.9; 35.29; 49.30; 50.12

**Madness** madness of Saul, 1 Sam. 16.14–23; David pretends to be mad, 1 Sam. 21.13–15; Nebuchadnezzar, Dan. 4; Jesus accused of madness, John 10.20; Paul accused of madness, Acts 26.24; see 'Devil 1.'

**Magdala** ($H$ = tower) town on the west shore of Lake Galilee, also called Magadan, Dalmanutha and Tarichea; some excavations about 3 miles north of Tiberias are not open to the public; in the first century, it was a fishing port with 40,000 inhabitants and 230 boats, Matt. 15.39; Mark 8.10

**Magdalene** (MAGG-duh-linn, $H$ = from Magdala) Mary Magdalene was among the women who stood near the cross; and were witnesses of the Resurrection, Matt. 27.56–61; 28.1; John 20.1–18. Jesus cast out seven devils from her; she was one of those who cared for Jesus from their possessions, Luke 8.2–3. Possibly the same person as Mary of Bethany and the woman who was a sinner in Luke 7.37

**Magi** (MAY-dj-eye, *G magoi*) usually translated 'wise men'; from a well-known sect of Persian astrologer-priests; gave gold, frankincense and myrrh to the infant Jesus at Bethlehem, Matt. 2.1–12; the belief that there were three is based on the gifts; the belief that they were kings is based on the predictions in Ps. 72.10–11; Isa. 60.6, see 'Star'. Elymas is described as a *magos* in Acts 13.6–8

**Magicians 1.** Of Egypt, compete with Joseph over Pharaoh's dream, Gen. 41.8, 24. **2.** Of Egypt, compete with Moses over the plagues, Ex. 7.11–12, 22; 8.7, 18–19; 9.11. **3.** Of Chaldea, compete with Daniel over a dream, Dan. 1.20; 2; 4.7–9; 5.11

**Magnificat** Latin name for the hymn of the Virgin Mary, from 'magnify', to praise the greatness of, Luke 1.46–55

**Magog** see 'Gog'

**Mahanaim** (*H* = two armies) where Jacob had a vision of angels; later the capital of Gilead; probably north of the Wadi Jabbok in Jordan, Gen. 32.1–2; 2 Sam. 2.8; 17.24–19.8; 1 Kings 4.14

**Maher-shalal-hash-baz** (*H* = haste spoil, speed prey) name given to Isaiah's son as a prophetic symbol of the coming Assyrian invasion, Isa. 8.1–4

**Malachi** (*H* = my messenger) (Mal.) The Book of Malachi (MAL-urk-eye), see p. **145**

**Malchus** (*G* form of *H Malluch* = ruler) slave of the High Priest, whose ear Peter cut off at Gethsemane, John 18.10; Jesus healed him, Luke 22.51

**Malta** see 'Melita'

**Mammon** (*Ar* = riches) untranslated Aramaic word, not a god but a personification of money, which must not compete for the worship we owe to God alone, Ecclus. (Ben Sira) 31.8; Matt. 6.24; Luke 16.9–13; see also 'Riches'

**Mamre** (*H* = fatness) see 'Hebron'; the oaks of Mamre were terebinths, Gen. 13.18

**Manaen** (MA-nee-un, *G* form of *H* Menahem) member of the church at Antioch, intimate friend or member of the court of Herod Antipas, Acts 13.1

**Manasseh** (*H* = causing to forget) **1.** Oldest son of Joseph, Gen. 41.50–52; 48.8–22; the tribes of Ephraim and Manasseh together counted as the Joseph tribe, Gen. 49.22–26; Deut. 33.13–17. Manasseh split into two parts on either side of the Jordan, Josh. 22.7–8. **2.** King of Judah 687–642 BC, for a while exiled in Babylon, 2 Kings 21; 2 Chron. 33. See Prayer of Manasseh, p. **148**

**Mandrake** (*H dudaim*=love-apple) probably *mandragora officinalis*, a low-growing plant with a forked root and a delicious-smelling reddish-yellow fruit; believed to be an aid to conception; the human properties attributed to it by western magic are not mentioned in the Bible, Gen. 30.14–16; S. of Sol. 7.13

**Manger** animals' feeding trough, where baby Jesus was put to lie down; houses in Bethlehem were built on a slope and the stables were probably in semi-caves under the house, like that in the Church of the Nativity, where the manger is cut into the rock, Luke 2.7–16; Isa. 1.3

**Manna** (*H* = what is it?) round white food which God provided to feed the Israelites during their wanderings in the wilderness; possibly a white substance exuded by insects which are found in tamarisk trees, Ex. 16; Num. 11.6–9; Deut. 8.3; Josh. 5.12; Ps. 78.24; John 6.31; Heb. 9.4; Rev. 2.17

**Manoah** (*H* = rest) father of Samson, who saw God and lived, Judg. 13

**Mansions** (from *L mansio* = inn, caravanserai) see 'Guest-room'

**Mantle** cloak of Elijah which was passed on to Elisha, his successor, 2 Kings 2.8, 14–15

**Manuscripts of the Bible** see p. **178**

**Maon** (*H* = dwelling) home of Nabal, now Tell Ma'in, about 8 miles south of Hebron, 1 Sam. 23.24–25; 25

**Marah** (*H* = bitterness) place in the Wilderness of Shur where bitter waters were made sweet, Ex. 15.22–27; Num. 33.8–9

**Marana-tha** (muh-RAH-nuh-THA, *Ar* = our Lord, come!) or **Maran-atha** (marruh-NAH-thuh, *Ar* = our Lord has come) familiar prayer which Paul saw no need to translate, 1 Cor. 16.22; Rev. 22.20

**Mark** (*G Markos* from *L Marcus* = hammer) John Mark, in whose mother's house the disciples met, cousin of Barnabas, companion of Paul until he deserted in Perga, Acts 12.12, 25; 13.5, 13; 15.37–39; Col. 4.10; 2 Tim. 4.11; Philemon 24; 1 Peter 5.13. Traditionally identified with the author of the Gospel according to Mark, and the young man who ran away naked, Mark 14.51

**Mark** (Mark) The Gospel according to Mark, see p. **150**

**Marriage** means a public commitment to a caring and lasting relationship; there were no state or church ceremonies or certificates in Bible times. Marriage is praised, Gen. 2.18; Ps. 128.3; Mark 10.5–9; 1 Tim. 5.14; Heb. 13.4. Polygamy was widely practised, especially by the kings, although forbidden in Deut. 17.17, but by the time of Jesus most marriages were monogamous. Wives are praised, Prov. 31.10–31; Jesus approved of wedding feasts, Matt. 22.1–13; Luke 12.36; 14.8; John 2.1–11; wives and husbands are to live together in mutual submission and self-sacrifice, 1 Cor. 7.1–5; Eph. 5.21–33; Col. 3.18–19; 1 Peter 3.1–7; marriage is compared to the loving relationship between Christ and his Church, Eph. 5.32; Rev. 21.9; property considerations and match-making no longer apply after the resurrection, Mark 12.25; heaven is described as the Marriage Supper of the Lamb, Rev. 19.7–9; see also 'Adultery', 'Divorce','Fornication', 'Levirate Marriage'

**Mars Hill** see 'Areopagus'

**Martha** (*H* = lady) sister of Lazarus and Mary at Bethany, rebuked by Jesus for over-concern with housework, was taught by him about resurrection, Luke 10.38–41; John 11.1–44

**Martyrs** (*G* = witnesses) people who willingly submit to execution rather than deny their beliefs. Martyrs were honoured by the Maccabeans, 1 Macc. 6; 2 Macc. 6–7; Stephen was the first Christian martyr, Acts 6–7; Antipas in Pergamon was another, Rev. 2.13; Rev. 17.6 foresees a time when the Roman Empire will have killed many more

**Mary** or **Miriam** (*H* = sorrow) **1.** Miriam the sister of Moses and Aaron; led the women in a song at the Exodus, Ex. 15.20–21; rebelled against Moses; was punished with leprosy, Num. 12; 20.1. **2.** See 'Virgin Mary'. **3.** Mary Magdalene, see 'Magdalene'. **4.** Mary of Bethany, sister of Martha and Lazarus; sat at Jesus's feet, Luke 10.39–42; saw Jesus raise Lazarus, John 11.19–45; poured ointment on his feet and wiped them with her hair, John 11.2; 12.3. **5.** Mary the wife of Clopas, John 19.25; mother of James (the younger) and Joseph (or Joses), stood by the cross, Mark 15.40; attended the burial, Mark 15.47; witnessed the Resurrection, Mark 16.1. **6.** Mary the mother of John Mark, in whose home the first disciples met, Acts 12.12. **7.** A woman in Rome to whom Paul sent greetings, Rom. 16.6

**Masoretic Text** see p. **178**

**Massah** (*H* = test) see 'Meribah'

**Master** see 'Rabbi'

**Masturbation** not mentioned in the Bible, but see 'Onan'

**Matthew** (short for Mattathiah, *H* = gift of Jah), see 'Levi 2.'

# Matthew

**Matthew** (Matt.) The Gospel according to Matthew, see p. **150**
**Matthias** (muh-THIGH-us, short for Mattathiah) chosen to take the place of Judas among The Twelve, Acts 1.26

---

**Measures of Capacity**, *approximately converted into Imperial, US and metric measures*

*Liquid Measures in the Hebrew Scriptures*
*kor* = 10 *bath* = 230 litres = 50.58 Imperial gallons = 60.74 US gallons, English translations 'cor' or 'homer', Ezek. 45.11, 14
*bath* (= daughter, the amount a girl could carry from the well) = 6 *hin* = 23 litres = 5.06 Imp. gallons = 6.07 US gallons, 'bath', 1 Kings 7.26, 38; 2 Chron. 2.10; 4.5; Isa. 5.10; Ezek. 45.10–14
*hin* = 3 *kabh* = 3.83 litres = 6.73 Imp. pints = 1.01 US gallons, Ex. 29.40; 30.24; Lev. 19.36; 23.13; Num. 15; 28; Ezek. 4.11; 45.24; 46.5–14
*kabh* = 4 *logh* = 1.28 litres = 2.25 Imp. pints = 1.35 US quarts
*logh* = 0.32 litre = 11.3 fluid ounces = 0.67 US pints, 'log', Lev. 14.10–24

*Dry Measures in the Hebrew Scriptures*
*homer* (= donkey, the load which one donkey could carry) = 2 *lethekh* = 230 litres = 6.32 Imp. bushels = 6.52 US bushels, Lev. 27.16; Isa. 5.10; Ezek. 45.13–14; Hos. 3.2
*lethekh* = 5 *ephah* = 115 litres = 3.16 Imp. bushels = 3.36 US bushels, 'half homer', Hos. 3.2
*ephah* = 3 *seah* = 23 litres = 20.25 Imp. quarts = 20.88 US quarts, Ex. 16.36; Lev. 5.11; 19.36; Num. 28.5; Prov. 20.10; Isa. 5.10; Ezek. 45.10–24; 46.5–14
*seah* = 3.33 *omer* = 7.7 litres = 6.78 Imp. quarts = 6.96 US quarts, 'measure', Gen. 18.6; Ruth 3.15–17; 1 Sam. 25.18; 1 Kings 18.32; 2 Kings 7.1, 16–18; and Hos. 3.2 in the Septuagint Greek translation only, where the word is *saton*, used in Matt. 13.33; Luke 13.21
*omer* or *issaron* (one day's ration of grain for a man) = 1.8 *kabh* = 2.3 litres = 2.02 Imp. quarts = 2.09 US quarts, Ex. 16.16–36
*kabh* = 1.28 litres = 2.25 Imp. pints = 1.16 US quarts, 'cab' or 'kab', 2 Kings 6.25

**Measures of Length** *in the Hebrew Scriptures*

*qaneh* (from which we get the word 'canon', the standard against which we measure which books are included in the Bible) reed = 6 cubits = 2.66 metres = 8 feet 9 inches, Ezek. 40.3–7; 41.8; 42.16–19; *kalamos* Rev. 11.1; 21.15
*'ammah* (the length of the forearm) = 2 spans = 44.4 cm = 1 foot 5.5 inches, translated as 'cubit', from the Latin for elbow, Gen. 6.15–16; Deut. 3.11; 1 Sam. 17.4; 1 Kings 6; 7; 2 Chron. 3; 4; Esth. 5.14; 7.9; Ezek. 40–48. The Greek translation *pechun* is in Matt. 6.27; Luke 12.25; John 21.8; Rev. 21.17
*zereth* (the width of the outstretched hand) = 3 palms = 22.2 cm = 8.75 inches, 'span', Ex. 28.16; 39.9; 1 Sam. 17.4; Ezek. 43.13; Isa. 40.12 imagines God measuring the heavens with his 'span'
*tophah* or *tephah* = 4 fingers = 7.4 cm = 3 inches, 'palm' or 'handbreadth', Ex. 25.25; 37.12; 1 Kings 7.26; 2 Chron. 4.5; Ps. 39.5; Ezek. 40
*etzeva'* = 1.85 cm = 0.73 inches, finger, Jer. 52.21
*Above is the Common Scale; for Ezekiel's Royal Scale multiply by 1.17*

---

sabbath day's journey = 1,109 metres = 3,637 feet, Acts 1.12
day's journey, Gen. 30.36; 1 Kings 19.4; Jonah 3.3–4; Luke 2.44
furrow's length, 1 Sam. 14.14
bowshot, Gen. 21.16
*tsemedh* = as much land as a team of oxen can plough in one day, 'acre', 1 Sam. 14.14; Isa. 5.10

**Measures in other systems**  see also 'Weights'
*metretes* = from 38 to 115 litres = 8–26 Imp. gallons = 10–30 US gallons, 'firkin', 'measure', Bel. 1.3; John 2.6. The amount of water turned into wine was therefore somewhere between 96 and 2,800 gallons!
*modios* or *modius* = about 8.49 litres = 14.95 Imp. pints = 7.68 US dry quarts, 'bushel', Matt. 5.15; Mark 4.21; Luke 11.33; it would be stupid to put a lighted oil lamp beneath the upturned basket used for measuring grain
*choinix* = about 1.08 litres = 38 fluid ounces = 0.98 US dry quarts, 'measure', 'quart', Rev. 6.6
*xestes* or *sextarius* = 0.53 litres = 0.93 Imp. pints = 0.96 US dry pints or 1.12 US liquid pints, 'pot', Mark 7.4
Roman mile or *milion* = 1.48 km = 1,615 yards, Matt. 5.41; this was the distance a Roman soldier was allowed to compel a bystander to carry his pack
*orgurias*, Greek fathom (fingertip to fingertip with both arms outstretched) = 1.84 metres = 6 feet 0.5 inch or just over a modern fathom, Acts 27.28
Greek furlong or *stadion* (the length of the running track in a stadium) = 202 yards = 184 metres, 2 Macc. 12.19–19; Luke 24.13; John 6.19; 11.18; Rev. 14.20; 21.16

**Meat offered to idols**  At private parties and trade-guild feasts, meat came from beasts which had been slaughtered in the temples and offered to the god of that temple. Some said that to eat such meat showed a belief in the power of that god. Paul points out that other gods 'do not exist': you need not ask about the source of your food. But for those who are uncertain, to see Christians eating such meat might lead them to assume that we worship other gods also. If you are challenged, says Paul, don't eat; better be vegetarian than cause someone to turn aside from Jesus, 1 Cor. 8; Rev. 2.20

**Medad**  prophesied with Eldad, Num. 11.26

**Medeba**  town of the Moabites, now Madaba in Jordan; a sixth-century AD mosaic map of Palestine can be seen in St George's Church, Num. 21.30; 1 Chron. 19.7; Isa. 15.2; see also 'Machaerus' 'Nebo 2.'

**Medes**  Aryan empire east of Assyria (2 Kings 17.6; 18.11) with its capital at Ecbatana; King Cyaxares (624–585 BC), together with Nabopolassar of Babylon, captured and destroyed Nineveh in 606; his son Astyages (584–550) was defeated by Cyrus, a Persian who formed a combined empire of the Medes and Persians, Isa. 13.17–22; Dan. 6.8–15; see Mesopotamia, p. **165**. People from Media were present on the Day of Pentecost, Acts 2.9

**Mediator**  Jesus, both human and divine, is the go-between bringing understanding between humans and God, 1 Tim. 2.5; Heb. 8.6; 9.15; 12.24

**Meek**  quiet; gentle; obedient; the humble who do not push themselves forward, and therefore often become the faithful poor; commended in Num. 12.3; Ps. 10.17; Isa.

11.4; 29.19; Gal. 5.23 (sometimes translated gentleness); Col. 3.12, James 1.21; 1 Peter 3.15–16. Jesus an example of meekness, Matt. 11.29; 21.5; 2 Cor. 10.1; he promised that those who submit humbly to suffering will inherit the land, Matt. 5.5 quoting Ps. 37.11

**Megiddo** city in the Valley of Jezreel (Esdraelon) where Ahaziah and Josiah were killed, Judg. 5.19; 2 Kings 9.27; 23.29–30; 2 Chron. 35.20–24; see 'Armageddon'. Impressive excavations reveal a mound with twenty successive layers of habitation, and a tunnel for fetching drinking water during a siege

**Melchizedek** (*H* = my king is righteous) priest and king of Salem (Jerusalem); blessed Abraham with bread and wine; Abraham paid tithes to Melchizedek; as his birth or death are not mentioned he is said to be 'eternal'; Gen. 14.18; Ps. 110.4; Heb. 5.6–10; 6.20; 7.1–17

**Melita** where Paul was shipwrecked; shook off a snake which attacked him; and was welcomed by Publius, correctly called the 'First Man' of the island. Usually identified as the Mediterranean island of Malta (see 'Adria'); a landing place at St Paul's Bay, a rich man's farm in San Pawl Milqi, and an expensive Roman house in Mdina can be seen. The small island of Mljet off the Croatian coast was also called Melita, but anyone travelling from there to Rome would not go via Sicily, Acts 27.39–28.10

**Members** the limbs and organs of the body; Paul said we are all organically interrelated to each other like limbs in the Body of Christ; so we must co-operate and not despise others, Rom. 12.4–5; 1 Cor. 10.17; 12.12–27; Eph. 3.6; 4.12; 5.23–30; Col. 3.15

**Memphis** (*Eg Men-nepher*, *H Noph*) city in Egypt, 13 miles south of Cairo, taken by Sennacherib in 671 BC, Isa. 19.13; Jer. 2.16; 46.14; Ezek. 30.13; Hos. 9.6

**Menahem** (*H* = comforter) son of Gadi, killed Shallum, became king of Israel 743–738 BC, 2 Kings 15.14–22

**Mene mene tekel and parsin** the writing on the wall at Belshazzar's feast, Dan. 5.5–28; the words are the names of weights, 'a mina, a mina, a shekel and half-minas'; but can also be translated 'counted, counted, weighed and divided', a judgement on the quality of the king's governance

**Menstruation** when not fully understood, was considered to make a woman 'unclean'; originally seclusion for hygienic reasons, the regulations became oppressive and applied to anything a woman touched for seven days after her period ended. A woman who had bleeding from a gynaecological problem for twelve years touched Jesus; he might have been angry; instead he healed her, Gen. 31.35; Lev. 15.19–33; Mark 5.25–34

**Mephibosheth** (called Merib-baal, *H* = contender with Baal, but 'shame' is substituted for the god's name, 1 Chron. 8.34; 9.40), lame son of Jonathan; cared for by David, 2 Sam. 4.4; 9.1–13; 16.1–4; 19.24–30; 21.7

**Mercy** characteristic of God, Ex. 34.6; Ps. 18.25; 37.26; 67.1; Jer. 3.12; Jonah 4.2; Luke 18.13; Heb. 2.17; 8.12; forgiveness which we should show to others, 2 Sam. 22.6; Prov. 11.17; Hos. 6.6; Matt. 5.7; 9.13; Luke 6.36. God requires mercy, not sacrifice, Micah 6.6–8. See also 'Forgiveness', 'Steadfast Love'

**Mercy-seat** the 'cover' of the Ark of the Covenant, but as to cover means to atone in Hebrew, some translations give this name to the throne of the invisible God, Ex. 25.17–22; 26.34; 37.6; Lev. 16.13; 1 Chron. 28.11; Heb. 9.5

**Meribah** (*H* = quarrel) where Moses brought water from the rock and the Israelites rebelled, Ex. 17.7; Num. 20.13, 24; Deut. 33.8; Ps. 81.7; 95.8; 106.32; called

Meribath-Kadesh, in the Wilderness of Zin, in Num. 27.14; Deut. 32.51; Ezek. 47.19; 48.28; or Massah, at Rephidim on Mount Horeb, Ex. 17.1–7; Deut. 6.16; 9.22; 33.8; Ps. 95.8. The life-giving rock symbolizes Christ, 1 Cor. 10.4; based on a legend in the Jewish commentary *Targum Onkelos* on Num. 21.17 that the rock followed Moses through the wilderness

**Merodach-baladan** (*Ak Marduk-apal-iddina* = Marduk has given a son) Chaldean who led a revolt against the Assyrian rulers of the Babylonian Empire, 2 Kings 20.12; sent envoys to Hezekiah king of Judah, asking for support, 2 Kings 20.12–19, see Mesopotamia, p. **165**

**Merom** waters where Joshua defeated a Canaanite alliance, probably near modern Meiron in Upper Galilee, Josh. 11.1–9

**Meshach** (*Ak Misha-Aku* = who is what the god Aku is?) originally called Mishael, see 'Abednego'

**Meshech** (*H* = drag) **1.** Son of Japheth, Gen. 10.2; 1 Chron. 1.5. **2.** Son of Shem, 1 Chron. 1.17. **3.** Associated with Kedar, Ps. 120.5. **4.** Associated with Tubal and Gog, Ezek. 27.13; 32.26; 38.2; 39.1

**Mesopotamia** (*G* = between rivers) area between the Tigris and the Euphrates, Acts 2.9; 7.2, see 'Aram-naharaim', Mesopotamia, p. **165**

**Mess of pottage** 'Esau selleth his birthright for a mess of pottage' was a chapter heading in the Geneva Bible, 1560, for the red lentil stew of Gen. 25.34

**Messiah** (*H* = anointed) Kings and priests were appointed by pouring oil on their head, 'anointing', 1 Sam. 15.1; 16.13; Lev. 6.20. The LORD's anointed was another way of describing the present king, David and his descendants, Ps. 2.2; 18.50. The kings were a disappointment; hope grew of a new anointed king, descended from David, who would restore the fortunes of the nation and defeat their enemies. He was referred to as the Messiah, the anointed one, Dan. 9.25. Other prophecies of a deliverer were attached to the term, such as Isa. 9.6; Jer. 33.15–16; it was believed he would usher in the kingdom of God. Frequent claimants appropriated the title, Matt. 24.5. Simeon, Luke 2.26; Peter, Matt. 16.16, even demons, Luke 4.41, recognized Jesus as the Messiah, but Jesus told them to keep it secret because he did not want a military role, Matt. 16.20; John 6.15. Challenged by the High Priest to say whether he was 'the Messiah, the son of the Blessed One', Jesus replied 'I am', Mark 14.62. The idea of a suffering Messiah, dimly foreseen in Dan. 9.26, was taught by Jesus, Luke 24.26, 46; then by Peter, Acts 3.18; and finally by Paul, Acts 17.3; 26.23. When Christianity moved into the Greek-speaking world, Messiah was translated as *Christos*, John 4.25; an unfamiliar word which some people confused with *chrestos* = virtuous. Paul proves that 'Jesus is the Christ', Acts 9.22; 18.5, 28; gradually the phrase 'Jesus who is called the Christ', Matt. 27.17, 22, becomes simply, 'Jesus Christ'; and the Gospels are written 'that you may believe that Jesus is the Christ', John 20.31. The 'Messianic Secret' is the theory that the Gospel-writers believed that only demons (and Peter) recognized that Jesus was the Messiah until after the Resurrection. See also 'Son'

**Methuselah** (*H* = man of the javelin) son of Enoch, who lived for 969 years; longevity was common in ancient legends, Gen. 5.21–27; 1 Chron. 1.3

**Micah** (*H* = who is like Jah?) (Micah) The Book of the Prophet Micah (MY-cuh), see p. **144**

**Micaiah** (*H* = who is like Jah?) prophet who pretended to give a favourable message to Ahab, but when challenged to tell the truth, prophesied disaster, 1 Kings 22.8–28; 2 Chron. 18.8

# Michael

**Michael** (*H* = who is like God?) archangel, prince who fights the Devil, Dan. 10.13, 21; 12.1; Jude 9; Rev. 12.7

**Michal** (feminine form of Michael) Saul's daughter who loved David and became his wife, was given to Paltiel and returned, criticized David for dancing and was punished, 1 Sam. 18.20–27; 25.44; 2 Sam. 3.13–16; 6.16, 20–23

**Michmash** (*H* = hidden) town near Bethel; the accuracy of the description enabled a British major using the same method as Jonathan to win a battle there in the First World War, 1 Sam. 13–14

**Midian** (*H* = strife) nomadic people, descended from Abraham, whose priest was Jethro, Moses' father-in-law; who roamed the Arabian desert, beyond Moab and Edom, as far as the Gulf of Aqaba. They tempted the Israelites to sin at Peor, and Moses swore to eliminate them. In the time of Gideon, nomadic Midianites made camel-raids, the first such raids in ancient literature. Gideon's defeat of their kings Oreb and Zeeb, Zeba and Zalmunnah became proverbial, Num. 25; 31.1–54; Judg. 6–8; Isa. 9.4; 10.26; 60.6

**Midwives** women who assist at childbirth; Shiphrah and Puah tricked the Egyptians when ordered to kill the Hebrew boy-children, Ex. 1.15–20

**Milcom** corruption of Molech, god of the Ammonites, 2 Sam. 12.30; Jer. 49.3; Zeph. 1.5

**Mile** distance a Roman soldier could compel a bystander to carry his pack, Matt. 5.41, see 'Measures in other systems'

**Miletus** seaport at the mouth of the River Meander, on the west coast of Asia Minor (Turkey). It has an impressive theatre, see 'God-fearers', and a fine gateway, now in the Pergamon Museum in Berlin. Paul called there on his third missionary journey, to speak to the elders of the church in Ephesus, Acts 20.16–38; 2 Tim. 4.20

**Mill** two stones, the upper one pushed over the lower for grinding grain into flour. **1.** The saddle-quern was a bar-shaped upper stone pushed by one woman over a rectangular lower stone, Deut. 24.6; Judg. 9.53; Isa. 47.2; Jer. 27.10. **2.** The hand mill, with horizontal circular stones, was worked by two women, one turning and the other pouring the grain, Matt. 24.41. **3.** The community mill had a vertical circular stone turned by a donkey; the lower millstone of this was massive; tied to a rope round a person's neck it would ensure they sank immediately, Job 41.24; Matt. 18.6; Rev. 18.21–22

**Millo** (*H* = filling) important defensive feature, perhaps a rampart, linking the City of David with the Temple Mount at Jerusalem, 2 Sam. 5.9; Solomon built it to 'fill up the gap', 1 Kings 9.15, 24; 11.27; Joash was killed there, 2 Kings 12.20; Hezekiah strengthened it, 2 Chron. 32.5

**Mind 1.** 'Love God with all your mind', Matt. 22.37. **2.** 'Who has known the mind of the Lord?' Rom. 11.34; 1 Cor. 2.16; quoting Isa. 40.13 in the Greek Septuagint translation. **3.** 'We have the mind of Christ', 1 Cor. 2.16. **4.** 'Let the same mind be in you that was in Christ Jesus', Phil. 2.5

**Ministers** those who serve. **1.** Angels, Ps. 103.21; Heb. 1.7 quoting Ps. 104.4. **2.** Priests, Ex. 28.35, 43 etc. **3.** The boy Samuel, 1 Sam. 2.11. **4.** The nation of Israel, Isa. 61.6. **5.** (*G leitourgos*, one who performs public service, including leading worship) Paul, Rom. 15.16; his assistants, Phil. 2.25; Christ, Heb. 8.2. **6.** (*G diakonos*, a domestic servant) Paul, 2 Cor. 3.6; 11.23; his assistants, Eph. 6.21; Col. 1.7; 4.7

**Miracles** literally 'things which make us admire God'; the Gospel according to John calls them 'Signs'. The writers of the Bible did not think they 'went against the laws of nature', because they did not know any laws of nature. For modern scientists, laws are a statement of the probability of certain consequences following certain causes in controlled and repeatable conditions, but they do not take into account the activity of God, which is not a factor mere humans can predict, Heb. 2.4; see The Life of Jesus, p. **168**

**Miriam** see 'Mary'

**Mishael** (*H* = who is what God is?) also called Meshach, see 'Abednego'

**Mite** (*G lepton*) the smallest coin, two of which were given by a poor widow, Mark 12.42; Luke 21.2; see 'Money'

**Mitre** see 'Turban'

**Mitylene** alternative name of the Aegean island of Lesbos, visited by Paul on his third missionary journey, Acts 20.14

**Mizpah** (*H* = watchtower) **1.** In Gilead, where Jacob met Laban, Gen. 31.49; Judg. 10.17. **2.** In Galilee, where Jabin fled, Josh. 11.3. **3.** In Judah, Josh. 15.38. **4.** In Moab, 1 Sam. 22.3. **5.** In Benjamin, where the Israelites assembled; remains have been found 7 miles north of Jerusalem at Tell en-Nasbe, Josh. 18.26; Jer. 41.3; 1 Macc. 3.46

**Moab** (*H* = descendants of father) **1.** Son of Lot, Gen. 19.37. **2.** Region south-east of the Dead Sea, probably inhabited by nomadic Arameans who overran the Amorite inhabitants, settled down and adopted their language. They were in constant dispute with the Israelites over the region between the Arnon and Jabbok Rivers, and their god Chemosh was abhorrent to the Israelites. They were conquered by the Babylonians c. 582 BC, Judg. 3.12–30; Ps. 60.8 = 108.9 (where the sea of Moab, i.e. the Dead Sea, is hardly big enough to serve as God's washbasin); Isa. 15–16; Jer. 48. **3.** Ruth the Moabitess was the ancestor of King David, Ruth 1; 4.17–22. **4.** The Moabite Stone, discovered in 1868 in Dibon (modern Dhiban) gives an account, in a language and alphabet not unlike Hebrew, of the wars of Mesha, king of Moab, around 870 BC, against Israel, the worshippers of YHWH, 2 Kings 3. Many of the names confirm the accuracy of those recorded in the Hebrew Scriptures. It is now in the Louvre Museum in Paris

**Modein** village 18 miles north-west of Jerusalem where the Maccabean revolt started, family home of the Hasmonean kings, 1 Macc. 2.1

**Molech** god of the Amorites, placated by human sacrifice, Lev. 18.21; 1 Kings 11.7; 2 Kings 23.10; Jer. 32.35

---

**Money** see also 'Riches', 'Weights'

*Until the Exile, value was expressed in number of sheep or weight of silver.*

*qesitah*, an uncoined piece of silver with the value of a small ewe, Gen. 33.19; Josh. 24.32; Job 42.11

*kikkar*, translated 'talent', 34.27 kg. or 75.6 lbs = 60 mina, 1 Kings 20.39; 2 Kings 5.22; 23.33; 2 Chron. 26.3

*maneh*, 'mina' = 50 shekel (or 60 shekel in Ezek. 45.12), 1 Kings 10.17

*sheqel*, 'shekel', weight of about 11.4 grammes or 0.4 ounces, Gen. 23.15–16; 24.22; Lev. 5.15; 27.1–7; 2 Sam. 24.24; 2 Kings 5.5; 6.25; Isa. 7.23; Ezek. 4.10; Hos. 3.2; Amos 8.5

The 'Sanctuary Shekel' or 'shekel by the King's weight' was apparently slightly larger, Ex. 30.13–15, 24; 38.25–26; 2 Sam. 14.26

*beka* or half-shekel, Ex. 30.11–16; 38.26

one-third shekel, 1 Sam. 13.21; Neh. 10.32

# Money-changers

quarter-shekel, 1 Sam. 9.8
*gerah* or one twentieth of a shekel, Ex. 30.11–16; Num. 3.47; Ezek. 45.12

*After the Exile, coins were used.*
*shekel*, Neh. 5.15; 1 Macc. 10.40–42. The 30 shekels of Zech. 11.12–13, the price of a man, are the basis of the 30 pieces of silver paid to Judas for betraying Jesus, Matt. 27.6

*Persian*
silver *minas*, worth 100 Median shekels, Ezra 2.69; Neh. 7.71–72
golden *darics*, issued by Darius, weighing 8.41 grammes or 0.3 ounces, 1 Chron. 29.7; Ezra 2.69; 8.27; Neh. 7.70–72
silver *darics*, weighing 5.6 grammes or 0.2 ounces, also called Median shekels, Neh. 5.15; 10.32

*Hellenistic*
*talanton*, translated 'talent' = 6,000 *drachmas*; a vast amount, over 15 years' wages for a labourer, 2 Macc. 8.11; 1 Esd. 1.36; Matt. 18.23–35; 25.15–28. When Jesus told the parables, 'talent' only meant a sum of money; because of the parables it came to mean ability or skill
*mna*, 'pound' = 100 *drachmas* = 3 months' wages, Luke 19.12–26
gold *stater* weighing 8.6 grammes or 0.3 ounces, also called *tetradrachma* = 4 drachmas
*didrachmon*, Latin *didrachma* = 2 drachmas, the coin paid in 'temple tax', Matt. 17.24–27
silver *drachme*, Latin *drachma*, 'piece of money', 'silver coin' = 3.41 grammes or 0.12 ounces, Tob. 5.15; 2 Macc. 4.19; 10.20; 12.43; 3 Macc. 3.28; Luke 15.8; Acts 19.19

*Roman*
silver *denarion*, Latin *denarius*, 'penny', 'denarius' = 3.43 grammes or 0.12 ounces, a day's wages for a labourer; the coin which was paid to the Emperor in poll-tax, or *tributum capitis*, see 'Image', Matt. 20.2, 10; 22.15–22; Mark 6.37; 12.13–17; 14.5; Luke 20.20–26; John 6.7; Rev. 6.6
bronze *assarion*, Latin *as*, 'farthing', 'penny' = 1/16 *denarius*; used in calculating the selling price of a sparrow, Matt. 10.29; Luke 12.6
bronze *kodrantes*, Latin *quadrans*, 'farthing', 'penny' = 0.25 *as*; the 'last farthing' for which your enemy will sue you, Matt. 5.26; Luke 12.59; the 'widow's mite', Mark 12.42
*lepton*, = 0.5 *quadrans*, two of which formed the 'widow's mite', Mark 12.42; Luke 21.2; the word still used in Greece for a hundredth of a Euro

**Money-changers** in the Temple, Roman coins with the image of the Emperor were considered idols, so had to be exchanged for half-shekels; Jesus objected that the money-changers occupying the outer court prevented Gentiles from worshipping there, Mark 11.15–17
**Months** see 'Calendar'
**Mordecai** (*H* = belonging to the god Marduk) protector of his cousin Esther, Esth. 2.5; discovered a plot against the king; incurred Haman's jealousy; promoted after Haman's downfall, Esth. 2–10

**Moreh** (*H* = teacher) **1.** Oak of, near Shechem, where YHWH appeared to Abram, Gen. 12.6. **2.** Hill of, Jebel Dahi, north of the spring of Harod, Judg. 7.1

**Moresheth-Gath** (*H* = possession of Gath) home of Micah; today Tell ej-Judeideh, 7 miles east of Gath, Jer. 26.18; Micah 1.1; 1.14

**Moriah** (*H* = Jah provides), mountain where Abraham had intended to sacrifice Isaac; where David sacrificed to end the plague; site of the Temple in Jerusalem, Gen. 22; 2 Chron. 3.1

**Morning Star** the bright planet Venus visible before sunrise. **1.** Symbolic of Jesus, 2 Peter 1.19. **2.** Metaphor for the king of Babylon, whose brightness will soon fade, Isa. 14.12. **3.** Isa. 14.12 in Latin is 'Lucifer'; similarity to Luke 10.18; Rev. 9.1–11, led to this name being given to the Devil

**Moses** (*H* = is born, probably from *Eg* Thutmose) leader of the Israelites at the Exodus from Egypt, teacher of monotheism and lawgiver. See 'Transfiguration', Pentateuch, p. **136**

**Most High** usual translation of *Elyon* (*H* = exalted), ancient West Semitic name of God, Ps. 21.7; 46.4; 47.2; Acts 7.48

**Mote** speck of dust in someone's eye, Matt. 7.1–5; Luke 6.37–42

**Mother 1.** To be honoured, see 'Parents'. **2.** Mother of Jesus, see 'Mary 2'. **3.** Motherhood of God, who loves us as a mother loves her children, Isa. 46.3–4; 49.14–15; 66.12–13; Matt. 23.37. **4.** Jerusalem the mother of us all, Gal. 4.26

**Mourning** sadness over the death of those we love, and over the sin and suffering of the whole world. **1.** Jacob mourns for his son, Gen. 37.34. **2.** David mourns for Saul and Jonathan, refuses to mourn for his child, 2 Sam. 1; 12.15–23. **3.** A time to mourn, Eccles. 3.4. **4.** Mourning not to be excessive, Ecclus. (Ben Sira) 38.16–23. **5.** God will wipe away all tears, Isa. 25.8–9. **6.** To comfort those who mourn, Isa. 61.2–3. **7.** Blessed are those who mourn, Matt. 5.4. **8.** Weep with those who weep, Rom. 12.15, see 'Comfort'

**Mule** sterile offspring of a male donkey and a female horse, 2 Sam. 13.29; Ps. 32.9. Jews were forbidden to breed them, Lev. 19.19; if Leviticus was in fact observed they must have been imported, Ezek. 27.14

**Murder** forbidden, Ex. 20.13; punishable by death, Gen. 9.6; to be executed by the next-of-kin, Num. 35.19; see also 'Eye for an eye'

**Murrain** the fifth plague in Egypt, a disease of cattle, possibly anthrax, Ex. 9.1–7

**Music 1.** Soothed Saul, 1 Sam. 16.23. **2.** Used in worship, 2 Sam. 6.5; 1 Chron. 15.28; 16.42; 2 Chron. 7.6; 29.25; Ps. 33; 81; 92; 108; 150; Dan. 3.5. **3.** Used at festivals, Isa. 5.12; 14.11; Amos 6.5; Luke 15.25; 1 Cor. 14.7. **4.** In heaven, Rev. 5.8; 14.2, see 'Hymn', 'Singing'

---

**Musical instruments** *probably identified as:*

Bells, fastened to robes, Ex. 28.33

Castanets?, literally 'wooden instruments', 2 Sam. 6.5

Cymbals, large, 1 Chron. 15.16–19; Ezra 3.10; Ps. 150.5

Cymbals, small, fastened to fingers, 2 Sam. 6.5; Ps. 150.5

Drum or tambourine, Gen. 31.27; Ps. 68.25; 149.3

Flute (recorder), Gen. 4.21; Ps. 150.4; Job. 21.12; 30.31

Gong, possibly a bronze vase to make an actor's voice resonate, 1 Cor. 13.1

Lute, guitar-like with 3 strings, 1 Sam. 18.6

Lyre, U-shaped harp held in one arm, with 3, 5 or 6 strings, Gen. 4.21; 31.27; Job 30.31; Ps. 150.3

Bass-Lyre with 10 strings, Ps. 33.2; 144.9
Bass-Lyre with 12 strings, often translated harp, 1 Sam. 10.5; 1 Sam. 16.16–23; 2 Sam. 6.5; 1 Kings 10.12; Ps. 81.2; 150.3; Rev. 14.2; 1 Cor. 14.7; Rev. 5.8; 14.2; 15.2
Psaltery or zither, horizontal harp beaten with two sticks, Dan. 3.5
Ram's horn, Ex. 19.13–16; Lev. 25.9; Josh. 6.5; Ps. 47.5; 81.3
Rattle made of pottery?, 2 Sam. 6.5
Pipe, reed instrument like a single or double oboe, 1 Sam. 10.5; 1 Kings 1.40; Ps. 150.4; Isa. 5.12; Jer. 48.36; Matt. 9.23; 11.17; 1 Cor. 14.7
Trumpet, of silver or bronze, Num. 10.2–10, 2 Kings 11.14; 12.13; 1 Cor. 14.8; 15.52; Rev. 1.10

**Mustard** the black mustard tree grows to 8 to 10 feet high; although birds do not nest in it, this is a quotation from Dan. 4.20–21, the birds representing the nations of the earth. The parable of the mustard seed teaches that, from small beginnings, the kingdom of God can grow to include all peoples, Matt. 13.31–32; even small faith produces great results, Matt. 17.20

**Mute** see 'Dumb'

**Muzzling the ox** covering the mouth to prevent it eating the grain, forbidden, Deut. 25.4; applied metaphorically to clergy stipends, 1 Cor. 9.9; 1 Tim. 5.18; see also 'Threshing'

**Myra** port, named from the myrrh traded there, in Lycia on the southern coast of Asia Minor, now known as Demre in Turkey, where Paul changed ships on his way to Rome, Acts 27.5–6

**Myrrh** (pronounced mur to rhyme with her) see 'Spices'

**Myrtle** shrub with beautiful branches, Neh. 8.15; Isa. 55.13; Zech. 1.8

**Mysia** district in the Province of Asia, Acts 16.7–8, see 'Adramyttium', 'Assos', 'Pergamon', 'Troas'

**Mystery religions** cults which revealed to the initiated a secret which, they claimed, explained the purpose of life. A mystery was something which had been a secret but is now revealed. Paul realized that God's plan to bring unity to the whole human race through the Church, was the 'mystery' which he had to reveal, Mark 4.11; Rom. 11.25; 16.25–26; 1 Cor. 4.1; 13.2; 15.51; Eph. 1.9; 3.3; 5.32; 6.19; Col. 2.2; 2 Thess. 2.7; 1 Tim. 3.16; Rev. 17.5

**Naaman** (*H* = pleasantness) Syrian official who contracted leprosy; asked King Ahab to heal him; was referred to Elisha; reluctantly washed in the River Jordan; was healed; asked for a bag of earth from Israel so that he could worship YHWH on his own soil, 2 Kings 5; Luke 4.27

**Nabal** (*H* = fool) shepherd with property in Carmel; his churlish response to David's request was redeemed by the gracious behaviour of his wife Abigail; he died on hearing what she had done, 1 Sam. 25

**Naboth** (*H* = fruits) man of Jezreel; owned a vineyard which Ahab wanted; stoned to death because of forged letters sent by Jezebel; Elijah pronounced God's judgement in Naboth's vineyard; Ahab and Jezebel met horrible deaths, 1 Kings 21–22; 2 Kings 9

**Nadab** (*H* = noble) **1.** Son of Aaron, Lev. 10.1–3, see 'Abihu'. **2.** Son of Jeroboam I, king of Israel 910–909 BC, 1 Kings 14.20; 15.25–28

**Nag Hammadi** city in Egypt 350 miles south of Cairo, where a jar of twelve papyrus books was found in 1945, including the Gospel of Thomas, see p. **162**

**Nahash** (*H* = snake) Ammonite king; threatened Jabesh-Gilead; defeated by Saul, 1 Sam. 11

**Nahor** Abraham's brother, grandfather of Rebekah, Gen. 11.26; 22.20; 24.10

**Nahum** (*H* = comforter) (Nahum) The Book of the Prophet Nahum (NAY-hum), see p. **144**

**Nain** (*H* = lovely) village now called Nein, in Galilee overlooking the Plain of Esdraelon, where Jesus raised the widow's son to life, Luke 7.11–17; 2 miles from Shunem where Elijah raised a boy to life, 2 Kings 4.8–37

**Name** represented the character of a person or a god, Gen. 3.13–15; Ex. 34.5–8; or their reputation, Prov. 22.1; Rev. 3.1; to know their name gave you power over them, Gen. 32.29; God's name is to be respected and not misused, Ex. 20.7; Matt. 6.9; Eph. 1.21; Phil. 2.10; God's new name, Isa. 62.2; Rev. 2.17; 3.12; a representative would come in the name of someone who sent them, Acts 3.6; Col. 3.17; to receive someone 'in the name of a prophet' means in the character of a prophet, or because they are a prophet, Matt. 10.41; to pray in the name of Jesus is to pray in the spirit of the character he showed, for things which he would have requested, and trusting him to give them, John 14.13; 15.16; to have life in his name is because of his power, John 20.31; Acts 4.12

**Naomi** (*H* = my joy) Bethlehemite widow of Elimelech; mother-in-law of Ruth, Ruth 1–4

**Naphtali** (*H* = my wrestling) one of the sons of Jacob, Gen. 30.7–8; ancestor of one of the twelve tribes of Israel, who occupied land north of Lake Galilee, Gen. 30.8; 49; Deut. 33; Judg. 1.33; Isa. 9.1, quoted in Matt. 4.13–16

**Nard** see 'Spices'

**Narrow** gate on the way that leads to life, Matt. 7.14

**Nathan** (*H* = gave) prophet who told David he could not build the Temple; condemned him with the parable of the ewe-lamb, for arranging the death of Uriah. He anointed Solomon, 2 Sam. 7.1–17; 12.1–15; 1 Kings 1.32–45

**Nathanael** (*H* = God gave) from Cana in Galilee; first to acclaim Jesus as Son of God and king of Israel, when Jesus saw him meditating under a fig tree; among those who saw the risen Christ while they were fishing on Lake Galilee, John 1.45; 21.2. Possibly another name for Bartholomew; possibly the Beloved Disciple.

**Nation** The nation, in the singular, usually means the Jews, Ps. 33.12; Isa. 9.3; 26.2; Luke 7.5; John 11.50–52. 'The nations', in the plural, means all the non-Jews, *goiim* in Hebrew and Gentiles in Latin, Ps. 2; Isa. 2.2–4; 49.6; Matt. 24.14; 25.32; Mark 11.17; Rev. 22.2

**Nazarene** or Nazorean, probably meaning Jesus from Nazareth, or his followers, Matt. 26.71; Acts 24.5. In Matt. 2.23 it could refer to nazirite, Judg. 13.5, or to *H netser* = a sprout, Isa. 11.1

**Nazareth** town in the Galilean hills overlooking the Valley of Jezreel, where the angel appeared to Mary; where Jesus was brought up in Joseph the carpenter's workshop. Several dwellings from the first century have been excavated, including one in the Church of the Annunciation described as Mary's kitchen, Matt. 2.23; 21.11; Mark 1.9; Luke 1.26; John 1.45–46; Acts 10.38

**Nazirites** (*H* = separated) those who had taken a vow not to cut their hair or drink alcohol, Num. 6; Judg. 16.17; 1 Sam. 1.11; Acts 18.18; 21.23–26

**Neapolis** (*G* = new town) port in Thrace where Paul and his companions first landed in Greece; now called Kavalla, Acts 16.11

**Nebo 1.** The second most important god of the Babylonians, son of Bel / Marduk, Isa. 46.1. **2.** Peak 6 miles north-west of Madaba in the Abarim range in Jordan northeast of the Dead Sea, which rises to 2,625 feet above sea level, 4,000 feet above the Dead Sea, now Jebel en-Neba; here Moses surveyed the Promised Land, then died, Deut. 32.49–34.5; see also 'Pisgah'

**Nebuchadnezzar** or **Nebuchadrezzar** (nebb-you-kuh-NEZZ-ur, *Ak Nabu-kudur-ri-usur* = the god Nebo protect my boundary) king of Babylon 605–562 BC; defeated the Egyptians at Carchemish in 605; in about 598 attacked Jerusalem and began deporting the Jews; see 'Exile', 2 Kings 24; 25; 2 Chron. 36.10–20; Jer. 20–34; 52; Ezek. 26.7; 29.19; Dan. 1–4; see also Mesopotamia, p. **165**

**Nebuzaradan** (*Ak Nabu-zera-iddina* = Nebo has given offspring) captain of Nebuchadnezzar's bodyguard, in charge of the destruction of Jerusalem, but showed kindness to Jeremiah, 2 Kings 25.8–20; Jer. 39.11–14; 40.1–6

**Neco II** (*Eg Neca-u*) Pharaoh of Egypt 610–595 BC, defeated Josiah at the Battle of Megiddo; defeated by Nebuchadnezzar in 605 at the Battle of Carchemish, 2 Kings 23.28–30; 2 Chron. 35.20–24; Jer. 46.2–12

**Negeb** see 'Wilderness'

**Nehemiah** (*H* = Jah comforts) (Neh.) (Nehemiah is called 2 Esdras in the Latin Vulgate; Ezra and Nehemiah are one book known as Esdras B in Greek) The Book of Nehemiah (Nee-him-EYE-ur), see p. **139**

**Nehushtan** (*H* = bronze) image of a snake, made by Moses, worshipped by the Israelites and destroyed by Hezekiah, Num. 21.8–9; 2 Kings 18.4, see 'Serpent 4.'

**Neighbour** recognizing the frequency of boundary disputes etc., the Hebrew Scriptures command us to love our neighbour; this was given the challenging addition that we are to love them as much as we love ourselves, Lev. 19.18; Matt. 19.19; 22.39; in practice it was restricted to people of the same race or village. Jesus made the astonishing suggestion that we are to behave in a loving way towards anyone, even of a different and hated race, who needs our help and whom we have an opportunity of helping, Luke 10.25–37; see also 'Samaria'

**Nergal-Sharezer** (*Ak Nergal-shara-utser* = the god Nergal protect the king) king of Babylon 560–556 BC, see Mesopotamia, p. **165**. The list of officials who released Jeremiah include two with this name; possibly one of them later became king, Jer. 39.3, 13

**Nero** Roman Emperor AD 54–68, to whom Paul made his appeal, Acts 25.11; whom Peter told Christians to honour, 1 Peter 2.17; traditionally executed Peter and Paul; see also 'Six hundred and sixty-six'

**Net** see 'Fish 2.'

**New 1.** New birth, John 3.3–8; 1 Peter 1.23. **2.** New commandment, John 13.34. **3.** New covenant, Jer. 31.31–34; 2 Cor. 3.6; Heb. 7.8–12. **4.** New creation, 2 Cor. 5.17; Gal. 6.15. **5.** New every morning, Lam. 3.22–33. **6.** New heavens and new earth, Isa. 65.17; 66.22; Rev. 21. **7.** New Jerusalem, Isa. 65.18–25; Rev. 21.10–27. **8.** New Moon Festival, Num. 10.10; 1 Sam. 20.5; Ps. 81.3; Isa. 1.13. **9.** New name, Isa. 62.2; Rev. 2.17; 3.12. **10.** No new patch on old clothes, no new wine in old wineskins, Matt. 9.16–17. **11.** A new song, Ps. 33.3; 96.1; 98.1; 149.1; Isa. 42.10; Rev. 5.9. **12.** New teaching, Mark 1.27; Acts 17.19. **13.** New Year, see 'Calendar'. **14.** Nothing new under the sun, Eccles. 1.9. **15.** I make all things new, Rev. 21.5

**The New Testament** see p. **149**

**Next-of-Kin** (nearest relative) obliged to care for his relations, their property and their widows, and avenge their death, Ex. 21.13; Lev. 25.25; Num. 35.9–34; Deut.

19.1–13; 24.16; Ruth 2.1; 4.1; Jer. 32.8–15, see also 'Eye for an eye', 'Redemption'

**Nicanor** (*G* = conqueror) **1.** General of Antiochus Epiphanes, 1 Macc. 3.38; 2 Macc. 8.9. **2.** One of the Seven Helpers, Acts 6.5

**Nicodemus** (*G* = conqueror of the people) elderly Pharisee who visited Jesus by night, defended him before the Jewish authorities, and helped with his burial, John 3.1–21; 7.50–51; 19.39–42

**Nicolaitans** group whose teachings are condemned, Rev. 2.6, 15. It is not known what they taught, or whether they were followers of Nicolas who was one of The Seven, but as his name in Greek means the same as Balaam in Hebrew, they may, as in Num. 25.2, have advised the believers to eat meat sacrificed to idols, see 'Meat'

**Nicolas** or **Nicolaus** (*G* = conqueror of the people) one of the Seven Helpers, Acts 6.5

**Nicopolis** (*G* = city of victory) town in western Greece, near modern Preveza, Titus 3.12–15

**Niger** (*L* = black) surname or nickname of Simeon, one of the prophets at Antioch who sent Paul and Barnabas out as missionaries; possibly of African origin, he might be the Simon of Cyrene who carried the cross for Jesus, Mark 15.21; Acts 13.1

**Nile** river of Egypt, which, by annual flooding, covered the land with fertile silt, Gen. 41; Ex. 7; Isa. 19; Amos 8.8

**Nimrod** grandson of Ham, a mighty hunter, founder of Babel and Nineveh, Gen. 10.9–11; 1 Chron. 1.10; Micah 5.6

**Nineveh** one of the oldest and largest cities on earth, the third capital of Assyria, and from 1300 until it was destroyed in 607 BC, the centre of the civilized world. The remains are on the outskirts of Mosul in Iraq, on the east bank of the Tigris. To the Jews, a symbol of pagan unbelief, therefore Jonah at first refused to preach there, Gen. 10.11; Jonah 1–4; Nahum 1–3; Matt. 12.41; Luke 11.32; see Mesopotamia, p. **165**

**Noah** (*H* = rest?) son of Lamech; built an ark to save his family and the animals from the flood; the dove returning with an olive branch showed him that the flood was nearly finished; the ark landed on Mount Ararat; God made a covenant with him never to flood the earth again; Noah sent his sons Ham, Shem and Japheth and the animals to multiply and populate the earth. The well-known story was retold to answer the common question, why does a loving and omnipotent God allow evil to flourish? Noah was also the discoverer of wine, Gen. 5–9; Isa. 54.9; Ezek. 14.14; Matt. 24.37–39; Heb. 11.7; 1 Peter 3.20

**Nob** sanctuary where the priest Ahimelech shared the holy bread with David; attacked by Saul; the site is unknown but was between Anathoth and Jerusalem, 1 Sam. 21.1–9; 22.6–19; Neh. 11.32; Isa. 10.32; Matt. 12.3–4

**Nobleman 1.** A nobleman – whose departure seeking to be made king could be modelled on the behaviour of Archelaus following the death of Herod the Great – lent money to his servants in the Parable of the Pounds, Luke 19.12–27. **2.** Better translated, 'king's officer', asked Jesus to heal his son, John 4.46–53; the title would include a centurion in the service of Herod, so this might be the same as the centurion in Matt. 8.5–13 and Luke 7.1–10

**Nod** (*H* = wandering) land to which Cain fled after murdering Abel, Gen. 4.16

**Non-Biblical Books** see p. **161**

**Numbers** (Num.) The Book of Numbers, see p. **136**

**Nympha** (*G* = sacred to nymphs) in whose house a congregation met, which she probably led, Col. 4.15

**Oaks** several species grow in Israel; six different Hebrew words are thus translated. **1.** Oaks or terebinths of Mamre, where Abraham was buried at Hebron, Gen. 13.18; 14.13; 18.1. **2.** Absalom caught by his hair in an oak tree, 1 Sam. 18.9–14. **3.** 'They will be called oaks of righteousness', Isa. 61.3. See also 'Terebinth'

**Obadiah** (*H* = servant of Jah) **1.** In charge of Ahab's palace; hid prophets of YHWH; carried a message to Elijah, 1 Kings 18.1–16. **2.** Author of The Book of the Prophet Obadiah. **3.** Seven other Obadiahs in Scripture

**Obadiah** (Ob.) The Book of the Prophet Obadiah (oh-bird-EYE-uh), see p. **144**

**Obed-Edom** (*H* = servant of Edom) man from one of several towns called Gath; cared for the Ark, 2 Sam. 6.10–15

**Obedience** to our Creator who knows the future consequences of our actions, Ex. 19.5; Deut. 11.26–28; Isa. 1.19; Heb. 11.8. Obedience is better than sacrifice, 1 Sam. 15.22. When Adam disobeyed God, it was the source of our troubles, so if we identify ourselves by faith with the obedience of Jesus, the Second Adam, on the cross, our relationship with God can be restored, Rom. 5.19; Phil. 2.8; Heb. 5.8–9

**Offence 1.** To offend someone, causes of offence, and rock of offence, see 'Stumblingblock'. **2.** Mount of Offence, the southern end of the Mount of Olives in Jerusalem, named from the idols erected there by Solomon, 1 Kings 11.1–8

**Og** see 'Bashan'

**Oholah** and **Oholibah** (*H* = tent, my tent in her) immoral sisters symbolizing Samaria and Jerusalem, Ezek. 23

**Oil** see 'Anointing', 'Lamp', 'Olive'

**Old** the elderly, Ps. 37.25; 71.18; 90.10; Prov. 22.6; John 21.18; Titus 2.2. Respect for old age, Lev. 19.32; Job. 30.1; Prov. 23.22; 1 Tim. 5.1. Old and young together, Wisd. 4; Joel 2.28, quoted in Acts 2.17. The description of old age in Eccles. 12.1–8 warns against leaving concern with God until it is too late. The darkness, and those who peer through the window, are probably failing eyesight; rain is tears; arms tremble and legs are bent; grinders are teeth; daughters of song are a powerful voice; almond tree blossom is white hair; you drag yourself along slowly like a grasshopper; silver cord, golden bowl, pitcher and wheel are probably different bodily organs and functions. See also 'New'

**Old Testament** The Hebrew Scriptures, see p. **133**

**Olive** major crop in Canaan; the fruit is removed from the tree by beating, Ex. 27.20; Deut. 24.20; its oil, produced by pressing the fruit under heavy weights, or with a screw, is used for cooking, 2 Kings 18.32; lamps, Lev. 24.2; and anointing, Ex. 30.24; Ps. 23.5; 45.7. Some of the trees now in Gethsemane are thought to be a thousand years old. Olive trees in visions, Zech. 4.3–12; Rev. 6.6; 11.4. Olive grafting, Rom. 11.17–24; leaf, Gen. 8.11; orchard, Ex. 23.11; 1 Sam. 8.14; Neh. 9.25; parable, Judg. 9.8–9

**Olives, Mount of or Olivet** range of hills east of Jerusalem, beyond the Kidron Valley; Gethsemane was one of the olive orchards which covered it, Mark 13.3; 14.26; Luke 21.37; 22.39; John 8.1. Here the Messiah was expected to appear, 2 Sam. 15.30–16.2; Zech. 14.4; Matt. 21.1–11

**Omega** (*G* = big 'o') written ω and Ω, final letter of the Greek alphabet, see also 'Alpha'

**On** city in Egypt also called Heliopolis, on the east bank of the Nile, where Joseph's father-in-law was a priest, Gen. 41.45, 50; 46.20; Jer. 43.15

**Omri** (*H* = my portion) one of the greatest kings of Israel 885–874 BC; founder of the Omrid dynasty, 1 Kings 16.16–28; Micah 6.16

**Onan** (*H* = vigour) refused to ensure the continuation of his brother's family, his obligation under the law of Levirate marriage, probably by premature withdrawal, Gen. 38.8–10

**Onesimus** (Oh-NEE-simm-us, *G* = useful) slave who ran away, and became a Christian when he met Paul, Col. 4.9, Philemon 2, see Philemon, p. **157**

**Onesiphorus** (Oh-nee-SIFF-or-us, *G* = bringing gain) Christian who helped Paul in Ephesus and Rome, 2 Tim. 1.16. Paul sends greetings to his household only, 4.19; so Onesiphorus may have been dead when Paul prayed for him, 1.18

**Open door** an opportunity for evangelism, 1 Cor. 16.9; Col. 4.3; Rev. 3.8

**Ophel** (*H* = mound) area south of today's Sion Gate in Jerusalem, west of the Kidron Valley, and north of the city of David, 2 Chron. 27.3; 33.14; Neh. 3.26–27; 11.21. Sometimes the word is erroneously used of the whole ridge as far as Siloam

**Ophir** (*H* = rich) proverbial source of gold, jewels and almug-wood, probably somewhere on the coast of Arabia, Africa or India, Gen. 10.29; 1 Kings 9.28; 10.11; 22.48; Ps. 45.9

**Ophrah 1.** See 'Ephraim 4'. **2.** Ophrah of Abiezer, home of Gideon, unknown site in Jezreel region, Judg. 6

**Oracle** (*L* = pronouncement) those who seek oracles from the dead are condemned, Lam. 2.14; Hos. 4.12; Micah 3.11. Hebrew prophets received brief 'words' from YHWH, which they memorized and later gathered into written collections called oracles, Isa. 13.1; Jer. 36.1–4; Nahum 1.1; Hab. 1.1; Mal. 1.1. When they predict bad times, oracles are sometimes called a 'burden', though Jer. 23.33–38 condemns the word. In the New Testament 'oracles' translates *logia*, the pronouncements of God, about the present as well as the future, Acts 7.38; Rom. 3.2; Heb. 5.12; 1 Peter 4.11; see 'Prophets'

**Orderliness** necessary in worship, 1 Cor. 14.26–40

**Oreb** (*H* = raven) **1.** King of the Midianites, killed by Gideon along with Zeeb. **2.** The rock where he died, Judg. 7.25; Isa. 10.26

**Orion** or **Arcturus**, the Bear, and **The Pleiades** the Seven Sisters (uh-RYE-un, ark-TYOO-rus, PLY-uh-dees or PLEE-uh-dees) are constellations of stars, Job 9.9; 38.31; Amos 5.8

**Ornan** see 'Araunah'

**Orpah** (*H* = raincloud?) like Ruth, a Moabite widow and daughter-in-law of Naomi, but she returned to Moab, Ruth 1.4–14

**Orphans 1.** Pitiable state of, Lam. 5.3. **2.** To be cared for, Ex. 22.22–24; Deut. 24.17–21; Job 29.12; Ps. 82.3; Isa. 1.17; James 1.27. **3.** Jesus promised 'I will not leave you orphaned' ('comfortless' in old translations), promising the Holy Spirit, John 14.18

**Osnappar** Assyrian king, historically either Shalmaneser or Sargon; but the name is probably a corruption of Assurbanipal, Ezra 4.10

**Ostrich** the largest living bird, though flightless; lays the largest eggs in the world; was wrongly believed to neglect its eggs, because it leaves them to be warmed by the sun during the day, and only sits on them at night, Job 39.13–18

**Othniel** (*H* = God is my might) captured Kiriath-Sepher (Debir); married Caleb's daughter; first of the 'Judges', Josh. 15.16–17; Judg. 1.13; 3.7–11

**Ox** (plural 'oxen') domesticated breeds of cattle used for meat and milk; the castrated male is docile, and used to pull a cart or plough in many places still, Ex. 20.17; 21.28–36; Luke 13.15; 14.19; Acts 14.13; 1 Cor. 9.9

**Oxyrhynchus** site 120 miles south of Cairo in Egypt, where a chest of ancient papyri, preserved by the dry desert conditions, included early fragments from the New Testament and other documents, with what are claimed as hitherto unknown sayings of Jesus

**P** the priestly editor, one of the sources believed by some to lie behind the books from Genesis to Numbers, see p. **135**

**Paddan-aram** (*H* = field of Aram, Hos. 12.12; or = way of Aram, see 'Haran') area in northern Mesopotamia, homeland of the Patriarchs, where Jacob went to find a wife, Gen. 25.20; 28.2–7; 31.18; 35.9

**Pain** was well known to the Bible writers, e.g. Job 16.6; Ps. 38.17; 69.29; Jer. 4.19; Jesus suffered appalling pain on the cross, yet was able to think of others, John 19.25–27; he promises an end, John 16.20–22, when there shall be 'no more pain', Rev. 21.4

**Palm 1.** Date-palms are frequently mentioned in the Bible, Ex.15.27; Ps. 92.12. **2.** Palm branches or leaves were waved to greet a conqueror, 1 Macc. 13.51; 2 Macc. 10.7; John 12.13; Rev. 7.9. **3.** 'I have inscribed you on the palm of my hands', Isa. 49.16, a tattoo of either the name of a loved one, or an architect's plans. **4.** Handbreadth, see 'Measures of Length'

**Palmer-worm** old translation for a development-stage of the locust, Joel 1.4

**Pamphylia** (*G* = all tribes) Hellenistic kingdom, then a Roman Province on the southern coast of Asia Minor, with its capital at Attalia, today Antalya in Turkey, Acts 13.13; 14.24; 15.38; 27.5. People from Pamphylia were present at Pentecost, Acts 2.10

**Paphos** see 'Cyprus 5.'

**Papias** (about AD 60–130) Bishop of Hierapolis; his writings have not survived, but are quoted by other writers; he said he had heard from John the Elder that Mark was Peter's secretary and translator, and that Matthew originally wrote in Hebrew; see also 'Philip'

**Papyrus** reed found by the Nile and used for boat-building and writing, Ex. 2.3; Job 8.11; Isa. 18.2; see p. **178**

**Parable** truth brought home by means of fiction; a story which enables the hearers to see a truth that they had not previously grasped, Matt. 13.34–35; found in the Bible from 2 Sam. 12.1–6 onwards. Parables are often humorous, when they make the hearers laugh and then realize they are laughing at themselves, Matt. 7.3–5. Usually they make only a single point, Matt. 13.45; though some become allegory, when every detail of the story has a symbolic meaning, Matt. 13.1–9, 18–23. See The Teaching of Jesus, p. **170**

**Paraclete** (*G parakletos* = someone called to come to one's side to help) translated Comforter, Advocate or Helper, meaning the Holy Spirit who helps us to speak for Christ, John 14. Also used of Christ, who speaks for us to God, 1 John 2.1

**Paradise** Persian word for the garden or park of a palace; used in Hebrew in Neh. 2.8; Eccles. 2.5; S. of Sol. 4.13, and in the Greek translation for the Garden of Eden. Hence it means God's dwelling, 2 Esd. 4.7; Luke 23.43; 2 Cor. 12.4; Rev. 2.7

**1 & 2 Paralipomenon** (*G* = things left out) see '1 & 2 Chronicles'

**Paralysis** or **Palsy** healed by Jesus, Matt. 4.24; 8.5–13; 9.2–8; Mark 2.1–12; and by his disciples, Acts 8.7; 9.33–34

**Paran** region around Kadesh-Barnea, Gen. 21.21; Num. 10.12; 13.26; 1 Sam. 25.1

**Parchment** skins of sheep or goats, washed and polished, for writing on, which replaced papyrus, see 'Pergamon'. Possibly the parchments in 2 Tim. 4.13 were Paul's citizenship documents

**Pardon** see 'Forgiveness'

**Parents 1.** To be honoured, Ex. 20.12; Prov. 1.8–9; 19.26; 23.22; Eph. 6.1–2. **2.** To show love and understanding for their children, Prov. 22.6; Luke 11.11–13; Eph. 6.4; Col. 3.21; Titus 2.4

**Parousia** (*G* = presence) usually translated coming. In the words of Jesus: Matt. 24.27, 37, 39. In the teaching of Paul: 1 Cor. 15.23; 1 Thess. 2.19; 3.13; 4.15; 5.23; 2 Thess. 2.1, see also Apocalyptic, p. **175**

**Parthians** tribe from Persia; independent from around 250 BC to AD 226; formed a threat to the Roman Empire, using the 'parting-' or 'Parthian-shot', fired over their horses' tails as they passed, Rev. 9.13–19; 16.12. People from Parthia were present at Pentecost, Acts 2.9; see Mesopotamia, p. **165**

**Passion** (*L* = suffering) the suffering of Jesus on the cross, Acts 1.3; described by each Gospel with slight differences in the Passion Narratives, Matt. 26–27; Mark 14–15; Luke 22–23; John 18–19. Probably there was an oral tradition with many details, from which the Gospel writers have each selected what they needed

**Passover, Paschal Lamb** (*H Pesach*) sacrificed at the annual festival commemorating the Exodus of the Hebrew slaves from Egypt under Moses. The animal's blood was smeared on the doorposts of the houses where Israelites lived, in the pattern of a T-shaped cross; then, when the firstborn of the Egyptians were killed, the angel of death would pass over that house, and those inside would be saved by the blood of the lamb, Ex. 12–13; Num. 9.2–14; 2 Chron. 35.1–19; Matt. 26.17–19; John 2.13; 18.28, see also 'Unleavened bread', 'Calendar'

**Pastoral Epistles** (1 & 2 Timothy, Titus), see p. **156**

**Patara** port in Lycia where Paul transhipped on his way home after his third missionary journey, now called Gelemiş in Turkey, with extensive remains, Acts 21.1

**Patience** shown by God in refraining from punishing, Ps. 86.15; Rom. 2.4; 9.22; 1 Peter 3.20. Commended in dealings with our neighbours, Eph. 4.2. Endurance, perseverance, 1 Thess. 1.3; Heb. 12.1–3. A fruit of the Spirit, Gal. 5.22

**Patmos** island where John had the vision recorded in Revelation; in the Greek Dodecanese south of Samos, it is only 30 miles from the Turkish coast and the churches he wrote to; such islands were often used for banishment at hard-labour of those considered politically dangerous, Rev. 1.9

**Paul** name adopted by Saul of Tarsus as he increasingly moved in a non-Jewish environment. For his life and teaching see A Time-Line of the Bible, p. **1**; The Acts of the Apostles, p. **151**; and the Letters of Paul, pp. **152–7**. Brought up in a multicultural environment in Tarsus, and trained as a Pharisee by Gamaliel, he persecuted the Christians but was converted on the road to Damascus. He was sent by the church in Antioch on three missionary journeys: the first to Cyprus and Galatia; the second to Galatia, Troas, Philippi, Thessalonica, Athens and Corinth; the third to revisit places where he already established churches, and also Ephesus and Miletus. He was arrested in Jerusalem, and eventually appealed to be tried by the Emperor in Rome. After leaving Crete he was shipwrecked on Malta, and eventually sailed to Sicily and Italy. The result of his trial is not recorded in the Bible, but there is a tradition that he was released, and later rearrested and beheaded in Rome. He called himself Apostle to the Gentiles, Rom. 11.13; and sought to proclaim the death of Jesus in terms which would draw Jews and Gentiles into a single Church community.

**Pavement** see 'Gabbatha'

**Peace** (*H shalom*) in the Hebrew Scriptures implies the prosperity which follows when a nation is not troubled by wars, Ps. 122.6; Isa. 26.3; 52.7; Jer. 6.14. In the New Testament it is more an internal peace of mind; brought by Jesus, Isa. 9.6; Luke 1.79; 2.14; John 14.27; one of the fruits of the Spirit, Gal. 5.22; Phil. 4.7. Peacemakers are called blessed, Matt. 5.9

**Pearls** formed inside the shells of oysters, and very expensive. 'Don't throw pearls before swine' probably means don't waste time arguing with mockers, Matt. 7.6. The 'pearl of great price' is the kingdom of God: any sacrifice is worthwhile to attain it, Job 28.18; Matt. 13.45; the gates of the heavenly Jerusalem are each formed of a single pearl, Rev. 21.21

**Pedagogue** (*G paidagogos*) slave who trained a young boy until he was ready to start lessons with a Grammarian, 1 Cor. 4.15; Gal. 3.24. Translated as custodian, disciplinarian, guardian, guide, instructor or schoolmaster

**Pekah** (*H* = open-eyed) king of Israel 737–732 BC, 2 Kings 15.25; 2 Chron. 28.6; Isa. 7.1

**Pekahiah** (*H* = Jah opens eyes) king of Israel 738–737 BC, 2 Kings 15.22

**Pelethites** (*H* = swift) see 'Cherethites'

**Pelusium** (*L* from *G* = mud) city in Egypt near the sea, east of the Nile delta, Ezek. 30.15–16

**Peniel** or **Penuel** (*H* = face of God) where Jacob wrestled with God by the River Jabbok, Gen. 32.22–32

**Penny** or **pence** see 'Money'

**Pentateuch** (*G* = five volumes) the first five books of the Bible, from Genesis to Deuteronomy, see pp. **134–7**

**Pentecost** (*G* = fiftieth) the fiftieth day after Passover, a festival with sacrifices, combined with the Feast of Weeks celebrating the wheat harvest, Lev. 23.9; Deut. 16.9; the day on which the Law was given to Moses, Ex. 19; the day on which the Holy Spirit was given to the first Christians, Acts 2. The traditional site of this is the upper room known as the Cenacle just outside the Sion Gate of modern Jerusalem; there is archaeological evidence that this may be on the site where the first disciples gathered in John Mark's mother's house, Acts 12.12, see also 'Calendar', 'Holy Spirit', The Holy Spirit, p. **174**

**Peor** (*H* = hole), **1.** Where Balaam blessed Israel, and later tempted the Israelites to sin by eating meat offered to idols; the last stopping place for the Israelites before they crossed the Jordan, probably Tell el-Hammam, above Wadi el-Kefrein in Jordan, Num. 23.28; Deut. 3.29; Hos. 9.10, see also 'Nebo 2.', 'Shittim 2.'. **2.** The god worshipped there, Baal-Peor, Num. 25.1–18; Ps. 106.28

**Perga, Perge** town near the Cestrus River in Pamphylia. The site is 11 miles north-east of Antalya on the southern coast of Turkey, with impressive remains. Paul and Barnabas disembarked nearby, sailing from Cyprus on their first missionary journey; here John Mark left them. They preached here on their way back, Acts 13.13–14; 14.25–26

**Pergamon** (*L* **Pergamum**) one of the 'Seven Churches of Asia' to which John was commanded by the Risen Christ to write, Rev. 2.12–17. It is now called Bergama in Turkey, 55 miles north of İzmir and 20 miles from the Aegean coast. An independent kingdom from 283 to 263 BC, it built up a library of 200,000 scrolls; here parchment (*L Pergamenta charta*) was invented. In 133 Pergamon voluntarily joined the Roman Empire. There is a steep acropolis, which was a centre for Emperor worship, with a large theatre, and a processional way to the Serapion or healing centre. The podium of the Temple of Zeus has been re-erected in the Pergamon Museum in Berlin

**Perizzites** (*H* = villagers) people living in the forested hills of Samaria before the Israelites arrived, Gen. 13.7; Josh. 17.15; Judg. 1.4–5; Neh. 9.8

**Perseverance** see 'Patience'

**Persia** area between the Caspian Sea and the Persian Gulf. The Persians were Zoroastrians, worshipping Ahura Mazda, whose prophet Zarathustra in the sixth century BC called them to make a free choice to side with good against evil; see Mesopotamia, p. 165

**Pestilence** epidemic, fatal disease spreading rapidly through the population, Ex. 3.3; Rev. 18.8

**Peter** (*G Petros*, translates *Ar kefa* = rock) nickname which Jesus gave to his disciple Simeon or Simon. Peter was a Galilean fisherman, the son of Jonah, Matt. 16.17; or John, John 21.15; brother of Andrew; Jesus called them both to fish for people, Matt. 4.18–19. It may have been a teasing nickname because of Simon's notoriously unstable character, Luke 22.31; he, or his faith, was to be the foundation stone of the Church, Matt. 16.18. He was one of The Twelve, and of the smaller group present at the Transfiguration, Matt. 17.1–13, and Gethsemane, 26.37. He was the first to acknowledge Jesus as the Messiah, 16.16. Asked by a servant girl whether he was a follower of Jesus, he three times denied that he even knew him, 26.69; the report of this, and his subsequent remorse, 26.75, can only have come from his own mouth. Jesus appeared to him personally after the Resurrection, 1 Cor. 15.5; and three times told Peter to be a shepherd to Christ's sheep, John 21.15–17. He preached at Pentecost, Acts 2.14–36; his missionary work is reported in Acts 3–5; 10–12. He baptized the Gentile Cornelius, Acts 10; at the Council of Jerusalem Peter argued for the admission of Gentiles to the Church, without requiring obedience to the Jewish law, Acts 15. Paul rebuked him for refusing to eat with Gentiles, Gal. 2.14; and some have seen the rivalry between their followers persisting in the early Church, 1 Cor. 1.12. There is early documentary evidence that he was martyred in Rome, and the archaeology makes it probable that his tomb is in the crypt of the present St Peter's Basilica in the Vatican. Christians disagree as to whether he passed on his primacy to his successors in Rome

**1 Peter** (1 Peter) The First Letter of Peter, see p. **158**

**2 Peter** (2 Peter) The Second Letter of Peter, see p. **158**

**Pharaoh** (FAIR-oh, *Eg* = great house) title of the kings of Egypt, Gen. 12.10–20; Gen. 39–50; Ex. 1–15; there is great debate, with little evidence, about which Pharaoh was involved with the Exodus, see also 'Hophra', 'Neco', 'Rameses', 'Shishak', 'So'

**Pharisees** (*H* = ?separated) religious movement who believed in resurrection, emphasized strict adherence to the Jewish law, and had their own traditions in addition. Mark links them with the scribes, criticized by Jesus for their obsession with purity, tithing and their own traditions, 2.1–3.6; 3.19–30; 7.1–23. Matthew links them with the Sadducees, 3.7; 16.1, 6; 21.43–46; they have the authority of Moses, but their teaching is dangerous, 15.14; 16.11–12; 23.2–3. Luke represents them favourably, 5.17–26; 13.31; Jesus criticized their self-satisfaction, and love of money, 11.42–54; 12.1; 16.14–15; 18.9–14, but continued to accept their hospitality, Luke 7.36–50; 11.37–41; 14.1–6. The Pharisee Gamaliel is praised, Acts 5.33–39; Paul, a former Pharisee, made use of their disagreement with the Sadducees over resurrection, 23.6–9. Jesus had much in common with the Pharisees; probably they were more varied and less rigid in Jesus's day than when they compiled the Mishnah (c.AD 175–c.220) and Talmud (c.220–c.400)

**Pharpar** (*H* = rapid) river near Damascus, see 'Abana'

**Philadelphia** (*G* = brotherly love) **1.** One of the Seven Churches of Asia to whom John was commanded by the risen Christ to write, Rev. 1.11; 3.7–13. King Attalus II of Pergamon, called Philadelphus because of his loyalty to his brother Eumenes, occupied a hill settlement in Lydia, on the border with Mysia and Phrygia; the remains of the ancient town are buried beneath the Turkish town of Alaşehir. **2.** See 'Rabbah'

**Philemon** (*G* = friendship) (Philemon) The Letter of Paul to Philemon (fill-EE-mon), see p. **157**

**Philip** (*G* = friend of horses) **1.** 'The apostle', one of The Twelve, who brought Nathanael, and later some Greeks, to Jesus, and asked him to show them the Father, Matt. 10.3; John 1.43–46; 12.20–22; 14.8–9. **2.** One of The Seven, Acts 6.5. **3.** 'The evangelist', who preached in Samaria, baptized the Ethiopian official, and together with his four daughters, gave hospitality to Paul, Luke and their companions, Acts 8.5–40. Acts 21.8–9 states that **3.** was the same as **2.**; but Papias, writing in the second century, who met Philip's daughters, insists that **3.** was the apostle, the same as **1.**, and that he was buried at Hierapolis. **4.** See 'Herod Family'

**Philippi** (FILL-ipp-eye) Roman colony in Macedonia, where Paul baptized Lydia, healed a slave-girl, and was released from prison, Acts 16.11–40; 20.1, 6; 1 Thess. 2.2

**Philippians** (Phil.) The Letter of Paul to the Philippians (fill-LIPP-yuns), see p. **155**

**Philistines** (*H* = wanderers) people who, in the thirteenth and twelfth centuries BC, came from the Aegean region; their pottery and writing are related to those of Mycenae and Crete. They settled in five towns, Ashdod, Askelon, Ekron, Gaza and Gath. They fought the Israelites from the time of the Judges, Judg. 3.31; 5.6; until the time of the Exile. In Samuel's lifetime Israel was defeated at the Battle of Ebenezer, Shiloh destroyed and the Ark of the Covenant captured, 1 Sam. 4.1–7.1; Jer. 7.12–14. Saul fought against the Philistines throughout his reign, 1 Sam. 14.47–52, and was victorious at the Battle of Michmash, 1 Sam. 13.2–14.30; David defeated Goliath the Philistine, and the Philistines killed Saul, 1 Sam. 17.1–4; 31.1–13. David defeated them, 2 Sam. 5.17–8.1; 21.18–22; but war continued until Uzziah's reign, when the Philistines were defeated by the Assyrians, 2 Chron. 26.6–7; 28.18; Isa. 9.12; 20.1; they were deported by Nebuchadnezzar II in 604 BC, Jer. 25.20

**Philosophers, Philosophy** (*G* = love of knowledge) in Classical Greece philosophy meant rational, logical thought, including morality and religion; Paul quoted approvingly from philosophers, Acts 17.18, 28; see 'Epicureans', 'Stoics'; but condemned the heresy which some Christians in Colossae called a philosophy, Col. 2.8

**Phinehas** (*H* = Nubian) **1.** High priest, grandson of Aaron, Ex. 6.25, Josh. 24.33; reconciled the tribes of Reuben and Gad with the other ten tribes, Josh. 22.10–34; joined in battle against the Midianites, Num. 31.6; gave the order to fight, Judg. 20.28; killed Zimri, Num. 25. **2.** A bad priest, see 'Hophni'

**Phoebe** (*G* = radiant) (FEE-bee), she was deacon of the church at Cenchreae, the port of Corinth; praised and commended by Paul to the church in Rome; presumably the bearer of the letter, Rom. 16.1–2

**Phoenicia** (fuh-NEE-shah) the eastern Mediterranean coastal region, inhabited by *ponnim* or Phoenicians, a Semitic people, with capitals in Tyre and Sidon, Obad.

1.20; 2 Macc. 3.5; 1 Esd. 2.17; Acts 11.19; 15.3; 21.2. They travelled widely by sea; the Phoenician community in Carthage in North Africa spoke a dialect called 'Punic'

**Phoenix** or **Phenice** (FEE-nicks) port on the south coast of Crete, Acts 27.12. The sailors carrying Paul as a prisoner to Rome tried to sail to Phoenix, but were blown off course by a gale. On Cape Mouros there are traces of an ancient town, with the resort of Loutro in a bay on the east side, and a chapel called Phoinika in another bay on the west

**Phrygia** (FRIDG-ya) kingdom with its capital at Gordion, where Alexander the Great cut the Gordion knot; the remains are at Yassıhöyük, 66 miles west of Ankara. Phrygian kings were called either Gordio or Midas. By Roman times it was a region spanning the border between the Provinces of Asia and Galatia. People from Phrygia were present at Pentecost, Acts 2.10; Paul passed through on his second and third missionary journeys, Acts 16.6; 18.23

**Phylacteries** (*H tefillin*) two small leather boxes, containing parchments with Ex. 13.1–10, 11–16; Deut. 6.4–9; and 11.13–21 inscribed on them, which devout Jews tie with leather straps to their forehead and left arm, fulfilling the commandment in Deut. 6.4–9 to bind the words of the law 'as a sign on your hand and as a frontlet on your forehead'. In Jesus's day most people only wore them during prayers, but the extra-pious wore them all day, and enlarged them to hold more Scripture passages, Matt. 23.5

**Physicians** who could prescribe herbal medicines and set fractures, were in great demand, Job 13.4; Jer. 8.22; Mark 5.26; Luke 8.43. Jesus was taunted with a proverb, 'Physician, heal yourself', Luke 4.23; but warned that his ministry was among the sinners who knew they needed it, 'Those who are sick need the physician, not those who are well', Matt. 9.12; Mark 2.17; Luke 5.31. Luke is called 'the beloved physician', Col. 4.14

**Pierced** 'they shall look on one whom they have pierced', describing Jesus on the cross in John 19.37; Rev. 1.7; quotes Zech. 12.10. The Greek translation of Ps. 22.16 reads 'they have pierced my hands and my feet'

**Pilate** (*L* = armed with a javelin) Roman Governor of Judea AD 26–36, Luke 3.1, who sentenced Jesus to death. An inscription found at Caesarea-Maritima, his headquarters, commemorates 'Pontius Pilatus, prefect of Judaea'. Contemporary writers describe him as cruel and corrupt, deliberately offending the Jews by using standards surmounted by eagles, which they regarded as idols, and using money given to the Temple to finance an aqueduct, remains of which can still be seen south of Jerusalem. He killed some Galileans at the very moment they were offering sacrifice, Luke 13.1. The Gospels, trying to smooth relations between Christians and the Empire, present him as fair but weak, and shift the blame for the death of Jesus onto the high priests, Matt. 27; Mark 15; Luke 23; John 18.28–19.38. He was deposed by the Legate of Syria and recalled to Rome when he massacred the Samaritans, and disappears from history.

**Pinnacle of the Temple** where the Devil took Jesus and tempted him to leap off, Matt. 4.5; Luke 4.9. The south-east corner of the outer court, where the ground drops steeply into the Kidron Valley, and the Herodian walls are still high, is the most likely place

**Pisgah** mountain in the Abarim range east of the River Jordan, where Balaam prophesied about Israel, Num. 23.14; and where Moses was allowed to view the Promised Land which he would never enter, Deut. 3.27; 34.1. It is identified with Ras es-Siyaghah, just north of Jebel en-Neba or Mount Nebo

**Pishon** one of the four rivers of Eden, Gen. 2.11; it could be the Indus, the Ganges, or a tributary of the Euphrates

**Pisidia** region in Galatia, north of the Taurus Mountains, see 'Antioch 2.'

**Pithom** see 'Rameses'

**Plagues** suffering of many forms, including epidemic illness; only in 1 Sam. 5–6, where rats and swellings are mentioned, can it be identified as bubonic plague. Ps. 78 lists seven; Ps. 105 lists eight plagues in Egypt; in Ex. 7–12 there are ten: blood; frogs; gnats; flies; cattle-disease; boils; hail; locusts; darkness; and the death of the firstborn. The story teaches the uniqueness of YHWH, Ex. 8.10; and the distinctiveness of Israel, 11.7

**Plain, Cities of the** Sodom, Gomorrah, Admah, Zeboiim, and Bela (or Zoar), Gen. 13.12; 14.1–10; 19.24–29; Deut. 29.23; Hos. 11.8, see also 'Siddim'

**Pleiades** see 'Orion'

**Plough** (USA Plow) simple wooden agricultural implement in Bible times, pulled by a yoke of oxen or other animals, who needed a man to direct them, and to bear down with his hand to keep the pointed ploughshare digging below the surface. The share was at first made of wood, then bronze, then iron; it needed frequent sharpening, 1 Sam. 13.19–22. It was possible to beat swords into ploughshares in times of peace, Isa. 2.4; Micah 4.3; contrast Joel 3.10. Jesus warned against lack of commitment, when he said that 'No man setting his hand to the plough and then looking back is fit for the kingdom of God', Luke 9.62

**Plumbline** or **Plummet** piece of lead on the end of a string, used for judging whether a wall is vertical, or testing the depth of water; an image of God testing and judging, Isa. 28.17; 34.11; Amos 7.7–9

**Pods** see 'Husks'

**Poetry** in Hebrew marked not by rhyme or scansion but parallelism. Two lines, each usually with three stressed syllables in each, will either say the same thing twice in different words, or, less frequently, will be a contrast of opposites. Three stresses followed by two is the metre for a lament. Sometimes there is a play on words: in Isa. 5.7 the word for 'justice' sounds like the word for 'bloodshed'; the word for 'righteousness' is like that for 'a cry'

**Politarchs** (G = rulers of the city) leaders in Thessalonica, Acts 17.6; this word was otherwise unknown until it was found inscribed on an arch from that city

**Pomegranate** evergreen tree with orange / scarlet-coloured flowers, S. of Sol. 7.12; and fruit like apples but full of pink seeds. The spies brought pomegranates among the evidence of the fruitfulness of the Promised Land, Num. 13.23. Images of pomegranate fruits were used as a decoration of the priests' robes, Ex. 28.33–34; and the Temple, 1 Kings 7.18–20

**Pontus** region on the southern shore of the *Pontus Euxinus* or Black Sea, in northeastern Asia Minor, part of the Province of Bithynia and Pontus. People from Pontus were present in Jerusalem at Pentecost, Acts 2.9; Paul's friend Aquila was a native of Pontus, 18.2. In 1 Peter 1.1–2 they are among the recipients of the letter

**Poor** those who were faithful to their religion remained poor, the unscrupulous became rich. Amos 2.6–7; 4.1; and 5.11 condemn those who oppress the poor; Ps. 41.1 praises those who help them. Jesus declared the poor to be blessed, Luke 6.20; and in Matt. 5.6, the 'poor in spirit' are those who have the same faithful spirit as the virtuous poor. James said the poor were not to be despised, James 2. Paul had to take up a collection for the poor Christians in Jerusalem, Gal. 2.10; Rom. 15.26

**Potiphar** (short for Potiphera, *Eg* = given by Ra, the sun-god) Joseph's employer, until Potiphar's wife tried to seduce Joseph, Gen. 37.36; 39.1–20

**Potsherd** (POT-shurd) shard or fragment of broken pottery, which Job scraped himself with, Job 2.18; gave its name to a gate in Jerusalem, Jer. 19.2; metaphor for dryness in the mouth, Ps. 22.15

**Pottage** see 'Mess of pottage'

**Potter** maker of clay pots by turning them on a wheel; metaphor for God's power over his creation, Ps. 2.9; Isa. 64.8; Jer. 18.2–11; Rom. 9.21

**Pounds** parable, Luke 19.12–27, and see 'Money'

**Power 1.** 'Powers that be', the authorities of the state, which must be obeyed, to avoid giving Christianity a reputation as a revolutionary organization, Rom. 13.1–7; Titus 3.1; 1 Peter 2.13–14. **2.** Heavenly powers, possibly heavenly representatives of earthly kingdoms, Matt. 24.29; Eph. 3.10; see 'Angels'. **3.** The power of God, Ps. 62.11; Matt. 24.30; Acts 1.8; Rev. 5.12

**Praetorium 1.** Where Pilate tried Jesus, and the soldiers mocked him, Mark 15.16; John 18.28; now believed to be Herod the Great's palace, where Pilate stayed when visiting Jerusalem, of which three towers remain standing, at the Citadel by the present Jaffa Gate. **2.** Herod's Palace in Caesarea-Maritima where Paul was detained; excavations near the theatre have shown its size, Acts 23.35. **3.** Soldiers guarding the Emperor, who heard about Jesus through Paul, their prisoner, Phil. 1.13

**Prayer** and **Praise** examples: **1.** Spontaneous exclamations, Acts 7.59–60. **2.** Conversations with God, Gen. 15.1–8. **3.** Personal prayer, Jer. 11.18–23; 12.1–6; Acts 10.2, 30. **4.** Public prayer, 2 Chron. 6.12–42. **5.** Poetic and ritual prayer and praise, Ps. 100.4. **6.** Thanksgiving, Phil. 4.6. **7.** Prayer for others, 1 Tim. 2.1. **8.** The Prayers of Jesus, Matt. 26.36–44; 27.46; Luke 6.12; 23.34, 46; John 17. **9.** Teaching on prayer, Matt. 6.5–13; Luke 11.1–13. **10.** The Lord's Prayer, Matt. 6.9–13; Luke 11.2–4. **11.** Exhortations to pray, Matt. 7.7–11, 1 Thess. 5.17

**Preaching** the Greek nouns for proclamation, *euangelion* and *kerygma*, apply to a herald who brings the good news of a victory and proclaims it to the bystanders. 'The messenger who announces peace, who brings good news', Isa. 52.7, was a model for the Christian evangelist, who heralded what God has done for us in Christ. *Kerygma* is apostolic proclamation of what God has done for us; *didache* is the teaching which was given to those who had been converted, instructing them how to live. Paul's letters contain *kerygma*, linked by the word 'therefore' to the *didache* which follows. See Matt. 4.17; Acts 5.42; Rom. 10.14–15; 1 Cor. 1.23; 9.16

**Predestination** the belief that God has decided beforehand what will happen, based on Rom. 8.29–30; Eph. 1.5. God created time and is 'outside' time, so he knows eternally things which to us, who live within time, seem not to have happened yet, Ecclus. (Ben Sira) 23.19–20. But to say that God causes everything to happen contradicts the doctrine of free will, and the feeling that we can make choices, Josh. 24.15. Jesus said 'You did not choose me, but I chose you', John 15.16; so the doctrine of 'election' (from *L elego* = choose) means we cannot claim any credit for being part of God's people. Few, however, believe in the opposite doctrine of 'reprobation', meaning that God has predestined some people to a punishment which they cannot avoid. God's chosen people are chosen for service, not for privilege, John 15.16

**Preparation** the day before the sabbath, on which Jesus was crucified according to Matt. 27.62; Mark 15.42; Luke 23.54. He was crucified on 'the day of Preparation for the Passover' according to John 19.14; many have understood this as the day before the day of Passover, but it is best interpreted as the day before the sabbath in Passover week

**Presence of God**  God is everywhere present, but in some places we are specially aware of his presence. Jacob became aware of the presence of the LORD in Bethel, Gen. 28.16, and a sanctuary was erected there. The Tent of Meeting and the Ark of the Covenant were places symbolizing God's presence, Ex. 25.10–30; 40.34–38. The Temple became the centre of God's presence, though Jeremiah warned against taking it for granted, 7.1–4. The Hebrew term for God's presence was his 'face'; to appear before him was to go before his face, Ps. 27.8; Adam and Eve hid from his face, Gen. 3.8; if he was displeased, God could withdraw his face, Ps. 27.9; but in his presence is the fullness of joy, Ps. 16.11. In John 1 the Word was God, and Jesus, the Word made flesh, came to put a face on God; God was in Christ reconciling the world to himself, 2 Cor. 5.19; Col. 1.15–20. See also 'Bread of the Presence', 'Parousia'

**Priest 1.**  Aaron and his descendants were priests, serving God in the Tabernacle and then the Jerusalem Temple; we have a full description of their robes and duties in Exodus to Deuteronomy, though these may have been edited at a later date, and describe aspects as being there from the beginning, which only evolved later, see Sources, p. **134**. **2.** The High Priests played an important role in the political life of the nation after the end of the monarchy, see 'Caiaphas', 1 & 2 Maccabees, p. **147**. **3.** By mediating between God and the human race, Jesus performs the function of a priest, Heb. 2.17, see 'Melchizedek'. **4.** Individual Christians are called elders (*G presbyteroi*) in the New Testament but not priests; all Christians share in Christ's task of mediation, and are called a kingdom of priests, 1 Peter 2.5; Rev. 1.6; 5.10; 20.6

**Prince 1.**  Another word for king, Ezek. 7.27. Tired of war, the Jews looked forward to a leader who would bring them peace, Isa. 9.6; Jesus by choosing a donkey rather than a war-horse to enter Jerusalem was claiming the title of Prince of Peace, Matt. 21.1–11. **2.** Daniel looks forward to an anointed prince who is to come, 9.25–26. **3.** Prince or ruler of the devils, Beelzebul, whose power Jesus is accused of using to drive out demons, Matt. 9.34; 10.25; 12.24, 27; Mark 3.22; Luke 11.15–19. **4.** Prince, or ruler, of this world, name for the Devil, John 12.31; 14.30; 16.11. **5.** Prince of the Power of the Air, name for the Devil, Eph. 2.2

**Principalities and powers**  spiritual beings, mostly malignant. From the Persian belief that every kingdom has its heavenly representative, the book of Daniel pictures each of the kingdoms known to the author as a different beast, which gives evil power to the kingdom it represents, and shows Michael, the heavenly representative of Israel, defeating them all, Dan. 7–12. Those to whom Paul wrote, suffering under bad rulers, blamed it on evil heavenly powers. He did not argue with these beliefs, but insisted that Christ had conquered every power, since Christ is seated at God's right hand, 1 Cor. 15.24; Eph. 2.1–7; 6.10–17; Col. 1.15–20; 2.8–15

**Priscilla**  diminutive of Prisca (*L* = ancient, 2 Tim. 4.19), see 'Aquila'

**Prisoner**  Joseph, Gen. 39.20–41.14; Samson, Judg. 16.21; Jeremiah, Jer. 37.15–18; John the Baptist, Matt. 11.2; 14.3–10; the apostles, Acts 5.18–25; Peter, Acts 12.3–17; Paul and Silas in Philippi, Acts 16.23–40; Paul in Caesarea, Acts 24.27; 25.14; Promise of release, Isa. 42.7; 61.1; Luke 4.18; Duty to visit, Matt. 25.36–44; Heb. 10.34; 13.3; Christ visited the spirits in prison, 1 Pet. 3.19, see 'Descent into hell', Captivity Epistles, p. **154**

**Prochorus**  (*H* = leader of the chorus) one of The Seven chosen to care for Greek-speaking widows in Acts 6.5; see Revelation p. **159**

**Proconsul** Roman official who has already served a term as a consul in Rome, and is sent for a one-year tour to administer a Province, see also 'Gallio', 'Sergius Paulus'

**Prodigal Son** parable told by Jesus, to teach that God is our Father, eager to forgive and be reconciled; also that 'virtuous' people need not be jealous of outcasts who are welcomed back, Luke 15.11–32

**Prophets** see also p. **141**. John the Baptist and Jesus are both described as prophets, Matt. 11.9; 14.5; and references to Agabus and others in Acts show the gift never died out, Acts 21.9–10. When prophecy is included among the gifts of the Spirit, 1 Cor. 12.10; we should perhaps think of inspired preaching, including comment on God's attitude towards the life of the nation in our own time

**Proselytes** (PROSS-uh-lights) those who have changed their religion. Some Jews were eager to welcome and convert the Gentiles, Isa. 44.5; Tob. 1.8; Matt. 23.15. Converts were divided into Proselytes of the Altar, who were circumcised and kept the complete Jewish law, Acts 6.5; 13.43; and Proselytes of the Porch, who kept the moral law but could not keep the ceremonial law, see 'God-fearers'. Proselytes were present at Pentecost, Acts 2.10

**Prostitutes** the Israelites were forbidden to allow their daughters to sell sexual intercourse for money, Lev. 19.29; or to marry prostitutes, Lev. 21.7, 14; but harlots were a normal part of society, Judg. 11.1; 16.1. Solomon judged between two prostitutes, 1 Kings 3.16–28; Rahab of Jericho was praised, Josh. 2.1–3; 6.17–25; Heb. 11.31; James 2.25. To have sex with a temple prostitute was considered by sympathetic magic to ensure the fertility of the crops, the herds and one's family. The excesses of these religions were abhorrent to the Jews, Gen. 38.15, 21–22; Ex. 34.14–16; Lev. 17.7; 19.29; Deut. 23.17; Hos. 4.14. Prostitution therefore became a metaphor for idolatry, Deut. 31.16; Jer. 5.7; Hos. 4.14; 9.1. Paul forbade Christian men to use prostitutes, 1 Cor. 6.15–16. Prostitutes were usually either women who had been sold as slaves, or who had been widowed or divorced and left with no other means of supporting themselves; Jesus was sympathetic to prostitutes, and said they would enter the kingdom before respectable people, Matt. 21.31; Luke 7.37–50

**Proverbs** (Prov.) The Book of Proverbs, see p. **140**

**Province** areas into which the Roman Empire was divided; most were ruled indefinitely by a legate responsible to the Emperor; Achaea, Asia and Cyprus were controlled by the Senate, who appointed a former consul or praetor for one year as proconsul; mountainous provinces like Judea and Thrace were under a procurator responsible to the legate of the nearest lowland province

**Psalm 151** following Psalm 150 in the Greek Bible, see p. **148**

**Psalms** (Ps.) The Psalms (pronounced sarmz, though in some places the a is shortened), see p. **140**

**Pseudepigrapha** (SYUE-duh-PIG-ruh-fuh) (*G* = falsely ascribed writings) comprehensive term describing many Jewish documents dating roughly from 200 BC to AD 200, not included in the canon of Hebrew Scriptures nor the Apocrypha or Deuterocanonical Books, see pp. **161–4**

**Ptolemais** (TOLL-uh-MAY-iss) see 'Akko'

**Publicans** (*L publicani*) tax-collectors, so called because they worked for the public service. (To call the host of a 'public house' a publican was a nineteenth-century joke)

**Publius** (*L* = popular) the Roman governor or 'First Man' of Malta, who cared for Paul when he was shipwrecked, Acts 28.7–10; the villa excavated at San Pawl Milqi may have been on lands he owned; the Grotto of St Paul in Rabat is alleged to be on the site of his town-house

**Pudens** (PYUE-denz) (*L* = modest) Christian in Rome who sent greetings to Timothy, 2 Tim. 4.21; he may be the Senator Pudens, the site of whose house was given to the church in AD 145 by his son, where the ancient Church of Santa Pudenziana now stands in the Via Urbana

**Pul** see 'Tiglath-Pileser III'

**Purification** ceremonies removing a wide range of barriers which disqualified people from joining in public worship, Lev. 13–16; Num. 19; 31.19–20; Acts 21.24; Heb. 9.13. The Purification of Women after Childbirth is a misleading name for the ceremony marking the point at which it was considered there was no longer risk of the mother suffering an infection, Lev. 12; Luke 2.22

**Purim** Jewish celebration of great jollity; its origins are told in the book of Esther, which is read on that day, Esth. 9.26; 2 Macc. 15.36, see also 'Calendar'

**Purple** juice of murex shells, gathered in Tyre, and expensive cloth dyed with it, Ex. 25.4. Jesus told a story of a rich man 'dressed in purple and fine linen', Luke 16.19; was wrapped in a soldier's purple cloak before the crucifixion, Mark 15.17. Emperor Nero tried unsuccessfully to restrict its use to the Imperial household; Lydia, the leader of the church in Philippi, was head of a large international trading company dealing in purple-cloth; Acts 16.11; she came from Thyatira where there was a guild of purple-dyers, though possibly there they used the madder root

**Puteoli** port in the Bay of Naples, where Paul landed on his way to Rome, and stayed seven days with the believers there, Acts 28.12. Now called Pozzuoli, it contains remains of the macellum or marketplace, the Amphitheatre of Augustus and the Temple of Augustus, all dating from Paul's time

**Q** source used by the Gospels of Matthew and Luke, see p. 149

**Qoheleth** (KOH-hell-ett, *H* = preacher) Hebrew name for the book called Ecclesiastes, see p. 140

**Quail** bird like a small pheasant, given to feed the hungry Israelites in the wilderness, Ex. 16.12–13; Num. 11.31–32; Ps. 78.27–29; 105.40. Until the 1930s they crossed the Mediterranean in large numbers on their annual migration, and, falling exhausted, were eaten by Bedouin

**Queen 1.** The wife or widow of a king, e.g. Ps. 45.9; Isa. 49.23. **2.** Female monarch, e.g. the Queen of Sheba, 1 Kings 10.1–13; 2 Chron. 9.1–12; Matt. 12.42; Luke 11.31, see 'Saba'. **3.** The Queen of Heaven, a fertility goddess, probably the Canaanite Astarte and the Mesopotamian Ishtar, Jer. 7.16–20; 44.17–25

**Quirinius** (kw-eye-RINN-ee-us) Publius Sulpicius Quirinius was legate or governor of Judea following the removal of Archelaus in AD 6, until his death in 21. Josephus reports that he conducted a census of Judea for tax purposes; this is confirmed by an inscription discovered at Aleppo; probably this is the census which caused an insurrection, Acts 5.37. Luke makes a census the reason for Jesus's parents' journey to Bethlehem, Luke 2.1–7, but Jesus was born in the lifetime of Herod the Great, Luke 1.5, who died in 4 BC. It is just possible that Quirinius supervised a census while he was in the east as a military commander, 10–7 BC, so either we must translate Luke 2.2 as 'this was the Census Quirinius took before he was Governor', or 'this was the census *before* that of Quirinius', or admit that, having no books of reference to consult, Luke got this historical detail wrong

**Qumran** (koom-RAHN) see Dead Sea Scrolls, p. 162

**Rabbah** or **Rabbath-Ammon** capital city of the Ammonites, now Amman in Jordan. The iron bed of Og, king of Bashan, could be seen there, Deut. 3.11. The royal city stood on a hill, and the 'city of waters' in the valley below, 2 Sam. 12.26–27. David captured the city and crowned himself in it, 12.30. It later supplied David with food and equipment, 17.27–29. King Ptolemy II Philadelphus (285–246 BC) renamed it Philadelphia; it was one of the towns of the Decapolis

**Rabbi** (*H* = my master) Jewish term of address for a teacher, equivalent to Master; used when speaking to Jesus, Matt. 25.26; Mark 9.5; John 1.38 (where its meaning is explained as Teacher). Jesus criticizes those who boast of the title, Matt. 23.7–12. Only after AD 70 was it restricted to officially ordained teachers

**Rabbouni** or **Rabboni** (*H* = my master) used instead of rabbi by Bartimaeus, Mark 10.51; and Mary Magdalene, John 20.16; maybe a dialect form

**Rabshakeh** (*Ak* = chief cupbearer) senior Assyrian official, 2 Kings 18.17–19.8; similar terms are **Rabsaris** (*Ak* = chief eunuch) 2 Kings 18.17; Jer. 39.3, 13; and **Rabmag** (meaning unknown) Jer. 39.3, 13

**Raca** an insult, probably an Aramaic word meaning 'stupid fool', Matt. 5.22; detailed interpretation of the verse is obscure, but the meaning is plain: anger is the cause of murder, and being verbally insulting to anyone is as bad in God's eyes as physically attacking them, because both have sinful uncontrolled rage as their motive

**Racing** see 'Games'

**Rachel** (*H* = ewe) daughter of Laban, younger sister of Leah. Jacob loved her and worked seven years for the right to marry her, then, when he was tricked, another seven years after that, Gen. 28–31; 35; she became the mother of Joseph and Benjamin, but died in childbirth; for the location of her tomb see 'Ephrathah'

**Rages** (RAH-geez) town in the hills above Ecbatana in Media, where Tobit hid 10 talents of silver, Tob. 4.1; 5.6; Judith 1.5; the ruins are south of modern Teheran

**Rahab** (*H* = wide) **1.** Sea-monster defeated by YHWH, out of which he created the world, Job 9.13; 26.12; Ps. 89.10; Isa. 51.9. **2.** Symbolic name for Egypt, Ps. 87.4; Isa. 30.7. **3.** Prostitute in Jericho, praised for hiding the Israelite spies, see 'Prostitutes'. **4.** Mother of Boaz, mentioned only in Matt. 1.5

**Rainbow 1.** Arc of colours formed in the sky by refraction of sunlight through raindrops. To Noah, God said that it was his battle-bow, hung up in the sky to show that he has disarmed, and will never destroy the human race, even though they deserve it; the rainbow is the sign of that promise, Gen. 9.8–17; Ps. 7.12; 18.7–15; Lam. 2.4; Hab. 3.9–11. **2.** A rainbow around the throne of God symbolizes his glorious majesty, Ezek. 1.28; Ecclus. (Ben Sira) 43.11–12; Rev. 4.3; 10.1

**Ramah** (*H* = height) **1.** Modern er-Ram, 5 miles north of Jerusalem, Josh. 18.25. Deborah decided disputes nearby, Judg. 4.5; Baasha, king of Israel, captured it; Asa of Judah got it back when Ben-hadad attacked Israel, 1 Kings 15.16–22; 2 Chron. 16.1–6; it was attacked, probably by Assyria, and its inhabitants deported to Babylon; Jeremiah represents Rachel weeping for her 'children', the exiled Benjaminites of Ramah, Jer. 31.15; Isa. 10.29; Hos. 5.8. **2.** Ramah of the Negeb, Josh. 19.8; 1 Sam. 30.27; unidentified. **3.** Town near Tyre, modern Ramieh, Josh. 19.29. **4.** Town in Napthali, Khirbat Zeitun er-Rameh, 8 miles south-west of Safed, Josh. 19.36. **5.** Ramathaim-Zophim (*H* = two heights of the Zuphites) in Ephraim, identified with Arimathea, 1 Sam. 1.1. **6.** Hometown of Samuel, probably either 1. or 4. above, 1 Sam. 1.19–20; 2.11; 7.17; 25.1. **7.** Short for Ramoth-Gilead, see below

**Rameses** or **Raamses** and **Pithom** area in Egypt where the Israelites settled, and built two of the store-cities for Pharaoh, Gen. 47.11; Ex. 1.11. From here they started the Exodus, Ex. 12.37; Num. 33.3, 5. Rameses II (1290–1224 BC), of the nineteenth dynasty, whom some identify with the Pharaoh of the Exodus, moved his capital north from Thebes to the delta town which was called Rameses in his honour. This was on the site of the modern Qantir or Khatana, 9 miles north of Fagus; Pithom was south of here in the Wadi Tumilat

**Ramoth-Gilead**  (*H* = heights of Gilead) city of refuge in Gad, which was captured by Ben-hadad, king of Syria, and fought over for many years, Deut. 4.43; 1 Kings 22.3–37; 2 Kings 9.1–10; its site is possibly Tell er-Ramith 4 miles south of Ramtha

**Ransom**  price paid to set a captive free; the Hebrew word is connected with 'to cover', used for atonement, Ex. 21.30; Num. 35.31–32; Ps. 49.7–8; Isa. 43.3. Jesus said he had come 'to give his life as a ransom for many', showing that he saw his death as a sacrifice in fulfilment of Isa. 53, to set us free from captivity to our sins, Matt. 20.28; Mark 10.45. Asking to whom it is paid would be pushing the metaphor too far

**Raphael**  (*H* = God heals) see 'Angel 4.'

**Rapture**  (*L raptio* = to catch up) term used of the last times, 'then we who are alive, who are left, will be caught up in the clouds together with them to meet the Lord in the air', 1 Thess. 4.17. Compare 2 Thess. 2.1–2. Some Christian denominations take this literally; most regard the language as metaphorical, see Apocalyptic, p. **175**

**Ras Shamra**  see 'Ugarit'

**Raven**  large black bird. Noah sent a raven to find dry land, Gen. 8.7; Elijah was fed by ravens, 1 Kings 17.4–6; Jesus pointed to them as examples of God's providence, Luke 12.24, referring to Job 38.41

**Rebekah**  (*H* = cattle) grand-daughter of Abraham's brother Nahor; helped Abraham's servant to water his camels at the well; chosen to be the wife of Abraham's son Isaac; mother of Jacob and Esau, Gen. 22.23; 24.11–67; 25.19–27; 27.5–46; 49.31. Spelt Rebecca in Rom. 9.10

**Rechabites**  descendants of Jonadab son of Rechab, 2 Kings 10.15–17, praised for keeping his commandment to abstain from alcohol, and an example to the people of Judah, who have disobeyed the commandments of the Lord, Jer. 35

**Reclining**  from Roman times, was how free people attended a feast. Three tables arranged in a U-shape, with couches so that the guests could lie with their heads near the table, formed a *triclinium*; a woman standing behind him could anoint Jesus's feet, which were raised off the floor on the couch, Luke 7.38; John 12.3. Diners supporting themselves on their left elbow, dipped the food in the dish with their right hand, John 13.26–27. At the Last Supper Judas would have reclined on Jesus's left and dipped into the same dish, Matt. 26.23. The Beloved Disciple, on Jesus's right, would have had to lean back almost into Jesus's bosom to speak to him, John 13.23–25. 'In Abraham's bosom' means in the place of honour on his right at the heavenly banquet, Luke 16.23. Jesus criticized those who took the places of honour nearest the host, Luke 14.7

**Reconciliation**  making two people who are enemies into friends again. 'God was in Christ reconciling the world to himself', 2 Cor. 5.19; God 'reconciled us to himself through Christ, and has given us the ministry of reconciliation', 2 Cor. 5.18. Christians, having accepted God's friendship, are to make our enemies our friends; to make those who are estranged friends with each other; and to make everyone friends of God, Matt. 5.24; Acts 7.26; Rom. 5; 11.15; Eph. 2.16; Col. 1.20–22

**Red Sea**  in modern terminology is the large gulf stretching south from the Sinai

Peninsula and separating Africa from Arabia, but it is never mentioned by name in the Bible. During the Exodus, when a strong wind blew the waters back, the Israelites crossed the 'Sea of Reeds': Lake Manzala on the Mediterranean coast near Port Said; the Bitter Lakes north of Suez; the Gulf of Suez; or the Gulf of Aqaba have been suggested, Ex. 10.19; 13.18; 15.4, 22; Ps. 136.13, 15. The Septuagint translated this into Greek as 'Red Sea', and other translations copied it

**Redemption** setting someone or something free from legal obligations, through a payment or ransom. The firstborn of donkeys and humans could be bought back from God, to whom they had been dedicated, Ex. 13.13; property could be bought back by the next-of-kin, when it had passed out of the family, Lev. 25.25–34; Ruth 4.1–12; and the next-of-kin was also obliged to pay to free a relative who became a prisoner or slave, Lev. 25.48–52; Job calls God his next-of-kin, saying, 'I know that my Redeemer lives', Job 19.25. God their Redeemer sets the Israelite slaves free from Egypt, Ex. 6.6; from famine and war, Job 5.20; from oppression and violence, Ps. 72.14; from enemies, Ps. 69.18; Jer. 15.21; from death, Ps. 49.15; Hos. 13.14; and from sin, Ps.130.7–8. When a slave's owner would set them free as a reward for faithful service, it was called manumission. Slaves could often save money, but could not legally own property, so could not buy their own freedom. They donated the money to a god, who then bought them from the slave-owner and set them free. Many Christian converts were slaves or ex-slaves, and understood that Jesus sets us free from slavery to sin and death, Luke 21.28; Rom. 8.23; Gal. 4.5; Eph. 1.7; Col. 1.14

**Reed 1.** Baby Moses was placed in a basket made of papyrus reeds, Ex. 2.3–5. **2.** Reeds bend with the wind and spring upright again, but John the Baptist was unyielding, Matt. 11.7. **3.** God will not break a bruised reed but allows emotionally damaged people to return to health, Matt. 12.20 quoting Isa. 42.3. **4.** The Rabshakeh of Assyria compared Egypt to a broken reed, which will pierce the hand of anyone who leans on it, 2 Kings 18.21. **5.** Mockers gave Jesus a reed to hold, because it resembles the rod or sceptre held by a king, Matt. 27.29–30. **6.** See 'Measures of length'

**Refining** process of heating metals in a furnace; 'noble metals', gold and silver, can be separated out from other minerals which are oxidized and skimmed off as 'dross'. An image of God testing his people in the furnace of adversity to see which are worthy, Prov. 17.3; 27.21; Jer. 6.27; 9.7; Zech. 13.9; Mal. 3.2–3; Wisd. 3.6; Ecclus. (Ben Sira) 2.5

**Refuge, cities of** places to which those who had killed a man could flee to escape the revenge of his relations, Josh. 20.7–9

**Rehoboam** (*H Rehav'am* = increase of people) son of Solomon; his severity provoked the rebellion of the northern tribes; he became the first king of the divided southern kingdom of Judah 931–913 BC, 1 Kings 11.43

**Reins** old word for 'Kidneys'

**Religion** (*L religare* = to bind) the principle which binds together the parts of one's life, and binds one to God. The Jewish religion, 1 Macc. 2.19; Acts 26.5. The Athenians praised for being religious, Acts 17.22. Pure religion is care for the needy, James 1.27

**Remaliah** father of King Pekah of Israel, 2 Kings 15.25; Isa. 7.1; Pekah is just called 'the son of Remaliah' in Isa. 7.4–5, 9; 8.6

**Remembrance** Jesus commanded us to break bread in remembrance of him; that we should remember how much he loves us, and to remind God that we depend on his sacrifice, 1 Cor. 11.24

**Remnant** It is promised that a small part of the people of Israel will survive calamity and return to their God; in spite of apostasy by the many, God's plan will be fulfilled through the faithful remnant, Isa. 10.21–22; 11.11–16; 37.4; Zeph. 3.12–13; Rom. 9.27, see also '*Shear-jashub*'

**Repentance** may include remorse for past sins, but is essentially a new attitude (*G metanoia* = change of mind). The Jewish general Josephus, urging his colleagues to stop relying on themselves and to trust him, said 'Repent and believe'; just what Jesus proclaimed in Mark 1.15. See also Job 42.6; Ezek. 14.6; 18.30–32; Mark 1.4, Acts 2.38

**Rephaim 1.** Race of giants, with King Og as the last, Deut. 2.11; 2.20; 3.11. **2.** Tribe associated with the Perizzites, Gen. 15.20; Josh. 17.15. **3.** Valley near Hinnom, Josh. 15.8; 18.16. **4.** Valley where the Philistines assembled, 2 Sam. 5.18; 23.13

**Rephidim** place on Mount Horeb where Moses struck water from the rock, Ex. 17.1–6, see 'Meribah'. Israel defeated Amalek at Rephidim while Aaron and Hur hold up Moses' hands, and Jethro advised delegation of judicial tasks, Ex. 17.8–18.27. Wadi Feiran and Wadi Refayid, near Jebel Musa in the Sinai peninsula; or Wadi Musa near Jebel Haroun in Jordan have been suggested, see also 'Horeb', 'Sinai'

**Resurrection** raising a dead person to life. After death we enter a ghostly life in a shadowy realm, according to the Hebrew Scriptures, see 'Hell 1.'. God will restore the life of the nation after its 'death' in defeat and exile, Ezek. 37 (the Valley of Dry Bones). Belief in individual resuscitation emerged later, Dan. 12.2. Belief in a return to a physical body on earth was held by the Pharisees, and rejected by the Sadducees, Matt. 22.23. Jesus raised Jairus' daughter, Matt. 9.18; the widow's son, Luke 7.11–17; and Lazarus to physical life, promising that those who believe in him, though they die, will live, John 11.25, 44. He predicted that he himself would rise on the third day in fulfilment of prophecy, Matt. 16.21; Mark 8.31; Luke 9.22; Job 19.26; Ps. 17.15; Isa. 26.19; Hos. 6.1–2. The Resurrection of Jesus is the core of New Testament faith, Rom. 1.3–4; 1 Cor. 15.12–15, with the empty tomb as its symbol, Matt. 28.1–10; Mark 16.1–8; Luke 24.1–11; John 20.1–10; the proof lies in his appearances, Luke 24.13–49; John 20.19–21.23; 1 Cor. 15.5–8. He could appear and disappear at will behind closed doors, John 20.19, and forbade Mary Magdalene to touch him, John 20.17; yet he ate fish and commanded the disciples to touch him, to prove that, unlike a ghost, he had flesh and bones, Luke 24.39–43. The life of believers is changed, Col. 2.12; 3.1. Paul rejected Greek belief in the ghostly immortality of the soul (Wisd. 1–6), Acts 17.31–32, and also rejected Jewish belief in the resuscitation of the corpse ('flesh and blood cannot inherit the kingdom of God', 1 Cor. 15.50). He invented a new term, 'spiritual body', suggesting life emerging from our earthly personality as a plant grows out of a seed; not a physical life, but one when we can, even more gloriously, recognize each other, communicate, and praise God, 1 Cor. 15.35–58

**Reuben** (*H* = behold a son) firstborn son of Jacob, Gen. 29.31–30.22; tried to support Joseph, Gen. 37–50; ancestor of one of the twelve tribes, Gen. 49; Deut. 33

**Reuel** (*H* = friend of God) see 'Jethro'

**Revelation** The Book of the Revelation to John, or **The Apocalypse** (Rev.), see p. **159**

**Revenge** see 'Eye for an eye'

**Revilers** who criticize others scornfully, cannot inherit the kingdom of God, Ps. 44.16; Isa. 51.7; Ecclus. (Ben Sira) 23.8; Matt. 5.11; 1 Cor. 6.10

**Rezin** king of Syria, joined with Pekah of Israel against the Assyrians, killed by them in 732 BC, 2 Kings 16.5–9; 2 Chron. 28.5; Isa. 7.1–9

**Rhegium** city on the 'toe' of Italy facing Sicily across the Straits of Messina, today called Reggio di Calabria. Paul stopped there for one day on his way to Rome, Acts 28.13

**Rhodes** (*G* = a rose) large island at the mouth of the Aegean Sea, belonging to Greece; Paul called there on his way back to Jerusalem after his third missionary journey, Acts 21.1

**Riblah** Syrian town on the River Orontes, where Jehoahaz was imprisoned, and Zedekiah judged, 2 Kings 23.33; 25.5–7

**Riches** come from God, 1 Sam. 2.7; 1 Kings 3.11–13; Ps.112.3; Prov. 10.22; Eccles. 5.19; to be used to help others, Job 31.16–21; Tob. 1.8; Matt. 19.21; Luke 16.9; 1 Tim. 6.18; temptations of, Ps. 62.10; Amos 6.1–7; Matt. 6.24; 13.22; Mark 10.23–27; James 5.1–6; Rev. 18; spiritual riches, Matt. 6.19–21; Rom. 11.33; Eph. 1.7; Phil. 4.19; Heb. 11.26

**Right hand** On a wide, bench-like throne an emperor might allow another king to sit beside him, to show that he shared his power with the other. Jesus is described as seated at God's right hand, to show his divine authority, 1 Kings 2.19; Ps. 110.1; Mark 14.62; Eph. 1.20; Col. 3.1; Heb. 1.3

**Righteousness** being the winner in a law-suit, Ps. 9.4; Gal. 2.21; the good behaviour which wins law-suits, Job 29.14–25; Ps. 1.6; 23.3; Amos 5.24; Matt. 5.20; the triumph of God's justice, Judg. 5.11; Matt. 5.6; James 1.20; see 'Justification'

**Rimmon** (*H* = thunderer) another name for the Syrian god Hadad; the House of Rimmon where Naaman worshipped was probably on the site now occupied by the Umayyad Mosque in Damascus, 2 Kings 5.18; Zech. 12.11

**River** Rivers out of Eden, Gen. 2.10; River Euphrates, Gen. 15.18; River Nile, Gen. 41.1; River Jabbok, Josh. 12.2; River Kishon, Judg. 5.21; Rivers of Damascus, 2 Kings 5.12; Province Beyond the River, Ezra 4.10; A tree planted by the river, Ps. 1.3; There is a river, Ps. 46.4; By the rivers of Babylon we wept, Ps. 137.1; I will make rivers in the desert, Isa. 43.19; Then your peace would have flowed like a river, Isa. 48.18; A river from the Temple, Ezek. 47.6–12; River Jordan Matt. 3.6; Rivers of living water, John 7.38; Rev. 22.1–2

**Robbers** Den of Robbers, Jer. 7.11; Matt. 21.13; Fell among robbers, Luke 10.30

**Rock** Water from the rock, see 'Meribah'; In the cleft of the rock, Ex. 33.22; The LORD our rock, Ps. 18.2; 62.2; 71.3; He will set me on a rock, Ps. 27.5; Rock that is higher than I, Ps. 61.2; Shadow of a rock in a dry land, Isa. 32.2; Remember the rock from which you were hewn, Isa. 51.1; House built on the rock, Matt. 7.24–25; On this rock I will build my church, Matt. 16.18; Rock of offence, Rom. 9.33; Called to the rocks, 'Fall on us', Hos. 10.8; Luke 23.30; Rev. 6.16; see also 'Stone'

**Rod** Aaron's rod, Ex. 4.4; Heb. 9.4; rod of iron, Ps. 2.9; Rev. 12.5; sparing the rod, Prov. 13.24; beaten with rods, Acts 16.22; 2 Cor. 11.25

**Romans** (Rom.) The Letter of Paul to the Romans, see p. **152**

**Rome** capital of the Roman Empire; their occupation of Judea and Galilee, beginning in 63 BC, was bitterly resented. People from Rome were present at Pentecost, Acts 2.10. Paul was taken to Rome when he appealed to be tried by the Emperor, Acts 27.16–31, and may have written Ephesians, Colossians, Philippians and Philemon from there. 1 Peter was probably written from Rome; traditionally Peter is regarded as the first Bishop of Rome. Tradition says Peter and Paul were both executed in Rome on 29 June, AD 67; Peter was crucified upside down in the circus where St Peter's Basilica now stands, and buried there; Paul was beheaded with a sword at Aquae Silva and buried where St Paul's Without the Walls is located; there is good evidence to regard their tombs as genuine. Other places associated with them are the Mamertine Prison, the 'Quo Vadis' chapel, and the churches of San Pietro in Montorio, San Paolo alla Regola, Santa Pudenziana, San Clemente and Santa Prisca

**Rose** probably the narcissus or the lily, Isa. 35.1; the rose of Sharon may be the meadow saffron, crocus or tulip, S. of Sol. 2.1. In Greek writings such as Wisd. 2.8; Ecclus. (Ben Sira) 24.14; 39.13; 50.8, 'rose' probably means the Phoenician rose or the oleander

**Rue** scented herb, which Pharisees tithed although the law did not require it, Luke 11.42

**Rufus** (*L* = red) one of the sons of Simon of Cyrene, Mark 15.21; apparently mentioned because known to the readers, he may be the Rufus greeted in Rom. 16.13

**Ruler of the synagogue** elder (not a scribe or rabbi) chosen to preside over the business, maintain order, and decide who was to conduct the services: Jairus, whose daughter Jesus raised, Matt. 9.18–26; Mark 5.22–43; Luke 8.41–56; Crispus, who became a believer in Corinth, Acts 18.8; Sosthenes, who was beaten in Corinth, Acts 18.17

**Ruth** (*H* = friend) (Ruth) The Book of Ruth, see p. **137**

**Saba, Seba, Sheba, Sabeans** kingdom and tribe in Arabia, Job 1.15; Ps. 72.10, 15; Isa. 45.14; Sabean incense, Isa. 60.6; Jer. 6.20; see also 'Sheba 2'

*Sabaoth* (sa-BAY-oth or sa-ba-OAT) see 'Hosts'

**Sabbath** the seventh day of the week. The concept of a seven-day week came from the Canaanite calendar; it was considered unlucky to work on the seventh day. The Hebrews turned this into a day of worship, 2 Kings 4.23; Isa. 1.13. It is represented as ordained at the time of the giving of the manna, Ex. 16.22–28, and included in the Ten Commandments, 20.8–11, because the LORD rested on the seventh day of creation, Gen. 2.2–3. It was a day of celebration, and with the emergence of synagogue worship after the Exile was a day for reading the scriptures, Luke 13.10; Acts 13.14. The law against sabbath-breaking was severe, Ex. 35.2–3; the Pharisees, whose interpretation of it was complex, criticized Jesus because on the sabbath he healed, Mark 3.1–6; Luke 13.10–17; 14.1–6; John 5.1–17; 7.21–24; 9.1–34; and picked ears of wheat, Mark 2.23–26. He objected that what was intended to be a blessing had become a burden, Mark 2.27; see also 'Law', 'Lord's day', 'Measures of Length'

**Sackcloth** rough material woven from goats-hair, Isa. 50.3; Rev. 6.12; or from camel's-hair, worn by John the Baptist and other prophets, Isa. 20.2; Mark 1.6; Rev. 11.3; it signified personal and national mourning and penitence, 2 Sam. 3.31; 1 Kings 20.32; 21.27; Job 16.15; Ps. 30.11; 35.13; Isa. 58.5; Matt. 11.21

**Sacrifice** offering something to another or to God, at some cost to oneself. When early humans considered they had met with a god in some place, their instinct, derived from the custom of hospitality, was to offer him food. An individual or the head of the family might make a sacrifice in a holy place; priests were appointed to bring the offerings of the community to a temple, Gen. 20.24. There were two types: food for the god – a holocaust, from Greek *holos caustos*, whole burnt – so that the god could feed on the smell, Gen. 8.21; Ex. 29.38–42; Lev. 1; and food for the worshippers, when they shared a sacramental meal with the god in the temple, 1 Kings 3.15; often both types were offered at the same time. The priestly documents of the Hebrew Scriptures provide detailed sacrificial rituals for: daily worship and great festivals, Lev. 16; 23; Num. 28–29; ordination of priests and Levites, Ex. 29; Lev. 8–9; Num. 8; dedication of the tabernacle, Ex. 40; Num. 7; childbirth, Lev. 12; skin-diseases, Lev. 13–14; vows, Num. 6; purification from bodily discharges, Lev. 15; and purification after contact with a corpse, Num. 19. In the Bible, sacrifices are not intended to propitiate or bribe an angry god, Ps. 50.8–13; 116.17. The prophets criticize using sacrifices as a substitute for moral behaviour, 1 Sam. 15.22; Isa. 1.11; Hos. 6.6. Three great sacrifices influenced Christian thinking: the Covenant-sacrifice at Sinai, when God promised protection and the people promised loyalty and obedience, 'signing' the contract with blood, Ex. 24.1–8; 1 Cor. 11.25; the Passover, when worshippers were saved from death by the blood of the Lamb, Ex. 12.1–13; 1 Cor. 5.7; and the Day of Atonement, when the people's sins were transferred to the scape-goat, Lev. 16; Heb. 9.11–14. The death of Jesus on Calvary is described under this metaphor: believers join themselves by faith to that sacrifice and make it their own, Rom. 6.3, 6; Gal. 2.19; 6.4; promising to live a life of self-sacrifice in the service of others, Rom. 12.1; Phil. 4.18; 1 Peter 2.5

**Sadducees** Jewish leaders at the time of Jesus, possibly taking their name from Zadok the priest. Together with the Pharisees they opposed Jesus, Matt. 3.7; 16.1–12. The high priest and his companions were Sadducees, Acts 4.1; 5.17; they did not believe in resurrection, Matt. 22.23–34; Mark 12.18; Luke 20.27–40; Acts 23.8

**Saints** God's holy people, set apart for his service, the whole community rather than particular individuals. Paul writes to 'all the saints throughout Achaia' etc., 2 Cor. 1.1, Eph. 1.1; Phil. 1.1; Col. 1.2; but also rebukes them for un-saintly behaviour, 1 Cor. 5.1; all Christians are saints, but we are also 'called to be saints', by making our lives more holy, Rom. 1.7; 1 Cor. 1.2

**Salamis** see 'Cyprus 4.'

**Salmon** (SALL-monn) see 'Zalmon'

**Salmone** (sall-MOH-nee) promontory at the north-east of Crete, passed by the boat carrying Paul on his way to Rome, modern name Akrotirio Sideros, Acts 27.7

**Salome** (suh-LOH-mee) (*H* = peaceable) **1.** Daughter of Herodias; danced for Herod; asked for the head of John the Baptist, Matt. 14.6; Mark 6.22; see 'Herod Family'. **2.** Wife of Zebedee; present at the crucifixion; helped prepare Jesus's body for burial, Matt. 27.56; Mark 15.40; 16.1

**Salt of the earth** just as food without salt is uninteresting, and in hot climates dangerous to health, so Christians are called to give life and interest to the world, Matt. 5.13. Salt cannot lose its savour; this is probably comic exaggeration to indicate the dangers of Christians becoming boring. Salt is also a preservative, which may lie behind Mark 9.50; Col. 4.6; and is used in sacrifice, Lev. 2.13; Mark 9.49

**Salvation** see 'Saviour'

**Samaria, Samaritan** (*H* = watchman) **1.** When Omri, in about 884 BC, moved the capital city of the Northern Kingdom from Tirzah to the city of Samaria, the region changed its name from Ephraim to Samaria. Excavations at Shomron, 10 miles north-west of Nablus, have revealed foundations from Omri's time to the Roman period, including the 'ivory palace' where Ahab and Jezebel lived, 1 Kings 16.21–2 Kings 17.21; Ps. 45.8; Isa. 7.9; Amos 3.15; 6.4. **2.** When the Northern Kingdom was conquered by Assyria in 722, some of the population was deported.

# Samos

Propagandists for the Southern Kingdom alleged that it was the majority, and that they were replaced by foreigners, 2 Kings 17; the Samaritans claim that it was a few only, who returned later. Their objection to the rebuilding of Jerusalem was an escalation of the ancient rivalry between the two kingdoms, Neh. 4. Herod the Great rebuilt the city and named it Sebaste (Greek for Augustus, to honour the Emperor). **3.** Samaritan Jews, claiming descent from Ephraim and Manasseh, built a sanctuary on Mount Gerizim, and kept part of the religion of Israel: the worship of YHWH, the Five Books of Moses, circumcision, the sabbath and festivals; but they rejected later developments of Judaism, John 4.20. This mixture of similarity and difference led to mutual loathing and enmity between Jews and Samaritans, John 4.9. Jews avoided the area, Matt. 19.1; Luke 17.11. **4.** Jesus healed ten lepers, praising the only Samaritan among them for returning to thank him, Luke 17.11–19. He refused to call down fire on Samaritan villages, Luke 9.51–55; and spoke freely to the Samaritan woman at the well, John 4. The Parable of the Good Samaritan who rescued a traveller on the road to Jericho, teaches that neighbourliness knows no boundaries of race or religion, Luke 10.25–37. **5.** Philip led a successful mission to Samaria, Acts 8.4–25

**Samos** Aegean island near Ephesus, visited by Paul on his third missionary journey, Acts 20.15

**Samothrace** island in the north-eastern Aegean, about 20 miles from the coast of Thrace; Paul's ship stopped there on their way from Troas to Neapolis, Acts 16.11. It is now the Greek island of Samothraki

**Samson** (*H* = sun) Israelite strongman in the period of the Judges; who vowed as a Nazirite never to cut his hair; his marriage; the riddle; torches tied to foxes' tails; the jawbone of a donkey; his marriage to Delilah, a Philistine woman. Trapped by her into revealing that his strength lay in his hair, he was imprisoned and blinded, but died when he pulled down a Philistine temple on himself and the worshippers, Judg. 13–16

**1 Samuel** (*H* = God hears) (1 Sam.) (1 Kingdoms in Greek) The First Book of Samuel, see p. **137**

**2 Samuel** (2 Sam.) (2 Kingdoms in Greek) The Second Book of Samuel, see p. **138**

**Sanballat** (*Ak Sin-ubal-lit* = may the moon god give life) governor of Samaria, opposed Nehemiah's attempts to rebuild the walls of Jerusalem, Neh. 2.10, 19; 4.1–15; 6

**Sanctification** process of making someone holy, John 17.19; 1 Cor. 1.2, 30; 2 Thess. 2.13; Heb.10.10

**Sandals, shoes 1.** To be taken off on holy ground, Ex. 3.5; Josh. 5.15; Acts 7.33. **2.** To be put on ready to travel, at Passover, Ex. 12.11. **3.** Taken off and exchanged as a sign of a contract of ownership, Ruth 4.8–9; Ps. 60.8 = 108.9. **4.** John the Baptist says he is not good enough to undo Jesus's shoes, Matt. 3.11; Mark 1.7; Luke 3.16; John 1.27; Acts 13.25

**Sanhedrin** (SAN-uh-drinn or san-HEED-rinn, *H* form of *G synedrion* = council) **1.** General term for a 'meeting' of a group, Luke 22.66. **2.** Various judicial courts, Matt. 5.22; 10.17; Mark 13.9. **3.** The supreme judicial and legislative assembly in Jerusalem, also known as the Council of Elders. There were 71 members from the priests, scribes and 'elders of the people'; with the High Priests presiding. They normally met in the Hall of the Sanhedrin on the roof of the southern portico of the Temple courtyard, Matt. 26.59; Mark 14.53–65; 15.1; Acts 5.21; 22.5. The meeting at night in the High Priest's house was informal and had no legal power. The power to pass death sentences had allegedly been taken away by the Romans, John 18.31, though this is disputed

**Sapphira** (*Ar* = beautiful) see 'Ananias 1.'

**Sarah** (*H* = princess), **1.** Original name **Sarai** (*H* = contention), wife of Abraham, mother of Ishmael and Isaac. During their visit to Egypt during a famine she was taken by Pharaoh as his wife until the situation was clarified. She was childless until, when 90 years old, she heard that she was to have a son, so she laughed; she died aged 127, and was buried at Hebron, Gen. 11–23; Isa. 51.2; Rom. 4.19; 9.9; Heb. 11.11; 1 Peter 3.6. **2.** Seven times widowed Jewess, rescued by Tobias, Tob. 3.7

**Sardis** capital city of the kingdom of Lydia, in Asia Minor; one of the churches addressed by the Risen Christ in Revelation 3.1–6. It had been the city of the legendary King Midas and the historically rich King Croesus, where Aesop wrote his Fables. Cyrus of Persia, attacking the steep acropolis, found the defenders asleep. The remains are in and around the hamlet of Sart, 59 miles from İzmir in Turkey; they include a few pillars and walls from a huge Temple of Artemis, rebuilt by Alexander the Great, and a restored gymnasium complex, with an adjoining synagogue

**Sarepta** Greek form, see 'Zarephath'

**Sargon II** (*Ak Sharru-ken* = the king is legitimate) king of Assyria (721–705 BC), Isa. 20.1; it was he, not Shalmaneser, who imprisoned Hoshea; ended the Northern Kingdom of Israel; deported some of the Israelites, 2 Kings 17.1–6; 18.9–12, see 'Shalmaneser', Mesopotamia, p. **165**

**Satan** (*H* = adversary) originally a human being who is an adversary, 1 Kings 11.14, 23; when Peter tries to tempt Jesus to avoid the way of crucifixion, he is rebuked as a satan, a tempter, Matt. 16.23. In later literature and the New Testament Satan is a spiritual being who opposes the work of God, see 'Devil'

**Satrap** (*H* and *Ar 'ahashdarpan* = protector of the land) governor of a province in the Persian Empire, Ezra 8.36; Esth. 3.12; 9.3; Dan. 3.2–3; 6.1–7

**Saturday** see 'Sabbath'

**Saul** (*H* = asked for) **1.** Saul, son of Kish, first King among the Israelites, c.1030–c.1010 BC; he came from the tribe of Benjamin, and his kingdom covered little more than their territory; but he laid the foundations for David to become king of all the Israelites. Born in Gibeah, he was anointed by Samuel, 1 Sam. 9; proclaimed king, 10; defeated the Ammonites, 11; fought the Philistines, 13–14; defeated the Amalekites but spared their king, 15; appointed David his harpist and armour-bearer, 16; tried to kill him, 18–20; Saul's son Jonathan befriended David, 19–20; Saul killed the priests at Nob, 22; his life was spared by David, 24, 26; Saul consulted the witch of Endor, 28; and killed himself after his defeat by the Philistines on Mount Gilboa, 31. **2.** Saul of Tarsus, also of the tribe of Benjamin, was probably named after King Saul, but took the name Paul when he became apostle to the Gentiles, see 'Paul'

**Saviour, Save, Salvation** One of the most important concepts added by the Israelites to world religion is belief in a God who saves, Isa. 43.3, John 4.22. Focusing on the Exodus, when God saved the Israelites from slavery in Egypt, Ex. 15.2, it became a principle that God gives us free will, which results in situations from which we cannot save ourselves, and then intervenes to save us from our trouble. This belief was applied to salvation from defeat in battle, Ps. 138.7; oppression, Ps. 107.39; poverty, Ps. 12.5; prison, Ps. 107.10; sickness, James 5.15; the consequences and the guilt of sin, Matt. 1.21; unjust accusations, Ps. 109.31;

# Scapegoat

physical death, Heb. 5.7, and eternal death, James 5.20. To begin with, the emphasis was on the salvation of communities, Ps. 144.10; then the realization grew that God is also our personal Saviour, Rom. 10.10. The name of Jesus means 'God saves', Matt. 1.21, and he is described as the Saviour of the world, John 4.42. Jesus saves us from our problems here and now, if only by giving us grace to bear them, 1 Cor. 10.13; but final salvation will be achieved in eternity, Heb. 5.9, when he gives us forgiveness for sin, 1 Tim. 1.15, and eternal life with him after we die, John 3.16

**Scapegoat** male goat on which all the sins of the Israelites were laid on the Day of Atonement, which was then sent off into the wilderness, Lev. 16.8–26. The meaning of the Hebrew word *azazel* is unknown, but 'scapegoat', from 'escape', meaning go away, entered the English language with the translation of William Tyndale (1494–1536). Isa. 53.6 may refer

**Sceptre** staff carried by a monarch to symbolize power, Gen. 49.10; Esth. 4.11; Ps. 60.7; Isa. 14.5; Wisd. 10.14; Heb. 1.8

**Sceva** Jew whose seven sons tried to exorcize demons 'by the Jesus whom Paul proclaims', but were overpowered by their patient, Act 19.13–16

**Scorpion** arachnid with eight legs, pincers and a tail which curves back, armed with a sting to paralyse its prey, Deut. 8.15; 1 Kings 12.11; Luke 10.19; 11.12; Rev. 9.3–10

**Scourging** beating with rods or whips, a punishment then thought suitable for children, Prov. 13.24; and slaves, Ex. 21.20–21; metaphor for punishing the nation, 1 Kings 12.11; Isa. 10.26. It was limited to forty strokes, in practice 39, to avoid killing the victim, Deut. 25.1–3; 2 Cor. 11.24. Roman citizens could claim the right to be punished with wooden rods by the lictors, Acts 16.22; 22.25; 2 Cor. 11.25. Jesus, tied by his hands to a pillar, was scourged with a leather whip; into the plaited straps were inserted sharp pieces of metal or bone to tear the flesh, Matt. 20.19; 27.26; Mark 15.15; Luke 23.16; John 19.1. Prisoners were often almost unconscious from the pain of this before they reached the place of execution

**Scribes** At first, all those who could read and write were called scribes, and used as secretaries, 2 Sam. 8.17; 2 Kings 12.10; 18.18; 19.2; 22.3–20; Jer. 36.10–32. After the Exile they become students of religion and interpreters of the Scripture, Ecclus. (Ben Sira) 38.34–39.11; 1 Macc. 7.12; 2 Macc. 6.18–20. In the Gospels, scribes are also called teachers or teachers of the law, Luke 2.46; 5.17. Some scribes were friendly to Jesus, Matt. 8.19; Mark 12.28–34; but mostly he condemned them, with the Pharisees, for excessive concern with the minutiae of tradition, Matt. 15.1–20; 23; Mark 10.33; Luke 6.6–11; 20. Nevertheless scribes are interpreters of Scripture, who will still be needed in the Church, Matt. 5.17–20; 13.52; 23.34

**Scriptures** meaning always the Hebrew Scriptures or Old Testament: inspired by the Holy Spirit, Acts 1.16; 2 Tim. 3.16; Heb. 3.7; 2 Peter 1.21; not to be altered, Deut. 4.2; Prov. 30.6; Rev. 22.18; to be used for teaching, Ps. 19.7; 119; expounded by Jesus, Matt. 4.4; Luke 24.27; John 7.42; explain the work of Jesus, Matt. 5.17; John 5.39; 19.24; Acts 10.43; 18.28; 1 Cor. 15.3

**Scroll** roll of papyrus or parchment for writing on, Ps. 40.7; Isa. 34.4; Jer. 36; Ezek. 3.1; Zech. 5.1–2; Luke 4.17–20; Rev. 5.1–9; 6.14; 10.9–10

**Scythians** or **Ashkenaz** cruel warriors who swept down from the north, in the area now called the Ukraine, east of the Caspian Sea, in the seventh century BC, and dominated Mesopotamia for 28 years until defeated by the Medes; helped the

Persians defeat Babylon in 538 BC, Jer. 51.27; 2 Macc. 4.47; yet even they can be one with us in Christ, Col. 3.11

**Sea 1.** Molten Sea in the Temple, 1 Kings 7.24; 2 Kings 16.17; 25.13; Jer. 52.17; bronze vessel supported by 12 bronze oxen, containing over 10,000 gallons of water, replacing the Laver, Ex. 30.18. It may have symbolized the waters under the earth. **2.** Sea of Glass, layer of crystal before God's throne, mixed with fire; graphic image for peace following persecution, Rev. 4.6; 15.2. **3.** Jews hated the sea, Rev. 18.17, looking forward to the day when 'There shall be no more sea', Rev. 21.1

**Seal 1.** Signet ring with a design engraved in it unique to the owner, Gen. 38.18; 41.42; Ecclus. (Ben Sira) 38.27; Rev. 7.2. **2.** Small lump of soft wax, in which a design is impressed with a signet ring; it then hardens, and is a proof of who wrote or authorized the document, 1 Kings 21.8; Esth. 3.12; 8.8; Jer. 32.10–14, 44; metaphorically John 6.27. **3.** Similar wax seal placed across the opening of a scroll, preventing unauthorized persons from opening it, Isa. 8.16; 29.11; Dan. 8.26; 12.4, 9; Rev. 5.1–9; or placed on the cord which tied up the top of a moneybag, Tob. 9.5. **4.** Closing up an entrance by placing soft clay as a mortar between the stones, then impressing the signet ring into it, or a cord could have been placed between the stones and a wax seal formed at each end, Dan. 6.17; Bel. 1.11–17; 2 Macc. 2.5; Matt. 27.66. **5.** Distinctive mark, tattoo or brand, on the skin of a slave, or the devotee of a god, as proof of ownership, Isa. 44.5; Ezek. 9.4; 2 Esd. 2.38; metaphorically of circumcision, Rom. 4.11; of the Holy Spirit given at baptism, the sign of those who belong to God, 2 Cor. 1.22; Eph. 1.13; 4.30; Rev. 7.3–8; 9.4

**Second Coming** these words occur nowhere in the New Testament, though in Acts 1.11 the angels tell the disciples that Jesus 'will come in the same way as you saw him go into heaven'. There are many references to the Coming of Christ, and even more to his *parousia* or presence. Many of his predictions were fulfilled in his death, resurrection and ascension, together with the destruction of Jerusalem in AD 70; and he comes to Christians in moments of decision every day of their lives, and at their death. Believers in 'realized eschatology' argue that we should concentrate on this; others, aware that Christ's work on earth is far from completed, expect another visible intervention in history, see also 'Parousia', Apocalyptic, p. **175**

**Seed 1.** Old word for human descendants, Gen. 3.15; 12.6; Luke 1.55. **2.** The Parable of the seed growing secretly, Mark 4.26–29, teaches the urgency of preaching the gospel, because the rapid growth of the kingdom of God is God's work. **3.** See 'Sower'. **4.** See 'Mustard'. **5.** The resurrection of the dead, in a different type of body but with their personality continuous, compared to beautiful plants growing from humble seeds, 1 Cor. 15

**Seir** (*H* = rugged) range of mountains now in southern Jordan, called Jebel esh-Sharah, formerly in Edom, where Esau settled; including one of the suggested sites of Mount Horeb, Gen. 32.3; Deut. 33.2; Josh. 24.4; Isa. 21.11; Ezek. 35

**Sela** (*H* = crag) city east of the Seir range, later called Joktheel, then Petra, 2 Kings 14.7

**Selah** probably a musical or liturgical instruction inserted in the text of the Psalms; meaning unknown

**Seleucia-ad-Piera** port for Antioch-on-the-Orontes, whence Paul sailed on his first missionary journey; scant remains are at Çevlik, 4 miles north of Samandağ, near the amazing Titus and Vespasian Tunnel, Acts 13.4

---

**Seleucid kings** *in Antioch-on-the-Orontes*
**312–280** BC Seleucus I Nicator
**280–261** his son Antiochus I Soter
**261–247** his son Antiochus II Theos, husband of Laodike
**247–226** his son Seleucus II Callinicus
**226–223** his son Seleucus III Soter or Ceraunus
**223–187** his brother Antiochus III the Great
**187–175** his son Seleucus IV Philopator
**175–163** his brother Antiochus IV Epiphanes
**163–162** Antiochus V Eupator, son of Antiochus IV
**162–150** Demetrius I Soter, son of Seleucus IV
**150–145** Alexander I Balas, usurper
**145–139/8** Demetrius II Nicator, son of Demetrius I
**139/8–129** Antiochus VII Sidetes, son of Demetrius I, married his brother's widow Cleopatra Thea
There were other rival kings until 65; see 1 Maccabees, p. **147**

---

**Self-control** fruit of the Spirit, Acts 24.25; 1 Cor. 7.5–9; 9.25; Gal. 5.23; 2 Peter 1.6
**Self-denial** commanded by Jesus of his followers: refraining from over-indulgence, and overcoming the self-centredness which cuts us off from God and our neighbour, Matt. 16.24
**Self-examination** before receiving Holy Communion, commanded by Paul, so that we recognize the body of Christ, in the bread, and in our fellow-worshippers, 1 Cor. 11.28
**Sennacherib** (*Ak Ain-ahhe-riba* = moon god replaced the brothers) king of Assyria; succeeded Sargon; reigned 705–681 BC; attacked King Hezekiah, 2 Kings 18–19; his own account of the siege of Jerusalem survives; murdered by his sons Adrammelech and Sharezer, 2 Chron. 32; Tob. 1.21–22; see Mesopotamia, p. **165**
**Sensuality, Sexual excess** condemned, Rom. 13.13; 2 Cor. 12.21; Gal. 5.19; Eph. 4.17–19
**Sepharvaim** otherwise unknown Mesopotamian city, 2 Kings 17.24, 31; 18.34; 19.13
**The Septuagint** Greek translation of the Hebrew Scriptures, see p. **178**
**Seraphim** (*H* = burning ones) **1.** 'Fiery snakes' which attacked the Israelites in the wilderness; fiery winged snakes surrounded the king's throne in Egyptian art, Isa. 14.29; 30.6; Num. 21.6–9; Deut. 8.15; 2 Kings 18.4. **2.** The seraphim in Isaiah's vision were spiritual beings, not snakes, Isa. 6.1–7. Two wings are for flying, two for covering their faces so that they should not look at God's face, and two for modestly covering their 'feet', a euphemism for the genitals. They brought charcoal from the altar to purify the prophet's lips; now it is what we say which makes us either unclean or holy
**Sergius Paulus** proconsul of Cyprus, Paul's most important Gentile convert, Acts 13.4–12; who may have given him the vision of converting the Roman Empire. A large residence at Pafos, with a mosaic of Theseus, is probably the Governor's Palace, from a slightly later date but on the same site. An inscription found at Antioch-of-Pisidia to 'Lucius Sergius Paulus the younger' shows that the family of the Cyprus governor had connections with that remote town; soon after their meeting Paul headed there, and changed his name from Saul to Paul

**Sermon on the Mount** ethical teaching of Jesus, Matt. 5–7. There is too much material for one sermon; probably Matthew collected together separate sayings, each the memorable climax of one sermon. The hilltop setting reminds us of Moses giving the law on Mount Sinai, though the teaching of Jesus consists rather of ideals to strive for. Luke 6.20–7.1 is a similar but shorter collection, often called the Sermon on the Plain, see 'Teaching of Jesus', p. **170**

**Serpent 1.** Snake in the Garden of Eden, who tempted Eve to eat the forbidden fruit, and is identified with Satan; Christians interpret Jesus as the 'descendant of Eve' who will crush the Devil, Gen. 3.1–7; 2 Cor. 11.3. **2.** Fleeing and twisting serpent, Isa. 27.1, see 'Leviathan' **3.** Rods of Moses and Aaron which turned into snakes, Ex. 4.3; 7.8–13. **4.** Bronze image of a snake, made by Moses to heal those bitten by fiery serpents, worshipped by the Israelites, destroyed by Hezekiah, Num. 21.8–9; 2 Kings 18.4; John 3.14. **5.** That Old Serpent, name for the Devil, Rev. 12.9; 14.15; 20.2

**Servant 1.** One who serves someone else, from a top court official, 2 Kings 22.12, to a domestic kitchen-maid, Luke 22.56; not a slave, but a 'hired servant', Luke 15.17–19; paid wages, Matt. 20.2. **2.** Speaking of oneself as 'your servant' is a gesture of humility, Gen. 19.2. **3.** Moses and others are described as 'servant of God', Num. 12.7. **4.** The Servant Songs of Isaiah are four poems about the Servant of the Lord, Isa. 42.1–9; 49.1–7; 50.4–11; 52.13–53.12. These describe the vocation of God's servant to restore Israel and bring justice to the nations, a 'light to the Gentiles', whose suffering benefits others. The Servant could mean the prophet himself, or someone such as Jeremiah, but the Songs are most likely a challenge to Israel to learn from its suffering during the Exile, and carry the message of a Saviour God to the rest of the world. Later they helped Jesus and his followers explain his suffering on the cross, understanding that anyone called to serve God may suffer, but self-sacrifice is redemptive

**The Seven** seven men from the Greek-speaking section of the church in Jerusalem, chosen to take charge of the daily distribution of food to poor widows, ensuring fairness between them and the Aramaic-speaking part of the community, Acts 6.1–6, 21.8. They were Stephen; Philip; Prochorus; Nicanor; Timor; Parmenus; and Nicolaus, a Gentile converted to Judaism. All have Greek names. See 'Deacon', 'Philip', 'Stephen'

**Seven Churches of Asia** see The Revelation, p. **159**

**Seven words from the cross** (1) 'Father, forgive', Luke 23.34; (2) 'Today you shall be with me in Paradise', Luke 23.43; (3) 'See, your Mother'; 'Mother, see, your son', John 19.26–27; (4) *'Eloi, Eloi, lema sabachthani'*, which see, Matt. 27.46 = Mark 15.34; (5) 'I thirst', John 19.28; (6) 'It is finished', John 19.30; (7) 'Father, into your hands', Luke 23.46

**Seventy 1.** Seventy elders chosen to accompany Moses up Mount Sinai, who received the Holy Spirit, Ex. 24.1, 9; Num. 11.16–30. **2.** Seventy missionary disciples sent out by Jesus to proclaim the Kingdom and to preach, Luke 10.1–20. In each case some manuscripts read 'seventy-two'

**Shadrach** (*Ak Shudur-Aku* = command of Aku, a moon god) one of three Israelites thrown into the fiery furnace in Babylon, originally called Hananiah, see 'Abednego'

**Shallum** (*H* = reward) **1.** Son of Jabesh, killed Zechariah, became king of Israel for 1 month in 743 BC; killed by Menahem; 2 Kings 15.10–15. **2.** Son of Josiah, king of Judah for 3 months in 609, Jer. 22.11–18, also called Jehoahaz, see 'Jehoahaz 2.' **3.** Fourteen other people in the Bible called Shallum

**Shalmaneser** or **Shalmanezer V** (*Ak Shulmanu-asharid* = Salman is leader) king of Assyria 726–722 BC; died while besieging Samaria; actions apparently attributed to him in 2 Kings 17–18 were in fact carried out by his successor, see 'Sargon', Mesopotamia, p. **165**

**Sharon** (*H* = plain) fertile plain on the Mediterranean coast south of Mount Carmel, 1 Chron. 27.29; Isa. 33.9; 35.2; 65.10. The 'Rose of Sharon' may be a meadow saffron, crocus or tulip, S. of Sol. 2.1. The inhabitants of Sharon turned to the Lord when Peter performed a miracle in Lydda, Acts 9.35

*Shear-jashub* (*H* = a remnant will return) son of Isaiah, named to indicate that only a minority of the Israelite army would return home from their failed attempt to besiege Jerusalem, Isa. 7.3–9; 8.18; see also 'Remnant'

**Sheba** (*H* = oath) **1.** Benjaminite who raised a rebellion against David, was pursued by Joab, and beheaded by the people of Abel Beth-Maacah, 2 Sam. 20. **2.** The Queen of Sheba visited Solomon, 1 Kings 10.1–13; 2 Chron. 9.1–12; Matt. 12.42; see also 'Saba'

**Shechem** (*H* = shoulder) ancient town in the strategic pass between Mount Ebal and Mount Gerizim; substantial remains dating from 4000 to 108 BC have been excavated, at a crossroads a mile east of modern Nablus (Roman Neapolis). Here Dinah was raped, Gen. 34; the tribes renewed their covenant, Josh. 24; Abimelech raised a rebellion, Judg. 9; Rehoboam was crowned, 1 Kings 12.1; Ps. 60.6; see also 'Sychar'

**Shekel** see 'Money'

*Shekinah* (shuh-KEE-nuh, *H* = dwelling) word used by later Jews for the bright cloud, the sign of God's presence; the brightness of God's glory prevented Moses seeing God's face, Ex. 3; 13.17–22; 25.8; 33.17–23; 1 Kings 8.10–11; Jesus made God visible, John 1.15, 18; see also 'Rainbow 1.', 'Transfiguration'

**Shem** (*H* = name) son of Noah, ancestor of the Semitic peoples, named after him. The Semitic languages – Hebrew, Aramaic, Akkadian (spoken in Assyria and Babylon), Ugaritic (Canaanite), Syriac, Arabic and Ethiopic – are all related, and the classification of the races in Genesis is more linguistic than ethnic, Gen. 5.32; 7.13; 9.1, 23–27; 10.21–31; 11.10–26

**Sheol** (shuh-OLE or SHE-oll, *H* from *Ak* = chamber) world of the dead, see 'Hell 1.'

**Shephelah** (shuh-FEE-luh) lowlands between the coastal plain and the Judean hills, Deut. 1.7

**Shepherd** image for a ruler, or God, caring for their people, Ps. 23. Shepherds protect the flock from thieves, John 10.1; from attack by wild animals; at the risk of their own lives, John 10.11; lead them through valleys of deep shadow, Ps. 23.4; to good pastures, Ps. 23.2–3; bringing them back to the fold at night, John 10.16; and lying down across the entrance themselves, John 10.7; caring for the expectant ewes and newborn lambs, Isa. 40.11; fetching back any that have gone astray, Matt. 10.16; Luke 15.1–7; using basic equipment: a rod, a staff, Ps. 23.4; a cloak, Jer. 43.12; a sling, 1 Sam. 17.40; and a sheepdog, Job 30.1. Because Israel had many bad leaders, they hoped that one day there would be a good shepherd, Ezek. 24.15; John 10.11

**Sheshach** code name for Babylon, Jer. 25.26; 51.41

**Sheshbazzar** (*H* = ?fire worshipper) either another name for Zerubbabel, or the name of another prince who started to build the Temple but did not complete it, Ezra 1.8; 5.14–16

*Shibboleth* (*H* = torrent) password used by Gileadite guards to test whether those approaching the River Jordan were Ephraimites, who could not pronounce the 'sh' sound, Judg. 12.5–6

**Shiloh** (*H* = place of rest) main sanctuary of the Israelites, in the northern hills of Ephraim, at Tell Seilun between Bethel and Nablus; where the Ark of the Covenant, the Tent of Meeting and the altar were kept, from Joshua's time until the time of Saul. Its priests claimed a succession from Phinehas, Aaron's grandson, and many priestly traditions may have originated there; there Eli the priest taught the boy Samuel, Josh. 18.1–10; 22.9–34; Judg. 21.19–23; 1 Sam. 1–4; 1 Kings 11.29. After David took the Ark to Jerusalem, Shiloh was regarded as heretical, 2 Sam. 6; Ps. 78.56–72. It is uncertain when Shiloh was destroyed, Jer. 7.12–15; 26.6–9

**Shimei** (*H* = famous) Saul's relative; cursed David, 2 Sam. 16.5–13; later begged for mercy, 19.16–23; David forgave him but remained suspicious; Solomon found an opportunity to put Shimei to death, 1 Kings 2.8–9, 36–46. There are eighteen other people with this name in the Bible

**Shinar** another name for Babylonia, Gen. 14.1; Josh. 7.21; Isa. 11.11; Dan. 1.1–2; Zech. 5.11

**Shishak** = Sheshonq I, Pharaoh of Egypt, invaded Israel, demanding the gold shields from the Jerusalem Temple as tribute from Rehoboam, confirmed by an inscription in Thebes, 1 Kings 11.43–12.22; 14.21–31; 2 Chron. 10.1–12.16

**Shittim** (*H* = acacia trees) **1.** See 'Acacia'. **2.** Alternative name for Peor, Num. 25.1; 33.49; Josh. 2.1; 3.1, Micah 6.5, see 'Peor 1.'. **3.** Wadi Shittim, probably Wadi en-Nar, the continuation of the Kidron Valley to the Dead Sea, Joel 3.18

**Showbread** see 'Bread of the Presence'

**Shunem** now called Sulam, east of 'Afula in Galilee; where Elijah raised a boy to life, 2 Kings 4.8–37; 8.1–6; and see 'Nain'. Abishag, a young woman from Shunem, cared for David in his old age, 1 Kings 1.1–4; the Shulammite woman, heroine of the Song of Solomon, 6.13, may have been a Shunammite, or this may be a feminine form of Solomon

**Shur** wilderness in the north of the Sinai peninsula, where the LORD appeared to Hagar, Gen.16.7–14; where the Israelites began their journey after crossing the Red Sea, Ex. 15.22. Also called Etham, Num. 33.8

**Siddim,Valley of** at the south end of the Dead Sea, possibly at various times covered by water, at others the site of the Cities of the Plain, Gen. 14.3, 8, 10

**Sidon** Mediterranean port, rivalling Tyre for leadership of the Phoenicians; now called Saida in Lebanon, 25 miles south of Beirut; there is nothing to see from Bible times. Paul called at Sidon on his way to Rome, Acts 27.3. See also 'Syro-Phoenician', 'Zarephath'

**Sign** event which points to God, such as the Exodus, Ex. 7.3; or prophetic symbolism, Isa.23; the Gospel of John has been called the Book of Seven Signs, see p. **150**; and the ministry of the apostles was accompanied by signs and wonders, e.g. Acts 2.22, 43; 4.30; 5.12; Rom. 15.19, 2 Cor. 12.12. 'Signs of the Times' are historical events indicating that God is at work, Matt. 16.3

**Signet** see 'Seal'

**Sihon** (SIGH-honn) Amorite king at Heshbon; refused the Israelites permission to pass through his land; attacked them at Jahaz (an unknown location), where he was defeated, killed and his land seized, Num. 21.31–32; Deut. 2.24–32; Ps. 135.11; 136.19

**Silas** shortened form of Silvanus (*L* = woodland), Christian from Jerusalem sent to inform the churches in Syria and Cilicia about their decision on Gentile Christians,

Acts 15.22–33; he then replaced Barnabas as Paul's companion on his second missionary journey, 15.40; he and Paul, both Roman citizens, were imprisoned together at Philippi, 16.19–40; separated when Paul went to Athens, but Paul sent for him, 17.15; they met in Corinth, 18.5; 2 Cor. 1.19; there he joined Paul in writing to the Thessalonians, 1 Thess. 1.1; 2 Thess. 1.1; later he probably carried Peter's letter from Rome, 1 Peter 5.12

**Siloam** (*H* = sent) in Jerusalem: **1.** Shiloah, waters which 'flow gently', Isa. 8.6. **2.** Lower pool, Isa. 22.9. **3.** Conduit of the Upper Pool on the highway to the Fullers' field, Isa. 7.3; 36.2. **4.** King's Pool, on Nehemiah's donkey-ride round the ruined walls, Neh. 2.14. **5.** Pool of Shelah in the King's Garden, Neh. 3.15. **6.** Pool of Siloam, where Jesus sent the blind man to wash, John 9.7. **1.–6.** could all be the same pool, south of the City of David, Birket Silwan, fed by water sent from Gihon Spring through Hezekiah's tunnel; or the water system could have passed through several pools of which no trace remains. **7.** The Tower of Siloam, probably part of the pool building, which collapsed, killing eighteen people, Luke 13.4

**Simon or Simeon** (*H* = hearing) **1.** Simeon, one of the sons of Jacob, Gen. 29.31–30.22; ancestor of one of the twelve tribes of Israel, Gen. 49; Deut. 33. **2.** Simon, called Thassi, high priest 143–135 BC, great-grandson of another Simeon; continued the fight against the Greeks after the death of his brother Judas Maccabeus, 1 Macc. 2.1–5; 9–16. **3.** Simon the Benjaminite, a temple official who betrayed its treasures to the Greeks, 2 Macc. 3–4. **4.** Righteous and devout man in Jerusalem who recognized baby Jesus as the Messiah, praised God in what is known as the 'Nunc Dimittis', and warned Mary, Luke 2.25–35. **5.** Simon of Nazareth, Mark 6.3; see 'Brothers of Jesus'. **6.** Simon Peter, see 'Peter'. **7.** Simon the Zealot or Cananaean, one of The Twelve, Matt. 10.4; Mark 3.18. **8.** Simon the Pharisee; invited Jesus to a meal; was judgmental about the woman who was a sinner, Luke 7.36–50. **9.** Simon the leper, a man in Bethany who had been healed of a skin disease; invited Jesus to a meal; was judgmental about the woman who anointed the feet of Jesus; possibly the same as 8., and / or Lazarus or one of his relations, Matt. 26.6; Mark 14.3. **10.** Simon of Cyrene, father of Alexander and Rufus, who carried the cross for Jesus, Mark 15.21; possibly ethnically African, and the same as 11. **11.** Simeon called Niger, prophet in Antioch, who sent Paul and Barnabas on their first missionary journey, Acts 13.1–3. **12.** Simon called Magus, baptized by Philip; wanted to buy the Holy Spirit; rebuked by Peter, Acts 8.9–24. **13.** Simon the Tanner; Peter stayed in his house at Joppa, even though his occupation made him unclean to observant Jews, Acts 9.43; 10.6, 32

**Sin** the disobedience of Adam is the first example, Gen. 3.1–7; Rom. 5.12; it includes 'missing the mark', i.e. failing to achieve the standards of love that God expects, Num. 15.27–29; transgressing the commandments of God and the terms of the covenant, Num. 15.30; a rebellious attitude, Isa. 1.2–20; Dan. 9.11–12; and 'all have sinned and fall short of the glory of God', 1 Kings 8.46; Rom. 3.23; 7.19; 1 John 1.8. The result is to break the relationship between humans and God, Isa. 1.4; Col. 1.21; God is eager that this relationship should be restored, Isa. 66.4; Hos.11.1–4; Luke 13.34; 15.11–32; God calls us to repent, Luke 5.32; and provides means, such as sacrifice, Gen.22.8; Heb. 9.13; for seeking his forgiveness, Ps. 130.3–4; which brings atonement, Ex. 32.30; and reconciliation with God, 2 Cor. 5.18–19. The death and resurrection of Jesus is the supreme sacrifice, Matt. 26.27–28; Eph. 1.7; which 'takes away the sin of the world', John 1.29. The 'sinners' in the Gospels were not wicked people, but those who had given up the attempt to live by the full Pharisaic code in ordinary life, Matt. 9.13; 11.9; Luke 7.37; 15.7

**Sin, Wilderness of** desert area which the Israelites crossed between Elim and Mount Sinai; there they were given manna and quails; location unknown, not the same as Zin, Ex. 16; Num. 11; 33.11–12, see also 'Sinai'

**Sinai** (*H* = bush, correct pronunciation SIGH-nigh, though most say SIGH-nee-eye) name of a mountain (in J and P sources), usually assumed to be the same as Horeb in E and D sources, see p. **135**; where the LORD gave the Ten Commandments. The Bible is not clear on its location, but since the fourth century AD it has been traditionally identified as Jebel Musa (and the nearby Jebel Katarin and Ras es-Safsaf) in the Sinai Peninsula of Egypt, Ex. 16.1; 19–24; 31.18; 34.2–4, 29–32; Num. 20.22, Ps. 68.8, 17; Acts 7.30, 38. Other passages imply a location further north-east, and Jebel Halal, west of Kadesh Barnea; Jebel Nabi Harun (Mount Hor); and the range around Mount Lawz, east of the Gulf of Aqaba, which contained active volcanos at the time, have all been suggested, Deut. 33.2; Gal. 4.24–25. See also 'Horeb', 'Rephidim'

**Singing** spontaneous response to God's goodness, or rehearsed element in worship, Judg. 5; 1 Chron. 25.7; Ps. 98.1; Isa. 5; 35.10; 1 Cor. 14.15; Eph. 5.19; Rev. 7.12

**Sion** see 'Zion'

**Sirach** = Ecclesiasticus (Ecclus. or Ben Sira) The Wisdom of Jesus Son of Sirach (SI-rack), see p. **146**

**Sirion** see 'Hermon'

**Sisera** leader of the army of Jabin, king of Hazor; killed by Jael, Judg. 4–5

**Six hundred and sixty-six** the 'mark of the Beast' in Rev. 13.18, code for 'Nero Caesar' written in Hebrew characters, each of which is also the sign for a number, and adding them together

**Slavery** widely practised and unquestioned throughout Bible times, Gen. 12.16; 1 Kings 9.21–22; Neh. 7.66; some suffered greatly, Ex. 2.23; 3.7; others rose to high positions, Ps.105.17; but had no choice and no freedom unless they were redeemed, Lev. 25.48. Israelites kept slaves, Deut. 15.13, 17; 23.15; provided they were from other races, Lev. 25.44; Josh. 9.23. Jesus mentions slaves in parables, Matt. 13.27–28; 18.23–33; 20.27; 21.34–36. Slaves should be obedient, 1 Cor. 7.21–23; Eph. 6.5; 1 Peter 2.8; slave-owners must treat their slaves leniently, Col. 4.1. His owner must treat the slave Onesimus as a Christian brother, Philemon 16. All are equal in Christ, 1 Cor. 12.13; Gal. 3.28; Col. 3.11; centuries later this teaching brought the abolition of slavery

**Sling** simple weapon, 2 Kings 3.25; also used by shepherds for driving away wild animals: a stone is inserted in a loop of cloth or leather, swung round and released, Judg. 20.16; 1 Sam. 17.40

**Smithy** described in Isa. 44.12; Ecclus. (Ben Sira) 38.28

**Smyrna** (*G* = myrrh) town on the west coast of Asia Minor, now the Turkish city of İzmir. The hill called Old Smyrna was settled about 3000 BC; Alexander the Great ordered the building of a stronghold on Mount Pagos, and in the first century AD Roman Smyrna was 'the Glory of Asia'; the impressive Agora can be visited, but the rest of the Roman city is underneath modern buildings. One of the seven letters in the book of Revelation is addressed to Smyrna, Rev. 2.8–11

**Snake** see 'Serpent'

**So** Egyptian 'king', though probably a general called Sive, 2 Kings 17.4

**Sodom and Gomorrah** two of the five Cities of the Plain, where Lot settled; rebelled against five kings; Abraham rescued Lot, Gen. 13.10–12; 14. They were

# Soldiers

guilty of every type of sin; Abraham pleaded with the LORD, Gen. 18; the inhabitants wanted to rape two angels; the wicked cities were destroyed by fire; the LORD rescued Lot; Lot's wife, looking back, became a pillar of salt, Gen. 19; Matt. 10.15

**Soldiers** John the Baptist's preaching, Luke 3.14; guarding Jesus, Matt. 27.66; 28.4, 12; at the crucifixion, gamble for Christ's cloak, John 19.2, 23, 32; guarding Paul, Acts 12.4; 23.10; 27.42; obedient to the centurion, Matt. 8.9; messenger for Cornelius, Acts 10.7; soldiers of Christ, 2 Tim 2.3, see 'Armour'

**Solomon** (*H* = peaceable) son of David and Bathsheba, third and last king of the united kingdom of Israel c.970–931 BC; responsible for building and dedicating the Jerusalem Temple and for other building works, 1 Kings 1–10; famous for his wisdom, as in the tale of the two prostitutes, 3.28; his reign was one of great wealth, demonstrated to the Queen of Sheba, 10.1–12. Later he built sanctuaries for the deities of his foreign wives, punished by the division of the kingdom after his death, 1 Kings 11. A much less critical account is in 1 Chron. 22–29; 2 Chron. 1–4. Archaeology showing rebuilding of Gezer, Hazor and Megiddo, all at the same period, apparently confirms the account of Solomon's work, though some question the date of these works. See 'Wisdom'

**Solomon's Portico** along the east side of the Temple courtyard, where Jesus taught, John 10.23; and the first Christians assembled, Acts 2.46; 3.11; 5.12

**Son 1.** Male offspring who inherit the father's property and position, Gen. 21.10; also descendants many generations later: Son of Abraham, Luke 19.9; Son of David, Luke 18.38–39; or a whole tribe or nation: sons of Israel, Deut. 23.17; a class or profession, sons of Aaron, Num. 10.8; sons of the prophets, 2 Kings 2.3. Because the Hebrew language is deficient in adjectives, 'son of' or 'daughter of' is used to describe residents of a place, or a quality or characteristic: daughters of Jerusalem (= Jerusalemites), S. of Sol. 1.5; son of virtue (= virtuous), 1 Kings 1.52; sons of thunder (= tempestuous), Mark 3.17; sons of Belial (= hellish), Judg. 19.22. This influenced the development of the following terms: **2.** God commanded Ezekiel, 'Son of man, stand up', emphasizing that he was merely mortal, Ezek. 2.1. After Daniel's descriptions of beasts, he then saw 'one like a son of man', a human figure who is the heavenly representative of Israel, coming to God on the clouds, Dan. 7.13–14. This is amplified in 1 Enoch 37–71, a Hebrew work which Jesus probably knew. Jesus may have used 'son of man' as a humble term for 'I', or even for the whole human race, Matt. 8.20; 9.6; but usually he meant it as a fulfilment of Daniel's prophecy: one who is more than merely human, ascending to God on the clouds, Mark 14.62. **3.** 'Sons of God' means divine beings, maybe recalling polytheism, though later regarded as angels, Gen. 6.2–4; Job 38.7; God says to the Kings of Israel, 'You are my son', 2 Sam. 7.14; Ps. 2.7; 89.27. So even among monotheistic Jews, a divine or godlike person could be described as a son of God, and the loving character of God our Father reflected in the life of Jesus is pointed out in a saying, 'like father, like son', Ps. 82.6; John 5.19–21; 10.36. Jesus praised Peter for recognizing him as Son of God, Matt. 16.16, and answered 'I am' when the high priest asked him 'Are you the son of the blessed One?', Mark 14.61–62. Paul emphasized that the Resurrection proved that Jesus is Son of God, Rom. 1.3–4. Later development of christological and trinitarian doctrine has its seeds in the language of the New Testament, John 3.16–17; 10.30

**Song 1.** Song of Moses, Ex. 15.1; Deut. 32; Rev. 15.3–4. **2.** Song of Deborah, Judg. 5. **3.** Song of the Lamb, Rev. 15.3. **4.** New song, Ps. 33.3; 96.1; 98.1; 149.1; Isa. 42.10; Rev. 5.9–10; see also 'Singing', Psalms, p. **140**

**The Song of Solomon** (S. of Sol. or Cant.) or The Song of Songs, see p. **140**
**The Song of the Three Jews** or **Three Children** or **Three Young Men** (The Prayer of Azariah and the Song of the Three Jews are together referred to by the abbreviation Song of Thr.), see p. **147**
**Sopater** (*G* = of sound parentage) from Beroea, went with Paul to Jerusalem carrying a gift from the Gentile churches, Acts 20.4; possibly the same as Sosipater, Paul's relative or compatriot, who sends greetings, Rom. 16.21
**Sorek, Valley of** modern Wadi es-Sarar, beginning 13 miles west of Jerusalem, where Delilah lived, Judg. 16.4. Khirbat Sariq may be the site of Sorek town, and Sar'ah is Zorah, Judg. 13.2; 16.31. Beth-Shemesh is Tell er-Rumeileh, 1 Sam. 6–7; 2 Kings 14.11. See also 'Timnah'
**Sosthenes** (*G* = safe in strength) Jew in Corinth, beaten by the mob, Acts 18.17; became a Christian, 1 Cor. 1.1, see 'Ruler of the synagogue'
**Soul 1.** In Hebrew *nephesh* is the breath of life which God breathed into Adam, Gen. 2.7; in animals, too, life differs from death in that live animals breathe, 1.20–21. It can refer to a 'person', 46.27; or to one's 'life', 1 Kings 19.4; and is the seat of the emotions, Ps. 86.4; it ends when breathing ceases at death. **2.** In Greek *psyche* refers to the whole person, Acts 2.41; or to one's life, Matt. 2.20; Mark 3.4; Luke 12.13–20. In some passages the soul may be thought of as surviving death, Luke 9.25; 12.4; 21.19. 'The souls of the righteous are in the hand of God', Wisd. 3.1
**Sower** parable or allegory teaching persistent evangelism, even if not all the seed is fruitful, Matt. 13.1–23; Mark 4.1–20; Luke 8.4–15
**Spain** Paul's wish to evangelize, Rom. 15.24, 28
**Span** see 'Measures of length'
**Sparrows** nest in the Temple, Ps. 84.3; Jesus said God cares for them, Matt. 10.29–31; Luke 12.6–7
**Speaking in tongues** see 'Tongues'
**Speck of dust** see 'Mote'

---

**Spices** Ex. 30.34 lists the ingredients of incense: stacte, a resin from the storax tree *Styrax officianalis*; onycha, from the wing shell, found in the Red Sea; galbanum, the dried sap from the root of a type of fennel; and frankincense, a resin formed from the sap of the *Boswellia sacra* tree, its name coming from the 'freedom' with which it gives off a perfume when burnt. The oil for anointing Ex. 35.8, 28, includes liquid myrrh, the sap of the *Commiphora myrrha* plant, probably dissolved in oil, now known as 'Balsam of Mecca'; cinnamon, the oil pressed from the fruit of the *Cinnamomum zeylanicum* tree (the bark produces an inferior oil); aromatic cane, sweet cane or calamus, juice from a reed called *Acorus calamus*; and cassia, oil pressed from the inner bark of the Indian *Cinnamomum cassia* tree. A different sort of cassia, from the *laurus cassia* tree of southern Arabia, perfumes the bride's robes, Ps. 45.8. The magi brought to Jesus gold, frankincense and myrrh, Matt. 2.11. Nard in an *alabastron* was used to anoint Jesus's feet, Mark 14.3; John 12.3; it is an ointment extracted from the *Nardostachys jatamansi* plant in the Himalayas, and is called spikenard from the shape of the leaves, though in both Gospels *pistikos* should be translated 'pure' or 'genuine'. Myrrh dissolved in wine was used as a pain-killer, Mark 15.23. At the burial of Jesus his body was anointed with myrrh and aloes, the bitter-smelling leaves of a succulent related to the well-known Aloe Vera, John 19.39

Spirit, spirits

**Spirit, spirits 1.** Evil spirits, 1 Sam. 16.14–16; Tob. 6.8; Matt. 8.16; Mark 1.23–27; Luke 4.33–36; Acts 19.12–16, see 'Demons'. **2.** Elemental spirits of the universe, Gal. 4.3, 9; Col. 2.8, 20. **3.** A person's spirit, Gen. 41.8; Ps. 31.5; Matt. 26.41; Rom. 8.16. **4.** Ghosts, spirits of the departed, Deut. 18.11; 1 Sam. 28.8; Job. 4.15; 1 Peter 3.19. **5.** Angels as spirits, Heb. 1.14. **6.** See 'Holy Spirit', The Holy Spirit, p. **174**

**Spiritual gifts** (*G charismata*, the normal word for presents or gifts) Because of the generous, loving grace (*charis*) of God, Christians are given the ability to do things they had never dreamt of doing. Examples in 1 Cor. 12–14 are wisdom, knowledge, faith, healing, miracles, prophecy, discernment of spirits, speaking in tongues, the interpretation of tongues, and love; but all come from the same Spirit. Rom. 12 adds ministry, teaching, exhortation, giving, leadership and compassion. Nobody has all the gifts, so we should respect those who have different gifts from those we have ourselves, and make nobody feel inferior; love and unity in the Church is more important than anything else, 1 Cor. 13

***Stadion*** see 'Measures in other systems'

**Star 1.** The stars were made by God, Gen. 1.16; see 'Orion'; not to be worshipped, Deut. 4.19; Amos 5.26; sometimes identified as angels, Job 38.7; Rev. 1.20; see 'Hosts'. Sometimes they are angelic representatives of other nations, or the Devil, and are cast down, Isa. 14.12–14; Dan. 8.10; Rev. 8.10; 9.1; 12.4; see 'Lucifer'. At the resurrection the righteous will shine like stars, Dan. 12.3. **2.** The Magi believed the star they saw was the counterpart or angel of a great king, Matt. 2.2. Jews identified the Star out of Jacob, Num. 24.17, with the Messiah. Jupiter and Saturn were in close conjunction three times in 7 BC; Halley's comet passed over the perihelion on 8 October, 12 BC; or there may have been an unrecorded supernova

**Steadfast love** in some translations 120 times in the Psalms, and frequently elsewhere in the Hebrew Scriptures, translating *hesed*, which other translations render as 'mercy' or 'lovingkindness'

**Stephen** (*G* = crown) one of The Seven, the first martyr, Acts 6.1–8.2; his speech in his own defence retells the history of the Jews, their importance in God's plan, their frequent rejection of their opportunities, and the call to move outward from focusing on the Temple to world mission; Saul of Tarsus was present and may have been one of those who disputed with him

**Stocks** device for trapping a prisoner's feet between two pieces of wood, to prevent him from escaping, cause him discomfort, and expose him to ridicule, 2 Chron. 16.10; Job 13.27; 33.11; Jer. 20.2–3; 29.26; Acts 16.24

**Stoics** (from their meeting-place, the *Stoa poikile* or painted colonnade in Athens) philosophers, followers of Zeno (336–264 BC), teaching that everything is a part of God, so everything happens because it is fated to; the cycle of history ends in flames and begins again; so we should bear our suffering bravely, Acts 17.18. Paul quotes the Stoic poet Epimenides in the first half of Acts 17.28; Titus 1.12; and Aratas of Cilicia (or perhaps Cleanthes) in the second half of Acts 17.28

**Stone 1.** Stoning, throwing stones at someone until they were dead, was the punishment for keeping dangerous animals, Ex. 21.28–32; human sacrifice, Lev. 20.2–5; witchcraft, Lev. 20.27; sabbath-breaking, Num. 15.32–36; idolatry, Deut. 13.6–10; 17.2–7; disobedient children, 21.18–21; adultery, 22.22–24. Stephen was stoned to death, Acts 7.58; stoning was threatened for Jesus, John 10.31; the apostles, Acts 14.5 (all of these for blasphemy); and see 'Adultery'. **2.** Christ the cornerstone, Isa. 28.16; Dan. 2.34; Matt. 21.42; Mark 12.10; Luke 20.17–18; 1 Peter 2.6. **3.** Precious stones, see 'Jewels'. **4.** The promise that we shall not strike our foot against a stone, Ps. 91.12; Matt. 4.6; Luke 4.11. **5.** Round yellow stones resemble loaves of bread, Matt. 4.3; 7.9. **6.** Many of the stones from Herod's Temple were thrown down when the Temple was demolished in AD 70, but some enormous stones remain in the Western Wall and its surroundings, Mark 13.1–2. **7.** First-century tombs sealed with rolling stones are common in Jerusalem: near the King David Hotel, at Bethphage, the tomb of Queen Helena of Adiabene, the Garden Tomb, John 11.39; 20.1. **8.** Tablets of stone, Ex. 24.12; 1 Kings 8.9; 2 Cor. 3.3. **9.** Christians built into God's temple as living stones, 1 Cor. 3.10–17; 1 Peter 2.5. **10.** Stony ground is where only a thin layer of earth covers the bedrock, so it quickly becomes hot and dry, Matt. 13.5. See also 'Rock'

**Straight Street** see 'Damascus'

**Stumblingblock** protruding stone causing walkers to trip, Lev. 19.14; metaphor for God testing our faithfulness, Jer. 6.21; Ezek. 3.20; metaphor for something which causes others to sin, or lose their faith, Ezek. 14.3–7; Ecclus. (Ben Sira) 31.7; Matt. 16.23; Rom. 14.13; 1 Cor. 8.9; Rev. 2.14. In older translations it is called The Rock of Offence, Rom. 9.32–33, quoting Isa. 8.14–15; 28.16; warning that Jews would stumble over putting their faith in Jesus, Matt. 21.44; 1 Cor. 1.23; 1 Peter 2.8

**Succoth 1.** The first place the Israelites came to after leaving Rameses in Egypt; site uncertain, Ex. 12.37. **2.** The Valley of Succoth is east of the Jordan, near the River Jabbok, Gen. 33.17; Ps. 60.6 = 108.7. **3.** See 'Booths'

**Suffer 1.** Old word for to cause, 'suffer the children' means 'cause the children to come to me', Matt. 19.14. **2.** Jesus taught that he would have to suffer, fulfilling Isa. 53; Matt. 16.21–28; 17.12; Mark 8.31–38; Luke 9.21–27; 24.46; Acts 3.18; see 'Redemption', 'Sacrifice'. **3.** Jesus's suffering helps us understand, endure, and offer to God our own suffering, Rom. 8.17; 2 Tim. 2.11–12; 1 Peter 2.21, see 'Evil'

**Sulphur** (USA Sulfur) see 'Brimstone'

**Sunday** see 'Lord's day'

**Susa** the capital city of the Susiana region from the fourth millennium BC; now called Shush in south-western Iran, north of Abadan; four mounds have been explored, and the site of the Palace of Darius I discovered; also what is called Daniel's Tomb. It was frequently overrun by the Elamites so it is wrongly described as being in Elam, Dan. 8.2; it was sacked by Assur-banipal in 646 BC, but the Persian kings had a summer palace at Susa, Ezra 4.9; Neh. 1.1; Esth. 1.2–9.18; see 'Elam', Mesopotamia, p. **165**

**Susanna** (*H* = lily) **1.** Woman who financially supported Jesus and his disciples, Luke 8.3. **2.** See p. **147**

**Susanna** (Sus.) The Story of Susanna (sue-ZANN-uh), see p. **147**

**Swaddling cloths** strips of fabric wound round an infant from the navel downwards, in the mistaken belief that this would make the legs grow stronger, Job 38.9; Ezek. 16.4; Wisd. 7.4; Luke 2.7, 12. They were also used for setting a broken limb, Ezek. 30.21

**Swearing 1.** Taking an oath, by the name of God, Isa. 65.16; some sacred object, Matt. 5.35; or one's life. This was permitted in the Hebrew Scriptures, Jer. 4.2; provided the oath was not taken for trivial purposes (taking God's name in vain), Ex. 20.7; or broken, Lev. 19.12. God makes promises, swearing by 'myself', Isa. 45.23. Jesus said we should be so honest and truthful that no oaths are needed, Matt. 5.34–37. **2.** Profane language is a sign of a weak character, or anger, which is disapproved of, but is not called swearing in the Bible, 1 Tim. 6.20; 2 Tim. 2.16, see also 'Blasphemy'

**Sweat** in Gethsemane, poured off Jesus as fast as blood from a wound; these verses are not in the best manuscripts, Luke 22.43–44

**Sword** when curved is for slashing; when straight is sometimes for cutting, Josh. 8.24; but more often for stabbing, Ps. 37.15; and the 'double-edged sword' is also for stabbing, with the tip honed on both surfaces for better penetration, Ps. 149.6; the word of God can even separate our motives, Heb. 4.12. Jesus said that those who live by the sword, also die by the sword, Matt. 26.52; Rev. 13.10. Swords were a much-feared weapon, Deut. 13.15; Jer. 6.25; Ezek. 11.8; a symbol for God's judgement, Gen. 3.24; Jer. 12.12; Matt. 10.34. Like the mouth they were called voracious, Isa. 1.20; or sated, 34.6; so the tongue was described as a sword, Ps. 57.4. The sword became a symbol of the word of God, Rev. 1.16; 19.15; Paul speaks of the sword of the Spirit, which is the word of God, Eph. 6.17

**Sychar** town near Jacob's Well; either modern 'Askar or ancient Shechem, John 4.5–6

**Sycomore tree** neither the European nor the American sycamore, which are species of plane, but a type of fig tree, *Ficus sycomorus*, which Amos was seasonally employed to cultivate; into which little Zacchaeus climbed, Amos 7.14; Luke 19.4

**Syene** (sigh-EE-nee) Egyptian town, now just below the Aswan dam, Ezek. 29.10; 30.6. On the island of Elephantine (ELL-ee-fan-TEE-nee) in the river, papyri have revealed a vigorous Jewish community

**Synagogue** (*G sunagoge* = a gathering; *H beth kenesseth*) Jewish place of prayer. Synagogues probably developed during the Exile, when Jews could not visit the Temple, Ezek. 11.16. Jesus went to the synagogue each sabbath, as was his custom; he read the Scriptures, preached and healed, Matt. 4.23; Mark 1.21–29; Luke 4.16–30; John 6.59. Paul began his mission in the synagogues, but when expelled he turned to the Gentiles, Acts 13.5, 14–46; 14.1; 15.21; 18.4–8. The synagogue service, with readings, psalms, exposition and prayers is the basis for the Christian liturgy. See also 'Freedmen'

**Synoptic Gospels** (not the same as 'synopsis' meaning a short summary) Matthew, Mark and Luke; which see the life of Jesus from the 'same point of view', different from that of John; the 'Synoptic Problem' is working out the relationship between them, see pp. **149–50**

**Syntyche** (*G* = fortunate) see 'Euodia'

**Syracuse** historic port in the south-east of the island of Sicily, visited by Paul on his way to Rome, Acts 28.12

**Syria** called Aram in the Hebrew Scriptures was an area east of the Jordan; kings Ben-Hadad, Hazael etc. fought Israel and Judah, 2 Sam. 8.10–2 Kings 16.7. In the Roman Empire, the Province of Syria, north of Galilee, was under a legate who supervised the rulers of the mountainous Province of Judea, Matt. 4.24. Paul began his ministry in the Syrian towns of Damascus and Antioch, Acts 9; 15.23; 18.18; Gal. 1.21. The Syriac language used in the Syrian Orthodox Church is close to the Aramaic that Jesus spoke. See also 'Damascus'

**Syro-Phoenician** (sigh-roh-fuh-NEE-shun) woman from the area around Tyre and Sidon. Jews referred to Gentiles as dogs; by her playful banter she overcame Jesus's objection that there was no time to start a Gentile mission in his lifetime, and he healed her daughter, Mark 7.24–30. Called a Canaanite in Matt. 15.21–28

**Syrtis** (SUR-tiss) now called the Gulf of Syrte or Sirt, from Leptis Magna to Benghazi on the Libyan coast, containing sandbanks on which Paul's shipmates feared running aground, Acts 27.17

**Tabernacle** (*L* = tent) portable sanctuary taken with them by the Israelites in their wanderings. A simple one is described in Ex. 33.7–11; Deut. 31.14–15; a much more elaborate one, which may reflect King David's time, in Ex. 30–31; 35–40; 2 Sam. 6.17. The simple one was a Tent of Meeting tended by Joshua, the elaborate one was God's dwelling, served by Priests and Levites, Num. 1.50. An ideal tabernacle is imagined in heaven where Jesus the High Priest mediates the new covenant, Heb. 8.1–6; 9.1–14; the Word became flesh and 'tabernacled' among us, John 1.14; 'the tabernacle of God is among men', Rev. 21.3

**Tabernacles, Feast of** see 'Booths', 'Calendar'

**Tabitha** see 'Dorcas'

**Tabor, Mount** (*H* = lofty) solitary mountain, 1,800 feet (562 m.) high, in the Valley of Jezreel, Judg. 4.6, 14; 8.18; 1 Sam. 10.3; Ps. 89.12; Hos. 5.1, see also 'Transfiguration'

**Tahpanhes** (TAH-puh-neez, *Eg* = fortress of General Penhase) town in Egypt where Jeremiah was taken; the site has been identified on Lake Manzala, beside the Suez Canal, Jer. 2.16; 43.6–9; 44.1; 46.14; Judith 1.9

**Talent** see 'Money'

**Talitha cum** (TAL-ee-thuh KOOM, *Ar* = little girl, get up) words of Jesus to Jairus's daughter, Mark 5.41

**Tamar** (*H* = palm-tree) **1.** Widow of Er, whose brother Onan refused to give her a child under levirate marriage laws; she posed as a prostitute and conceived twins, Perez and Zerah, by her father-in-law Judah; she was an ancestor of David, and of Jesus, Gen. 38; Ruth 4.12; Matt. 1.3. **2.** Daughter of David, raped by her half-brother Amnon and avenged by her brother Absalom, 2 Sam. 13. **3.** Absalom's daughter, 2 Sam. 14.27. **4.** City in the wilderness fortified by Solomon, 1 Kings 9.18. **5.** Site on the south-eastern border of the ideal Israel, also called Hazazon-Tamar, probably En-Chatseva 25 miles south-west of the Dead Sea, Gen. 14.7; Ezek. 47.18–19. **6.** Hazazon-Tamar is also an alternative name for En-Gedi, 2 Chron. 20.2

**Tammuz** legendary murdered Sumerian shepherd, Dumuzi, for whom women mourned annually in a popular Mesopotamian ritual, Ezek. 8.14; Dan. 11.37; weeping for Jephtha's daughter may be a variant of this, Judg. 11

**Tares** probably darnel, *Lolium tremulentum*, a weed which, when it is growing, looks like wheat, but is poisonous; wheat and tares cannot be separated until full-grown. Answering the question, 'Why doesn't God destroy evil?', Jesus's parable suggests that good and evil are too intertwined in the heart of each of us, Matt. 13.24–30, 36–43

**Targums** translations of the Hebrew Scriptures into Aramaic; at first memorized; written down from the second century AD onwards

**Tarshish 1.** Faraway kingdom, which sent riches by a distinctive type of ship to Tyre and Joppa, Ps. 72.10; Isa. 23.14; 66.19; Ezek. 27.12, 25; Jonah 1.3; probably Tharsis and the Rio Tinto mines, north of Huelva in south-western Spain, well known to the Phoenicians for metal and jewels. **2.** Ships of this type sailing other trade routes, 1 Kings 10.22; 22.49; Isa. 2.16

**Tarsus** capital city of the Roman Province of Cilicia, strategically placed below the pass known as the Cilician Gates, on the road from Rome to the East; birthplace of the Apostle Paul. Cleopatra sailed her barge up the Cydnus River to meet Mark Antony there in 41 BC, when he made it a free city with the power of granting citizenship. It was a university town, so Paul became familiar with Greek and Roman culture. A well is allegedly on the site of his family home; a fine Roman street is where he will certainly have walked, Acts 9.30; 11.25; 15.41; 18.23; 21.39; 22.3

**Tax** in the Hebrew Scriptures is collected by means of a census, Lev. 27.1–8; 2 Sam. 24; 2 Kings 12.4–18; 15.20; 23.35. In the Roman Empire, land-tax and poll-tax were called 'tribute'; Christians should pay these and also indirect taxes, Matt. 22.17; Rom. 13.6–7. Jews suffered double-taxation, having to pay temple-tax, Matt. 17.25. See also 'Money'

**Tax-collectors** Under the system known as 'tax-farming', they bought at auction a contract to collect taxes in an area, paid the agreed price to the Roman authorities, then were totally unscrupulous in collecting more than that from the tax-payers and keeping the profit. They were hated, as oppressors of their own people and traitors who collaborated with the Roman occupation. Jesus enjoyed their company, and influenced many to become reformed characters, Matt. 11.19; 21.31–32; Luke 5.27–32; 18.10–14; 19.2–10

**Teachers** of the law see 'Scribes'

**Tears** see 'Mourning'

**Teeth 1.** See 'Eye for an eye'. **2.** 'Children's teeth set on edge' (literally 'made insensitive') teaches individual responsibility, Jer. 31.29. **3.** 'Gnashing (grinding) of teeth', gesture of rage and despair, Matt. 8.12

**Tekoa** town located at Khirbat Tequ'a between Bethlehem and Hebron; birthplace of the prophet Amos, 2 Sam. 14.2–9; 2 Chron. 11.6; 20.20; Jer. 6.1; Amos 1.1; 1 Macc. 9.33

**Tell** or **Tel** mound revealing the site of an ancient city, see 'Amarna'

**Tema** oasis, now called Teima, about 200 miles NNE of Medina, Job. 6.19; Isa. 21.14; Jer. 25.23

**Teman** (*H* = southern) city of Edom, 3 miles east of Sela (Petra), Gen. 36.11, 34; Jer. 49.20; Ezek. 25.13; Amos 1.12

**Temple 1.** From earliest times, humans have marked places of encounter with the holy, by stones, trees, open altars or sacred enclosures. **2.** To monotheistic Israelites, the temples of other gods were abhorrent. **3.** David intended to build the Temple at Jerusalem on the threshing-floor of Araunah the Jebusite, where the plague had stopped, 2 Sam. 7.1–5; 24.16–25; 1 Chron. 21.15–27; 22.1; this was identified with Mount Moriah where Abraham had been willing to sacrifice Isaac, Gen. 22.2–14. The rock at the centre of the Muslim Dome of the Rock, which is probably where the Holy of Holies stood, may have been the threshing floor. The first Temple was built by Solomon, 1 Kings 6; 8; 9; 2 Chron. 3–7. **4.** The temples to YHWH at Dan, Bethel and Shiloh focused the worship of the Northern Kingdom, but as the Hebrew Scriptures were finally edited by those from the Southern Kingdom, they regarded these as rebellion against the command to have a single sanctuary. **5.** After the Exile the Second Temple was built by Zerubbabel, but the people wept because it was smaller than Solomon's, Ezra 3.12–13; 6.3–5, 13–16; Hag. 2.1–3. Herod the Great extended the platform on which it stood until it was the largest in the world, and decorated the Temple with precious materials. After the Romans destroyed it in AD 70, all that remains is the Western Wall, the steps up to the southern gates, the south-east corner, and some parts of the foundations, Mark 13.1–2. See also 'Money-changers'. **6.** Christians are the New Temple, 1 Cor. 3.16; 6.19

**Temptation 1.** Wanting to do something you know to be wrong, 1 Tim. 6.9; James 1.12. **2.** 'The Tempter' is one of the names of the Devil, Matt. 4.3; 1 Thess. 3.5, but if we give way to temptation the blame is ours alone. **3.** The Temptation of Jesus, to gain followers by feeding them, fascinating them, or forcing them, instead of following the way of the cross, Matt. 4.1–11; Mark 1.13; Luke 4.1–13; he was tempted exactly as we are, Heb. 4.15. **4.** Jesus replied, quoting Deut. 6.16, meaning instead of testing God's love by asking him to support our plans, we should be trying to discover his. **5.** We pray, 'lead us not into temptation', probably a reference to the testing times of the Last Days, remembering that God as a good parent allows our will and determination to be tested, but gives us the grace to bear it, Matt. 6.13; 1 Cor. 10.13

**Ten Commandments** the 'small print' in the contract between God and the Israelites: the covenant was that God would lead them and care for them, provided they observed the basic minimum of behaviour needed for life together as a community. Our duty to God comes before our duty to our neighbour. The Commandments are not legislation imposing penalties, but headings, listing areas in which we must make moral choices, Ex. 20; Deut. 5; see also 'Covenant'

**Tent-making** profession which Paul shared with Priscilla and Aquila; included tents for soldiers and nomads and awnings for shops and theatres, made of goats-hair or leather, and gave an opportunity for 'gossiping the gospel', Acts 18.3; 20.24; 1 Cor. 4.12; 9.14–15

**Teraphim** household idols, used for fortune telling, Gen. 31.19–35; Judg. 17–18; 1 Sam. 19.13; 2 Kings 23.24; Ezek. 21.21; Zech. 10.2. Documents found at Nuzi in Mesopotamia show that a man could inherit his father-in-law's property if the teraphim were given to him

**Terebinth** large deciduous tree of the genus *Pistacia*, Gen. 12.6; Deut. 11.30; Isa. 6.13; Hos. 4.13; Ecclus. (Ben Sira) 24.16; see also 'Oaks'

**Tertius** ($L$ = third) wrote Paul's Letter to the Romans at his dictation, and added his own greetings, Rom. 16.22

**Tertullus** professional orator brought in to prosecute Paul before Felix; he follows the standard format of Roman rhetoric, Acts 24.1–8

**Testament** see 'Covenant'

**Tetragrammaton** ($G$ = four letters) YHWH, see 'Lord'

**Tetrarch** originally ruler of one-fourth of a kingdom, applied to several vassals appointed by Rome to rule provinces, see 'Herod Family', 'Judea'

**Thaddaeus** called in some manuscripts Lebbaeus, see 'Judas 4.'

**Theatre** open-air auditorium for dramatic performances, originally religious, later competitive; also for public debates, as in the riot concerning Paul in Ephesus, where the fine theatre survives from his time, Acts 19.29–41

**Thebes** (theebz) Egyptian city on the Nile 300 miles south of Cairo, destroyed by the Assyrian king Ashurbanipal, Jer. 46.25–26; Ezek. 30.14–16; Nahum 3.8–11; noted today for Karnak, Luxor and the Valley of the Kings

**Thebez** town in Ephraim where a woman dropped a millstone on Abimelech's head, Judg. 9.50–54; 2 Sam. 11.21; probably Tubas, 10 miles north-east of Nablus

**Theophilus** ($G$ = lover of God) name, or pseudonym, of a Gentile to whom the Gospel of Luke and the Acts of the Apostles are both addressed. His title 'Your excellency' indicates a high official, maybe a lawyer or judge at Paul's trial in Rome, Luke 1.3; Acts 1.1, see p. **150**

**1 Thessalonians** (1 Thess.) (stress on the 'o', which is long in 'Thessalonians' and short in 'Thessalonica') The First Letter of Paul to the Thessalonians, see p. **156**

**2 Thessalonians** (2 Thess.) The Second Letter of Paul to the Thessalonians, see p. **156**

**Thessalonica** (*G* = victory in Thessaly) port city, capital of the Roman Province of Macedonia; Paul visited Thessalonica on his second missionary journey and was driven out by a riot; to the church there he addressed two letters, Acts 17.1–9; Phil. 4.16. Frequently destroyed by fire and earthquake, all that can be seen from biblical times in modern Thessaloniki is the Roman Forum, see 'Politarchs'

**Theudas** leader of a failed revolutionary movement, mentioned by Gamaliel, Acts 5.36

**Thief** Thief at midnight, Luke 12.39; Sheep-stealer, John 10.1; Judas, John 12.6; Crucified with Jesus, Matt. 27.38; Mark 15.27; Luke 23.32; Jesus comes like a thief, 1 Thess. 5.2; 2 Pet. 3.10; Rev. 3.3; 16.15; see also 'Robbers'

**Third Day** the Resurrection of Jesus fulfilled Hos. 6.12; Matt. 16.21; John 2.1; Acts 10.40; 1 Cor. 15.3–4

**Thomas** (*Ar* = twin) also called Didymus (*G* = twin) one of The Twelve; stayed apart, doubting that Jesus was risen, but when he joined the others was the first to acclaim him as 'My Lord and my God'; traditionally he travelled to India, Matt. 10.3; John 11.16; 14.5; 20.24–29; 21.2

**Thorns 1.** Jesus said you can no more expect good deeds from bad people than grapes from thorns, Matt. 7.16. **2.** Crown of thorns, see 'Crown 3.'. **3.** Paul had a nagging pain (some say a human adversary) which he describes as a 'thorn in the flesh', 2 Cor. 12.7

**Three Taverns** place on the Appian Way where Christians came 30 miles from Rome to meet Paul; probably underneath modern Cisterna di Latina; the Roman *taberna* sold food and provisions, Acts 28.15

**Threshing** separation of the grain from the straw and chaff on a hard threshing floor, either by an animal walking on it, Deut. 25.4; 1 Cor. 9.9; with a flail (hinged rod) or a sledge (heavy block of wood embedded with stones which is dragged over the grain, by a donkey or ox), Judg. 6.37; Ruth 3.1–18; 2 Sam. 24.16–25; 1 Kings 22.10; Isa. 28.27; 41.15; Micah 4.13; Amos 1.3; see also 'Muzzling', 'Winnowing'

**Thyatira** (THIGH-uh-TIE-ruh) one of the seven churches addressed in the Revelation; the modern city of Akhisar stands over the site, 60 miles north-east of İzmir in Turkey. Thyatira had many trade guilds, which required their members to join in feasts at pagan temples; it was a centre for purple dying, Lydia the purple-cloth merchant in Philippi came from Thyatira, Acts16.14; Rev. 1.11; 2.18–29

**Tiberias** Hellenistic city founded by Herod Antipas on the west shore of Lake Galilee, also called Lake Tiberias; people from Tiberias came to hear Jesus, John 6.1, 23; 21.1

**Tiberius** (*L* = son of the River Tiber) Roman Emperor AD 14–37, throughout Jesus's ministry, Luke 3.1; his image was on the tribute money, Mark 12.17

**Tiglath-Pileser III** (*Ak Tukulti-apil-esharra* = my trust is in the heir) also called Pul, king of Assyria 745–727 BC; attacked the Northern Kingdom of Israel, and deported some of the population, 2 Kings 15.19–20, 29; 16.5–10; see Mesopotamia, p. **165**

**Tigris** river in Mesopotamia, Gen. 2.14; Dan. 10.4; Tob. 6.2–3; Ecclui. (Ben Sira) 24.25

**Time** see 'Eternity'

**Timnah** (*H* = allotted portion) town identified as Tel Batash, 28 miles west of Jerusalem in the Sorek Valley; it changed hands several times between the Israelites and the Philistines; Samson married a Philistine woman there; Delilah's home was nearby, Gen. 38.12–14; Josh. 15.10; Judg. 14–15; 16.4; 2 Chron. 28.18

**Timothy** (*G* = honours God) Christian from Lystra whose mother Eunice and grandmother Lois were Jewish, but his father was Greek and Timothy had not been circumcised. He accompanied Paul on his journeys and became his representative, Acts 16.1–5; Rom. 16.21; 1 Cor. 4.17; 16.10–11; Phil. 2.19–23; 1 Thess. 3.1–6; Heb. 13.23

**1 Timothy** (1 Tim.) The First Letter of Paul to Timothy, see p. **157**

**2 Timothy** (2 Tim.) The Second Letter of Paul to Timothy, see p. **157**

**Tirzah** (*H* = beauty) capital of the Northern Kingdom until Omri established Samaria. Here Zimri assassinated Elah, and died 7 days later when Omri besieged Tirzah. The site is at Tell el-Farah, 7 miles north-east of Nablus, 1 Kings 14.17–16.24; 2 Kings 15.14; S. of Sol. 6.4

**Tithe** giving one tenth of one's harvest or income to the work of God, Lev. 27.30–33; Deut. 14.22–29; Matt. 23.23

**Tittle** see 'Jot and tittle'

**Titus** a Greek disciple, who carried one or more of Paul's letters to the Corinthians; textual variants make it uncertain whether he was circumcised; he went to Dalmatia; his tomb is at Gortyna in Crete, Gal. 2.1–3; 2 Cor. 2.13; 7.14–16; 8.16–23; 12.18; 2 Tim. 4.10

**Titus** (Titus) The Letter of Paul to Titus (TIE-tus), see p. **157**

**Tobias** (*H* = Jah is good) see p. **145**

**Tobit** (Tob.) The Book of Tobit (TOE-bit), see p. **145**

**Tombs** see 'Absalom', 'Calvary', Ephrath, 'Hebron', 'Resurrection', 'Rome', 'Stone 7.', 'Titus'

**Tongues** 'speaking in tongues' is an experience of ecstatic prayer, when sounds pour from the mouth of the worshipper which go beyond language. It is a gift of the Spirit, and encourages those to whom it is given, though Paul says it is less important than love and must not be divisive, 1 Cor. 13.1; 14.1–40. At Pentecost it is represented as overcoming the divisions caused by language, Acts 2.8–11

**Topheth** (*H* = hearth) altar of child-sacrifice in the Hinnom Valley, 2 Kings 23.10; Jer. 7.31–32

**Torah** (*H* = law) Hebrew name for the Pentateuch, and YHWH's instructions on how his people should live

**Tower of Babel** Gen. 11.1–9, see 'Babel', Mesopotamia, p. **165**

**Tradition 1.** The tradition of the elders was criticized by Jesus where its interpretation of the law went against the spirit of the law, Matt. 15.1–20; Mark 7.1–22. **2.** Paul claimed to pass on the tradition of what he had been taught about Jesus, 1 Cor. 11.2–16, 23–24; 15.3–7; 2 Thess. 3.6

**Transfiguration** when Peter, James and John on a mountaintop saw Jesus shining with divine brightness, accompanied by Moses and Elijah, who spoke about the 'exodus' (*G exodos*) he was to about to accomplish; traditionally on Mount Tabor, but Mount Hermon is more likely, Matt. 17.1–8; Mark 9.2–8; Luke 9.28–36, see '*Shekinah*'

**Tribes** the twelve tribes of Israel, descendants of the sons of Jacob, are Reuben, Simeon, Levi, Judah, Dan, Naphtali, Gad, Asher, Issachar, Zebulun, Joseph (Ephraim and Manasseh) and Benjamin, Gen. 29; 30; 35; Deut. 33

**Tribunal** wherever a Roman governor instructed his tribune to set up his standard, usually on a raised platform or *bema*, was the tribunal, where he heard lawsuits, Matt. 27.19; John 19.13; Acts 18.12–17; 25.6–21; see also 'Praetorium'

**Tribute** see 'Tax'

**Trinity** While a developed doctrine of the Trinity is not found in the Bible, the description of God the Father, the Spirit of God, and Jesus the Son of God, and the statement that 'I and my Father are one', cannot be summarized without using language about three persons in one God, Matt. 12.28; 28.19; John 10.30; 14.16–17

**Troas** city founded on the coast when the estuary at Troy silted up, called Alexandria Troas; there are a few scattered ruins near the village of Dalyan, south of the Dardanelles in Turkey; here Paul received his vision of a man from Macedonia calling him; set sail towards Greece; healed a young man who had fallen from a window, Acts 16.6–11; 20.4–12; 2 Cor. 2.12–13; 2 Tim. 4.13

**Trophimus** (*G* = fosterchild) uncircumcised Gentile Christian from Ephesus, who accompanied Paul to Jerusalem, and provoked a riot when suspected of crossing the dividing wall into the Temple Court of Israel, Acts 20.4; 21.29; Eph. 2.14

**Trumpet** both the *shofar*, the ram's-horn, and the later metal trumpet, were used as a battle signal, Josh. 6.4; Judg. 3.27; 2 Sam. 2.28; 18.16; Jer. 4.19; 51.27; 1 Cor. 14.8; to celebrate victory, 1 Sam. 13.3; in worship, Lev. 23.23–25; 25.9; Num. 29.1–6; Ps. 98.6; 150.3; and to warn of God's judgement, Hos. 5.8; Joel 2.1; Amos 2.2; Zeph. 1.16; 1 Cor. 15.52; 1 Thess. 4.16; Rev. 8.2

**Tryphaena, Tryphosa** (*G* = dainty, delicate) two women, possibly sisters, who worked for the church in Rome, to whom Paul sent greetings, Rom. 16.12

**Tubal-Cain** the first smith, Gen. 4.22

**Tumours** which broke out on the people of Ashdod when they put the Ark of the Covenant in the temple of their idol. Called 'Emerods' (haemorrhoids) in the King James Version, they were more likely the swellings symptomatic of bubonic plague, 1 Sam. 5; 6.4–18

**Turban** called a mitre in old translations, part of the vestments of the priests, Ex. 28.4, 37, 39

**Turtle** see 'Dove'

---

**The Twelve** selected by Jesus to represent the twelve sons of Jacob as leaders ('judges') of the new Israel, Matt. 19.28, see 'Apostles'. Harmonizing the lists in Matt. 10.2–4; Mark 3.16–19; Luke 6.14–16; Acts 1.13; they are:

Simon Peter = Cephas
Andrew, Peter's brother
James, son of Zebedee
John, son of Zebedee
Philip
Bartholomew = Nathanael
Thomas called Didymus or the twin
Matthew = Levi, the tax-collector
James the Less, son of Alphaeus
Thaddeus = Judas, son (or brother) of James
Simon the Cananaean or Zealot
Judas Iscariot, replaced by Matthias

---

**Twin Brothers** figurehead of the ship carrying Paul to Rome, are Castor and Pollux, sons of Zeus and Leda, Acts 28.11

**Tychicus** (*G* = fortunate) trusted colleague of Paul, from the Province of Asia, who carried his letters to their destination, Acts 20.4; Eph. 6.21–22; Col. 4.7; 2 Tim. 4.12; Titus 3.12

**Tyre** Phoenician port on an island, now as-Sur in Lebanon, see 'Hiram', 1 Chron. 22.4; Ezek. 27–28; Mark 7.24–31

**Ugarit** huge ancient commercial city, excavated at Ras Shamra, north of the Syrian port of Lattakia. A vast library of inscribed tablets was found in several different languages; Ugaritic is a Semitic language, and they revealed many insights into Canaanite culture at the time the Israelites emerged as a people. Cycles of myths include the defeat of the sea-god Yamm by the storm-god Baal, and Baal's conflict with his brother Mot or death; he is brought back to life and the supreme god, El, restores the regular cycle of fertility

**Unforgivable sin** see 'Blasphemy 2.'

**Unknown god** to whom an altar was seen by Paul in Athens; he used it to preach that he was not introducing a new god, but telling them something they had not hitherto known about the God they already worshipped, Acts 17.22–31. During a plague, the Athenians were told to release a flock of sheep, and sacrifice each to the god whose altar they lay nearest to; it is possible that one lay down near no known shrine, and a special altar was erected 'to the unknown god'

**Unity of the Church** Jesus taught us to love each other uncritically and share a common table with those of a different cultural and social background, Luke 14.12–14; John 10.16; Paul faced some very deep divisions on matters of principle, but he still worked and wrote for unity between Jewish and Gentile Christians, Gal. 3.28; Eph. 1.10; 2.19; 4.1–6, 13; to split the Church is to tear the Body of Christ limb from limb, see 'Members'; Jesus prayed for the unity of the Church 'that the world may believe', John 17.20–21

**Unleavened bread** without any yeast, used at the Passover because there was no time to wait for it to rise when the Israelites fled from Egypt, and annually at the Feast of Unleavened Bread to remind them of the Exodus and wandering, Ex. 12.39–13.10; 29.2; Lev. 2.4; Deut. 16.1–8; Ezra 6.22; Matt. 26.17; 1 Cor. 5.6–8, see also 'Calendar', 'Leaven'

**Upper room** see 'Pentecost'

**Ur of the Chaldees** (*Sumerian* = flame) original home of Abraham's family; identified as Tell al-Muqayyar 120 miles north of Basra in modern Iraq, which has yielded numerous grave-goods giving a vivid impression of Mesopotamian culture from the fifth millennium until around 400 BC, Gen. 11.27–32; see Mesopotamia, p. **165**

**Uriah** (*H* = Jah is my light) **1.** The Hittite, husband of Bath-sheba, whom David arranged to have murdered, 2 Sam. 11. **2.** The High Priest, 2 Kings 16.10–16; Isa. 8.2. **3.** The Prophet, murdered by King Jehoiachim, Jer. 26.20–23

**Urim and Thummim** probably stones which functioned like dice, for casting lots to find the Lord's answer to yes/no questions; originally available to all the Levites, they were later used only by the High Priest and kept in his breast-plate, Ex. 28.30; Num. 27.21; Deut. 33.8; 1 Sam. 14.41

**Usury** lending money in order to receive interest; lending is praised in Ps. 17.26; 112.5; Ecclus. (Ben Sira) 29.2; Luke 6.35; taking interest is condemned, Ex. 22.25–27; Lev. 25.36–37; Ps. 15.5; Ezek. 18.8; 22.5; charging interest to fellow-Israelites is condemned, Neh. 8; when lending to foreigners it is allowed, Deut. 23.20; and Prov. 28.8 is a paradox. Banking is accepted, Matt. 25.27; Luke 19.23. Interpreters either say that only exorbitant interest is disallowed, or that in the changed circumstances of today, old prohibitions no longer apply

**Uzzah** son of Adinadab, who tried to steady the Ark of the Covenant when the oxen pulling it stumbled, and died for his presumption – God can look after himself, 2 Sam. 6.1–7

**Uzziah** (*H* = Jah is my strength) see 'Azariah 1.'

**Vanity** old translation of Hebrew *hevel*, puff of wind or small cloud, something which does not last for long; it has nothing to do with arrogance. In Ecclesiastes, expresses the transitory impermanence of the material world and its glories, Eccles. 1.2

**Veil of the Temple** curtain hanging before the holy of holies; only the High Priest could pass through it once a year on the Day of Atonement to enter God's presence. Torn in two when Jesus was crucified, symbolizing intimate access to God available to every believer at all times through the death of Christ, and the redundancy of the Temple ritual, Ex. 26.31–33; Lev. 16.12–15; Matt. 27.51; Heb. 10.19–20

**Vial 1.** Flask containing oil for anointing, 1 Sam. 10.1; 2 Kings 9.1. **2.** Broad, shallow bowl; some full of incense, symbolizing prayer; others containing the wrath of God, Rev. 5.8; 15.7–8; 16; 21.9

**Vine.** Noah was the legendary discoverer of wine, Gen. 9.20; spies brought back grapes from Eshcol, Num. 13.23–24. In a vineyard, the ground had to be prepared; a wall built; and a watchtower constructed, Ps. 80.8–14; Mark 12.1; surplus branches pruned so that the remainder bore abundant grapes, Isa. 2.4; 18.5; at vintage-time, grapes were carried to a winepress, often a trough cut from solid rock, and trodden out, Isa. 63.1–6; Rev. 14.19–20. The juice was fermented in vats, then poured into an earthenware amphora or a leather bottle, Ps. 4.7; Isa. 16.10; Joel 3.13; Mark 2.22. Ideally, every family should have its own vine, Micah 4.4. The 'Song of the Vineyard' compared Israel to a choice vine which would be destroyed because it bore sour fruit, Isa. 5.1–7. Jesus is the vine; we, the branches, can only bear the fruit of good works if united by faith to Jesus the trunk; even then we must be 'pruned' by suffering, John 15.1–17. Jesus compared his teaching to new wine, Matt. 9.17; told parables about vineyards, 20.1–16; 21.33–41; and used wine as a symbol of the blood of the covenant, at the Last Supper, 26.28; Paul advises against abstaining from wine, 1 Tim. 5.23

**Vinegar** cheap acidic wine which soldiers drank; offered to Jesus at the crucifixion, Ps. 69.21; Matt. 27.48; Mark 15.36; Luke 23.36; John 19.29

**Vipers** snakes whose bite is poisonous; John the Baptist compares Pharisees trying to escape God's wrath to a nest of young snakes fleeing a forest fire, Matt. 3.7; 12.34; a viper bit Paul's hand in Malta but did not harm him, Acts 28.3–6, see also 'Asp'

**Virgin** mistranslation of the Hebrew word for a young woman, Isa. 7.14. Isaiah prophesies to Ahaz that a young woman who will soon become pregnant, perhaps Ahaz's new wife, will be so thankful for the promised deliverance that when the child is born, she will call him 'God-is-on-our-side'. In the Greek translation, this verse, predicting the virgin-birth of a child called 'God-with-us', became an ideal text to proclaim the birth of Jesus, God incarnate, born 'not of the will of the flesh, nor of the will of man, but of God', Matt. 1.18–23; Luke 1.27–38; John 1.13; 2 Cor. 5.19; see also 'Miracles'

**Virgin Mary** husband of Joseph, Matt. 1.16–20; visited by Gabriel, Luke 1.27–38; visited Elizabeth, Luke 1.39–56; sang Magnificat, Luke 1.46–55; went to Bethlehem, Luke 2.5; mother of Jesus, Mark 6.3; welcomed the shepherds, Luke 2.16–19; welcomed wise men, Matt. 2.11; her sorrow predicted by Simeon, Luke 2.34; fled to Egypt, Matt. 2.13–21; took Jesus aged 12 to the Temple, Luke 2.41–52;

attended the wedding at Cana, John 2.1–12; tried to dissuade him, Mark 3.31–35; stood by the cross, John 19.25–27; prayed with the believers, Acts 1.14.

**Vision** seeing a scene which is not physically present but has symbolic meaning; hallucinations come from inside the brain, visions are sent by God, Ps. 89.19. More generally, vision is insight into God's purposes, Isa. 1.1; Prov. 29.18; see also 'Transfiguration', Apocalyptic, p. **175**

**Visitation 1.** Time when God visits us, bringing a special opportunity for repentance; if we miss it, it may be too late, Luke 1.68; 19.44; 1 Peter 2.12. **2.** The visit which the Virgin Mary paid to her cousin Elizabeth, Luke 1.39–48

**Voice of God** aural equivalent of a vision, when a thunderclap, a psychological experience, or a conviction of knowing God's viewpoint, leads a prophet to proclaim, 'Thus says the Lᴏʀᴅ', Ex. 19.19; 1 Kings 19.13; Ps. 18.13; Isa. 7.7; Matt. 3.17; 17.5; John 12.28; Acts 9.4; Rev. 1.10

**Vow** solemn promise made to God, Lev. 27; Ps. 22.25; 132.2; Paul probably made or supported a temporary Nazirite vow, Num. 6.1–21; Acts 18.18; 21.23–26

**Wadi** Arabic for brook or small river, often a dry riverbed in summer with flashfloods in winter, 1 Sam. 17.40

**Walls** of a city, for defence, also called bulwarks and ramparts, with towers or a fortified citadel enclosure, a smooth sloping glacis to make approach difficult, and double or triple gateways, Josh. 6; Ps. 48.13. Double walls are casemates. Lookouts or watchmen were posted on the walls, Hab. 2.1

**Water 1.** From the rock, see 'Rephidim'. **2.** Jesus is living water, John 4. **3.** From within the believer, living water, John 7.38. **4.** See 'Baptism', 'Life'

**Wave Offering** means of offering sacrifices by waving them before the altar, Ex. 29.22–24; especially at the Feast of First-fruits, Lev. 23.9–11, see 'Calendar'

**Weeds** see 'Tares'

**Weeks, Feast of** see 'Calendar'

---

**Weights** see also 'Measures'

**1.** Hebrew

*gerah*, 0.57 grammes; 0.02 oz., Ex. 30.13

*beka*, half-shekel = 10 *gerah*, 5.7 g.; 0.2 oz., Gen. 24.22; Ex. 30.13–15; 38.26

*pim* = 1.33 *beka*, 7.8 g.; 0.27 oz., 1 Sam. 13.19–21

*shekel* = 2 *beka*, 11.4 g.; 0.4 oz., Gen. 24.22; see also 'Money'

*kikkar* = 50 *shekels*, talent, Ex. 25.39; 37.24; 38.27; 2 Sam. 12.30; 1 Chron. 28.2

The 'Sanctuary Shekel' or 'shekel by the King's weight' was slightly larger, Ex. 30.13–15, 24; 38.25–26; 2 Sam 14.26

**2.** Greek and Roman

*mina* = 50 *shekel*, 571.2 g.; 1.26 lb., see also 'Money'

*talent* = 60 *mina*, 34.27 kg.; 75.6 lb., see also 'Money'

*litra*, Latin *libra*, translated 'pound', 340 g.; 12 oz., John 12.3; 19.39

---

**Western Text** group of early manuscripts of Acts from the western Roman Empire, giving additional information and different readings in many passages from the Alexandrian text in most Bibles

**Wheels** see 'Cherubim'

# Whipping

**Whipping** see 'Scourging'
**Widow** 1. Caring for, Ex. 22.22–24; Job 29.13; Acts 6.1; 1 Tim. 5.3–16; James 1.27. 2. Widow whose oil-jug was never dry, 1 Kings 17. 3. Widow who gave a tiny coin, Mark 12.42
**Wife** see 'Marriage'
**Wilderness** uncultivated region, with no permanent inhabitants, though nomads can sometimes find sparse grazing for their animals; whereas a desert is arid and bleak, Job 1.19; 38.25–27; Ps. 78.40; 105.41; 106.14. The 'howling wilderness' was the haunt of demons, Deut. 32.10; Matt. 12.43. John the Baptist preached; Jesus was tempted; he retreated to pray; he fed the crowd; and Paul was in danger in the wilderness, Matt. 3.1; 4.1; 14.13; 15.33; 2 Cor. 11.26. Clouds from the Mediterranean, west of Israel, drop their rain before reaching the high ground, so eastern slopes are mostly dry, forming the Wilderness of Judea, west of the Dead Sea, Matt. 3.1; the Rocks of the Wild Goats near En-Gedi, 1 Sam. 24.2; and the Arabah, 1 Kings 19.4. The Wilderness of Beersheba is now called the Negeb, Ps. 126.4. Next are the Wilderness of Zin, also known as the Wilderness of Kadesh, Num. 33.36; the Wilderness of Paran, Num. 13.26; the Wilderness of Sin, Ex. 16.1; and the Wilderness of Shur, east of Egypt, 1 Sam. 15.7. Together these make up the Sinai Desert. Prophets envisaged the wilderness becoming fertile at the last, Isa. 35.1–10; 40.3–5; 41.18–19; 43.19–20
**Willows, Wadi of the** see 'Zered'
**Wine** see 'Vine'
**Winged creatures** see 'Cherubim'
**Winnowing** after threshing, throwing the grain into the air with a fork or shovel; useless chaff and straw, caught by the wind, is blown aside, where it can be burnt; the heavier grain falls direct to the ground; used as a symbol of God's judgement when he separates out worthless people 'by wind and fire', Ruth 3.2; Isa. 30.24; Jer. 15.7; Matt. 3.11–12; see also 'Threshing'
**Wisdom** following the example of Egyptian administrators, was seen as a desirable quality for King Solomon, 1 Kings 3; 10; and all who worked for the king, Eccles. 8.1–5; Jer. 18.18; it was practical common sense learnt by copying out proverbs, Prov. 1.2–6; 8.32–36. Reverence for the LORD is the beginning of wisdom, Job. 28; Ps. 111.10; Prov. 9.10; Ecclus. (Ben Sira) 1.11–27. Wisdom was also needed by those who serve God; it is the gift of God, Prov. 2.6; Isa. 11.2–3; Wisd. 9.17. The 'Wisdom Literature' was written by and for this class of scribe; biblical examples include Job, Proverbs, Ecclesiastes, Ecclesiasticus and the Wisdom of Solomon, and passages in other books also. God's Wisdom is one with God, and assists in creation, Ps. 104; Prov. 8.22–31; Jer. 51.15; yet has a life of her own, Prov. 1.20–33; 8; 9.1–12; used as a model for thinking about Jesus, the Holy Spirit, and their relationship to God the Father, Acts 6.3; 1 Cor. 1.24; 12.8
**The Wisdom of Solomon** (Wisd.) see p. 146
**Wise men** see 'Magi'
**Women** in a patriarchal society nevertheless had considerable authority in and around the home, Prov. 31.10–31; women's initiative plays a significant part in the biblical narrative, see 'Deborah', 'Rebekah', 'Sarah', etc. The Bible absorbs some of the assumptions and language of the society around it, but Jesus gave women a higher position than his contemporaries: accepting their aid, defending them against the oppression of casual divorce, healing those whom others would have counted unclean or mad, treating with respect society's outcasts; he made women the first

witnesses of his resurrection, then sent them out, the true meaning of 'apostle'; he could not make them members of The Twelve, as those had to symbolize the sons of Jacob. Paul accepted Lydia as the natural leader of the church in Philippi, and addresses several women on terms of equality as co-workers, see 'Apostle'. To avoid scandal, he insisted on head-covering, 1 Cor. 11.2–16. 'Women should keep silence', 14.34–35, may be to encourage families to discuss the sermon at home; it contradicts 1 Cor. 11.5; the verses may be a late addition, not by Paul. 'Women not to teach' (1 Tim. 2.12) is very negative; if it is by Paul, it must be for a specific situation, for it is clear that Chloe, Dorcas, Euodia, Julia, Junia, Lydia, Nympha, Persis, Phoebe, Priscilla, Syntyche, Tryphaena, Tryphosa and many others had considerable authority in the early Church. In Eph. 5.21–32 Paul quotes the common belief that the relationship between Adam and Eve is a pattern for that between Christ and the Church. His readers assumed that meant that wives must obey their husbands; Paul argues that it also means that husbands must sacrifice themselves completely to their wives. In Gal. 3.28 he said that 'there is no longer male and female; for all of you are one in Christ Jesus'

**Word of God** When God speaks in the Hebrew Scriptures, his word is eternal and takes on a life of its own, Gen. 1.3; Isa. 40.8; 55.11; Ezek. 12.25–28; Wisd. 18.14–16; so John 1.1–18 describes Jesus as the eternal and powerful Word. But the Greek word used, *logos*, also means logic and reason, so we see that the Divine logic, by which the world was created, dwelt among us, 1 John 1.1; Rev. 19.13

**Work, works 1.** Human labour is valued by God, 'In their work is their prayer', Ecclus. (Ben Sira) 38.24–34. **2.** The work of God, in creation, Job. 14.15; Ps. 8.6; 145; in salvation, Ex. 14.31; Isa. 5.12; through Jesus, John 5.17; 8.41; 10.25; 14.10–12. **3.** Christians are instructed to bring forth the fruit of good works, Matt. 5.16; Rom. 2.6–7; 2 Cor. 9.8; Col. 1.10; 2 Thess. 2.17. **4.** We cannot earn a place in the Kingdom by 'the works of the law', by keeping all the commandments of the Hebrew Scriptures. Jew and Gentile alike can only find justification by grace through faith, not works, Gal. 2.16; Rom. 3.21–26. **5.** This does not excuse us from trying to do good, 'I will show you my faith by my works', James 2.14–26

**Wormwood 1.** Bitter herb of the genus *Artemisia*, used as a tonic and stimulant, and in making vermouth; metaphorically, bitterness, Deut. 29.18; Prov. 5.4; Jer. 9.15; 23.15; Lam. 3.15; Amos 5.7. **2.** Star which fell from heaven, turning a third of the waters bitter, Rev. 8.11

**Worship** or 'worth-ship', is showing what is worth most to you. God does not need our worship, but we need to put ourselves in a relationship of dependent gratitude with God, Gen. 22.5; Ps. 95.6; 100.2; Dan. 3.5; John 4.23–24; Rom. 12.1

**Wrath** God's determined opposition to all that is evil. Because God loves the whole creation, God's wrath is shown against any part of it which hurts or harms another, 2 Chron. 19.2; Ps. 90.7–8; Rom. 1.18; 2.7–8. Not to be compared to capricious human anger, Prov. 14.17; James 1.20; the power of God's wrath is the power of his love, Isa. 54.8; Zech. 8.2. Fear of God's wrath should turn us from evil, Ps. 90.11; Matt. 3.7; John 3.36. God is quick to forgive, Ps. 103.8–9; Jonah 4.2; Micah 7.18; the death of Christ enables God to redeem evil instead of destroying it, Rom. 5.9; 1 Thess. 1.10

**Xerxes** see 'Exile', Mesopotamia, p. **165**.

**Yarmuk** see 'Jarmuth'
**Year** see 'Calendar'

Yeast

**Yeast** see 'Leaven'

**YHWH** or **Yahweh** the name of God, see 'LORD'

**Yoke** shaped piece of wood placed across the shoulders of one or two domestic animals so they can pull a plough etc., 1 Kings 19.19; Luke 14.19. It would not work efficiently if the animals were of a different size, Deut. 22.10; 2 Cor. 6.14. Jews refer to the yoke of the law, Ecclus. (Ben Sira) 6.24–30; Jesus said his yoke is easy, Matt. 11.28–30

**Young** advice for, Prov. 1.8–19; Eccles. 11.9–12.1; young and old together, Ps. 148.12; Joel 2.28; dying young, Wisd. 4

**Zacchaeus** (*H* = pure) chief tax-collector in Jericho, climbed a sycamore tree to see Jesus; when Jesus dined with him, he promised to pay back those he had defrauded, Luke 19.1–10, see also 'Tax-collectors'

**Zadok** (*H* = righteous) high priest in Jerusalem alongside Abiathar under David, anointed Solomon king; when Solomon exiled Abiathar, Zadok became the sole High Priest and ancestor of all subsequent High Priests, 2 Sam. 8.17; 15.24–36; 17.15; 1 Kings 1.8, 26–45; 2.35; Ezek. 40.46, see also 'Sadducees'

**Zalmon** (*H* = shady) in Judg. 9.48–49 possibly another name for Mount Ebal or Gerizim; in Ps. 68.14 possibly Mount Hermon

**Zalmunnah, Zeba** and **Zeeb** (*H* = protection withheld, sacrifice and wolf) kings of the Midianites killed by Gideon, Judg. 7.25; 8.5–21

**Zarephath** (*H* = dye) Elijah was cared for by a widow of Zarephath near Sidon, today called Sarafand in Lebanon; the widow's cruse never ran out of oil; Elijah raised the widow's son, 1 Kings 17.8–24; Luke 4.25–26

**Zarethan** probably Tell es-Sa'idiyah, 14 miles north of Adam by the River Jordan, Josh. 3; 1 Kings 7.46

**Zealot** (*G* = one who is zealous) those who opposed Roman rule were called zealots, 4 Macc. 18.12; nickname of Simon, one of The Twelve, Luke 6.15; Acts 1.13; translation of the Aramaic word spelt Cananaean, Matt. 10.4, Mark 3.18

**Zeba** see 'Zalmunnah'

**Zebedee** (short for Zabediah, *H* = Jah's gift) Galilean fisherman, the father of James and John, and husband probably of Salome, Matt. 4.21; 27.56; Mark 1.19; Luke 5.10; John 21.2

**Zeboiim** see 'Plain'

**Zebulun** son of Jacob and Leah, Gen. 30.20; ancestor of one of the twelve tribes of Israel, Gen. 49.13; Deut. 33.18–19

**Zechariah** (*H* = Jah remembers) **1.** Son of Jeroboam, king of Israel 6 months in 743 BC, killed by Shallum, 2 Kings 14.29; 15.8–14. **2.** Son of the priest Jehoiada, who rebuked Joash and was stoned to death in the Temple, 2 Chron. 24.20–22, Luke 11.51. **3.** Son of Barachiah, author of the Book of the prophet Zechariah; Matt. 23.35 confuses him with 2. above. **4.** Priest, father of John the Baptist; struck dumb in the Temple for doubting God's promise; spoke again after naming his son John, and sang a song called the Benedictus, Luke 1.5–24, 57–80; and 28 other Zechariahs in the Bible

**Zechariah** (Zech.) The Book of the Prophet Zechariah (zeck-ur-EYE-uh), see p. 145

**Zedekiah** (*H* = Jah is righteousness) **1.** False prophet; made horns of iron; promised Ahab success, 1 Kings 22.11; 2 Chron. 18.10, 23. **2.** Last king of Judah 598–587 BC, appointed by Nebuchadnezzar to replace King Jehoiachin, 2 Kings 24.17–19. In 588, Zedekiah rebelled, Nebuchadnezzar besieged Jerusalem, Zedekiah was blinded and deported, 2 Kings 25.1–7; see 'Exile'. **3.** False prophet during the Exile in Babylon, rebuked by Jeremiah, Jer. 29.21–23

**Zeeb** see 'Zalmunnah'

**Zephaniah** (*H* = Jah has hidden) (Zeph.) The Book of the Prophet Zephaniah (zef-urn-EYE-uh), see p. **144**

**Zered, Wadi** watercourse entering the Dead Sea at its southernmost end; border between Moab and Edom; now called Wadi al-Hesa, Num. 21.12; Deut. 2.13–14. Possibly the same as 'Wadi of the Willows', Isa. 15.7; 'Wadi Arabah', Amos 6.14; 'this wadi', 2 Kings 3.16

**Zerubbabel** (*H* = offspring of Babylon) leader among the returning exiles, governor of Judah under Persian supervision; started to restore the Temple, Ezra 3.8–13; 4.1–5, 24; 5.13–6.12; Hag. 1; 2; 1 Esd. 3–4. It was hoped he would become the Messianic King, Zech. 4.6–10; Hag. 2.20–23; but after Darius and his army passed through in 519 this hope faded and the prophecies were altered, Zech. 6.9–14; 1 Chron. 3.16–19; Matt. 1.12; Luke 3.27; see also 'Exile'

**Zeruiah** mother of Joab, Abishai and Asahel, 2 Sam. 2.18

**Zeus** the highest god of the Greeks, corresponding to Roman Jupiter; Barnabas was called Zeus by the priest in Lystra, Acts 14.12–13

**Ziba** (*H* = branch) servant of Saul; brought Mephibosheth to David and was made his servant after Saul's death, 2 Sam. 9.1–11; when Ziba criticized Mephibosheth, David gave all Saul's property to Ziba, 16.1–4; later Mephibosheth accused him of slander and deception, so the property was divided between the two of them, 19.24–30

**Ziklag** town in the south of Judah, given to David by King Achish of the Philistines, burnt down by Amalekites; possibly Tell Sera', about 10 miles north-west of Beer-Sheba, 1 Sam. 27.6; 30; 2 Sam. 1.1; 1 Chron. 12.1

**Zilpah** (*H* = dripping of balsam) Leah's maid, mother of Gad and Asher, Gen. 29.24; 30.9–13

**Zimri** (*H* = my song) king of Israel in 885 BC, treacherously killing Elah and seven days later committing suicide by burning the palace at Tirzah; succeeded by Omri, 1 Kings 16.9–20

**Zin, Wilderness of** part of the Wilderness of Paran, including Kadesh Barnea. Here Moses struck water from the rock (but see 'Meribah'); the Israelites sent out spies; Miriam was buried, Num. 13.1–20.22; 27.14; Josh. 15.1; Deut. 32.51; Ps. 29.8

**Zion, Mount** or **Sion** spur or hill on which the Jebusite city of Jerusalem was built, 2 Sam. 5.6–9. David kept the name when he captured the city, 1 Kings 8.1; when the Temple was built, Zion was applied to the Temple Mount, Ps. 9.11; 76.2; Isa. 2.2–3. It remained a symbolic name for Jerusalem and its people, the sons of Zion and daughters of Zion, Isa. 2.3; 3.16; 33.14; Lam. 4.2; Heb. 12.22; Rev. 14.1. In Byzantine and modern times the name was moved again to apply to the south-western hill where the Cenacle stands, see also 'Pentecost'

**Ziph, Wilderness of** (*H* = furnace) area where David hid from Saul, identified with Tell Zif, 3 miles south-west of Hebron, 1 Sam. 23.14–24

**Zipporah** (*H* = sparrow) daughter of the priest of Midian; wife of Moses, Ex. 2.16–22; 4.20–26; 18.2–5

**Zoan** (*Eg Dja'ne* = storm; the Greek name was Tanis) capital of Egypt around 1000–800 BC, at San el-Hagar in the eastern Delta, 15 miles north of Rameses (Qantar) the Egyptian name is The Fields of Zoan; here Moses performed his miracles before Pharaoh, Ps. 78.12, 43; Isa. 19.11–25; 30.4; Ezek. 30.14

## Zoar

**Zoar** (*H* = little) or Bela, city to which Lot escaped when Sodom and Gomorrah were destroyed; it survived into the Middle Ages in the Wadi Zered, Deut. 34.3; Isa. 15.5; Jer. 48.34; see 'Plain'

**Zophar the Naamathite** (*H* = fledgling) one of Job's 'friends', Job 2.11; 11; 20; 42.9

# The Bible Book by Book

## The Canon of Scripture

The Bible consists of the Hebrew Scriptures (which Christians call the Old Testament), in Hebrew and Aramaic; the Apocrypha, and the New Testament, concerning Jesus, in Greek. Over the course of several centuries, separate books or scrolls were gradually collected together. The Canon of Scripture is the agreed list of books which it was eventually decided to include.

## The Hebrew Scriptures or Old Testament

The Masoretic text, see p. **178**, of the Hebrew Scriptures is regarded as final and authoritative by Jews. The books are arranged in three sections, and often named by the first few words.

**The Law:** Genesis ('In the beginning'); Exodus ('Names'); Leviticus ('And he called'); Numbers ('In the Wilderness'); Deuteronomy ('Words').

**The Prophets: The Early Prophets:** Joshua; Judges; Samuel; Kings.

**The Later Prophets:** Isaiah; Jeremiah; Ezekiel; Hosea; Joel; Amos; Obadiah; Jonah; Micah; Nahum; Habakkuk; Zephaniah; Haggai; Zechariah; Malachi.

**The Writings:** Psalms ('Praises'); Proverbs; Job; The Song of Songs; Ruth; Lamentations ('How'); Ecclesiastes ('Preacher'); Esther; Daniel; Ezra–Nehemiah; Chronicles.

### The Septuagint and Vulgate

Meanwhile Jews living outside Israel needed a Greek translation; traditionally this was made by seventy scholars in Alexandria between 285 and 246 BC, and is called the Septuagint or LXX from the Latin word for seventy, see p. **178**. The Septuagint also contains several chapters or books which were not included in the Hebrew Bible, shown below in *italics*, and known as the *Deuterocanonical Books* (*G* = second canon). This became the recognized Bible of the early Christians, and many of the quotations from the Old Testament in the New Testament are in the form of the Septuagint readings; it is still the Old Testament used by the Greek Orthodox Church. Greek names were given to the books, and were kept when the Bible was translated into Latin as the Vulgate translation, for centuries the official Bible of the Roman Catholic Church, see p. **178**. Both the Septuagint and Vulgate include:

# The Bible Book by Book

**The Five Books of** (or about) **Moses**, or **Pentateuch:** Genesis; Exodus; Leviticus; Numbers; Deuteronomy.

**History Books:** Joshua; Judges; Ruth; 1 Samuel (1 Kingdoms in Greek); 2 Samuel (2 Kingdoms in Greek); 1 Kings (3 Kingdoms in Greek); 2 Kings (4 Kingdoms in Greek); 1 Chronicles (1 Paralipomenon in Greek); 2 Chronicles (2 Paralipomenon in Greek); Ezra (Ezra is called 1 Esdras in the Latin Vulgate and the sixteenth-century English translations; Ezra and Nehemiah are one book known as 2 Esdras in Greek); Nehemiah; (Nehemiah is called 2 Esdras in the Latin Vulgate and the sixteenth-century English translations); *1 and 2 Maccabees.*

**Stories:** Esther *(with additions)*; *Judith*; *Tobit*.

**Poetry:** Psalms; Proverbs; Ecclesiastes; Song of Solomon ('Canticles' in Latin); Job; *The Wisdom of Solomon*; *Ecclesiasticus (ben Sira* or *Sirach).*

**Major Prophets:** Isaiah; Jeremiah; *Baruch*; Lamentations; *Letter of Jeremiah*; Ezekiel; Daniel *(with additions).*

**Twelve Minor Prophets:** Hosea; Joel; Amos; Obadiah; Jonah; Micah; Nahum; Habakkuk; Zephaniah; Haggai; Zechariah; Malachi.

**Apocryphal Books** (incorporated in the text of the Greek and Slavonic (Russian) Bibles, but in an appendix in the Vulgate): 3 Esdras (called Esdras A in Greek and 2 Esdras in Slavonic); 4 Esdras (called 3 Esdras in Slavonic, not in the Greek Bible); 3 Maccabees; The Prayer of Manasseh; Psalm 151; and (in an appendix to the Greek Bible only) 4 Maccabees.

## The Apocrypha

At the Reformation Martin Luther included the *Deuterocanonical Books and Apocryphal Books* (which are in the Greek Bible but not the Hebrew Scriptures) separately, bound between the Old and New Testaments, called **The Apocrypha** and many Protestant and Ecumenical Bibles do the same. The names of the books above are as given in the English King James Version.

## Context

Some of the stories and songs in the Hebrew Scriptures were first told to explain the names of places and tribes, and the origins of leagues and enmities. They passed down by word of mouth in the family and around the camp-fire for centuries, possibly improving with each telling, and surviving in several different versions before they were written down. They were then edited several times, each editor trying to draw out the meaning of the story for the Jews of his day. Any serious doctrine of inspiration must consider the possibility that all the story-tellers and editors were in various ways themselves inspired, see Interpreting the Scriptures, p. **176**.

## Sources

No one can be sure what really happened in the early days, but one version goes like this: Ethnically indistinguishable Semitic people covered the whole area from Mesopotamia to the Mediterranean. Wandering nomads settled among the resident population of Canaan and were absorbed, but brought their stories and their religion with them. A band of slaves in Egypt were brought out by Moses. These entered Canaan from the south and joined the tribes settled in Hebron.

**10–9 centuries BC:** When David moved the capital to Jerusalem, in about 1000 BC, the traditions of the southern tribes were collected in a document called **J**. (J for Judah, Jerusalem, and Jahweh or YHWH). J included early legends of the creation and the patriarchs, as well as the account of the Exodus. It was not afraid to speak of YHWH in human terms, and emphasized his promise to give land to the Israelites. Twelve tribes made a covenant with each other and with YHWH at Shechem. Following Solomon's death, the nation split into Southern and Northern Kingdoms.

**9–8 centuries:** The ten northern tribes, called Ephraim, collected their traditions, including stories of the patriarchs and a covenant experience at Horeb, south of the Dead Sea, into a document called **E** (for Ephraim, and Elohim, the name by which they called God). The northern tribes had sanctuaries at Bethel, Shechem, Shiloh and Dan. Both kingdoms produced great prophets.

**8–7 centuries:** Samaria fell to the Assyrians in about 700 BC; writers in Judah sought unity between what was left of the two kingdoms, and combined their holy books into **JE** which placed Horeb somewhere on the route of the Exodus and called it Sinai.

**7 century onwards:** Meanwhile another document was produced, retelling the story of the Exodus, and continuing with the stories of the two kingdoms, emphasizing the importance of the one sanctuary in Jerusalem, and suggesting that the northern sanctuaries had been heretical. We call this document **D** from Deuteronomy, because Deut. 12–26, and possibly 5–11, may be based on the new law-book found during repairs to the Temple during King Josiah's reign; new books were added: Joshua, telling the story of the arrival of the twelve tribes in Canaan as though they had all invaded from the east; and Judges, Samuel and Kings. These books all portray national disasters as God's punishment for sin.

**6 century:** Next to fall was Jerusalem, and most of the people of Judah were taken into exile in Babylon. During the Exile a new Priestly Code was written, **P**. P gathered and developed several collections of laws, emphasizing the ritual of the Jerusalem Temple, the sabbath, the covenant, and holiness.

**Post-exilic:** After the return of the exiles to Jerusalem in about 538 BC, to draw together those who originated in the Northern and Southern Kingdoms, all these documents were edited together into **JEPD** comprising the books from Genesis to Kings as we now know them. Where accounts of the same events were found in two or more documents they were both included; Gen. 1–11 are from J and P, Lev. is entirely P, Deut.–Kings is D. In addition, **Psalms** from various sanctuaries were combined into one book; the **Priesthoods** at each (possibly Zadokite at Jerusalem, Aaronite at Shechem and Levitical at Dan) were amalgamated, and the new office of High Priest established.

**Advantages:** There are several variants of the multiple-source theory, and other scholars deny that these sources were written documents, referring instead to strands of oral tradition. The multiple-source theories of the Old Testament can never be proved, but they do explain, for instance, why there are two accounts of creation side by side at the beginning of Genesis, one calling God 'the LORD' and the other speaking of him as 'Elohim', and many other doublets and inconsistencies; and it is still possible to believe that God was speaking to us through the work of the editors. It also avoids the implication that God really wants us to use violence to seize our neighbours' land. The emphasis on Judaism as obedience to the law enabled ethical monotheism to survive, even when the Temple was destroyed and the land occupied by their enemies.

# The Bible Book by Book

## The Pentateuch or Books of Moses

**Genesis** (*G* = beginning)
1–2: Two stories of Creation. 3: The Garden of Eden. 4: The murder of Abel by Cain. 5: The descendants of Adam. 6–9: Noah's Ark. 10: Nations descended from Noah. 11: The Tower of Babel. 12: The call of Abram; Abram pretends Sarai is his sister. 13–14: Lot chooses the Jordan Valley, is captured and rescued by Abram; Abram is blessed by Melchizedek. 15: God's covenant with Abram. 16: The birth of Ishmael. 17: Circumcision, the sign of the Covenant. 18–19: Promise of a Son; Destruction of Sodom and Gomorrah. 20: Abraham pretends Sarah is his sister. 21: The birth of Isaac; Hagar and Ishmael; covenant with Abimelech. 22: God commands Abraham to sacrifice Isaac, but provides a ram instead. 23: Sarah's death. 24: Marriage of Isaac and Rebekah. 25: Death of Abraham; Esau sells his birthright to Jacob. 26: Isaac pretends Rebekah is his sister. 27–28: Isaac blesses Jacob and Esau; Esau marries Ishmael's daughter; Jacob's dream at Bethel. 29–30: Jacob marries Leah and Rachel; the sons of Jacob. 31: Jacob and Laban. 32–33: Jacob and Esau; Jacob wrestles at Peniel. 34: The rape of Dinah. 35: Jacob returns to Bethel; birth of Benjamin and death of Rachel; death of Isaac. 36: Esau's descendants. 37: Joseph's dreams; he is sold by his brothers. 38: Judah and Tamar. 39: Joseph and Potiphar's wife. 40–41: Dreams of two prisoners and of Pharaoh; Joseph's rise to power. 42–45: Joseph's brothers go to Egypt. 46–50: Jacob comes to Egypt, blesses his sons and dies.

**Exodus** (*G* = way out)
1: Oppression of the Israelites. 2: Birth of Moses, adoption by Pharaoh's daughter. 3: The Burning Bush. 4: Return to Egypt. 5: Bricks without straw. 6: Moses and Aaron. 7–11: The plagues of Egypt. 12–13: The Passover. 14: Crossing the Red Sea. 15: The Song of Moses. 16: Quails and Manna. 17: Water from the rock. 18: Jethro's advice. 19: Mount Sinai. 20: The Ten Commandments. 21–23: Sundry laws. 24: The blood of the covenant. 25–31: The Tabernacle. 32: The Golden Calf. 33–34: New Tablets. 35–40: More regulations.

**Leviticus** (*G* = Levite traditions)
1–7: Sacrifices. 8–9: Ordination. 10: Unholy fire. 11–15: Purity laws. 16: The Day of Atonement. 17–26 The Law of Holiness: 17: Blood. 18: Sex. 19–22: Holiness. 23: Festivals. 24: The Lamp; Shewbread; Blasphemy. 25: Jubilee Year. 26: Rewards and Penalties. 27: Votive Offerings.

**Numbers**
1–2: Census returns. 3: Duties of Levites; Redemption of the Firstborn. 4: Temple servants. 5: Uncleanness; Restitution; Adultery. 6: Nazirites. 7–8: Offerings. 9: Passover at Sinai. 10: Trumpets. 11: Longing for the fleshpots; Seventy Elders; Quails. 12: Aaron and Miriam's Jealousy. 13: Spies in Canaan. 14: Punishment for rebellion. 15: Various laws. 16: Revolt. 17: Aaron's Rod. 18: Priests. 19: The Red Heifer. 20: Water from the rock; death of Aaron. 21: The Bronze Serpent; Sihon and Og. 22–24: Balaam. 25: Worshipping Baal-Peor. 26–30: Census and offerings. 31: Midian. 32–34: Boundaries. 35: Levites; Murder and Revenge. 36: Female Heirs.

**Deuteronomy** (*G* = second law)
This book is presented as the farewell speech of Moses, and perhaps the law book discovered by Josiah, 2 Kings 22.8. 1: Israel at Horeb. 2: The Wilderness Years. 3: Og, Moses' view from Pisgah. 4: Obedience. 5: The Ten Commandments. 6: 'Hear,

O Israel'. 7: A chosen people. 8: Dangers of Prosperity. 9: Rebelliousness. 10: New Tablets. 11–14: One sanctuary. 15: Jubilee Year. 16: Festivals. 17–18: More laws; a new prophet. 19–28: More laws. 29: The Covenant renewed. 30: Choose Life! 31: Joshua succeeds Moses. 32: The Song of Moses. 33: Moses' Blessings. 34: Description of the death of Moses.

## History books

### Joshua

An account of the occupation of Canaan by the twelve tribes of Israel by military conquest under the generalship of Joshua. As Jericho, Ai and Gibeon appear to have been almost unoccupied at the time; only two out of the sixteen towns described as destroyed show any archaeological signs of destruction; and the cities listed in Josh. 21 were not occupied until five hundred years later; many scholars consider this a collection of unconnected battle stories made to justify the occupation of tribal areas, which had actually come about by peaceful migration.

1–6: Crossing the Jordan; Jericho. 7: Achan. 8: Ai; Renewal of the Covenant at Shechem. 9: Trickery of Gibeonites. 10: The Sun stands still; Five Kings. 11–13: Canaanite kings; summary of the conquest. 14–19: Allocation of Territory. 20: Cities of refuge. 21: Levites. 22: Eastern tribes. 23–24: Renewal of the Covenant; Death of Joshua.

### Judges

Judges here are leaders, not legal functionaries. Ancient stories are told: 3.7–11 Othniel. 3.12–30 Ehud kills fat Eglon. 3.31 Shamgar. 4–5: Deborah and her song. 6–8: Gideon, the fleece, soldiers who lap. 9: Abimelech. 10: Tola and Jair. 11: Jephtha and his daughter. 12: Ibzan, Elon and Abdon. 13–16: Samson. 17–18: Establishment of Dan. 19–21: Benjamin's crime and punishment.

### Ruth

The delightful story of a widowed woman from Moab who accompanies her mother-in-law to Bethlehem, and persuades Boaz, a relative of her late husband, to marry her under the laws of levirate marriage. The sting is in the tail: written in the time of Ezra around 390 BC, when the Jews had become ultra-nationalistic and racist, it points out that even David, the ideal king, had a foreign great-grandmother.

### 1 Samuel

The story of Samuel and Saul; from this point the historical books are largely based on contemporary court records.

1–3: Samuel's birth, the child in the temple at Shiloh. 4–6: The Ark of the Covenant is captured. 7: Samuel as judge. 8: The demand for a king. 9–10: Saul anointed king. 11: Saul defeats the Ammonites. 12: Samuel's farewell. 13: Saul's sin. 14: Jonathan, Saul's son, defeats the Philistines. 15: Saul defeats the Amalekites. 16: David anointed king, plays the harp for Saul. 17: David and Goliath. 18–19: Jonathan, David and Michal. 20: David and Jonathan. 21: David and the Holy Bread. 22–23: David flees from Saul; the Cave of Adullam; the Wilderness of Ziph. 24: David spares Saul's life. 25: Death of Samuel; David and Nabal's wife. 26: David spares Saul's life again. 27: David in Gath. 28: The witch of Endor. 29–30: David and Ziklag. 31: Death of Saul and Jonathan.

## 2 Samuel

The story of David.

1: David's lament. 2: David anointed king of Judah; the battle of Gibeon. 3: Abner defects to David; he is killed by Joab. 4: Ishbaal assassinated. 5: David king of all Israel; Jerusalem captured and becomes the capital. 6: The ark brought to Jerusalem. 7: God's covenant with David. 8–10: David's wars. 9: Mephibosheth. 11: Adultery with Bathsheba, Uriah killed. 12: Nathan condemns David; parable of the one ewe lamb; birth of Solomon. 13–14: Amnon rapes Tamar; Absalom kills him and flees; he returns and David forgives him. 15: Absalom usurps the throne, David flees. 16–17: Shimei, Ahitophel, Hushai. 18–19: Defeat and death of Absalom, David mourns his son, returns to Jerusalem; Shimei; Mephibosheth; Barzillai. 20: Revolt of Sheba. 21: Slaughter of the Gibeonites. 22–23: David's song and last words. 24: The census; the plague stops on the threshing floor of Araunah.

## 1 Kings

The story of Solomon and the kings of Judah and Israel (listed with approximate dates on p. 1).

1: Solomon anointed king. 2: David's instructions and death; Solomon disposes of rivals. 3: Solomon's prayer for wisdom. 4: Wealth and Wisdom. 5–8: Building and dedication of the Temple. 9: God appears to Solomon. 10: The Queen of Sheba. 11: Solomon's idolatry and death. Division of the kingdom; Jeroboam king of Israel. 13: The doom of Bethel. 14–15: Death of Jeroboam; Rehoboam, Abijam and Asa kings of Judah. 15–16: Nadab, Baasha, Elah, Zimri, Omri, Ahab kings of Israel; Ahab moves the capital to Samaria and marries Jezebel. 17: Elijah predicts a drought; the widow's jar; the widow's son. 18: Elijah's contest on Mount Carmel with the prophets of Baal. 19: Elijah meets God at Horeb; Elisha becomes his disciple. 20: Ahab, the Syrians and the prophets. 21: Naboth's vineyard. 22: Death of Ahab; Jehoshaphat king of Judah.

## 2 Kings

1: Death of Ahaziah, king of Israel. 2: Elijah's ascension; Elisha his successor. 3: Jehoram king of Israel. 4: Elisha and the widow's oil; the Shunammite's son. 5: Naaman the leper. 6–7: More miracles. 8: The Shunammite's land; Jehoram and Ahaziah kings of Judah. 9: Jehu anointed; deaths of Joram, Ahaziah and Jezebel. 10: Massacre of religious and royal rivals; death of Jehu. 11: Athaliah king of Judah. 12: Jehoash (Joash) king of Judah repairs the Temple. 13: Jehoahaz and Jehoash, kings of Israel; death of Elisha. 14: Amaziah king of Judah; Jeroboam II king of Israel. 15: Azariah and Jotham kings of Judah; Zechariah, Shallum, Menahem, and Pekahiah kings of Israel. 16: Ahaz king of Judah. 17: Hoshea king of Israel; end of the Northern Kingdom. 18: Hezekiah king of Judah; Senaccherib's invasion. 19: Hezekiah consults Isaiah. 20: Death of Hezekiah. 21: Manasseh and Amon kings of Judah. 22: Josiah king of Judah finds a law book. 23: Josiah's reforms; Jehoahaz and Jehoiakim kings of Judah. 24: Nebuchadnezzar captures Jerusalem; exiles many Jews; Jehoiachin and Zedekiah kings of Judah. 25: Judah exiled to Babylon.

## 1 Chronicles

The Chronicler, writing after the return from exile, retold the story of Israel, changing the account in Samuel and Kings to show that the destruction of the Temple was a punishment for Judah's failures in holiness. He is dismissive of Saul; David and Solomon can do no wrong; the Northern Kingdom is still part of the covenant, and must return to worship at the Jerusalem Temple, uniting the Priests and Levites.

1–9: Family trees and lists. 10: Death of Saul. 11–14: David. 15–16: The Ark of the Covenant brought to Jerusalem. 17: God's covenant with David. 18–20: David's wars. 21: Census, plague, the site of the Temple chosen. 22: David's instructions. 23–27: Priests and temple officials. 28–29: Solomon is instructed to build the Temple.

## 2 Chronicles

1: Solomon's prayer for wisdom. 2–7: Solomon builds and dedicates the Temple. 8: Solomon's activity. 9–11: The Queen of Sheba; death of Solomon; division of the kingdom. 12: Death of Rehoboam. 13–16: Abijah and Asa kings of Judah. 17: Jehoshaphat king of Judah. 18: Death of Ahab. 19–20: Jehoshaphat king of Judah. 21: Jehoram king of Judah. 22–23: Ahaziah, Athaliah and Joash kings of Judah. 24: Joash repairs the Temple. 25: Amaziah king of Judah. 26–28: Uzziah, Jotham and Ahaz kings of Judah. 29–31: Hezekiah's reforms. 32: Sennacherib's invasion. 33: Manasseh king of Judah. 34–35: Josiah discovers the law book. 36: Jehoahaz, Jehoiakim and Jehoiachin; exile and return.

## Ezra–Nehemiah (called 1 Esdras and 2 Esdras in the Latin Vulgate)

Originally a single book (called Esdras B in the Greek Septuagint), telling of the return from exile, when many of the patterns of later Jewish life and thought were established. Ezra is said to have arrived in Jerusalem 'in the seventh year of King Artaxerxes', 7.7; if this means Artaxerxes I that is 458 BC, in which case it is strange that Nehemiah does not mention him; so it is usually taken to be 398, in the reign of Artaxerxes II, which involves rearranging the material as follows.

**538** Cyrus II signed an edict for the return of the Jews, Ezra 1

**537** Zerubbabel started to restore the Temple, Ezra 3.8–12; but the work was interrupted, Ezra 4.1–5, 24

**520** work resumed on the Temple, with permission from Darius, Ezra 5.13–6.12

**516** restoration of the Temple completed, Ezra 6.15–22

**486–458** opposition to the Jews continued under Xerxes I and Artaxerxes I, Ezra 4.6–23

**445** Nehemiah became governor of Judah, rebuilt the walls of Jerusalem, Neh. 1–7; 12–13

**433** Nehemiah paid a visit to Persia, Neh. 13.6

**398** Ezra returned to Jerusalem, to reform the Jewish nation and its worship, Ezra 8.31–10.5; Neh. 8–11. He instructed them to divorce their foreign wives, Ezra 10.6–44.

## Esther

The story, written in about 125 BC, of a Jewish girl in exile in Persia, who is invited to replace Queen Vashti as the bride of King Ahasuerus (Xerxes). Haman, a court dignitary, was offended that Esther's guardian and relative Mordecai refused to bow to him, and persuaded the king to pass an edict to destroy the Jews. Esther spoke up for them, and Haman himself was hanged on the gallows he had erected for Mordecai. This event is commemorated in the feast of Purim, when the book of Esther is read.

# The Bible Book by Book

## Poetry books

### Job

One of the finest verse-dramas in the ancient world, which grapples with the problem of innocent suffering. Job, an Edomite, is prosperous and religious; one of the heavenly beings, called *ha-satan* (*H* = the accuser), tells God that Job is only religious because he is rich; so God gives him permission to take away Job's health and wealth, and as one disaster follows another Job is left sitting among the ashes scraping his sores; but he refuses to 'curse God and die.' Three friends come to reason with him, telling him that the innocent never suffer, so because he is suffering he must be guilty. Eventually God speaks to Job and reveals the grandeur of creation. Job accepts that many things he will never understand, but keeps his faith in God's love and is rewarded by a return to prosperity.

1–2: Prose introduction. 4–5, 15, 22: Eliphaz speaks. 3, 6–7, 9–10, 12–14, 16–17, 19, 21, 23–24, 26–31: Job speaks. 8, 18: Bildad speaks. 11, 20, 25: Zophar speaks. 32–37: a fourth friend, Elihu, speaks. 38–41: The LORD speaks. 42: Prose conclusion.

Famous quotations: 1.21: 'Naked I came from my mother's womb, and naked I shall return; the LORD gave, and the LORD has taken away.' 19.25: 'I know that my Redeemer lives' (see 'Redemption'). 28: Hymn to wisdom. 38.2: 'Who is this that darkens counsel by words without knowledge?' 38.4: 'Where were you when I laid the foundation of the earth?' 40.15: *Behemoth*, probably the hippopotamus. 41: Leviathan, a sea monster, maybe the crocodile.

### The Psalms

The hymnbook of the Second Temple. Some but not all claim to be by David; the remainder are written in his style to honour him. There are Royal psalms, psalms to be sung by individuals and the whole community, psalms for use in processions, psalms of praise, petition, lament, cursing, and triumph. The headings are mostly later than the psalms, giving traditions about who wrote them, the circumstances of composition and musical instructions. Protestant Bibles and most modern translations follow the numbering of the Psalms in the Hebrew Bible. The Greek and Latin translations join Pss. 9–10 and 114–115, and divide 116 and 147. As a result, the numbers of Psalms 11–113 and 117–146 are one less in the Septuagint and Vulgate than in the Hebrew.

### Proverbs

Practical guidance in common-sense behaviour. Some but not all claim to be by Solomon, see 'Wisdom'.

### Ecclesiastes

The title is a Greek form of the Hebrew name, *Qoheleth*, The Preacher, and should not be confused with Ecclesiasticus or Sirach. 1.1 says that the author was a 'son of David' but the language shows that it was written not long before the time of Christ. A pessimistic book, it warns against putting your trust in material things, which it says are 'vanity', or 'a breath'. 3.1–8: 'There is a time for everything under the sun'. 12.1–8: 'Remember your creator in the days of your youth' followed by a famous description of old age, see 'Old'.

### The Song of Songs (Canticles)

A beautiful love poem, in dramatic form, with the alternating voices of the lover, called Solomon, the beloved, who is 'dark but lovely', their friends, and the women of Jerusalem. Solomon is mentioned several times, but the book may be a collection of poems and dramas from subsequent centuries. As well as being a celebration of human love it has been seen as an allegory of the love between God and his people.

## The Prophets

Prophets speak on behalf of God. At first they were in groups attached to a sanctuary, 2 Kings 2.3, 5; and may have received their oracles in a trance-like state as did the prophets of Baal, 1 Kings 18.26–29. Those whose names we know: Deborah, Judg. 4.4; Samuel, 1 Sam. 10.1; Nathan, 2 Sam. 12.1; Elijah, 1 Kings 17.1; and Elisha, 1 Kings 19.19, have developed a highly critical involvement in national politics. In Isaiah, Jeremiah and Ezekiel we have prophets who cast their oracles in poetic form and wrote them down or dictated them, sometimes several years later, Jer. 36.2–4. On many occasions they use 'prophetic symbolism', when by acting out in a stylized way what they are proclaiming they believe they are helping to bring it about, Jer. 13. The twelve 'Minor Prophets' all have different roles in the society of their time, but share a conviction that God is in charge of history, and warns his people through his prophets what his view is on contemporary events. There has been much debate about whether the prophets were 'foretelling' the future or 'forthtelling' God's view of the present; either way they challenge their hearers to make a response here and now, Jer. 21.8.

### Isaiah

Prophet in Judah about 740–700 BC; courtier at the court of King Uzziah and Hezekiah; promised deliverance for Judah but warned against seeking alliances with Egypt. His words are in Isa. 1–39, mixed up with some later material (Isa. 11.10–16; 13; 14.1–21; 21; 24–27; 35). Three hundred years later an anonymous prophet wanted to reassure the Jews that the LORD would bring them back from Exile. It was dangerous to say so openly, so he 'tacked on' another section to the scroll of Isaiah, which we know as 'Second Isaiah', Isa. 40–55. Chapters 56–66 were to encourage those who were settling back into the promised land. Famous passages: 5: The Song of the Vineyard; 6: 'Holy, holy, holy', Isaiah's call; 7: Immanuel; 11: A shoot from the stump of Jesse; 35: The ransomed of the LORD shall return; 40: Comfort my people; a voice crying; 42.1–9; 49.1–7; 50.4–11; 52.13–53.12: Four Servant Songs, see 'Servant'; 45: Cyrus, God's anointed; 52.7: How beautiful upon the mountains; 53: Who has believed what we have heard?; a man of sorrows and acquainted with grief; 55: Ho, everyone who thirsts; 60: Arise, shine, for your light has come; 61: The spirit of the LORD God is upon me.

### Jeremiah

A priest from Anathoth in Judah about 630–586 BC, Jeremiah wrote some of the most intimate autobiographical passages in the whole of ancient literature.

**609** Jehoahaz, whom Jeremiah called Shallum, reigned 3 months, 22.11–17.

**609–598** Jehoiakim, 22.18–23; 26; 35; Jeremiah dictated his poems, to Baruch; Jehoiakim burnt the scroll, 36; 45.

**605** Jeremiah began to predict the Exile, 13.15–27; 25.1–14.

**599** Nebuchadnezzar deported 3,023 Jews to Babylon, 52.28.

**598** King Jehoiachin reigned 3 months in Jerusalem; Jeremiah called him Jeconiah,

24; and Coniah, 22.24–30; 37.1; he was exiled to Babylon; Jeremiah wrote to the exiles advising them to work for the prosperity of their new home, 29.

**598** Zedekiah enthroned, 52.1–3. Jeremiah calls him the 'Righteous Branch', 23.1–8; 33.14–26. Zedekiah reneged on a promise to free all slaves, 34.8–22; sent messengers to Jeremiah, 21; 37; those left in Jerusalem were rotten figs, 24.

**588** Zedekiah rebelled; Nebuchadnezzar besieged Jerusalem, 32.1–2; 52.3–6. Jeremiah confined; bought a field, to show that life would go on after the war, 32–33; 37.11–38.28; Zedekiah blinded; he and 832 people deported, 39.1–10; 52.7–11, 29; died in captivity 34.1–7.

**588** The Babylonians appointed Gedaliah governor of Jerusalem; Jeremiah released, 39.11–18; taken to Ramah, then set free, 40; insurrection against Gedaliah, 41–42.

**587** Jerusalem destroyed, 52.12–14; temple furnishings taken to Babylon; priests and others killed, 52.15–27.

**583** 745 Jews deported, 52.15–16, 30; Jeremiah taken to Tahpanhes in Egypt, 43–44.

**562** Jehoiachin received by Evil-Merodach, 52.31–34.

### Lamentations

Called in some versions the Lamentations of Jeremiah, this lament for the destruction of Jerusalem in 587 is quite different from his style of denunciation. It consists of five poems for three voices: the commentator, Jerusalem, and the voice of hope. Lamentations has been used by Christians to meditate on the crucifixion: 'Is it nothing to you, all you who pass by? Look and see if there is any sorrow like my sorrow,' 1.12

### Ezekiel

Written by a Jewish priest in Jerusalem and then in Babylon, to encourage the hopeless exiles, about 587–575 BC, in the form of a series of visions, see Apocalyptic p. **175**.

1; 10: The chariot of God carried along by living wheels, to remind the exiles that God had not remained behind in Jerusalem but had travelled to Babylon with them. 2–9, 11–17, 19–23, 33: Destruction of Jerusalem a punishment for sin; Israel a faithless bride, fruitless vine. 34: The kings of Judah were greedy shepherds, God the Good Shepherd. 18: Punishment for the individual's sins only. 33: The prophet will be blamed if he does not warn the people. 24: Prophetic symbolism. 25–32, 35: Judgements against the nations. 11.14–25; 17.22–24; 36–37: Return to Jerusalem; reunion of Southern and Northern Kingdoms. 37: See 'Bones'. 38–39: See 'Gog'. 40–46: A new Temple; God's return to Jerusalem. 47–48: An enlarged land to live in after the return from exile.

### Daniel

Describing the faithfulness of Jews to God in the corrupting court at Babylon, it was probably written some three and a half centuries later, just before the death of Antiochus Epiphanes in 163 BC, mostly in the late dialect of Aramaic, to encourage Jews to resist the corrupting Hellenistic ways of the Seleucid conquerors.

1: Four Israelites prefer vegetables to the rich food of court. 2: Daniel interprets Nebuchadnezzar's dream: feet of clay. 3–4: Three Jews thrown into the fiery furnace. 4: Nebuchadnezzar's dream; his seven years' madness. 5: Belshazzar's Feast, the writing on the wall. 6: Darius 'the Mede' signs a 'law of the Medes and

Persians' that anyone who worships a god other than him shall be thrown in the den of lions; Daniel prays to his God; God's angel shuts the lions' mouths.

7–12: Apocalyptic visions: 7: Lion, bear, leopard, and beast with ten horns probably represent the empires of Babylon, Medes, Persians, and Seleucids. The horns are Seleucid kings, and the little horn is Antiochus Epiphanes, given three and a half years (from 168 to 165 BC), then destroyed; the kingdom given to a human figure 'like a son of man', representing Israel, 'the holy ones', (Jesus took it as a prediction of himself). 8: The two-horned ram is the empire of the Medes and Persians; the goat is Macedonia, with Alexander the first horn and the other four horns his successors Ptolemy of Egypt, Seleucus of Babylon, Lysimachus of Thrace, and Antigonus of Asia Minor. The little horn is Antiochus Epiphanes, who set up a pagan altar (the 'abomination of desolation') in the Jerusalem Temple, and forbad Jewish worship for three and a half years (2,300 evening and morning sacrifices were missed). 9: Seventy weeks represent 490 years after the return from exile, until the kingdom of God is established. 10: God explains the future: 11.1–2: Persian kings Darius I, Xerxes and Artaxerxes. 11.3–4: Alexander the Great and his successors. 11.5: Ptolemy and Seleucus. 11.6: Berenice, daughter of Ptolemy II, married Antiochus II; they and her son were assassinated. 11.7–9: Ptolemy III and Seleucus II. 11.10: Seleucus III and Antiochus III. 11.11–12: Ptolemy IV and Antiochus III. 11.13–16: Antiochus III captured Palestine from Ptolemy V. 11.17: Antiochus married his daughter Cleopatra to Ptolemy V. 11.18–19: Antiochus attacked Asia Minor and Greece; was repelled by a Roman commander and killed by the people of Elymais. 11.20: Seleucus IV. 11.20–39: Antiochus IV Epiphanes. 11.40–45: Prediction of the imminent death of Antiochus in Palestine. Actually Antiochus died ten years later in 163 BC in Persia, see 1 Maccabees, p. **147**. 12: After almost ten years of persecution all will end in the resurrection of the dead. See Apocalyptic, p. **175**; Additions to the Book of Daniel, p. **147**, 'Seleucids'

## The Twelve Minor Prophets

### Hosea

Writer in Israel about 760–740 BC. 1–3: In order to illustrate, and bring about, the analogy that God is like a faithful forgiving husband of Israel, Hosea enacts the poetic symbolism in his own life, marrying a prostitute and forgiving her. 4–9: Israel worships foreign idols and is unfaithful to her own God; a call to repentance, for 'on the third day he will raise us up', (6.2). 10–13: God's fatherly compassion, 'it was I who taught Ephraim to walk!', (11.3). 14: Israel repents and is forgiven.

### Joel

Prophet in Jerusalem after the return from Exile, fifth century BC. 1.1–2.17: A plague of locusts, compared to the Day of the LORD; a call to fast and repent in sackcloth. 2.18–32: God forgives the people; pours out his Spirit on everyone. 3: Judgement of the Nations in the Valley of Decision.

### Amos

Prophet in Israel about 790–750 BC, when peasants were being made landless by a centralized state. 1–3: God's judgment circles around Israel's enemies, then homes in on them. 4–6: 'Grinding the faces of the poor', (4.1); condemnation of those who enjoy riches and ignore the needy; God is not interested in their worship, unless accompanied by compassion: 'Let justice roll down like waters, and righteousness like an ever-flowing stream', (5.24). 7–8: God's judgement symbolized by locusts, fire, a plumb-line, a basket of fruit. 9: Destruction of Israel, restoration of David's kingdom.

### Obadiah

Prophet in Jerusalem after the return from Exile, about 500 BC. A condemnation of Edom, a people who have occupied Israel's land: 'You should not have gloated over your brother on the day of his misfortune; . . . as you have done, it shall be done to you', verses 12–15.

### Jonah

Probably written in response to Ezra's nationalistic reforms around 390 BC. After running away from a call to preach to Nineveh, a famously heathen city, Jonah was swallowed by a fish; whales are not able to swallow large objects, although there are recorded cases of men brought out alive after being swallowed by sharks. Then he was returned to land and commanded again to preach to the Ninevites. The story is best seen as a parable of the Jews swallowed up, at the Exile, by Babylon (who worshipped a fish-god), as a punishment for refusing to share their faith with the rest of the world. The Ninevites repent and are forgiven, to Jonah's intense annoyance; he cannot believe that God can love anyone other than an Israelite, least of all their enemies. He grieves that the plant under which he is sheltering from the sun has died, and God replies: 'You are concerned about the bush . . . should I not be concerned about Nineveh, in which there are more than a hundred and twenty thousand persons who do not know their right hand from their left, and also many animals?' (4.10–11).

### Micah

Prophet in Judah about 730–720 BC, around the same time as Isaiah, condemning the greed of the rich rulers (though chapters 4–7 are mostly from the period of the Exile). 1.1–6: Destruction of Samaria. 1.8–16: 'Tell it not in Gath,' (quoting 2 Sam. 1.20) begins a series of puns on place names getting closer and closer to Jerusalem as the enemy troops advance. 2: Condemnation of those who increase their land–holdings to the detriment of others. 3: Wicked rulers and prophets. 4.2: 'Many nations shall say: ". . . out of Zion shall go forth instruction, and the word of the LORD from Jerusalem." ' 4.6–13: Return from exile. 5.2: A ruler from Bethlehem. 5.7–15: The remnant. 6.8: God's controversy with Israel: 'What does the LORD require of you but to do justice, and to love kindness, and to walk humbly with your God?' 7: Corruption; penitence; restoration and forgiveness.

### Nahum

Prophet in Judah about 610 BC. Condemnation of Nineveh.

### Habakkuk

Prophet in Judah about 600 BC, crying out for justice. 1.2: 'O Lord, how long shall I cry for help, and you will not listen?' 2: The prophet is a watchman on the walls; God answers 'Write the vision: make it plain on tablets, so that a runner may read it . . . wealth is treacherous, the arrogant do not endure.' 2.4: 'The righteous will live because of their faith'. 3.17–18: A Psalm of God's judgement; 'Though the fig tree does not blossom, and no fruit is on the vines . . . yet I will rejoice in the Lord, I will exult in the God of my salvation.'

### Zephaniah

Prophet in Judah during Josiah's reign, 640–609 BC. 1: Judgement on Judah;

punishment of corrupt officials on the day of the LORD – although the language sounds like the end of the world, Zephaniah is describing the destruction of Jerusalem. 2: Judgement on their enemies. 3: Judgement on the officials, judges, prophets and priests of Jerusalem; all nations will worship with the humble and lowly Jews in Jerusalem.

### Haggai

Prophet in Jerusalem; he heard the LORD speak between 29 August and 18 December 520 BC, see 'Exile'. Reassurance to Zerubbabel and the returning exiles that they should rebuild the Temple.

### Zechariah

Prophet in Jerusalem after the return from Exile, about 525 BC, see 'Zerubbabel'. 1.1–6.8: Eight visions to encourage the remaining exiles to return to a purified Jerusalem. 6.9–15: Coronation of Joshua the High Priest. 7–8: The right and wrong ways to fast; many races will worship in Jerusalem. 9–14: Oracles about the Day of the Lord, possibly from a later period.

Predictions fulfilled by Jesus: 9.9: 'your king comes riding on a donkey'; 11.12: 'thirty pieces of silver'; 12.10: 'they shall look on the one whom they have pierced'; 13.6: 'the wounds I received in the house of my friends'; 13.7: 'strike the shepherd, that the sheep may be scattered'; 14.4: 'his feet shall stand on the Mount of Olives'; 14.8: 'Living waters shall flow out from Jerusalem'; 14.21: 'there shall no longer be traders in the house of the Lord'.

### Malachi

Anonymous prophet in Jerusalem after the return from Exile, about 500 BC, Malachi means 'My Messenger'. 1–2: Corrupt priests and a profaned covenant. 3: God says, 'I will send my messenger to prepare the way before me . . . the LORD whom you seek will suddenly come to his temple'. 4: The Day of the LORD; 'the sun of righteousness shall rise, with healing in its wings'; Elijah to come before the day of the LORD to reconcile parents with their children.

## The Apocrypha or Deuterocanonical Books

See p. 134.

### (a) Books and Additions that are in the Roman Catholic, Greek and Slavonic Bibles

### Tobit

Story, probably written in Aramaic between 200–125 BC, of a family of Jews during the Exile, who, in spite of many adversities, remain faithful to God and perform acts of charity. 1.1–3.6: Tobit's piety in Jerusalem, and exile to Nineveh; his blindness and his prayer. 3.7–17: Sara daughter of Raguel, at Ecbatana in Media, has had seven husbands each of whom was killed by a demon on their wedding night (compare Mark 12.20–22). 4–6: Tobit sends his son Tobias to fetch back some money he has left in Media, and Raphael accompanies him. 7–8: Tobias stops at Ecbatana and marries his relative Sara, driving away the demon. 9–10: Recovery of the money and return journey. 11–13: Tobit sees again, Raphael reveals he is an angel, everyone praises God. 14: Last words and death of Tobit.

# The Bible Book by Book

### Judith
Story, probably written in Hebrew during the Maccabean revolt, 150–125 BC, of a Jewish woman who saved Jerusalem by killing Holofernes, general of the Assyrian forces who were invading Judah. 1–6: Struggle between Assyrians and Medes, the expedition of Holofernes. 7: Holofernes attacks the town of Bethulia. 8–9: The widow Judith offers to assassinate him. 10–12: She arranges to be captured and taken to Holofernes. 13–15: Judith beheads Holofernes and returns home; the Assyrians flee in panic. 16: Judith's song of praise.

### Additions to Esther
Chapters written in Greek in around 100 BC, and added to the Greek translation of the Hebrew text of Esther, they contain A: Mordecai's dream; B: The King's letter; C: Mordecai's and Esther's prayers; D: Esther's reception by the king; E: The decree of Artaxerxes; F: Final postscript. Whereas the original Book of Esther does not mention God, the additions reflect on the religious implications of the events.

### The Wisdom of Solomon
Written in Greek in the style of the Hebrew Wisdom Literature, probably in about 50–30 BC, when Greek-speaking Jews in Alexandria felt their religion was overshadowed by Greek philosophy. It honours King Solomon by presenting him as the author, but gives a philosophy of history from a later century. 1: 'Love righteousness'. 2: The viewpoint of the wicked. 3: 'The souls of the righteous are in the hand of God'. 4: It is better to die young and virtuous than old and wicked. 5: The final judgement. 6–9: Kings need wisdom. 10–12: Wisdom at work in history. 13–15: Foolishness of worshipping nature or idols; benefits of worshipping God. 16–19: Wisdom in the history of the Jews.

### Ecclesiasticus or The Wisdom of Jesus Son of Sirach (or Ben Sira)
Jesus (= G form of Joshua) Ben-Sirach was a teacher in Jerusalem around 175 BC; he wrote in Hebrew but it was translated into Greek and other languages, with variations shown in the footnotes of modern English editions. Ecclesiasticus (not to be confused with Ecclesiastes) is Latin for 'the church book', because of its interest in Temple worship.
Translator's prologue. 1: Wisdom is praised. 2–4: Duties to God; parents; the poor; rewards of wisdom. 5–8: Proverbs. 9: Women and friends. 10: Rulers, and who should be honoured. 11–13: Practical advice. 14: Wealth. 15–17: God rewards virtue and punishes sinners; God's wisdom seen in creation. 18–19: God's majesty; almsgiving; self-control; gossip; true wisdom. 20–23: Practical advice. 24: Wisdom speaks about herself. 25–26: Good and bad women. 27–34: Practical advice. 35: The Law, sacrifices and justice. 36: Prayer. 37: True and false friends; true and false wisdom. 38–39: Physicians; mourning; craftsmen; scribes; praise. 40: Joy and sorrow. 41–43: Death; contrasts; daughters; nature. 44–50: Ancestors: 'Let us now praise famous men'. 50: Prayer.

### Baruch
Selection of Jewish prayers and hymns from about 150 BC, true wisdom is obedience to the law.

### Letter of Jeremiah
A diatribe against idolatry, dated between 300 and 100 BC; the Latin Vulgate, and the King James English translation, show this as Baruch chapter 6.

### Four additions to the Book of Daniel

Probably stories circulating in the second century BC, at the same time as those included in the Book of Daniel, but only included later.

### 1. The Prayer of Azariah and 2. The Song of the Three Jews or Three Children or Three Young Men

Azariah was the Hebrew name of Abednego, one of the three Jews who were thrown into the fiery furnace; his prayer and their song, sometimes called the *Benedicite*, were inserted between 3.23 and 3.24 of some manuscripts of Daniel.

### 3. Susanna

Story dating from around 130 BC, though maybe based on earlier folk-tales, forming chapter 13 of the Greek version of Daniel: two elders attempted to rape Susanna, but when she cried out they alleged that they found a young man with her, and she was sentenced to death for adultery; Daniel demanded a retrial and the elders were convicted of giving false evidence.

### 4. Bel and the Dragon

Stories dating from around 130 BC, though maybe based on earlier folk-tales, forming chapter 14 of the Greek version of Daniel: Daniel refused to bow to the idol Bel, and tricked the priests who were trying to prove that it was a god; he refused to worship a serpent, and fed it a cake which made it explode.

### 1 Maccabees

History of the Jews between the Old and New Testaments, written c.110 BC in Hebrew, though only the Greek translation survives; see also 'Hasmoneans', 'Seleucids'.

**334–323** Alexander the Great, a Greek from Macedonia, conquered Asia Minor, Persia, Syria, Egypt and parts of India, 1 Macc. 1.1–7. On Alexander's death his empire was divided between the Ptolemies, Antigonids and Seleucids, all of them Greeks, 1.8–9.

**198** Seleucids under Antiochus the Great took control of Syria (including Judea) from the Ptolemies.

**187–175** Seleucus IV; Rivalry between families of Onias, the High Priests, and Tobias, the Financial Officers; revolt of Simon the Benjaminite, 2 Maccabees 3

**175** Antiochus IV Epiphanes; Jews who wanted Greek culture sought permission to erect a gymnasium in Jerusalem, 1 Macc. 1.11–15.

In the absence of Onias III the High Priest, his brother Jason paid Antiochus to appoint him instead; he tried to introduce Greek culture, 2 Macc. 4.

An outsider, Menelaus, paid a higher price for the High Priesthood; Jason fled; Menelaus assassinated Onias; with his brother Lysimachus he stole and sold some of the Temple vessels.

**169** The Jews rioted; Jason returned and drove out Menelaus. Antiochus returned, reinstated Menelaus, and plundered the Temple, 2 Macc. 5.

**167** Persecution of the Jews; martyrdom of Eleazar and seven brothers, 2 Macc. 6–7. Pollution of the Temple, 1 Macc. 1.10–62. Mattathias, a priest from Modein, and his five sons, John Gaddi, Simon Thassi, Judas Maccabeus (= hammer), Eleazar Avaran and Jonathan Apphus, led the resistance, then Mattathias died, 1 Macc. 2.1–70

**166–160** The Jewish Revolt, led by Judas Maccabeus, 1 Macc. 3–9; 2 Macc. 8

**164** Jerusalem captured and the Temple reconsecrated, 1 Macc. 4.52; 2 Macc. 10. Around this time the Book of Daniel was written to encourage the Jews.

**163** Last campaign and death of Antiochus Epiphanes, 2 Macc. 9.

**163–162** Under Antiochus V Eupator the fighting continues.

**162–150** Demetrius I took control of the Empire. Judas defeated the Syrian general Nicanor, 2 Macc. 14–15

**160–142** Jonathan Apphus, 1 Macc. 9.23–12.48

**152** Jonathan appointed high priest, 10.21

**142** Simon recognized by Demetrius, 13.34–40

**142–134** Simon Thassi, 13–16

**134–104** John Hyrcanus I, 16.18–24

### 2 Maccabees

A shortened version, from between 106 and 63 BC, of a history, now lost, in five volumes by Jason of Cyrene, with two letters; using exaggeration and miracle stories to arouse sympathy for the characters. 1–2: Two letters and the preface. 3: Revolt of Simon the Benjaminite. 4: Jason appointed High Priest. 5: Antiochus Epiphanes robbed the Temple. 6: Suppression of Judaism, martyrdom of Eleazar. 7: Martyrdom of seven brothers. 8: Revolt of Judas Maccabeus. 9: Death of Antiochus. 10: Purification of the Temple and establishment of Hanukkah. 11, 13: Under Antiochus Eupator the fighting continued. 12: Martyrs and the hope of resurrection. 14–15: Demetrius I, took control of the Empire; Judas defeated Nicanor.

### (b) Books in the Greek and Slavonic (Russian) Bibles; not in the Roman Catholic Canon

**1 Esdras** (called 1 Esdras in English Bibles; Esdras A in the Septuagint; 2 Esdras in Slavonic, and 3 Esdras in the Appendix to the Latin Vulgate), dating from c.150 BC. Esdras is the Greek form of the name Ezra: this book is a selection from 2 Chronicles, Ezra and Nehemiah, translated into Greek. The only new material is in chapters 3–4, where Zerubbabel wins a debating competition in the Persian court, proving that 'Great is truth'; probable date 150–100 BC.

**Prayer of Manasseh** (in the Appendix to the Latin Vulgate)

Claiming to be the prayer offered by King Manasseh when he was a prisoner in Babylon, 2 Chron. 33.12–13. It is a prayer for pardon; only found in a few manuscripts, it is not certain what the original language was, nor when it was written.

### Psalm 151

Following Psalm 150 in the Greek Bible, but found nowhere else, it is not clear where this short poem about David and Goliath comes from.

### 3 Maccabees

Life of a religious minority in Alexandria in the first century BC, balancing observance of the Jewish law with the requirements of a non-Jewish state.

### (c) In the Slavonic Bible and in the Latin Vulgate Appendix

**2 Esdras** (called 2 Esdras in English Bibles; 3 Esdras in Slavonic; and 4 Esdras in the Appendix to the Latin Vulgate)

Chapters 3–14, consist of a series of visions, brought by Uriel to Ezra, see Apocalyptic, p. **175**; they were probably written in Hebrew or Aramaic as late as AD 100, but only the Latin and Russian translations survive. Chapters 1–2 and 15–16 are probably written by a Christian in the second or third century AD; the book is unknown in Greek

## (d) In an Appendix to the Greek Bible

### 4 Maccabees

Philosophical discussion, written in Greek between AD 18 and 37, showing that reason is more important than emotion in religion, encouraging readers to keep the law even in difficult circumstances; it describes the blood of the martyrs as an expiatory sacrifice.

## The New Testament

See also 'Covenant'.

## The Synoptic Gospels

'Gospel' in English, *euangelion* in Greek, means 'good news'. The four books telling the story of Jesus are not just biographies but Gospels, Mark 1.1. They are objective about facts, but their purpose is to persuade the reader to accept the good news of God's love which Jesus proclaimed, and that the life of Jesus was itself good news. The first three Gospels see the life of Jesus from generally the same point of view, so they are called 'Synoptic' ($G$ = viewing together). Traditionally the authors are known as Matthew, Mark and Luke; they are not named in the text.

### Sources

The Gospels are not written by eyewitnesses, but claim to be based on eyewitness evidence, Luke 1.2; John 21.24. The words of Jesus were passed down by word of mouth for several years, but people who do not write much have an astonishingly accurate verbal memory. Some of his sayings are in poetical form to make them easily memorable, Matt. 7.7. Quite soon, individual stories and sayings may have been written down, in Aramaic or Greek. Later they were gathered into collections. The four-source theory holds that:

**Mark** was the earliest Gospel; most of Mark was copied by Matthew and Luke almost word for word into their Gospels;

**'Q'** from the German *Quelle* meaning 'source', was a collection consisting only of sayings of Jesus without any narrative; these were inserted into Mark in different places by Matthew and Luke, again almost word for word, though not in the same order;

**L** is Luke's special source, from which he draws material not found in any other Gospel, or which is so different in wording that it is unlikely that he copied it from Mark or Q;

**M** is a similar special source for Matthew.

This theory explains why so many passages are verbally identical in two or three Gospels, but not all scholars accept it.

If 'Q' did exist, it would have contained at least the following verses from Luke's Gospel (verses in brackets are uncertain), and the parallel passages from Matthew:
Luke 3.7–9; 3.16–17; 4.1–13; 6.20b–23; 6.27–49; 7.1–10; 7.18–35; 9.57–60; 10.2–16; 10.21–24; 11.2–4; 11.9–20; 11.21–22; 11.23–26; 11.29–35(36); 11.39–52; 12.2–12; 12.22–31(32); 12.33–34; 12.39–46; 12.(49)51–53; 12.57–59; 13.18–21;

13.23–30; 13.34–35; 14.11 (= 18.14); 14.16–24; 14.26–27; 14.34–35; 15.4–7; 16.13; 16.16–18; (17.1–2); 17.3–4; 17.(5–)6; 17.23–24; 17.26–30; 17.33–37; 19.12–27; 22.28–30

## The Gospel according to Matthew

The most Jewish of the four Gospels, Matthew begins with a genealogy: Jesus was a descendant of Abraham, and born in Bethlehem because he is a descendant of David. Then, like Moses on Mount Sinai, Jesus stands on a 'mountain' to deliver the new law, the Sermon on the Mount. See The Life of Jesus, p. **168**; The Teaching of Jesus, p. **170**.

## The Gospel according to Mark

Traditionally based on the reminiscences of Peter, about whose failings it is impressively frank; John Mark is said to have been his secretary, see 'Mark'. 1: The good news begins with the Baptism of Jesus by John, a brief mention of his temptation, and the call of the first disciples. 2–9: His ministry around Lake Galilee. 10: He travelled to Jerusalem. 11–12: His triumphal entry; cleansing the Temple; teaching in Jerusalem. 13: Teaching about the Destruction of Jerusalem and the Coming of the Son of Man. 14–15: Jesus is betrayed, arrested, tried, crucified and buried. 16: The Resurrection of Jesus. The chapter ends rather abruptly in verse 8 'for they were afraid'. Possibly some text has been lost from the end of the scroll. Two attempts have been made to round it off satisfactorily: the shorter ending which is the rest of verse 8; and the longer ending, verses 9–20, culminating with Jesus ascending into heaven; these are often shown as footnotes.

## The Gospel according to Luke

Written for someone called Theophilus, 1.1–4; the same as in Acts 1.1–5; so Luke–Acts is a two-part book, see below. The Gospel is intended for Gentiles, and emphasizes Jesus's concern for Gentiles, women, the outcast and the sick. His birth was witnessed by humble shepherds, and accompanied by the songs known as Magnificat, Benedictus and Nunc Dimittis. His genealogy goes back to Adam, the ancestor of all races. Luke includes parables about lost sheep, a lost coin and a lost son. Pilate's responsibility for the crucifixion is minimized, and the Resurrection is explained on the walk to Emmaus. Luke claims to have aimed at accuracy, but see 'Quirinius'.

## The Gospel according to John

The fourth Gospel tells the story of Jesus in a very different way. There are three visits to Jerusalem; there are long speeches which would have been hard to memorize. All four Gospels are the fruit of theological reflection, but many see John as the result of a lifetime's meditation on the meaning of the events. Possibly the author took a saying of Jesus, e.g., the Light of the World, Matt. 5.14, and wove it into a long discourse, John 8; many of these begin with the words 'I am', the name of God, Ex. 3.14. Miracles are called 'Signs', which point to God in action. The Gospel claims to be based on the testimony of an eyewitness known as 'The Beloved Disciple', John 21.24.

(The seven 'signs' are printed in **bold,** the seven 'I am's' in *italic*)

1: Prologue, the Baptist, Jacob's Ladder.

2: **The Wedding at Cana.** Cleansing the Temple.

3: Born of the Spirit. The Baptist. Coming from above.

4: The Samaritan woman and Living water. 'I am'. **Healing a boy.**

5: **Healing at Bethesda.** The sabbath. The Law.

6: **Feeding the 5,000. Walking on the water.** *I am the bread from heaven.* Words of life.

7: The Law and the Messiah. Living Water.

8: [Adultery] *I am the Light.* Death. Abraham.

9: **The man born blind.** Spiritual blindness.

10: *I am the good shepherd. I am the gate.*

11: *I am the Resurrection and the Life.* **The raising of Lazarus.**

12: Anointing. Triumphal entry. Teaching on death.

13: Foot-washing. The New Commandment.

14: *I am the Way, Truth, Life.* The Holy Spirit.

15: *I am the true vine.* Suffering.

16: The Holy Spirit. Joy, peace.

17: The High Priestly prayer.

18–19: The Passion.

20–21: The Resurrection.

The story of the woman taken in adultery in chapter 8 may be true, but not originally a part of John's Gospel. The Synoptics, with their accurate details, and John with his broad sweep, have been compared to a photograph and a portrait painting: the first is more factually true, the second brings out the truth of character.


## The Acts of the Apostles

The story of the growth of the Church, a continuation of the Gospel of Luke, Acts 1.1–5. Traditionally both written by Luke the beloved physician, Col. 4.14; Philemon 24; 2 Tim. 4.11; who was present at the events described in verses known as 'we' passages: Acts 16.10–17; 20.5–16; 21.1–18; and 27.1–28.16. Opinions vary between those who suggest that Luke–Acts were written to form part of the evidence at the trial of Paul in 64, the point at which Acts comes to an end; and those who say Acts and the Gospels were written in the eighties and nineties of the first century, to put Paul's side in a dispute between his followers and those of Peter. There is a discrepancy in the number of visits Paul made to Jerusalem: three in Acts and two in Galatians.

1–5: Acts of Peter and the other members of The Twelve. At Pentecost the gospel spread from its Galilean beginnings to include overseas Jews and proselytes.

5–8: Appointment of The Seven. Martyrdom of Stephen. Acts of Philip. Inclusion of Greek speaking Jews, Samaritans, and legally disqualified God-fearers (e.g. eunuchs).

9: Conversion of Paul.

10–12: Peter baptized the Gentile God-fearer Cornelius. The church in Antioch-on-the-Orontes preached to Gentiles. James was killed and Peter released from prison.

13–15: Paul's First Missionary Journey. Sent by the church in Antioch-on-the-Orontes with Barnabas and John Mark to preach in synagogues in Cyprus and Perge. Mark left them. They visited Antioch-of-Pisidia (where they 'turn to the Gentiles'),

Iconium, Lystra, Derbe and back to Antioch-on-the-Orontes. The Council in Jerusalem decided that Gentiles were allowed to become Christians.

16.1–18.22: Paul's Second Missionary Journey. Paul and Silas took a letter, reporting the decision of the Council in Jerusalem, through Tarsus, to the Galatian churches he had visited on his first journey; collected Timothy in Lystra; was prevented from going to Ephesus; had a vision in Troas; visited the Macedonian cities of Philippi, Thessalonica and Beroea, the Greek cities of Athens and Corinth, then returned via Ephesus, where he left Priscilla and Aquila.

18.23–21.16: Paul's Third Missionary Journey. Disturbed by reports that 'Judaizers' were demanding that Gentile Christians be circumcised, Paul visited Galatia and Phrygia. He spent three years in Ephesus. Driven out by a riot, he revisited Macedonia, Greece, Macedonia again and Troas. In Miletus he bade farewell to the Ephesian elders.

21.17–27.31: Paul returned to Jerusalem, was arrested, imprisoned in Caesarea, tried, appealed to Caesar, was shipwrecked in Malta and travelled on to Rome.

## The Letters

Paul wrote letters to the churches he visited on his journeys. All agree that the letters to the Romans, 1 and 2 Corinthians, Galatians, Philippians, 1 Thessalonians and Philemon were dictated by Paul; there is disagreement about Ephesians, Colossians and 2 Thessalonians; and most scholars think that 1 and 2 Timothy and Titus are not by Paul.

### The Letter of Paul to the Romans

Probably written from Corinth or Ephesus at the end of his third missionary journey, Acts 20, to prepare for an anticipated first-time visit to Rome. There was a deep division there between the Jewish Christians and the Gentile Christians, and he makes a passionate plea for unity.

1.1: All alike, Jews and Gentiles, need God's forgiveness, only found through faith in Jesus. This is the good news that Paul preached. 1.18: Jews despise Gentiles for worshipping idols, and 'unnatural' sex. But greed, jealousy, competitiveness, lying, pride, disobedience, and breaking promises – vices found among Jews as well as Gentiles – are against the will of God and equally unnatural. 2.1: The most unnatural vice of all is judging others. 2.17: Jews and Gentiles alike deserve a guilty verdict. The Law was an essential part of God's plan, to show us that he cares about the way we treat each other. 3.9: Ps. 14.1–3 and 53.1–3 say that nobody is righteous. 3.21: God will regard us as good, even though we are not, and admit us to his chosen people, if we have faith in Jesus. 4.1: Even Abraham was not justified by the Law, but by faith, (Gen. 15.6). So he became, not just the ancestor of the Jews, but also the father of many 'Nations' – Gentiles. 5.12: We are all guilty because we are descended from disobedient Adam; but we are all regarded as good because of our faith in obedient Jesus. 6.1: Our guilt was killed when Jesus was nailed to the cross. We had been contracted as slaves to our sinful habits; Jesus has set us free. Our only obligation now is to live a good life in gratitude for what he has done. 7.1: After the person who makes a contract dies, nobody is bound by it. We are part of the body of Christ, and Jesus has died, so we are no longer bound by our contract as slaves to sin. 7.7: To live a good life we have to struggle against our selfish desires; this is possible if we are controlled by the Holy Spirit. 8.1: The Old Testament Law was powerless to restrain our natural selfishness, but the Spirit empowers us to live in a loving way. Freed from the negative restrictions of the law we can live in a positive and loving manner. 8.31: Jesus, our advocate, pleads for us with God the judge, who declares us not guilty, even though we are guilty. 9.1: The Jews are God's chosen people, even though many have rejected Jesus. 10.5: God's plan is to bring the Gentiles to faith through the teaching of the Jews, then to bring the Jews to faith through the example of the Gentiles. 12.1: The result must be love for our fellow Christians, limbs in the body of Christ; 12.14: for our enemies; 13.1: the state authorities, even when hostile; 13.8: our neighbours; 14.1: Jewish and Gentile Christians, who may have different dietary customs; 15.1: and those whose faith is weak. 15.7: Paul is the apostle to the Gentiles so that the Church can be a community of people united in love despite their differences. He hopes to visit Rome soon, after he has carried some money collected by the Christians in Greece to the poor Christians of Jerusalem. 16.1: Personal greetings to leading Christians he knows there.

### The Letters of Paul to The Corinthians

*There were four versions of Christianity in Corinth (1 Cor. 1.12):*

1. Palestinian Jews, claiming to be followers of Peter, said it was impossible for a Greek to become a Christian without obeying the full Jewish law.

2. Some of Paul's followers said that we are free of the law and of all moral restraints.

3. Followers of Apollos from Alexandria thought that Christianity was a school of philosophy, only properly understood by the highly intelligent.

4. Another group claimed that special spiritual gifts are given to those who are 'of Christ', and those without these gifts are not true Christians.

*In his letters Paul diplomatically agrees with each of these groups in turn, and then subverts their cherished superiority by showing that each of them is incomplete without the others. During his three years in Ephesus, AD 52–54, some believe that Paul wrote at least four letters to Corinth; probably the first two were written from Ephesus:*

**1. The 'Previous Letter'** mentioned in 1 Cor. 5.9. Reports had reached Paul of immorality among the Christians in Corinth. Part of his reply may be contained in 2 Cor. 6.14–7.1, warning the Corinthians not to be 'unequally yoked with unbelievers'. Then Chloe's household reported on party spirit in Corinth, with a list of written questions.

**2. 1 Corinthians** is Paul's reply.

Chapters 1–4: Party spirit. It is essential to unite the different parties, or they will destroy the church.

5: Immorality: a man was living with his stepmother. The 'Previous Letter' did not mean withdrawal from the world.

6: Christians must not take each other to court.

7: Marriage and divorce. Jesus was opposed to divorce, because it drove divorced women into prostitution.

8: Meat offered to idols.

9: Paul is entitled to be paid for his ministerial work. But for the time being, he will not take advantage of this freedom, so as not to offend weak consciences.

10: Greed at the love feast which preceded Holy Communion.

11: Head-covering: prostitutes were the only women who publicly went bare-headed.

12: Spiritual gifts. We are like limbs in a body, which can only function when united to all the others, see 'Tongues'.

13: The great Hymn to Love, arising from the squabbles of the different parties.

14: Spiritual gifts must not interrupt orderly worship (14.34–35 appear in different places in different manuscripts, so may be a later addition, see 'Women').

15: See 'Resurrection'.

16: The collection for the Jerusalem church, Paul's plans, and final greetings.

*1 Corinthians was sent by sea, while Timothy went to Corinth by land; he returned with bad news. Paul wrote*

**3. The 'Severe Letter'** (2 Cor. 10–13) calling for moral behaviour, and respect for the apostle; it was carried by Titus (2 Cor. 2.4).

*Paul met Titus in Thessalonica, who reported that the Corinthians were willing to conform, and by a majority vote had censured the member who insulted Paul.*

**4. The Final Letter** *may be 2 Cor. 1–9.* It expresses forgiveness, and appeals for a practical demonstration of the unity between Jewish and Gentile Christians by taking up a collection for Paul to carry to the Christians of Jerusalem, who were in dire poverty because of a famine (Acts 11.28).

*But there are several other theories about the divisions of 2 Corinthians.*

## The Letter of Paul to the Galatians

Paul made converts in the Galatian towns of Antioch-of-Pisidia, Iconium, Lystra, Derbe and maybe others in North Galatia. When he left he had made it possible for non-Jews to accept the good news of God's forgiveness in Christ, without having to earn forgiveness by obedience to a code of law. Soon he heard that Jewish Christians had followed him to Galatia, and told his new Gentile converts that to be acceptable as Christians they must be circumcised, and keep the whole Jewish law, including the food laws. Gentile converts would not be admitted to eat with Jewish Christians at the Holy Communion meals until they had been instructed in Judaism and changed their whole lifestyle. That would have resulted either in two churches who did not share table fellowship, or more likely the death of Gentile Christianity. In a fury Paul shot off a letter blazing with passion, as he pleads with the Galatians not to reject their freedom to follow Christ in their own way. It is not clear how many times Paul visited Jerusalem, or whether he wrote this letter before or after the Council in Jerusalem.

1.1–5: Introduction. 1.6–10: Why turn to another gospel? 1.11–2.14: My gospel is not of human origin. Paul's relationship with the Jerusalem leaders. 2.15–21: I have taught justification by faith, not by works of the law. 3.1–5: Does the Spirit come by means of the law? 3.6–9: The faith of Abraham. 3.10–14: The curse of the cross frees us from the curse on law-breakers, and extends Abraham's blessing to the Gentiles. 3.15–18: The analogy with a will. 3.19–29: The analogy with a schoolteacher. 4.1–11: The freedom of sons and slavery to spirits. 4.12–20: Imitate my sincerity, not my opponents' insincerity. 4.21–31: The analogy with Hagar and Sarah. 5.1–12: The demand for circumcision hinders Christian freedom. 5.13–26: But do not abuse your freedom: the works of the flesh and the fruit of the Spirit. 6.1–6: Bearing one another's burdens. 6.7–10: Sowing what you reap. 6.11–18: Personal postscript.

## The Letter of Paul to the Ephesians

**The Captivity Epistles** (Ephesians, Philippians, Colossians and Philemon), all state that they were written from prison. The only imprisonments we know about from Acts were in Philippi (overnight only), Caesarea-Maritima and Rome. Ephesians was probably written when Paul was under house arrest in Rome.

**Ephesians** contains no personal greetings, and in some manuscripts does not mention Ephesus. It was probably a circular letter to be taken by Tychicus, 6.21, to a number of churches in the Province of Asia, perhaps at the same time as Colossians (Col. 4.7, 16) and Philemon. There are many echoes of Colossians in Ephesians, so some suggest that Ephesians is not by Paul; but whereas Colossians was an argument, responding to a specific crisis, Ephesians seems to be a reflection on the same themes, in the form of a prayer. Paul's vision: a world won for love, by means of a Church united in love.

1.1: Thanksgiving that God has called us to be part of his people, the Church. 1.10: God has revealed to us a 'mystery': his plan to bring the whole of creation together in Christ. 1.15–23: A prayer that we may know God in Christ, the head of the Church, which is his body. 2.1–10: We are saved from sin and become members of the Church, not by earning it, but through God's undeserved grace and kindness. 2.11–22: God even includes non-Jews in his Church, which is built into a single structure like a temple. 3.1–13: Paul's ministry: to reveal God's plan for Jews and Gentiles to be united in the Church. 3.14–21: He prays that we may know the greatness of God's love. 4.1–5.20: Therefore work hard to show love and unity in the Church. 5.21–32: Examples of reconciliation: relationships between husbands and wives; 6.1–4: children and parents; 6.5–9: slaves and masters. 6.10–17: Paul, guarded by soldiers wearing Roman armour, writes that we are under attack from the divisive forces of the universe, so we must defend ourselves with the armour of God. 6.18–23: Paul asks for prayer that he may be able to carry this message to the Roman rulers, and prays for his readers.

### The Letter of Paul to the Philippians
One of the Captivity Epistles written from prison, most likely from Rome, 1.13; 4.22; yet its keynote is joy.

1.13: Paul's love for the church that he had founded. 1.21: He would prefer to die, to be with Jesus, but may have to stay alive to continue his work.1.28: He reassures them of God's love; 2.2: and exhorts them to unity. 2.5–11 apparently quotes an early Christian hymn, about Jesus 'emptying himself' of his glory to come to earth. 3.12: Beware of Judaizers, who say Gentile Christians must be circumcised. The effort to live a moral life compared to runners in a stadium. The Philippians, proud to be a Roman colony, are also a colony of heaven. 4.2: Please stop quarrelling! 4.4: 'Rejoice', the conventional word for 'farewell', used literally. 4.8: Concentrate your thoughts on good things. 4.10: Thanks for the gift that they had sent to him in prison.

### The Letter of Paul to the Colossians
The church at Colossae was probably founded by Epaphras under Paul's guidance, Col. 1.7; 4.13. Colossians is one of the Captivity Epistles, Col. 4.18; maybe Epaphras and Onesimus had brought news to Paul in his prison of the 'heresy' which was disturbing the church in Colossae. This probably combined pagan mythology, speculative philosophy and mystical Judaism. It claimed to be a philosophy better than Christianity; that the material world was evil and opposed to the spiritual world of the angels. It demanded observance of festivals, kosher diet, asceticism and self-denial, and worshipping angels. They thought that the human Jesus could only represent a part of the nature of God. Paul taught the pre-eminence of Jesus Christ,

the image of God and the creator of everything, including the angels. The fulness of the Church leads us to the fulness of Christ who is the fulness of God. Gentiles reach God not by circumcision but by baptism, in which we are raised with Christ; so we must 'seek the things which are above', meaning, not the angelic powers, but loving behaviour.

1.1–2: Greetings. 1.3–8: Paul thanks God for the love and hope of Christians in Colossae. 1.9–14: He prays for their growth in good works, endurance, and in knowledge of God who has rescued us from the powers of darkness. 1.15–20: Christ is the head of all things: this is a typically Jewish exploration of the first words of the Bible, 'in the beginning God', which in Hebrew could mean 'in, through or by the head is God'. 1.21–23: Paul is a minister of the gospel of reconciliation. 1.24–2.4: He reveals to Gentile nations the mystery that Christ is in us. 2.6–23: The fulness of God is found in Christ 'bodily', not in the Colossian heresy. 3.1–17: Because of your baptism you have died to earthly things, so clothe yourselves in love; then there are no distinctions between people but all are one in Christ. 3.18–4.1: Mutual submission of wives and husbands, parents and children, slaves and slave-owners. 4.2–18: Further instructions and greetings.

### The Letters of Paul to the Thessalonians

On his second missionary journey in about AD 50, Paul made converts in Thessalonica. Rioting caused his departure, but on reaching Athens he sent Timothy back to encourage the new Christians. Timothy rejoined Paul in Corinth, reporting that they had understood that they would all live to see 'the day of the Lord', and were puzzled that some had died already. Paul wrote his First Letter to the Thessalonians. Soon afterwards, hearing that some had misunderstood the first letter, and had stopped work, thinking that the 'day of the Lord' had passed already, he wrote a Second Letter to the Thessalonians. See Apocalyptic, p. **175**.

**1 Thessalonians** 1.1–10: Greetings and thanksgiving. 2.1–13: Paul's self-defence. 2.14–16: The Christians of Thessalonica had suffered persecution from their fellow-countrymen, just as Paul and Jesus had from theirs. 2.17–3.5: Paul longed to see them again, but could not, so he sent Timothy to encourage them. 3.6–13: Timothy has reported their faithfulness. 4.1–12: Live a life pleasing to God, avoid fornication, love your fellow-Christians. 4.13–18: Don't worry about Christians who have died; at the 'coming of the Lord' they and we will rise together to be with the Lord forever. 5.1–11: Not knowing when 'the day of the Lord' will come, we must always be ready. 5.12–28: Exhortations and prayers: obey your leaders; don't be idle; discriminate between, but do not quench, spiritual gifts.

**2 Thessalonians** 1.1–4: Greetings and thanksgiving. 1.5–12: When Jesus is revealed from heaven, God will reward the afflicted and punish their persecutors. 2.1–12: The Day of the Lord has not yet come; it is delayed until the 'man of lawlessness' is revealed; he is being held back by 'the restraining power'; when that is removed Jesus will destroy him. 2.13–17: So stand firm. 3.1–15: A request for prayer, and a rebuke to idlers. 3.16–18: Paul's final greetings.

### The Pastoral Epistles

Paul's personal First and Second Letters to Timothy and his Letter to Titus are quite unlike the letters which he wrote to congregations. The style and language is different; the teaching of Paul and his opponents is more rigid; and it is not clear whether he is giving basic training to young missionaries or reminding senior bishops of his earlier instructions. He seems to quote from earlier Christian authorities, and is more legalistic, particularly on the position of women. Therefore, many think they reflect the rigid structures of the Church and of moral teaching in the second century, and were written in Paul's name to honour him and give his authority to the new developments; though they may contain some verses borrowed from otherwise unknown letters. If they are by Paul, he must have written them late in his life, perhaps after he was arrested for a second time in AD 67.

## The First Letter of Paul to Timothy

Addressed to the young assistant who had joined Paul at Lystra, and is now in charge of the church at Ephesus; possibly Paul wrote from Macedonia (1.3).

1.1–3: Greetings. 1.3–11: Warning against false teachers and those who reject the law. 1.12–20: Gratitude for God's mercy. 2.1–15: Instruction in prayer. 3.1–13: The qualifications of bishops and deacons; they must be the husband of one wife. 3.14–16: Paul quotes a formula which he describes as the mystery of our religion. 4.1–5: Warning against false asceticism; 6–16 instruction to a young minister. 5.1–6.2: Advice on dealing with different groups within the congregation. 6.3–21: False teaching, true riches and fighting the good fight of faith.

## The Second Letter of Paul to Timothy

Written when Paul was a prisoner, 1.8; possibly in Rome, 1.17; he believes he is near the end of his life, 4.6.

1: Greetings, thanksgiving and encouragement. 2.1–13: Paul urges Timothy to be a good soldier. 2.14–26: A worker approved by God. 3.1–4.8: Godlessness and false teaching in the last days. 4.9–22: Final instructions; Paul wants Timothy to come to him.

## The Letter of Paul to Titus

The Letter of Paul to Titus is addressed to a Greek disciple, Gal. 2.3; who is in charge of the church in Crete, 1.5–16. Paul writes from Nicopolis: 3.12–15. The letter contains exhortations to sound doctrine and good deeds, and advice for dealing with old and young in his congregation, slaves and those who cause divisions.

## The Letter of Paul to Philemon

In this short personal letter, Paul writes about a runaway slave named Onesimus. A slave who asked his owner's friend to seek a reconciliation could not be punished as a fugitive. Because a slave had no legal rights and was the property of his owner, Paul sends Onesimus back to his slave-owner. Traditionally Philemon was thought to be the slave-owner, but it has been ingeniously suggested that he was the supervisor, living in Laodicea, of several churches in the Lycus Valley; the letter was written to him first, to be forwarded (Col. 4.12–16) to Archippus, the actual owner, in Colossae nearby. Onesimus is described as 'one of you' in Col. 4.9; he is said to have become Bishop of Ephesus, see 'Slavery'.

## The Letter to the Hebrews

More correctly 'A Letter to Jewish Christians' by an anonymous author, this book is not, as older translations suggested, by Paul; it proclaims the gospel in terms which would appeal to Alexandrian Jews, with their emphasis on Moses and angels, and could have been by Apollos. It assumes a thorough knowledge of the Old Testament in the Greek translation, and uses the sacrifices in the Jerusalem Temple as a metaphor to explain the effects of the death of Christ on the cross.

1.1–2.9: God has spoken through Jesus, who is more important than the angels.

2.10–18: Jesus became like us, so that his suffering might be a sacrifice of atonement. 3.1–4.13: Jesus is greater than Moses; therefore do not reject God's offer of eternal rest, as the followers of Moses did. 4.14–5.10: Jesus is a high priest, not of the family of Aaron, but like Melchizedek (Gen. 14.17). 5.11–6.20: Persistence leads to hope. 7.1–28: A priest for ever like Melchizedek; mediator of a new covenant. 9.1–22: Like Plato's 'ideas', there is a perfect sanctuary in heaven, of which the Temple at Jerusalem is an imperfect copy. 9.23–10.39: In the heavenly sanctuary the sacrifice of Jesus on the cross is accepted to remove the sins of all people. 11.1–12.13: Examples of faith. 12.14–29: Do not reject God's grace. 13.1–19: The Christian way of life. 13.20–25: Final greetings.

## The Letter of James

For authorship see 'James'. It is written for Jewish Christians who read Greek, but are suspicious of Paul's insistence that justification is by grace through faith alone; he counterbalances it with Jewish teaching on the importance of good works.

1: Faith, wisdom, poverty, riches, temptation, hearing and doing the word. 2: No favouritism for the rich; faith without works is dead. 3: Taming the tongue; true wisdom. 4: Friendship with the world; judging others; boasting about tomorrow. 5: Warning to the rich; patience in suffering; what to do when sick; the power of prayer.

## The Letters of Peter

**The First Letter of Peter** is a circular letter to be carried by Sylvanus – probably the same as Silas who travelled with Paul – to Christians in northern Asia Minor, 1.1; it was written from 'Babylon', 5.13; which is often a symbolic name for Rome (Rev. 17.5, 9). Some see it as a sermon delivered by Peter at an Easter baptism service.

1 Peter 1: Thanksgiving for the Resurrection of Jesus; a call for reverence. 2.1–17: We are living stones in God's temple, so we must live as slaves of God. 2.18–3.7: The relationship of slaves to masters, and of husbands and wives. 3.8–4.19: We must be willing to suffer for being a Christian. 5: Leaders in the Church are to be shepherds of the flock.

**The Second Letter of Peter** mentions the letters of Paul (3.15); which were probably not collected until after his death; therefore many think this letter, intended to honour Peter, was written by someone else much later, based on the letter of Jude.

2 Peter 1.1–15: We are called to share in the nature of God. 1.16–21: We were eyewitnesses of Christ's glory. 2.1–22: Warning against false prophets. 3.1–13: In spite of the promises of Jesus delivered through the apostles, the day of the Lord has been a long time coming, but it will come. 3.14–18: In the meantime you are to grow in grace.

## The Letters of John

Three short letters, the author of whom is only identified as 'the elder' in 2 John 1 and 3 John 1; the style and language are very similar to those of the Gospel according to John, so they probably have the same author.

**1 John** Some members have left the Christian community, whom the author describes as antichrists, deceivers and false prophets, who did not confess that Jesus is the Christ and the Son of God, or that Jesus Christ has come in the flesh, 2.18–27; 4.1–6; probably they are the ones who say that they have no sin, 1.8; who do not love, 4.8; and claim to possess the Spirit, 4.1–6. God is love, 4.8; the heart of Christianity is that we should love, 2.10; 3.11; but this is only possible if we believe that Jesus was God become human, 3.23; 4.2, 19. The argument seems to go round and round, but always coming closer to God.

**2 John** To 'the elect lady and her children' probably a sister congregation where the false teaching has not yet come, warning them not to give it house-room.

**3 John** To 'Gaius', warning against 'Diotrephes' and commending 'Demetrius'.

### The Letter of Jude

This claims to be by Jude the brother of James, see 'Jude, Judas'. It warns against false teachers, 'who pervert the grace of God into licentiousness and deny our only Master and Lord, Jesus Christ', 4.

## The Revelation or The Apocalypse

The author tells us his name is John and he is writing from the island of Patmos, 1.1, 9. He is called Saint John the Divine, the old English word for a theologian. A life of John, claiming to be written by his secretary Prochorus, one of The Seven (Acts 6.1–6), states that John, son of Zebedee, one of The Twelve, was the Beloved Disciple who was asked by Jesus to look after his mother (John 19.26–27); that John wrote the Gospel of John and the three Letters of John in Ephesus; then, under the persecuting Emperor Domitian in AD 95, he was exiled to Patmos, where he received a vision in a cave and dictated it to Prochorus as The Book of Revelation; John returned to Ephesus after the death of Domitian and died there aged over a hundred. 'The Acts of John by Prochorus' is now regarded as being from the fifth century, but the traditions on which it is based go back to the second century.

Modern scholars are sceptical whether The Gospel and The Revelation could have been written by the same person, because the style and approach are so different; and that either could have been written by a Galilean fisherman. John was a common name. 'Revelation' could have been written under Diocletian or during the persecution under Nero in AD 68. see 'Six hundred and sixty-six'.

Almost every verse contains a quotation from the Hebrew Scriptures, reapplied in a new way to encourage the Church to stand firm under persecution.

1.1–8: John sends greetings to the seven churches. 1.9–19: John's vision of the Risen Christ. Letters from the Risen Christ to the 'angel' (heavenly representative, human messenger, or bishop?) of seven churches in the Province of Asia. The letters refer to specific local circumstances in each town. 2.1–7: Ephesus. 2.8–11: Smyrna. 2.12–17: Pergamum. 2.18–29: Thyatira. 3.1–6: Sardis. 3.7–13: Philadelphia. 3.14–22: Laodicea. 4: A vision of heaven opened, and God worshipped by twenty-four elders, representing the twelve tribes of Israel and the church, the new Israel; and four living creatures, based on Ezek. 1.1–14, representing the rest of the animal kingdom. 5: A scroll sealed in seven places with wax, and only the slaughtered Lamb (Jesus) is worthy to break the seals and unroll the scroll. 6: Four horsemen representing warfare and its consequences: one on a white horse representing a conquering invader, possibly the Parthians; one on a red horse with a sword, representing bloodshed; one on a black horse representing famine; one on a pale horse representing plague and death. The lament of the martyrs. Natural disasters. 7: Representatives of Israel and of all the Gentile nations are marked with a sign to show that they are not to be destroyed. 8–9: The seventh seal, the golden censer, and seven trumpets announcing seven woes – disasters seen as punishment for rejecting God. 10: John eats a bitter scroll. 11: Two witnesses, Moses and Elijah, are persecuted by the Gentiles for three-and-a-half years, following Dan. 12.7–12; predicting the length of time that the Romans would persecute the early Church. The seventh trumpet. 12: A woman representing Israel gives birth to a son representing the Messiah; Michael and his angels, defenders of (the Church, the new) Israel, defeat the powers of evil. 13: A beast representing the Roman Empire, with seven heads representing emperors, one of which, Nero, was expected to return from the dead, as another beast, a false messiah, with the number 666. 14: The Lamb and the martyrs. Three angels predict the fall of Rome, code-named Babylon. Reaping the harvest of death. 15–16: The seven last plagues. 17: Rome portrayed as a prostitute seated on seven hills, and a beast representing the emperors. 18: The fall of Rome / Babylon. 19: Rejoicing in heaven. Jesus on a white horse defeats the persecutors. 20: Satan imprisoned for a thousand years; the souls of those who have been beheaded rule with Christ. Destruction of Satan. Judgement of the dead. 21: New heaven, a new earth, and the New Jerusalem. 22: The river of life. Final promises.

## Interpretation

We can interpret Revelation as a literal prediction of the end of the world. But it is usually misleading to apply the Bible to our own times, without first seeing what it meant to its first readers, see Apocalyptic, p. **175**. We know much about the life of the churches to which Revelation was addressed, the persecutions and temptations to which they were subject, and the difficulty of maintaining a distinctive witness amidst many competing religions. The picture of the heavens opened, and the world of their day as God saw it, using Old Testament imagery, was an encouragement to the readers for whom it was intended. Interpreted as metaphor, it is a superb sequence of poetic symbols, tailor-made to give hope to Christians in the seven churches in the first century. The Roman Empire, under which they were suffering persecution, was under the judgement of God, and would not last for ever. If they would remain faithful to their Christian faith, they would receive their reward, if not in this life, then after their death, because they were playing their small but important part in a huge cosmic drama. The Risen Christ is telling us, too, that although we shall have to suffer in this life, God is ultimately in charge of this world and the life to come.

# Non-Biblical Books

**The Books of Enoch** Three books, translating *elohim* in Gen. 5.22 as 'angels', containing the visions Enoch saw during the three hundred years he walked with them. The New Testament Letter of Jude, verses 14–15, quotes from 1 Enoch as though it were inspired Scripture.

**1 Enoch** known as Ethiopic Enoch, is a collection of five books and several additions, written in Aramaic and translated into Greek. At one time, they were very influential, but were later ignored; the only complete version is a translation into ancient Ethiopic.

*Book of the Watchers*, third century BC, based on Gen. 6.1–4. 200 angelic 'Watchers' took human wives and produced a race of giants, who ate so much that God sent an archangel to destroy them and restore earth's fruitfulness. Enoch pleaded for the Watchers but they were imprisoned; Enoch visits the corners of the earth and several places of everlasting punishment.

*Similitudes*, just before or after the time of Christ. Three parables describe a judge in the last days called the Righteous One, the Chosen One, or the Son of Man; they may have influenced Jesus's use of these terms.

*Astronomical Book*, third century BC or possibly earlier. Enoch's tour of the heavens; the solar year of 364 days harmonized with the lunar year of 354 days.

*Book of Dreams*, a dream describing the judgement of the wicked at the time of Noah's flood. A second dream describing the history of the world up to about 165 BC through an allegory: different animals represent different nations; the Jews are sheep under God their shepherd; the Second Adam comes as a white bull, and good Jews and Gentiles are changed into his likeness.

*Epistle of Enoch*, second century BC. The rich and powerful will be punished for their oppression of the righteous.

**2 Enoch** known as Slavonic Enoch, is an Aramaic book translated through Greek into Slavonic, the only version which survives, and dates from around the time of Christ. It teaches monotheism and ethics, and contains an account of Enoch's ascent into heaven, and the secrets of the heavens, the calendar, the stars and the last things.

**3 Enoch** known as Hebrew Enoch, was written in the fifth or sixth century AD and is a work of Jewish rabbinic mysticism.

**The Book of Jubilees** a rewriting of Genesis and Exodus, proposing that many of the laws of the Torah were given to the patriarchs before the covenant at Mount Sinai, and exhorting contemporary readers to be faithful in living according to the law. It is probably dated around 150 BC.

**The Psalms of Solomon** composed in Hebrew in the first century BC, survive in Greek translation and were included by Codex Alexandrinus as canonical Scripture.

They give an eyewitness reaction to the Roman occupation of Israel, with a clear view of the Jewish expectation of the coming of a military 'Lord Messiah', and a call to rebellion.

**The Dead Sea Scrolls** Many Hebrew manuscripts have been found in caves near Qumran, on the west cliff of the Dead Sea, in the past half-century. Some were connected with a religious community, possibly of the Essenes, described by Josephus, who buried their library prior to the Roman victory in AD 70; the *Manual of Discipline* and the *War of the Sons of Light with the Sons of Darkness* are the most important of these. Many others were manuscripts of Hebrew Scriptures, dating from some four hundred years before the earliest complete manuscripts previously discovered. Several of the guesses which scholars had made about errors in the Hebrew text were confirmed. But they showed that the text of the Hebrew Scriptures in the early centuries was much more fluid than had been imagined: several books existed in two or more versions which were regarded as equally genuine. Moreover the canon of Scripture was equally unsettled: many of the books we dismiss as pseudepigrapha were regarded by the scribes at Qumran as Scripture, of equal inspiration with the books which later came to be recognized and accepted. Most of the scrolls refer to the political situation at the time; it was obvious that there was a multitude of Jewish sects at the time of Jesus, most of them opposed to the Temple authorities in Jerusalem, and his attacks on the Temple will have been seen by many of his contemporaries as nothing out of the ordinary. Also many 'Greek' ideas, such as the contrast between light and darkness, were common in Hebrew thought long before they were used in the Gospel according to John.

**The Gospel of Thomas** Coptic document found near Nag Hammadi in Egypt, translated from a Greek original, fragments of which, from AD 140, were found at Oxyrhynchus. It is a collection of sayings of Jesus, over half of them also in the four canonical Gospels, though in 'Thomas' they are often in a simpler and therefore probably earlier version. The remainder emphasize the unity of the human race, and the need to look for the kingdom of God within us. It claims to have been written by 'Didymos Judas Thomas', who might be the same as Thomas, one of The Twelve. It could well have been a collection of genuine sayings passed down by word of mouth quite independently of the canonical Gospels, and written down as early as AD 50, though later modified. It is important evidence for picturing the historical Jesus; the difficulty with this and the canonical Gospels is to know on what grounds you decide that a saying genuinely consists of the words he spoke. 'Thomas' claims to be a collection of 'secret' sayings; 'Gnosticism' is a name for systems of Christianity which reveal secret knowledge only available to the initiated, but 'Thomas' seems too early for this term to be applicable.

**The Hebrew Gospel of Matthew** Following Papias (c. AD 60–130), who believed that the canonical Gospel of Matthew was a translation from the Hebrew, several Hebrew versions of the Gospel have been examined as possible originals, in particular one quoted in full by the fourteenth-century Spanish Jew, Shemtob.

**The Gospel of the Ebionites** from the Aramaic *ebyonim*, meaning poor, the name given to a group of Jews who believed Jesus was the Messiah, but not the Son of God. Several writers refer to a Gospel in Aramaic, which possibly contained a Jewish-Christian form of the good news, but nothing of it survives; the Syrian Church uses a much later version of the Gospels.

**The Gospel of the Nazoreans** another Jewish-Christian Gospel, written in Aramaic or Hebrew; Eusebius, Origen and Jerome, amongst others, had seen copies in Hebrew characters. The brief quotations show that it resembled Matthew's Gospel but was independent of it, both drawing on a common strand of verbal tradition among Jewish Christians.

**Josephus** a priest, originally named *Yoseph bar Mattatyahu*; Jewish general during the revolt against Rome in AD 66–74; surrendered to the Romans in 67; adopted the name Flavius Josephus; wrote in Greek to persuade the Romans that the majority of Jews were not opposed to the Empire. His *Jewish Wars* argued that only a few young hotheads had been behind the revolt, and that the Jewish God had not been defeated. God used the Romans to punish the rebels. His *Antiquities* is a retelling of the history of the Jews from the Scriptures and continuing up until the eve of the revolt. He gives almost the only evidence outside the New Testament for Jewish beliefs and practices at the time of Jesus, and the Jerusalem Temple, and mentions Pontius Pilate, John the Baptist and James the Just. He almost certainly mentioned Jesus also, but this passage has been so corrupted by Christian additions that we can only guess at what Josephus originally wrote.

**The Epistle of Barnabas** an anonymous sermon, to which the name of Barnabas was later supplied, from the period between AD 70 and 135. It is written by a Gentile Christian who sees Judaism as a threat.

**The Odes of Solomon** a Christian hymnbook from the end of the first century AD revealing the state of theology in the early Church.

**The First Letter of Clement** by a leader in the church at Rome, giving advice to the church in Corinth; his reply to their query had been delayed, probably by the persecution under Domitian, which would imply a date near the end of the first century. It mentions the martyrdom of Peter and Paul, and calls for humility and godly peace in the divided congregation at Corinth. He mentions 'presbyters' and 'bishops' interchangeably, always in the plural; and unlike the Revelation, is positive about the values of Roman society.

**The Sibylline Oracles** a collection of predictions attributed to an old wandering prophetess of Greek tradition; by the first century BC there were believed to be at least ten different Sibyls. A new collection was made after the original was destroyed by fire in 83 BC, and both Jews and Christians added sections to it. Jews held that Sibyl was a daughter-in-law of Noah; Christians believed that although she was a pagan she predicted the coming of Jesus Christ. She is referred to in the hymn *Dies Irae*.

**The Didache** (DID-uh-key, *G* = teaching) or **The Teaching of the Lord to the Gentiles through the Twelve Apostles** edited between AD 70 and 150, contains a description of 'The Two Ways' (the way of living that leads to eternal life, and the way to destruction); of baptism; and of Holy Communion in the early Church, when it has moved out of the chaos described by Paul into an ordered structure based on familiar phrases, though without a full written liturgy yet. The Didache includes the famous prayer asking Christ to 'come with the dawning of the day and make yourself known in the breaking of the bread.'

**The Shepherd of Hermas** visions seen by a Christian, possibly Jewish, in Rome in the first half of the second century, followed by twelve commandments and ten parables. He calls for *metanoia*, repentance or conversion, and warns against double-mindedness.

**The Gospel of the Hebrews** a book written in Egypt around AD 150, probably in Greek; we have no complete copy though it is quoted by several early Christian writers. It appears to have contained a full life of Jesus with an account of his pre-existence, a resurrection appearance to James the Just, and several sayings of Jesus which are not in the canonical Gospels, and seems to be an independent witness not dependent on other writers.

**The Protevangelium of Saint James** an account of the life of the Virgin Mary, probably written in Greek towards the end of the second century by someone with little knowledge of Galilean geography or Jewish customs. Mary was miraculously conceived and born to a childless couple, Joachim and Anna. She was dedicated to the Temple at the age of three, and when she reached puberty the priests betrothed her to a much older widower, Joseph; the 'brothers of Jesus' are really his half-brothers, children of Joseph by his first marriage. The midwife Salome doubts Mary's virginity, and her hands are burnt when she tries to examine her; but they are miraculously healed when she touches the baby.

**The Infancy Gospel of Thomas** collection of stories about the childhood of Jesus, resembling folk-tales, probably from the end of the second century.

**The Gospel of Peter** second-century work found only in fragments dating from 200 onwards. All that survives is from the trial before Pilate to an appearance of the risen Christ in Galilee. Some claim that it contains an early 'Cross Gospel', the source of all four canonical passion narratives; others say that 'Peter' is copied from the canonical Gospels with the addition of stories passed down by word-of-mouth.

**The Acts of Peter** second-century work containing the story of how Peter, fleeing persecution in Rome, met Jesus on the Appian Way and asked him, *Domine, quo vadis?* (*L* = Lord, where are you going?) Peter returned to Rome and was crucified upside down.

**The Acts of Paul** historical novel from the late second century, telling of a woman, Thekla, who was converted by Paul's preaching, with her travels, suffering and death. It contains what may be a genuine reminiscence of Paul's physical appearance, and his beheading by Nero with a sword.

**The Second Letter of Clement** sermon by a Gentile Christian writing in the middle of the second century.

**The Story of Veronica** recounts an early legend of a woman who gave Jesus a cloth to wipe his face with on the way to Golgotha, and received it back marked with a portrait of Jesus: the incident has become one of the Stations of the Cross.

**The Gospel of Pseudo-Matthew** Latin work of the sixth or seventh century; it is the first to mention the ox and the donkey in the stable at Bethlehem, and gives a full account of the miracles performed during the journey of Mary, Joseph and Jesus to Egypt.

**The Gospel of Nicodemus** in manuscripts from the twelfth century, contains both *The Acts of Pilate*, giving additional details of the trial of Jesus before Pontius Pilate, which could be the same as a book mentioned by Justin Martyr in the late second century; and also a separate description of *Christ's Descent into Hell*.

# The History of Mesopotamia and Persia

**Mesopotamia** (*G* = between the rivers) lies between the Tigris and Euphrates, and to the east and west. **Persia** is southern Iran; **Media** is northern Iran. The Israelites had ancestors from this region, often fought Mesopotamian kings, and were exiled there. The following simplified overview aims to clarify the background to the Bible:

**Around 5000** BC in Mesopotamia, hunter-gatherers settled down as agriculturalists; invented cuneiform writing. The earliest towns were around Uruk and Ur, in the south, settled by the *Sumerians*.

**2350** Semi-nomadic Semitic *Akkadian* people, under *Sargon I*, formed an empire with its capital at Akkad in central Mesopotamia. Their language and script were related to but distinct from Sumerian.

**2193** The Akkadian Empire began to break up under threat from Semitic, nomadic *Amorites*; Akkadians, Sumerians, Amorites and a people called *Gutians* continued to co-exist.

**2112–2004** The *Ur III* period in southern Mesopotamia; ziggurats (stepped towers) built at Ur and Uruk. The last king of Ur captured by Elamites, from east of the Persian Gulf.

**2112** *Assyria* emerged in northern Mesopotamia; mostly Semitic; at first a province of Ur III; its capital was Assur; Nineveh and Arbela were important cities.

**2017–1794** The *Old Babylonian* period, in central and southern Mesopotamia; mostly Akkadian and Amorite peoples; cities in Isin and Larsa. No more is heard of the Sumerians. Traditional stories like the *Gilgamesh Epic* were edited and written down.

**1792–1750** The Amorite king *Hammurabi*, with his capital in Babylon, captured Larsa, and much of southern Mesopotamia and Elam. The *Code of Hammurabi* was a collection of case-law decisions.

**1595** *Hittites*, Indo-Europeans who in c.2300 settled in Anatolia, invaded Babylon; dethroned the last of Hammurabi's dynasty; then withdrew. *Kassites* from western Iran took control of Babylonia, but fought constantly against their eastern neighbours the *Hurrians* (founders of the kingdom of Mitanni) and *Urartu*.

**1560–1440** The Kassites and Hurrian / Mitanni people controlled southern Mesopotamia; Assur in northern Mesopotamia was their satellite. At spring festivals, the *Enuma Elish* creation legend was recited.

**1295–1264** The Assyrians ruled all of Mesopotamia; but soon lost much of it to the Hittites.

**1263–1234** The Assyrian king *Shalmanezer I* attacked the Urartu in southern Armenia, fought the Hittites and the southern Babylonians. He founded the city of Kalakh, later known as Nimrud, and made it his capital.

**1155** The *Elamites* destroyed the Kassite dynasty in Babylon.

**1119–1098** The Babylonian *Nebuchadrezzar I* conquered the Elamites.

# The History of Mesopotamia and Persia

**1115–1077** The Assyrian *Tiglath-Pileser I* fought Babylon; both survived.

**c.900** Aryan invaders, including Cimmerians, Scythians, Medes and Persians, from east of the Caspian settled in what is now north-western Iran.

**858–824** The Assyrian *Shalmanezer III* fought the Syrians, whose capital was at Damascus; in 853 at the battle of Karkar he defeated *Ahab* king of Israel and others; he had the *Black Obelisk* carved, now in the British Museum, which shows *Jehu* king of Israel paying him tribute.

**810–783** The Assyrian king was a minor; his mother was regent; Greek authors romanticized her as *Semiramis*.

**745–727** The Assyrian *Tiglath-Pileser III*, in 734 invaded Philistia as far as the Egyptian border. *Ahaz* king of Judah, and *Menahem* king of Israel paid him tribute, but in 733 he annexed a large part of Israel; in 729 he captured Babylon.

**726–722** *Shalmanezer V*, his son, succeeded him; in 724 he marched against *Hoshea* king of Israel; he began to attack Samaria.

**721–710** *Merodach-Baladan*, a Chaldean, seized Babylon.

**721–705** *Sargon II*, king of Assyria, in 721 completed the defeat of Samaria and the deportation of the upper class, replacing them with a mix of Syrians and Babylonians; annexed Carchemish; attacked King Midas in Cilicia; Judah paid him tribute. Merodach-Baladan fled from Babylon; Sargon became its governor. He made a new but short-lived capital at Dur-Sharrukin, now Khorsabad in Iran.

**704–681** Sargon killed in battle; his son *Sennacherib* succeeded him as king of Assyria; made Nineveh his capital.

**703** Merodach-Baladan returned to Babylon; sent envoys to Hezekiah king of Judah; next year he was defeated.

**701** Sennacherib marched against Egypt, and on the way besieged Jerusalem; King Hezekiah of Judah refused to surrender; Sennacherib withdrew due to an epidemic.

**700** Sennacherib put his son in charge of Babylon; Elamites conquered it; in 689 Sennacherib destroyed it.

**680–669** Sennacherib assassinated by Addramelech and Sharezer, two of his sons, who then fled; *Esar-haddon*, another son, succeeded him; rebuilt Babylon; used it as the Assyrian capital. In 671 he took the Egyptian capital of Memphis.

**668–627** The Assyrian king *Ashurbanipal* invaded Egypt; destroyed Thebes; took Manasseh king of Israel to Babylon in chains; besieged Babylon 652–648, when his brother the Governor rebelled; the brother died in the burning palace. In 646 Ashurbanipal defeated Elam, destroying *Susa* in Susiana which they had annexed. In 635 he withdrew to Haran while his twin sons fought for the succession. Detailed records of astronomical observations were begun.

**626** *Nabopolassar*, vassal king of *Chaldea* to the south of Mesopotamia, revolted against his Assyrian masters and seized the throne of *Babylon*; from this time the term 'Chaldea' meant Babylonia.

**625** The *Medes*, with their capital at Ecbatana in northern Iran, united under *Cyaxares* (reigned 653–585), who freed them from Scythian rule. Cyaxares and Nabopolassar formed an alliance against Assyria, taking Assur, Kalakh and Nineveh.

**605–562** The Babylonian king Nabopolassar died and was succeeded by his son *Nebuchadrezzar II*, who defeated the Egyptians and Assyrians at *Carchemish* in 605; Assyria disappeared from history.

**598** Nebuchadrezzar, known in the Bible as Nebuchadnezzar, attacked *Jerusalem*; king Jehoiakim died; 3,000 exiles taken to Babylon, see 'Exile'.

**587–586** Jerusalem destroyed; the rest of the population taken into exile. Babylon became the richest and largest city in the world, Nebuchadnezzar built the Hanging Gardens for Cyaxares' grand-daughter, whom he had married; the ziggurat of Elemenanki was probably the model for the Tower of Babel.

**561–560** Babylon ruled by *Evil-Merodach*, son of Nebuchadrezzar, who released Jehoiachin from prison.

**559–556** *Nergal-Sharezer*

**556–539** *Nabonidus*. In 552 he left to live in Tema in Arabia, appointing *Belshazzar* his viceroy, Dan. 5.

**549–529** *Cyrus II* (son of Cambyses I, king of *Persia* in southern Iran, and a Median princess), in 549 led a revolt against his Median grandfather, and in 550 annexed Media, forming a united kingdom of the Medes and Persians. In 538 he invaded Babylonia, and in 539 he defeated Nabonidus to become king of Babylon, when the priests of Marduk let him in without a battle; ruled there until 530; allowed all the subject people to return to their homelands; defeated wealthy Croesus of Lydia and annexed the whole of Asia Minor (modern Turkey). Now Persians were in political control of Babylon, but the remaining Babylonians, Arameans and some Jews carried on the commerce; Aramaic was the common language.

**529–522** Babylon ruled by his son, *Cambyses II*; conquered Memphis; captured Egypt, Cyprus and the Greek Islands; his throne was seized by one of the *magi* called Gaumata.

**522–486** *Darius I* executed Gaumata at Ecbatana; built a new capital at Persepolis, and summer palace at Susa; allowed the returning exiles to rebuild the Temple in Jerusalem; Darius won against the Greeks at Thermopylae; was defeated at Marathon in 490.

**486–465** Babylon ruled by *Xerxes I*, called Ahasuerus in Esther; attacked Greece in 480; defeats at Salamis, Miletus and Plataea forced him to withdraw. Successive Persian kings were *Artaxerxes I*, called Longimanus, (465–425), who allowed Nehemiah to rebuild Jerusalem, Neh. 1–7; 12–13; *Xerxes II* (424–423); *Darius II* (Nothus, 423–404, referred to in Dan. 6); *Artaxerxes II* (Mnemon, 404–358) who in 398 sent Ezra to reform the Jewish nation and its worship, Ezra 8.31–10.5; Neh. 8; *Artaxerxes III* (Ochus, 358–338); and *Arses* (338–336).

**336–331** *Darius III (Codomannus)* defeated by Alexander the Great at the Battle of Issus in 333, 1 Macc. 1.1.

**321** *Seleucus I Nicanor*, Alexander the Great's general, given Babylonia, see 'Seleucids'.

**315–312** *Antigonus I Monophthalmos* seized Mesopotamia; by 305 Seleucus was back; he founded Antioch-on-the-Orontes as his capital.

**323 BC – AD 226** Following Alexander's death in 323, Parthians seized control of Persia, with their capital in Ctesiphon. In 40 BC they invaded Roman-controlled Syria and placed Antigonus (40–37) on the throne of Jerusalem. The Parthians were succeeded by Sassanians (AD 223–651).

# The Life of Jesus

Jesus was a historical figure, mentioned in several non-Christian first-century authors. A full account of his life is given in the four Gospels, which are written by believers seeking to persuade others to believe in Jesus, and form one of the best bodies of near-contemporary evidence for the life of any person in ancient history. The writers of the Gospels claimed to have received their information from eye-witnesses, and that there were still eyewitnesses alive who would correct them had they been inaccurate.

Jesus was born during the reign of Herod the Great, i.e. before 4 BC; the tradition that he was born in AD 1 is due to a miscalculation by a sixth-century monk called Dionysius Exiguus. According to Matthew and Luke he was born in Bethlehem and his mother Mary was a virgin when he was conceived. He was brought up in Nazareth, where he was known as the carpenter's son.

His public ministry began when he was baptized by his cousin John the Baptist in the River Jordan. After a period of temptation in the wilderness he returned to Nazareth, where he was rejected.

He travelled around Lake Galilee, calling fishermen and tax-collectors to follow him, preaching that 'the kingdom of God has come near: repent, and believe in the good news'. He healed the sick, cast out demons, forgave sins and enjoyed parties with the social outcasts. He chose The Twelve to be close to him, and to be leaders among his followers; he sent seventy disciples on a trial mission, from which they returned reporting dramatic success.

Around thirty-eight miracles performed by Jesus are reported in the Gospels. Most of them are healing miracles; in addition there are the Catch of fishes, John 21.1–14; Fig-tree cursed, Mark 11.13–14, 20–24; Five thousand fed, Mark 6.30–44; Four thousand fed, Mark 8.1–9; Jairus' daughter raised, Mark 5.21–43; Lazarus raised, John 11.38–44; Passing through the crowd at Nazareth, Luke 4.28–30; Passing through the crowd in the Temple, John 8.59; Soldiers falling back, John 18.5–6; Stilling the storm, Mark 4.35–41; Tribute money provided, Matt. 17.24–27; Walking on water, Mark 6.47–52; Water into wine, John 2.1–11; Widow's son at Nain raised, Luke 7.11–17.

Sometimes Jesus crossed into Gentile territory: the Decapolis, or Tyre and Sidon, and on two occasions he healed Gentiles. In the first three Gospels, Christ's ministry in Galilee seems to be accomplished in a year; John, however, tells of him going to Jerusalem to celebrate the annual Passover festival on three separate occasions.

Jesus finally went up to Jerusalem for Passover in about AD 30. He rode into Jerusalem on a donkey while the crowd waved palm branches and shouted 'Hosanna'. He drove money-changers and traders out of the Temple, though John places this at the beginning of his ministry. He taught in the Temple, held a Last Supper with his disciples where he washed their feet, said of the bread 'this is my body', and of the wine, 'this is my blood of the covenant'.

Jesus prayed in the Garden of Gethsemane, was betrayed by Judas Iscariot, arrested and brought before the High Priests and the Council by night. They asked him, 'Are you the Messiah, the Son of the Blessed One?', and he replied 'I am'. He also spoke of himself as the Son of Man coming to God on the clouds. They pronounced him guilty of blasphemy, then took him to the Roman Governor, Pontius Pilate, accusing him of treason against the Emperor. Pilate reluctantly condemned him to death.

Jesus was executed on the Friday before the Passover sabbath by the standard Roman means of crucifixion, the most painful method yet invented for killing someone. After carrying his cross or at least the horizontal beam through Jerusalem, he was nailed to the cross by Roman soldiers at a place called 'The Skull' outside Jerusalem and left there until he died.

Then the body of Jesus was taken down and buried in a nearby cave-tomb, with a heavy stone rolled across the entrance. On the Sunday morning some women coming to anoint the body found the tomb open and empty. They returned to tell the other disciples, several of whom visited the tomb and confirmed that the body of Jesus was not there. Jesus was then seen alive by many people; Paul mentions over five hundred who saw him.

After forty days of appearances, Jesus ascended into heaven to indicate his authority, and that he would no longer be physically present on earth. Then on the Feast of Pentecost, fifty days after Passover, his disciples had an experience of the Holy Spirit, and knew that Jesus was still with them spiritually, empowering them to spread his message across the world, working and worshipping together as the fellowship of his Church.

# The Teaching of Jesus

The teaching of Jesus comes to us mostly in the form of parables: stories, often humorous, demanding a judgement from the listeners, which enable them to see themselves in a new light. He also taught in short, easily memorable sayings, often with a poetic structure. The main themes are the presence and growth of the kingdom of God; the need for decision; the Fatherhood of God; God's readiness to forgive and to heal; the requirement to love God and love our neighbour, forgiving those who have offended us; never to judge other people, but share table-fellowship with the outcast; and finally, suffering and self-sacrifice.

## The parables of Jesus

Barren fig tree  Luke 13.6–9
Blind leading the blind  Matt. 15.14
Bread of life  John 6
Bridegroom  Matt. 9.15; John 3.29
Camel and the needle's eye  Mark 10.25; Luke 18.25
Children in the marketplace  Matt. 11.16–19; Luke 7.31–35
City on a hill  Matt. 5.14
Counting the cost  Luke 14.28–33
Divided kingdom  Matt. 12.25–28; Mark 3.23–26; Luke 11.17–20
Drag net  Matt. 13.47
Faithful and unfaithful slave  Matt. 24.45–51
Fig tree  Matt. 24.32–33; Mark 13.28–29; Luke 21.29–31
Friend at midnight  Luke 11.5–8
Good Samaritan  Luke 10.25–37
Good and evil treasure  Matt. 12.35; Luke 6.45
Great supper  Luke 14.16–24
Guests at a banquet  Luke 14.8–14
Hen and chickens  Matt. 23.37; Luke 13.34
Hidden Treasure  Matt. 13.44
House built on rock  Matt. 7.24–27; Luke 6.48–49
I do not know you  Luke 13.25–27
Importunate widow  Luke 18.1–8
Labourers in the vineyard  Matt. 20.1–17
Lamp under a bushel  Matt. 5.15–16; Mark 4.21–22; Luke 8.16–17; 11.33; John 8.12

Leaven (yeast)  Matt. 13.33; Luke 13.20
Leaven of the Pharisees  Matt. 16.6
Lilies of the field,  birds of the air  Matt. 5.26–29; Luke 12.24–28
Living water  John 4; 7.37–38
Lost sheep  Matt. 18.12; Luke 15.1–7
Lost coin  Luke 15.8–10
Master and slave  Luke 17.7–10
Measure you give  Matt. 7.2; Mark 4.24; Luke 6.38
Mote and beam  Matt. 7.3–5; Luke 6.41–42
Moving mountains  Matt. 17.20; 21.21; Luke 17.5–6
Mustard seed  Matt. 13.31–32; Mark 4.31–32; Luke 13.18–19; cp. Luke 17.6
Narrow and wide  Matt. 7.13–14; Luke 13.24
New wine, old bottles  Matt. 9.17; Mark 2.22; Luke 5.37–38
New and old treasure  Matt. 13.51
New and old wine  Luke 5.39
New patch on old garment  Matt. 9.16; Mark 2.21; Luke 5.36
Oxen released on sabbath  Luke 13.15; 14.5
Pearl of great price  Matt. 13.45, 46
Pearls before swine  Matt. 7.6
Pharisee and tax-collector  Luke 18.9–14
Plentiful harvest  Matt. 9.37–38
Pounds  Luke 19.12–27
Prodigal son  Luke 15.11–32
Prudent steward  Luke 12.42–48
Pupil not above teacher  Matt. 10.24; Luke 6.40
Returning demon  Matt. 12.43–45; Luke 11.24–26
Rich fool  Luke 12.16–21
Rich man and Lazarus  Luke 16.19–31
Salt  Matt. 5.13; Luke 14.34
Seed growing secretly  Mark 4.26–29
Settling with your accuser  Luke 12.57–59
Sheep among wolves  Matt. 10.16
Sheep and goats  Matt. 25.31–46
Shepherd and sheep  John 10
Shrewd manager  Luke 16.1–13
Signs of the times  Luke 12.54–56
Slave of two masters  Matt. 6.24; Luke 16.13
Straining out a gnat, swallowing a camel  Matt. 23.24
Sower  Matt. 13.1–23; Mark 4.1–20; Luke 8.4–15
Sparrows  Matt. 10.29–31; Luke 12.6–7
Stones for bread  Matt. 7.9
Strong man's house  Matt. 12.29; Mark 3.27; Luke 11.21–22
Talents  Matt. 25.14–30
Tares  Matt. 13.24–30
Ten bridesmaids  Matt. 25.1–13
Thief at midnight  Luke 12.39
Treasure in heaven  Matt. 6.19–21; 19.21; Mark 10.21; Luke 12.33; 18.22
Tree and fruit  Matt. 7.15–20; 12.33; Luke 6.43–44
Two sons  Matt. 21.28–32

# The Teaching of Jesus

Two debtors  Luke 7.41–42
Unmerciful servant  Matt. 18.23–35
Vine and the branches  John 15
Watchful slaves  Luke 12.35–38
Watchful household  Mark 13.34–37
Wedding banquet  Matt. 22.1–10
Wedding garment  Matt. 22.11–14
Wicked tenants  Matt. 21.33–43; Mark 12.1–9; Luke 20.9–16

# The sayings of Jesus

Adultery  Matt. 5.27–30; John 8.1–11
Almsgiving  Matt. 6.1–4
Anger  Matt. 5.21–26
Ask, search, knock  Matt. 7.7; Luke 11.9
Beatitudes, blessings, woes  Matt. 5.1–12; Luke 6.20–26
Children, true greatness  Matt. 18.1–5; 19.13–15; 20.20–28; Mark 9.33–37; 10.13–16, 35–45; Luke 9.46–48; 18.15–17; 22.24–30
Come to me  Matt. 11.28–30
Counting the cost  Luke 9.57–62; 14.25–33
Death  Matt. 16.21–28; 17.22–23; Mark 8.31–38; 9.30–32; 10.32–34; 14.3–9; Luke 9.21–27, 43–45; 18.31–34
Divorce  Matt. 5.31–32; 19.1–10; Mark 10.1–12; Luke 16.18
Enemies  Matt. 5.43–48; Luke 67.27–35
Faith  Matt. 8.10–13; 9.2, 22, 29; 14.31; 15.28; 16.8; 21.22; Mark 2.5; 4.40; 5.34; 10.52; 11.22 etc.
Families divided  Matt. 10.35; Luke 12.49–53
Fasting  Matt. 6.16–18; Matt. 9.14–17
Fatherhood of God  Matt. 6.9; 11.25–27; Mark 14.36
For or against  Mark 9.40; Luke 9.49–50
Forgiveness  Matt. 18.15–22; Mark 2.1–11; Luke 7.36–49
Gentiles  Matt. 8.5–13; 15.21–28; Mark 7.24–30; Luke 7.9; 24.47
Golden Rule  Matt. 7.12
John the Baptist  Matt. 11.7–18; 14.1–12; Mark 9.9–13; 11.27–33; Luke 7.18–35; 20.1–8
Jonah  Matt. 12.38–42; Luke 11.29–32
Judging  Matt. 7.1–5; Luke 6.36–37
Last Supper  Matt. 26.20–35; Mark 14.17–31; Luke 22.14–38; John 13–17; 1 Cor. 10.16; 11.23–25
Law  Matt. 5.17–18; 22.40; 23.23; Luke 10.26; 16.14–17; John 7.19, 51
Light  Matt. 5.14–16
Love  Matt. 7.1–29; 22.34; Mark 12.28–34; Luke 10.27
Messiah  Matt. 16.13–20; 22.41–46; Mark 12.35–37; 14.62; Luke 20.41–44; 24.26, 45
Mission, The Twelve, Fishers for People  Matt. 10.1–15; Mark 1.16–20; Luke 4.42–44; 5.1–11; 9.1–6; 10.1–12 17–23; 24.47
Money  Matt. 6.24; 13.22; 19.21; Mark 10.23–27; Luke 16.1–13
Oaths  Matt. 5.33–37

# The Teaching of the Bible

### Progressive revelation

The beliefs of the Jewish people, which are also a necessary foundation for the New Testament, were arrived at through their experiences over more than a thousand years. God could only reveal his compassionate nature to them gradually, as each generation built on what previous generations had learnt, and overcame their earlier errors about him by experiencing his salvation. This theory of 'progressive revelation' explains why early generations were allowed to persist in some crude misunderstandings of the nature of God.

### Ethical monotheism, covenant, a God who saves

Slowly they arrived at a belief in 'ethical monotheism', meaning an understanding that there is only one God, who cares about right and wrong and how we treat each other. This was expressed in the idea of 'covenant'. God will care for his people if they will contract to be faithful to him and behave morally. Especially through the experience of the Exodus, they also learnt that God is a God who saves. he gives us free will to disobey him, but then intervenes to rescue us from the mess we have got ourselves into. Although masculine language is usually used of God, God has feminine characteristics also.

### Jesus

The New Testament builds on this, teaching that the life of Jesus reflects the character of God. God cares so much for the world that he became incarnate in Jesus, to enable us to love him, and to give his life as a sacrifice which would bring us forgiveness for our sins. Words like 'Atonement', 'Justification', 'Reconciliation' and 'Redemption' are used to describe this new relationship between the believer and God. Jesus claimed that he was one with the Father; anyone who claims that is either mad, bad or right. So his followers called him the Word of God made flesh, and said that God was in Christ reconciling the world to himself. Their purpose in telling the story of his life and recounting his teaching was to win people to believe that his teaching on the love of God came from God himself, and to accepting Jesus as their friend and Saviour in this world and sharing eternal life with him in the world to come.

### The Holy Spirit

The experience of the early Christians was that God works in and through us: the Holy Spirit, which was given to selected people at particular times in the Hebrew Scriptures, is now available to all believers at all times, giving them power to speak and work for God in love.

## Story and poetry

God reveals himself through his saving acts and their inspired interpretation. The Bible teaches that God has worked through history in the past, is doing so now and will continue to do so in the future. It also uses the language of story and poetry to convey God's truth. Some stories are fiction, but told in such a way as to convey profound truth; some poems communicate truths which could never be expressed in prose.

## Prophecy

The language of Prophecy and Apocalyptic is used to show God's view of the present and his plans for the future, see 'Prophets'

## Eschatology

Eschatology is the study of what the Bible has to say about the 'End Times'. Some Christians, assuming that it is a prediction of what will happen 2,000–3,000 years later, try to work out exactly what events are foretold and when they will occur. Others interpret it as metaphor about the present.

## Apocalyptic

Apocalyptic means revealing, unveiling or uncovering what was hidden; apocalyptic visions often begin 'I saw the heavens opened'. At first, people believed that the gods lived above the clouds in 'the heavens'. Most Jewish people by the time of Christ understood that God is everywhere. They believed that those who have died are sleeping in a place called Sheol, and the Pharisees thought that they would be resurrected to life again on earth. In the Greek and Roman world the gods were thought to live on Mount Olympus, and the dead to have a ghost-like existence in the world of the shades (Hades). The Greek philosopher Plato had given another interpretation to the idea of heaven: it was an ideal world where the perfect ideas existed of everything in the material world. Many Jewish books have been discovered in recent centuries which show how common it was to write of a vision of heaven. What was seen in the vision was a series of symbols which imparted a true understanding of what was happening on earth. These visions are a form of prophecy. Examples in the Bible are parts of Ezekiel, Daniel and Zechariah; Mark 13 and parallels; 2 Thessalonians 2; and the Book of Revelation. In predictions like those in Mark 13, Jesus warned his fellow-Jews that as their relations with the Romans deteriorated, the destruction of Jerusalem was inevitable; eventually it happened in AD 70. When he wrote to the Thessalonians, Paul assumed that Day of the Lord, and the physical resurrection of believers on earth, was coming very soon. But some Christians gave up work altogether as they thought the end was near, so by the time he wrote 1 Corinthians 15, Paul had moved to a more metaphorical view: 'flesh and blood cannot inherit the kingdom of God', he wrote. Possibly neither Paul nor the writer of The Book of Revelation thought it important to distinguish between literal prediction and metaphorical interpretation of history, even if they would have understood the question. Maybe neither should we, so long as nobody makes of apocalyptic an excuse for being idle, making elaborate speculations, ignoring contemporary politics, or postponing a decision to follow Christ.

# Interpreting the Scriptures or 'Exegesis'

To hear what God is saying to us through the Scriptures we must first understand what they meant to the people who first heard them, and then work out what that means in the changed circumstances of today. You cannot miss out either step, and Jesus commanded us to love God with all our mind. Of course simple believers can hear God by taking the surface meaning of the words, but they must always be willing to have misunderstandings corrected by those who have studied the background; by the use of this dictionary with a good commentary or a set of Bible reading notes, nobody should find this beyond them.

## The inspiration of the Bible
Those who first heard the Scriptures read aloud will have already been familiar with that type of literature. They will have been in no doubt that the Scriptures are inspired by God (2 Tim. 3.16), but what did they mean by inspiration? Did they mean that God 'breathed into' the writers to give them an inspired understanding of how God sees the world and the people in it, and what he is doing to change it, then left them to express that in their own words? Or did they mean that he took away their free will, and controlled the actual words they wrote down? Most modern interpreters take a position somewhere between these extremes.

## The history of biblical interpretation
We see from the Dead Sea Scrolls and the Gospels that at the time of Jesus there were several ways of interpreting the Hebrew Scriptures. Those who first heard the letters of Paul respected them as personal letters from a revered missionary, and soon began to regard them as inspired Scripture on a level with the Hebrew Scriptures; a similar development occurred with the Gospels. This was followed by a process of deciding which of the many writings which were circulating should be regarded as inspired and admitted to the Canon of Scripture, and which should not. It was the Church which made these decisions, and gradually the Church came to be regarded as the proper authority for deciding what was the right way to interpret the Scriptures; lay people were discouraged from reading and interpreting the Bible for themselves.

## The Reformation
In reaction against this, at the Reformation the Protestant teachers placed the Bible above the Church. They insisted that inspiration was mechanical and plenary: that the writers were merely the 'pens' of the Spirit, and were given not only the impulse to write, but also the matter and the words. They claimed that Scripture has authority, efficacy, contains all that is necessary for salvation (without the Church making

additional requirements which are not found in Scripture), and that difficult passages make sense when understood in the light of the whole Bible.

## Fundamentalism

The Reformation attitude to the Scriptures was challenged by the growth of scientific thinking, which in its extreme form regards nothing as true unless it can be demonstrated by experiment. In particular, geological discoveries about the age of the rocks, and Darwin's suggestions about the evolution of species, challenged those who wished to interpret the first few chapters of Genesis as a scientific statement. Coupled with a belief that the Second Coming of Christ was imminent, this led to the rise of Fundamentalism. It took its name from a series of tracts called *The Fundamentals*, published between 1910 and 1915 in the United States. The Fundamentalists challenged the spread of Darwinian evolutionary theory and the higher criticism of the Bible, both of which were accepted in the more liberal parts of the Protestant churches. Fundamentalism, through television evangelists, has gone on to play an important part in politics also. The Evangelical Alliance demands belief in 'the divine inspiration, authority, and sufficiency of the Scriptures; and the right and duty of private judgment in the interpretation of them'. But many Evangelicals do not insist on literal inerrancy. Considerable ingenuity was needed to resolve the apparent contradictions within the Bible, and its conflict with observable fact; and it was clear that Jesus, Paul and the Council at Jerusalem had all stated that the whole of the Old Testament Law was not binding upon Christians.

## Liberalism

Some Christians felt that new movements in philosophy, and the development of science, had made it impossible to adopt an unquestioning attitude to the Bible. The emphasis was put upon the individual reader's emotions and feelings about God. At its extreme, Liberalism said that the Bible should be read just like any other piece of ancient literature, an attitude which could be comfortably taken by an atheist. Yet it is hard to see how anyone can appreciate a book if they are completely out of sympathy with the person who wrote it. Rudolf Bultmann argued that it was necessary to 'demythologize' the Scriptures; others said that there are some truths which cannot be expressed in any other way than through a myth. The Higher Criticism, studying the literary form of the biblical books and their historical background; and the Lower Criticism, studying the accuracy of the text and the meaning of the words, have given modern Christians a deeper understanding of the original meaning of the Scriptures than has been possible at any other time since they were first written; criticism in this context does not mean condemnation but intelligent discernment. There are many passages, e.g.'the marriage supper of the Lamb', Rev. 19, which cannot possibly be taken as literal descriptions, and must be understood symbolically. Others (e.g. the wedding at Cana, John 2, in which the inner meaning is about replacing a search for purity with a joyful celebration of God's love) make arguments about the mechanism of the miracle irrelevant. The question for the reader of the Bible, then, is how much weight to put on the historical accuracy of the Scriptures (which has been confirmed to an extent that would have astonished sceptics of the nineteenth century) and how far to accept that many passages were never meant to be factual, but are to be understood as poetry and metaphor, stirring us with profound truths that science could never convey.

# Bible Manuscripts, Versions and Translations

## The Masoretic Text

The Hebrew Scriptures were written for many centuries showing only the consonants, no vowels; readers had memorized most of the text and only used the consonants to help their memory when reading aloud. The Dead Sea Scrolls have shown us that there were sometimes several competing versions of the consonantal text. Between about AD 600 and 950 groups of Rabbis, known as Masoretes, produced what were regarded as definitive versions of the Hebrew text, including the vowels.

## The Septuagint

The Hebrew Scriptures were translated into Greek. Traditionally this translation was made by seventy-two elders for the library in Alexandria between 285 and 246 BC, so it is known by the Latin word for seventy. Septuagint or LXX. It contains many books or parts of books that are not in the Masoretic text, see The Canon of Scripture, p. 133. It worked from the consonants before the vowels were added, and sometimes makes a different interpretation of what the words mean, or even seems to be working from a different text. Modern English translations put the abbreviation Gk in the footnotes to show that they have preferred the Septuagint reading over the Masoretic Text. It was the version quoted in the Greek New Testament, and regarded as superior to the Hebrew text by the early Church. Some of the Septuagint readings in the Pentateuch are confirmed by the Samaritan Version.

## The Vulgate

Many different translations of the Bible were made into Latin; they are referred to as Old Latin versions. Pope Damasus asked Saint Jerome (347–420) to prepare a new translation into Latin from the Septuagint, and it was called the *vulgata editio*, 'edition prepared for the public'. At the Council of Trent in 1546 it was made the official version for the Roman Catholic Church.

## Papyri

Copies of the New Testament were written on papyrus, and many fragments, from a few verses up to complete books, survived in the dry sands of Egypt; they were written in Greek Uncial (Capital) letters. $\mathfrak{P}^{52}$, now kept in the John Rylands Library in Manchester, consists of John 18.31–33 and 37–38, and is dated around AD 130–140;

$\mathfrak{P}^{66}$ in the Bodmer Library near Geneva contains almost all of John and dates before the end of the second century; $\mathfrak{P}^{45}$, $\mathfrak{P}^{46}$ and $\mathfrak{P}^{47}$, in the Chester Beatty Library in Dublin, contain between them third-century copies of most of the New Testament. $\mathfrak{P}^{104}$ is a fragment of Matthew which some scholars allege to be from the first century.

## Codices

A codex is a manuscript folded into the pages of a book.

*Codex Sinaiticus*, known as 'S' or by the Hebrew character Aleph, was discovered in 1859 at the Monastery of Saint Catherine on Mount Sinai. It is an almost complete fourth century manuscript of the Bible; now kept in the British Library in London.

*Codex Vaticanus*, or 'B', in the Vatican Library, dates from the mid-fourth century.

*Codex Alexandrinus*, or 'A', is an early-fifth-century manuscript containing most of the New Testament; it is kept in the British Library

*Codex Bezae Cantabrigiensis*, or 'D', is a fifth-century bilingual text, with Greek and Latin pages facing each other, containing most of the four Gospels and Acts. It is kept in the University of Cambridge, in England.

## Textual criticism

The differences between these manuscripts are mostly quite small. Apart from the beginning of John 8 or the end of Mark 16, they consist usually of differences in a few letters or a word or two, which do not substantially alter the meaning. Some modern editions of the Greek and Hebrew text are published with a full 'critical apparatus', i.e. footnotes showing which words occur in which manuscripts, and a set of rules has evolved which enables scholars to weigh the external and internal evidence in order to choose which reading is most likely to have been in the original. The footnotes in some modern translations indicate where there are important variations between the manuscripts.

## English translations of the Bible

Early translations of the Bible were made into Aramaic (known as Targums), Syriac, Coptic, Ethiopic, Armenian, Georgian and Latin. The Latin Vulgate was used throughout the Western Church, and the clergy were reluctant to allow unqualified laypeople to read the Scriptures in their own language. John Wyclif published an English translation of the New Testament in 1380, and the Old Testament in 1382, translating from the Vulgate. William Tyndale started the first English translation from Hebrew and Greek in 1523; under persecution he fled to Cologne; eventually his New Testament, translated directly from the Greek, was printed in Worms in 1525–8, and the Pentateuch in Marburg in 1530. He achieved a graceful style of English, following closely the Hebrew sentence structure, and this style and many of Tyndale's phrases dominated other translations for four hundred years. Miles Coverdale's translation was printed in 1535, and his version of the Psalms remained in use in the Book of Common Prayer long after the rest of his work was superseded by Matthew's Bible in 1537; the Great Bible 1539; the Geneva Bible 1560 and the Bishops' Bible 1568. In 1604 King James I of England ordered a distinguished team of scholars to make a new translation, direct from the original languages. The King James Version was published in 1611; because the title page proclaimed that it was authorized for use in churches, it is known in England as the Authorized Version. Increasing knowledge of the original text and languages caused revisions of this to be made in the nineteenth and twentieth centuries, but changes in the English language led to a host of modern translations, attempting to put the Bible into a form which could be understood by contemporary readers. The conservative translations aim at 'formal equivalence', finding modern words but keeping the original sentence structure as far as possible. More innovative translators attempt 'dynamic equivalence', finding phrases which sound natural in modern English and have the same overall meaning as the sentences of the original languages. 'Common language' translations aim at a form of language which will be equally understandable to the highly educated and to those for whom English is not their first language. The best way to understand the meaning of the Bible, if you cannot follow it in the original Hebrew and Greek, is to have two or more translations in front of you, then compare and contrast.

# Bible Study on the Internet

If you enter almost any word in the Bible in one of the Internet Search Engines you will find thousands of sites. Among those I have found useful are:

Texts and translations of the Bible:
   http://www.htmlbible.com
   http://www.biblia.com/bible/
Search the Bible by subject:
   http://bible.christiansunite.com/Naves_Topical_Bible
Archaeology of the Bible:
   Liberal: http://www.bib-arch.org
   Conservative: http://www.bibarch.com
Dictionary of Mythology:
   http://www.pantheon.org/mythica.html
Dictionaries of the Bible:
   http://www.christiananswers.net/dictionary
   http://www.newadvent.org/cathen
   http://www.searchgodsword.org
   http://www.studylight.org
Maps of Bible Lands:
   http://www.culturalresources.com/Maps.html
Photos of Bible places:
   http://www.BiblePlaces.com
   http://www.holylandphotos.org
Photos of the Holyland Hotel model of Jerusalem:
   http://www.j30ad.org
Society in New Testament Times:
   Edersheim, *The Life and Times of Jesus the Messiah*, full text on
     http://philologos.org
   Complete works of Josephus on http://bible.christiansunite.com/
     josephus/josindex.shtml
Towns addressed in Revelation:
   http://www.sevenchurches.org

# Maps

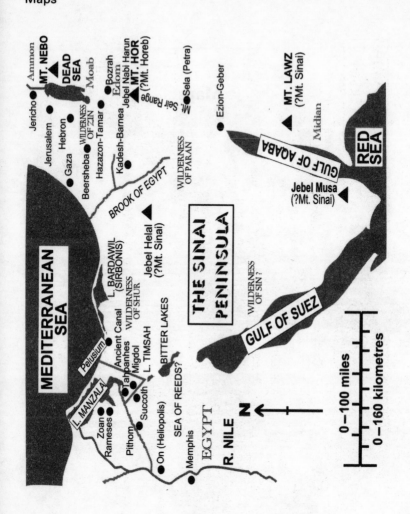

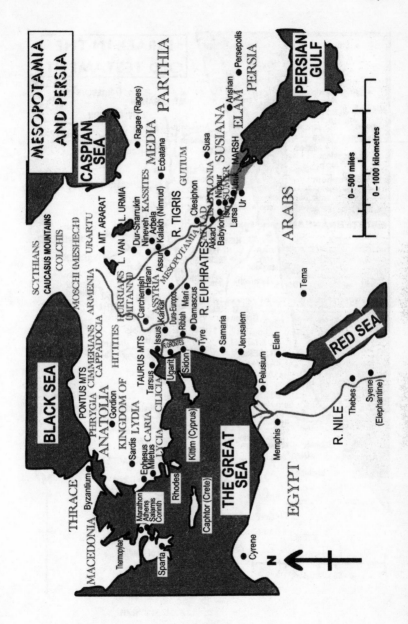

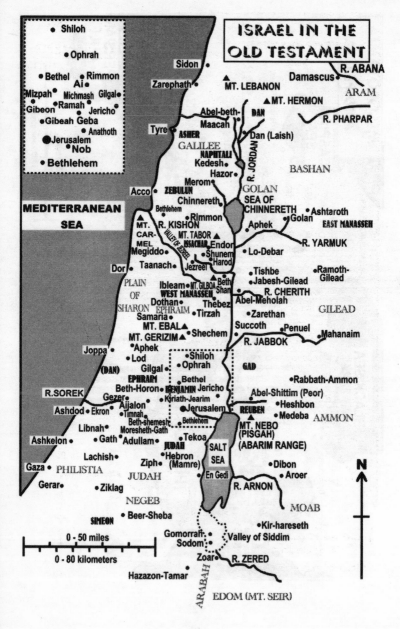

ISRAEL IN THE OLD TESTAMENT

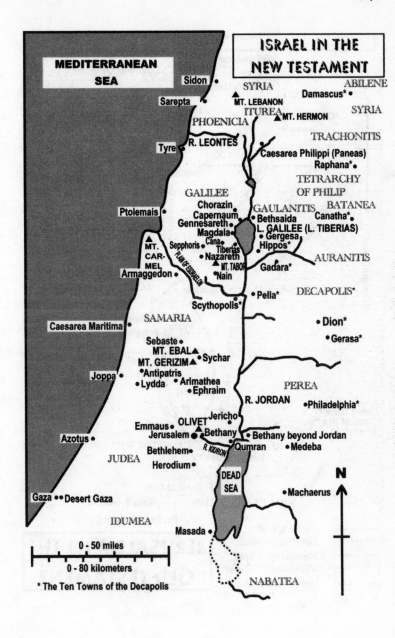

187

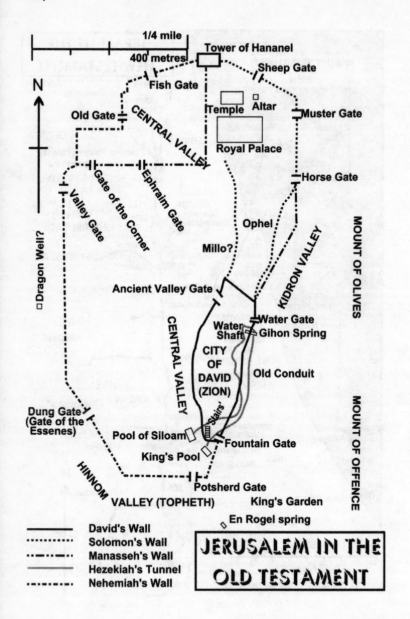

JERUSALEM IN THE OLD TESTAMENT

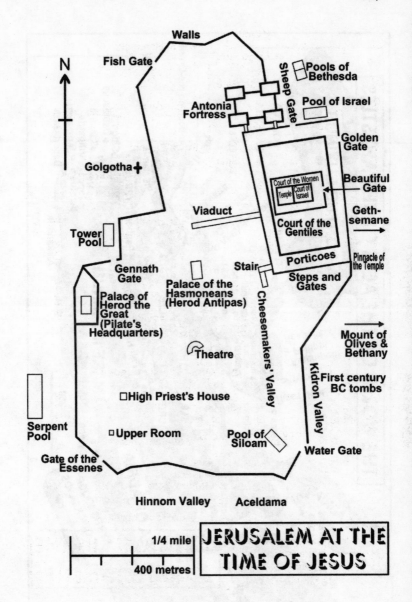

N

Walls
Fish Gate
Pools of Bethesda
Sheep Gate
Pool of Israel
Antonia Fortress
Golden Gate
Golgotha
Court of the Women
Temple
Court of Israel
Beautiful Gate
Viaduct
Court of the Gentiles
Geth-semane
Tower Pool
Porticoes
Pinnacle of the Temple
Gennath Gate
Stair
Steps and Gates
Palace of the Hasmoneans (Herod Antipas)
Palace of Herod the Great (Pilate's Headquarters)
Cheesemakers' Valley
Mount of Olives & Bethany
Theatre
First century BC tombs
High Priest's House
Kidron Valley
Serpent Pool
Upper Room
Pool of Siloam
Water Gate
Gate of the Essenes

Hinnom Valley          Aceldama

1/4 mile
400 metres

**JERUSALEM AT THE TIME OF JESUS**

Maps

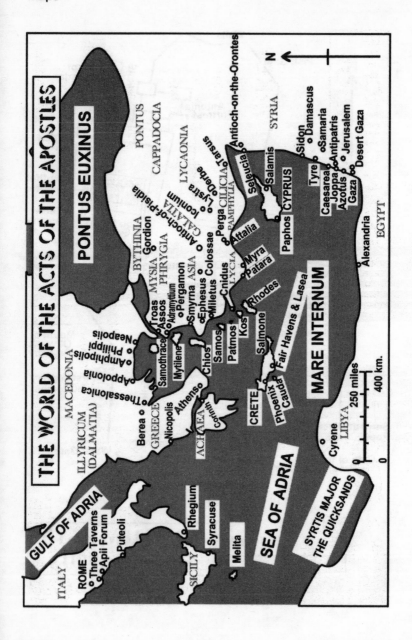

190

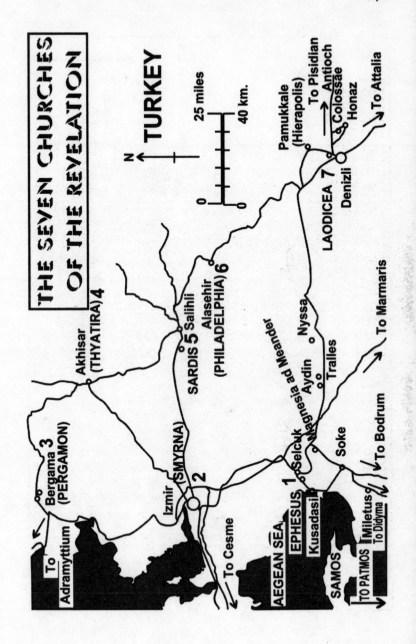

THE SEVEN CHURCHES
OF THE REVELATION

TURKEY